THE PEAKS OF LYELL

THE PEAKS OF LYELL

The Peaks of Lyell

GEOFFREY BLAINEY

ST. DAVID'S PARK PUBLISHING

St. David's Park Publishing
GPO Box 307c
Hobart Tasmania Australia 7001

First published 1954, and re-printed 1959, 1967 and 1978
by Melbourne University Press.

This fifth up-dated edition published by St. David's Park
Publishing, Hobart, 1993.

National Library of Australia
Cataloguing-in-Publication Data

Blainey, Geoffrey Norman, 1930—
The Peaks of Lyell.

Index
Bibliography
ISBN 0 7246 2265 9

1. Mount Lyell Mining and Railway Co. Ltd.
2. Copper Mines and Mining — Tasmania. I. Title.

338.76'2234'3'0994'6

Printed and bound in Tasmania by Government Printing Office

Preface to Fifth Edition

This book first appeared in 1954. For the second and third editions it was considerably updated. For this fifth edition two new chapters have been written, mainly on events of the the last quarter of a century when the mining field faced crisis after crisis. Some deletions have been made to make way for new chapters.

March 1993

PREFACE

This is the history of the Mount Lyell Mining and Railway Company—the first, the last, and the dominant company on a great Australian copper-field, a field that has yielded £174 million at present mineral prices. In its scope, however, this story is more than a company history. It is the story of a wild region of mountains and mines—some mines rich, many poor. It is the story of men who found them, floated them, worked them, and died in them.

As the field is barely seventy years old, much of its history is still preserved in the minds of men who blazed and cleared the trail. On the west coast of Tasmania I gathered information from H. J. Clarke (Strahan), G. Eaves, R. Griffiths, R. Kean, W. Lyden, B. B. Morrison, A. J. Sargeant, Owen Paice, E. Tripp and Joe Williams sen., and also from the late L. K. Hudspeth, the late A. P. Chaperon, and the late W. L. Rhodes (all three of whom had worked on the west coast in the last century). By the fire at Bowers' I enjoyed many reminiscences with old

Jimmy Elliott who was prospecting in the forest near Lyell before there was a Lyell, and whose pick cracked open the bonanza at Lynchford that led to the discovery of the field. I thank all these, and also the following: G. F. Jakins (Davenport), C. J. Coltheart, E. Pilling, G. W. Stokoe, E. J. Wedd, K. A. Rae, G. White, P. S. Kennedy, G. Schapira, G. Hine, C. Bradshaw, J. Booton, E. O. Barwick, T. J. Murphy and other Lyell men who recall the west coast of forty or fifty years ago; Robert Sticht jun. (Melbourne), H. W. Kelly, T. W. Haynes, G. Nabb, N. Kirton, E. L. Frazer (Victorian Parliamentary Librarian), Dr Loftus Hills (Hobart), John Reynolds, Miss Linda Monks, R. L. Sharman (State Archivist) and his assistant, P. E. Eldershaw, T. F. Nankivell (Queenstown), R. J. Ralph, C. Harris, M. Rush, Jim Beattie and Mrs M. A. Downie.

It is not possible to list all members of the Mt Lyell Company staff who helped me, but I should mention H. M. Murray, R. V. Parsons, G. F. Hudspeth, D. H. Wilsdon, W. Duff, V. Foster, H. J. Hodgson, W. C. Mainwaring, A. Canning, A. G. Cairnduff, J. Boyd, D. MacGregor, W. Flaherty, L. G. Naismith, G. Hiam, and Miss Betty Naylor.

I profited from the knowledge and criticism of H. M. Murray, the general manager, and G. F. Hudspeth, the mine superintendent, both of whom are well versed in the lore of the field. They read the manuscript several times, pointing out technical errors and obscurities. Mr W. E. Bassett (the chairman) and R. V. Parsons (the secretary) and F. Peter Johns (a director) also read the manuscript and offered constructive criticism in many places.

Sir Robert Knox and Mr and Mrs Bassett have taken a keen interest throughout the writing of the history; it was Mr Bassett who approached Professor R. M. Crawford of the University of Melbourne, and together they arranged that I should write the history. Its compilation has taken two and a half years. Except for an initial research grant from the University, the entire cost of writing has been met by the company. I thank the directors for their constant support and their willingness to give me a free hand in interpreting the history. To the best of my knowledge Mt Lyell is the first company in Australia to make available all its records for historical research.

October 1954

Contents

CONTENTS

PART 3: 1903-1922

PART 4: 1922-1954

PART 5: 1954-1992

Illustrations

MAPS

1

The Golden Mirage

On 22 November 1642 Abel Janszoon Tasman, three months out from Java in search of new trade routes, remarked in his journal: 'We found that our compasses were not so steady as they should be, and supposed that there might be mines of loadstone about here'. Two days later, in the sunny afternoon, a sailor saw high land to the north-east, now the peaks of Heemskirk and Zeehan, landmarks on the mountainous west coast of Tasmania. Tasman gave the sailor a pot of arrack rum and called the new land 'van Diemenslandt'.

Buried on the slopes of Mt Heemskirk within sound of the ocean were millions of tons of black magnetite, 66 per cent iron. Millions more outcropped in mountains to the north. It is unlikely, however, that these massive loadstones gave Tasman an omen that land lay ahead when his compasses varied 'eight points from one moment to another'. But his supposition of mineral wealth was true, for Heemskirk yielded tin and Zeehan silver two and a half centuries later. And twenty miles from the coast was more copper than the Dutchman's world had ever seen, the copper of Mt Lyell, which was to lie unmined until the age of railways and electricity.

Tasman did not land on the west coast of Tasmania. He sailed to the east coast, where he raised the Dutch tricolour, discovered New Zealand, and sailed back to Batavia, but with neither gold nor silver. The commercial failure of Tasman's voyages crippled Dutch exploration in southern seas, and left New Holland, New Zealand and 'van Diemenslandt' for the British.

The years rolled by and only the wandering blacks heard the roar of the surf until 1798 when Bass and Flinders sailed around

I

Tasmania, naming the peaks which Tasman saw, after his two ships, *Heemskerck* and *Zeehan*. Seventeen years later, James Kelly and four companions sailed up the west coast in an open whale-boat and found the two sheltered ports of the coast, Port Davey and Macquarie Harbour. On 28 December 1815 they entered Macquarie Harbour, a narrow sheet of water twenty miles long, with the smoke of bushfires in their eyes and the clamour of the blacks in their ears. 'Had the Natives Seen the Boat passing through the Narrow Entrance', wrote the twenty-four-year-old explorer, 'it is possible they would have killed every person on Board by Volleys of Stones and Spears, in thair usual Way'.

This was no land of lightly timbered hills and fertile plains. Here was a wild ocean, squally south-westerlies, bleak mountain ranges capped with white quartzite or pink conglomerate rock, winter snow, tangled forest and scrub so thick that a mile a day was often good travelling; a land of heavy rainfall, swampy button-grass plains and swift rivers that cut through mountains like a knife. Sixty or seventy miles of wild country isolated this western coast from the outback shepherd huts of the east.

But if the west coast was unfit for sheep and cattle, it was fit for convicts; in 1821 the first shipload sailed from Hobart Town to Macquarie Harbour, there to make a new hell on Sarah Island. Logging and shipbuilding were the mainstay of several hundred convicts, who found poor coal seams, traces of copper, and even gold in quartz if rumour was true.

Escaping convicts were the first explorers. Stealing off with a few crusts and meat-bones into eighty miles of wild mountain, their journeys were more heroic than those of many glamourized explorers. Convicts must have crossed the mineral region, for rusty leg irons were found on Mt Darwin, and the skeleton of a convict was discovered at the 'Sisters', a range near the silver-field of Zeehan, by a notorious prospector named 'Jack the Savage' who extricated the bones from the winding roots of a tree and carried them in a bag to the port of Strahan.

One convict possibly discovered gold near the Jane River, the scene of a small gold rush in this century. Just before the Victorian gold rushes a feeble old Irish convict, seeing brass filings in a smith's forge at Port Arthur, said casually to the overseer,

'I can tell you where you can get plenty of that'. When rich nuggets were found in Victoria the overseer remembered the remark and questioned the old prisoner, who recalled that he had seen heavy yellow grains at the bottom of the drinking pool while escaping from Sarah Island eastwards to the town of Hamilton. In 1866 the overseer sent the story to the Tasmanian government, which was searching energetically for gold. But his letter was merely filed, and he received no reward.

It was inevitable that the convicts would report few discoveries. They were too weak and bereft of hope to become excited prospectors or specimen collectors at the sight of a speck of gold or a lode of galena. Moreover, most of the hundred odd men who absconded did not live to tell the tale. Thus, in January 1834, when the convict settlement at Sarah Island was abandoned and the west coast was deserted by all but the few ships that came to fetch ancient logs of Huon pine, the charts bore only one reference to the convict explorers—the Pieman River. This noble stream was named after a famous man-eater and Hobart pie vendor, Jimmy the Pieman, who three times escaped from Sarah Island and assuaged his hunger with the flesh of his trusting mates. The first time he was recaptured on the banks of the river which honours his name; his last journey came to an end near the mouth of the King River, within shouting distance of the present Mt Lyell railway. There he brained his companion with an axe, ate the tastiest morsels, and calmly signalled to a passing schooner to take him to Hobart and the gallows.

The timber-cutters who sailed to the Pieman River and Macquarie Harbour had no more success than the convicts in finding minerals, though their axes rang in gullies which years later were to hear the thud of the gold-diggers' picks. Working from dawn to dusk, often drenched to the skin, the axemen had neither the time nor the desire to clamber over rotten logs and break through sodden undergrowth in search of gold-bearing gravel. Gold-seekers made the major gold discoveries in Australia, and nothing was found on the west coast until the adventurous digger made his desperate search for minerals. Nevertheless, specimens of mineral found in the forest at the eastern end of Macquarie Harbour indicated that parts of the region were mineralized. Thus Joseph Milligan found manganese near

Frenchman's Cap and galena near the Franklin River, and sent specimens to the Great Exhibition in London in 1851.

As the first thousands swarmed through the huge glass pavilions and gave, maybe, a passing glance at the exhibits from Tasmania, Hargraves had just electrified Australia with the news of rich gold at Bathurst. The great Victorian diggings were discovered in the same year, and thousands of Tasmanians sailed for the golden shore. Within twelve months half the free men of the island had crossed to the Victorian diggings, leaving behind deserted farms and shuttered shops. For a few fleeting months the little island caught the limelight when gold was found at Lefroy and Fingal, but the diggings were poor and yielded little gold in the following decade.

An Anglican parson, William B. Clarke, did more than any man to encourage the search for mineral wealth in Tasmania. He had studied geology in Cambridge under Professor Sedgwick before rheumatic fever exiled him to Sydney, where he taught school, preached sermons, and studied the local geology. In his geological writings he predicted that a goldfield would be found near Bathurst. When Hargraves struck it rich the renown of the parson spread far beyond his parish on the north shore of Sydney.

Clarke believed that gold would be found in Tasmania along the 146th meridian of longitude—a line extending from Blythe near Burnie to Port Davey in the south—and he advised prospectors to try the Gordon River and the Eldon Ranges. Such advice from the oracle of Australian mining caused a stir in Hobart, and merchants sent diggers to Macquarie Harbour where they found unpayable gold along the shore in 1854. Other parties visited the harbour, hacked their way inland, and returned empty-handed after spending hundreds of pounds in chartering vessels and buying provisions. The mighty Frenchman's Cap, twenty miles south-east of Mt Lyell, yielded gold-bearing quartz; four pounds of quartz gave the astonishing assay of over 600 ounces to the ton, but the sample was small and unrepresentative.

In 1856 the Tasmanian government asked Clarke, who was resting in the midland village of Green Ponds, to report on the auriferous districts of the island. Clarke was in poor health and refused. Two years later he declined an invitation to become government geologist, and advised the government to write to England and consult Sir Roderick Murchison. Murchison selected Charles Gould, one of the young geologists engaged on his geological survey of Great Britan, to carry out a similar survey in Tasmania—a survey that was to lead him to Mt Lyell.

When Gould reached Hobart the island was in the midst of depression. Population was stagnant; prices of the grain, fruit and mining timber shipped to Victoria had fallen. Gold had made Victoria the wealthiest and most populous colony in Australia, and a magnet for both the cream and scum of Tasmania's colonists. Tasmania would stagnate until gold enticed the people back; and in November 1859 bankers, merchants and politicians were so alarmed that they petitioned the government to send an experienced party of bushmen to search for gold in the Eldon Ranges.

In Hobart the *Mercury* took up the cry with a popular version of Clarke's theory: 'We have every right to believe that from the Eldon Range, all the gold hitherto found in the Esk, the Tyne, the Inglis, the Forth, the Hellyer and the other rivers taking their rise in the 146th parallel has been originally detached. This is more than a presumption. The gold must have come from somewhere'. The Executive Council at length despatched two expeditions, one from the north and one from the east, to explore the ranges.

Ronald Gunn led the northern expedition, but most of his men decamped and the expedition was abandoned. Meanwhile Charles Gould led the eastern party of twenty bushmen and miners out of Hobart in December 1859. Starting at Lake St Clair, the frontier of the highland sheep runs, where bullock teams had unloaded four months' rations, he followed one of Clarke's favourite lines—the 42nd parallel—to the west. His miners dug holes, diverted creeks, fired scrub, hacked and pushed through sodden undergrowth, and found only barren pyrites and some white quartz specked with gold. Gould returned with his gold pouch empty, and began to study the geology of eastern Tasmania.

Among the many who awaited Gould's return was Gabriel Read, a young Tasmanian who had washed gold in California and Victoria, and returned to his native land in the late fifties when the golden summer of the Victorian alluvial was almost over. He was still gripped by gold fever, and he must have eagerly scanned the small print of the newspapers for news of Gould's search in the Eldons. When Gould returned, and when rumours of other Tasmanian goldfields were dispelled, Read decided to try New Zealand, which, like Tasmania, gave promise of rich gold but had yielded little hitherto. He sailed from Hobart in January 1861.

In May, Read found rich gold in Otago. At first the exodus of Australians to Gabriel's Gully was slight. Then Tasmania caught the fever in September, and in one week five ships left Hobart, 'freighted with adventurers who paid £6 steerage or £10 cabin to reach Dunedin. Hobart's wharves were crowded with barrels of dried apples, flour, potatoes, palings, shingles, and hundreds of stabled cart horses—all for New Zealand. In Victoria, coaches packed with diggers were jolting down from Bendigo and Ballarat day and night. In a year twenty thousand Victorian diggers crossed the waters to Otago and chilled the stern-faced elders of this Scottish province. Twenty years later, many of these New Zealand diggers were to wash gold in Tasmania's west.

Patriotic Tasmanians reading of Otago's conversion from a sparsely settled sheep run to a populous Eldorado renewed the clamour for a Tasmanian goldfield. The government equipped a second expedition and ordered Gould to explore the land between the Eldon Ranges and Macquarie Harbour. Two depots were established, one where the King River empties into Macquarie Harbour, the other near the Eldon Range. From his inland depot Gould walked south along the marshy flats of the King River, setting the scrub ablaze as he went. Fording the river, he tried to penetrate the Comstock gap in the west coast range. Dense scrub drove him south a mile and he entered the valley known today as the Linda and looked west to the low mountain ridge, to be scarred and honeycombed in time with tunnels, shafts and open cuts, mining copper on a two-mile front. It was 16 February 1862.

> I found the valley to be about three miles long, winding westerly between two high quartzose mountains with rugged summits. There was a good deal of tea-tree scrub in the bottom of the valley

but the slopes of the mountain were barren. I named that on the right hand going up Mt Lyell, on the left Mt Owen. The valley I named Chamouni and the stream the Linda.* The ground rises considerably towards the head of the valley and it was nearly sundown before I reached the saddle and got a view of the country towards the coast. I was much disappointed by its appearance, for with the exception of a small plain distant about two miles on the other side of a set of frightful ravines or gullies there was no open land visible.

Meanwhile, the wind fanned the fires which Gould had lit, and drove a sheet of smoke and flame towards the head of the valley. Gould lit a firebreak, and when the fire passed he retreated to the King River. Next morning he climbed three thousand feet up Mt Owen, waited in vain for the mists to clear and returned when the clouds lifted on the following day. Seeing at a glance that the vale of Chamouni was the best gap through the long mountain range, he sent men back to the depot for supplies. His miners pitched their tents in the gully, halfway between the present mining towns of Linda and Gormanston, and less than half a mile from the tumbled iron boulders that lay across a great sepulchre of copper, gold and silver. They stayed in the valley for twelve days, the richest valley in Tasmania. They found nothing.

On the last day of February they mounted the ridge between Mt Owen and Mt Lyell and saw Macquarie Harbour, like a long lake, fifteen miles beyond the sea of scrub. They went down a ravine into dense forest, crossed the River Queen where the mining town of Queenstown stands today, and cut their way up to Misery Flat, a mass of tangled scrub, cutting grass and thread vines, held up by saplings and weighted down by dead logs.

Twenty-five days later the *Swansea Packet* anchored near the mouth of the King River, learned at the depot that Gould had not reached the harbour, and sailed for Hobart with a cargo of pine. When the ship reached Hobart with no news of Gould there was great alarm. It was common knowledge that Gould must travel wild country and ford rivers often swollen by sudden floods. Did his party have enough food to stay out all these

*Like the famous French valley of Chamonix, this Tasmanian Chamouni was an old glacial valley of great beauty. When he named the stream, possibly Gould had in mind the recent opera, *Linda di Chamounix,* composed by the Italian, Donizetti.

months? Not even the government which had despatched the expedition could answer that question. Tasmania dreaded a disaster greater than that of the Burke and Wills expedition which had stirred Australia early that summer. On 7 April the government sent out a search party under Burgess who guessed Gould's route from the burnt country stretching west. A second party sailed for Macquarie Harbour in the *Swansea Packet,* with orders to fire a rocket and burn a blue light each night from the depot at the mouth of the King River, and to make smoke signals and leave provisions along the beach towards the River Pieman. Hobart waited breathless for news.

Meanwhile Gould's men, cut, bruised, and drenched, had broken through the jungle of undergrowth. In four days they had battled forward two miles, and on many a day they had moved less than a mile. At nightfall on 24 March, having spent twenty-five days travelling little more than fifteen miles, they had reached the harbour where Strahan stands today just in time to see the *Swansea Packet* sail behind the headland, bound for Hobart.

Gould's men made their way along the shore to the depot, gathered supplies, and rowed across the harbour to the Gordon and Franklin Rivers, where they began to prospect for gold. When Gould learned that the *Swansea Packet* had just returned with a search party on board and that Burgess was walking over-land, he crossed the harbour and hurried along the Chamouni track to meet Burgess' party. He found them cut off by flood-waters at the King River, and sent Burgess hotfoot with a special despatch to Hobart.

Tasmania, tense with another month's silence since the search parties hurried off, throbbed with excitement when Burgess dashed in with news of Gould. More stirring, Gould had found a promising mineral district with traces of copper, gold and lead. In his despatch he reported gold in the Franklin and Gordon Rivers, and predicted that part of the country between Cham-ouni and Macquarie Harbour might be auriferous. His first message was guarded in its promises, but the Hobart *Mercury* had no qualms. 'We want an immediate accession of population on the very spot itself . . . We want a rush', it shouted. Tas-manians were certain that the exodus to the New Zealand diggings would turn to western Tasmania, that the western sky would glow with the camp-fires of thousands of diggers, winning the yellow metal in a new Gabriel's Gully beyond the mountains. In May the government accepted a tender to clear the trees that had sprouted on the unused road from Dunrobin's Bridge to the great bend of the Gordon. Politicians talked of rewarding the discoverer of a payable goldfield with £20,000. But there was no stampede to the west. Tasmania's adventurers had long left for Victoria and New Zealand where gold was more than just a topic of conversation and national debate.

Parliament was still determined to find gold in western Tasmania if there was gold to be found. It granted £3,000 and engaged a surveyor, two assistants, thirteen miners, twelve bushmen and labourers, a blacksmith, a hunter, a runner and some carrier pigeons. The party sailed for Sarah Island and landed at the rotting wharves of the old convict settlement while Gould and two men tramped overland through Chamouni and inspected the country visited in the preceding summer. On Boxing Day 1862 Gould announced his safe arrival at Duck Creek, near the present port of Strahan. 'Here we are again in the land of cold and rheumatism, anxiously longing for fine weather.' When the weather finally cleared, the miners sank holes around the shores of the harbour, near Frenchman's Cap, and along the banks of the rivers King and Gordon. The slate rock on the lower reaches of the King River impressed Gould, but when winter set in it was the old, old story, 'gold, but not payable'. The government, despairing of finding payable gold in the west, gave up the search; and the colony slept on.

Why Gould failed to find gold at Mt Lyell is a mystery. For several weeks his miners camped and walked in a valley where most creeks yielded gold in years to come. And they certainly prospected some of the creeks, for twenty years later the 'new-chum' prospectors who discovered the first gold in the valley saw an old prospecting hole within shouting distance of the shattered outcrop that covered the rich Mt Lyell mine. Gould probably found copper at Mt Lyell, for we know that he found traces of copper in 1862, and there is no other known copper-bearing country along the route of his journey. In this wilderness, however, a copper mine would need to be extremely rich to justify the heavy expense of mining, and Gould naturally was not swept off his feet by the sight of a few copper-stained rocks.

Sturt crossed Broken Hill almost forty years before the discovery of the great silver-field. Hunt and Forrest passed over the Western Australian goldfields almost thirty years before gold was found, and Forrest was quite blunt when told that this was strange. 'Young man', he retorted, 'I was exploring for pastoral country, and that means that my eyes were not on the ground a few inches ahead of my boots.' Gould had no such excuse; his eyes were glued to the ground. But his party was ill-equipped and he knew it. When he was asked to lead the third expedition he replied indignantly that he was a geological surveyor, not a prospector for gold. He could tell by the rocks whether a region was likely to contain mineral wealth, but he could not pin-point the exact spots where gold or copper might be hidden; that was the task of the mining geologist. He urged the government to entrust prospecting operations to a professional mining man and make him responsible for the result. Had this outburst been heeded, an experienced mining expert might have recognized the iron outcrop on the hillside as the capping of a large deposit of copper.

Perhaps it was good luck that Gould found nothing. As Mt Lyell had no large quantity of rich ore, the field might have been worked on a small scale for a few years, become too low grade and been abandoned. Lying dormant for another thirty years, however, it gained the immeasurable benefit of improved techniques in mining, smelting and transport; and when the first bars of copper reached the markets of the world, the field was ready for a long and wealthy life.

Gould left one lasting legacy from his expeditions; he named the peaks of the west coast range after famous British scientists of his day. He left England in 1859, the year in which Darwin published his revolutionary book *The Origin of Species,* and he seems to have opposed Darwin's theory of evolution, for he named the three massive mountains—Sedgwick, Owen, and Jukes—in honour of bitter opponents of Darwin's theory. In stark contrast, he gave to three smaller mountains which lay between the giants the names of Darwin and his faithful disciples, Lyell and Huxley. But later prospectors unwittingly redressed the balance in favour of the Darwinians, calling the field Mt Lyell though the first mine was nearest Mt Owen. And so Australia's richest copper-field honours 'the father of modern geology', Sir Charles Lyell, even though it was named long before evidence of mineral wealth was found.

After Gould's farewell the search went on, sporadic but full of hope. In 1866 the Eldon Ranges Prospecting Company was formed in Hobart to prospect those parts favoured by Clarke and Gould. Four miners went to Macquarie Harbour and inspected a well timbered shaft near the mouth of the King River where, some years previously, Victorian diggers had bottomed on a few specks of gold. Wary of the prospect of finding gold in the river drifts, they went towards the Frenchman's Cap, but flooded rivers forced them back. The shareholders received back half of their money.

The western El Dorado seemed a myth. Governments and companies had spent £10,000 in finding gold that would fill a tobacco tin. Between 1854 and 1866 rarely a summer passed without some gold-seekers coming to Macquarie Harbour. In the following ten years, the search was virtually abandoned.

2

A Mountain of Tin

While Marcus Clarke's *For the Term of His Natural Life* was damning the west coast and its convict past in the eyes of most literate Australians of his day, 'Philosopher' Smith was in the forest sixty miles north of the overgrown ruins of Sarah Island, opening a new era in Tasmanian history. On 4 December 1871 he discovered Mt Bischoff, the richest tin mine in the world.

James Smith was a 44-year-old farmer who had learned to carry heavy loads on his back when he worked as a small boy in a Launceston flour mill. In 1851 he rushed to the Victorian diggings, dug a little gold, and eventually rode in the gold escort. Returning to Tasmania in 1853, he selected virgin land at Forth, on the north coast. He was not a successful farmer; he was happier with a pick and a prospecting dish than with a plough. In 1859, the year of the Eldon Ranges excitement, he began the first of his long, lonely expeditions into the wild gorges at the back of his farm. He always returned, weary and exhausted, laughed at and pitied, but with his vision of wealth in his native land undimmed. His farm was a supply base, as essential for prospecting in wild country as for feeding armies in wartime, and a meagre livelihood to which he could always return.

'The Philosopher' believed in the Reverend William Clarke's theory that gold would be found where slates or schists with a north-south strike existed alongside certain hornblendic rocks near the 146th meridian. He worked in this theory long after geologists had become a laughing-stock on many Victorian fields. Near Mt Bischoff he found that the schists struck east and west, so he turned from gold to search for tin and other minerals. He discovered a black heavy mineral which he believed was tin, prospected the side of the mountain and sold out to a Launceston company in 1873. He received 4,400 shares in the Mt Bischoff Tin Mining Company and £1,500 in cash; other investors bought the remaining 7,600 shares at a pound a share. Within a quarter of a century the original capital had· been repaid two hundred times over.

The rich ore was carted by bullock teams to Burnie and shipped to Launceston, where the new tin smelters were fired in January 1875. The company put back all its early profits into the mine and smelters, spending £100,000 before its initial programme was completed. It paid its first dividend in 1878, the year the mine was linked to Burnie by a wooden tram and the year Clarke died in Sydney—an octogenarian whose faith in the west was justified at last.

'The Philosopher' returned to his farm, sat awhile in the Legislative Council and accepted an illuminated address and a sum of money for his services to the colony. A stern critic of the company's management, he gave away or sold his shares at trifling prices before he received one dividend. But this did not worry him. True to his name, he loved the simple pleasures of the bush more than security and riches; and when Mt Bischoff was a flourishing mine he often arrived in the horse tram from Burnie and carried his pack far into the wilds. Thirteen years after his famous discovery he was prospecting a vein of silver near the Whyte River, and ten years later, when he was nearly three score and ten, he longed to join the rush to the Western Australian goldfields.

Smith was tall and lean, with iron-grey hair and flowing white beard. He was religious and kind, ascetic and grave. 'I cannot remember ever hearing him laugh', his son once wrote, 'but occasionally he would smile at something amusing or pleasing.' The old patriarch of mining died in 1897, having seen his mine pay £1,500,000 in dividends and surpass all but two Australian mines in that wonderful century.

'The Philosopher' had revolutionized the island's mining. Two years before his discovery, fifteen men were mining in Tasmania and they won only 137 ounces of gold. Inspired by his success, Renison Bell found rich stream tin in the north-east, the Dallys found a dazzling reef at Beaconsfield, and the Lefroy goldfields

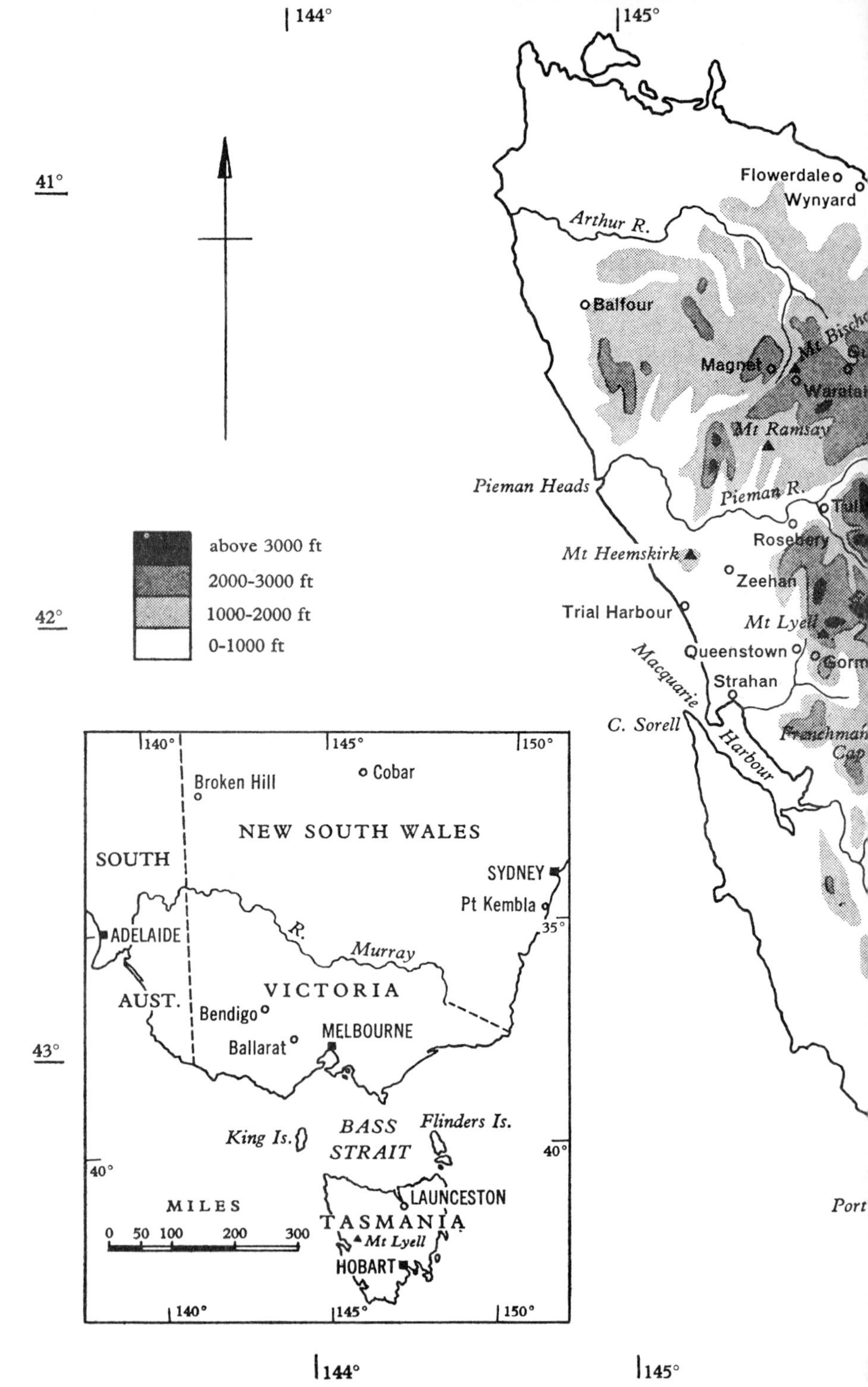
144°
145°
41°
42°
43°
Flowerdale
Wynyard
Arthur R.
Balfour
Mt Bischo
Magnet
Warataf
Mt Ramsay
Pieman Heads
Pieman R.
Tull
Rosebery
Mt Heemskirk
Zeehan
Trial Harbour
Mt Lyell
Queenstown
Gorm
Strahan
Macquarie
C. Sorell
Harbour
Frenchman
Cap
Port
above 3000 ft
2000-3000 ft
1000-2000 ft
0-1000 ft
140°
145°
150°
Cobar
Broken Hill
NEW SOUTH WALES
SOUTH
SYDNEY
Pt Kembla
35°
ADELAIDE
R.
Murray
AUST.
VICTORIA
Bendigo
MELBOURNE
Ballarat
King Is.
BASS
Flinders Is.
STRAIT
40°
LAUNCESTON
MILES
TASMANIA
Mt Lyell
0 50 100 200 300
HOBART
140°
145°
150°
144°
145°

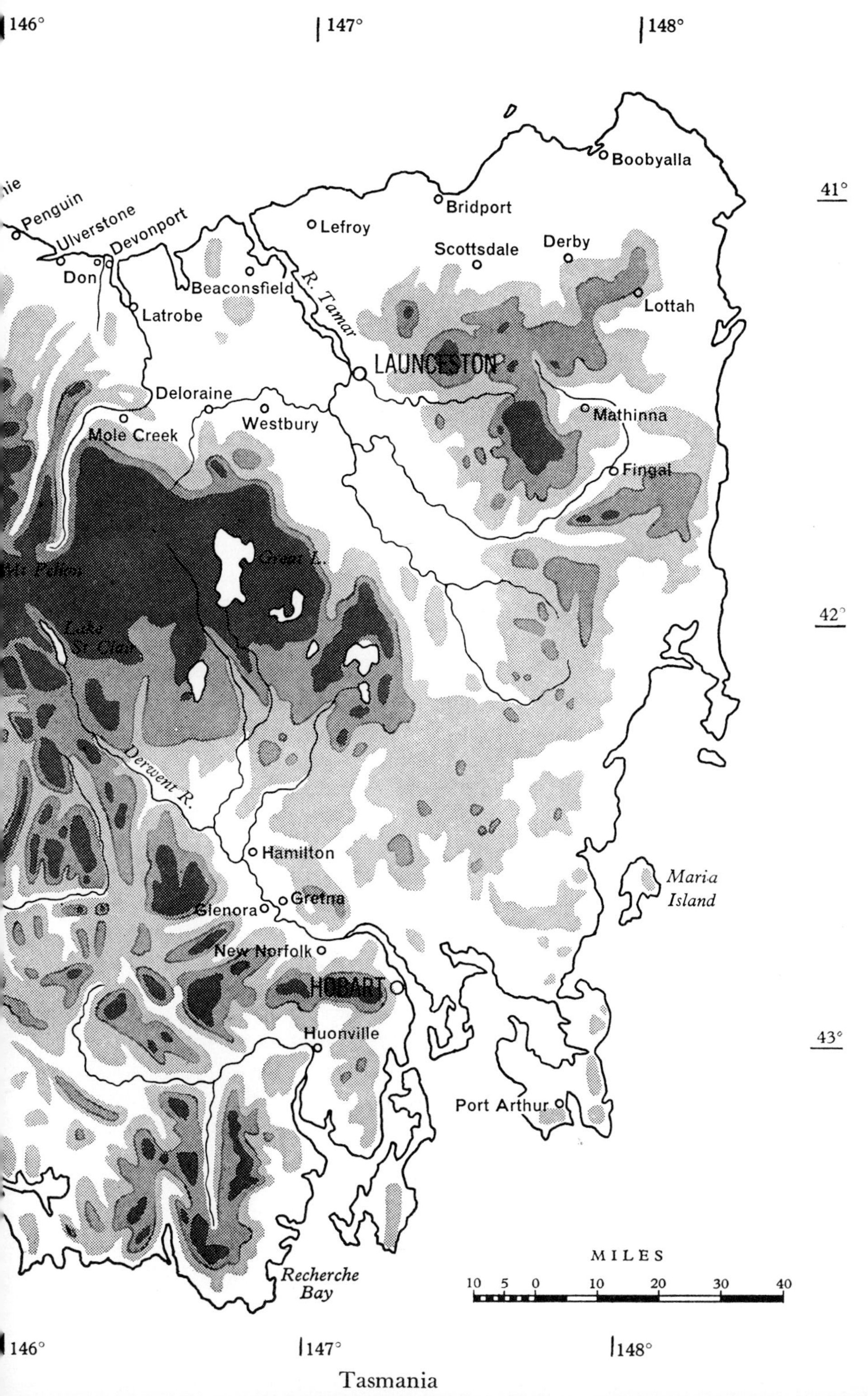
146°
147°
148°
41°
42°
43°
Boobyalla
Bridport
Lefroy
Scottsdale
Derby
Penguin
Ulverstone
Devonport
Don
Beaconsfield
Latrobe
Lottah
R. Tamar
LAUNCESTON
Deloraine
Westbury
Mole Creek
Mathinna
Fingal
Mt Pelion
Great L.
Lake
St Clair
Derwent R.
Hamilton
Maria
Island
Gretna
Glenora
New Norfolk
HOBART
Huonville
Port Arthur
Recherche
Bay
MILES
10 5 0   10   20   30   40
Tasmania

revived. A virile industry, employing thousands of miners, sprang up along the north coast and a fleet of ketches and schooners sailed up the winding Tamar with tin and gold for Launceston.

The influence of Mt Bischoff on western mining was slower but more decisive. If Smith had found a ten-ounce nugget instead of a great tin mine, thousands would have rushed the myrtle forests around the mountain and then swarmed south. Gold, the glamour metal, offered sudden fortunes. Tin usually required capital and patience, and therefore its discovery was less infectious. Nevertheless Waratah, the town at Mt Bischoff, was a supply base from which prospectors could push out into the unexplored beyond, an outpost on the advancing frontier thirty miles from the coast.

In 1873 Charles Gould and J. R. Scott found tin at Mt Ramsay, about twelve miles south of Mt Bischoff, but the deposits were not payable. In February 1876 Charles Sprent, the government surveyor, and four companions hacked their way even further south, crossed the Pieman River on a large log and found traces of tin and gold near Mt Heemskirk. Sprent's favourable report roused Tasmanian investors, and they sent three parties to Heemskirk in the following spring. Owen Meredith, a young Tasmanian who had won his spurs in the golden gullies of New Zealand, pegged the first ground on the west coast, the St Dizier lease at North Heemskirk, on 15 February 1877. In his eagerness to apply for a lease he walked through the scrub to the Pieman and rowed an old punt known as the 'Black Maria' miles downstream in a desperate effort to hand his application to the master before the ketch *Coral* set sail for Hobart. Winter came and Heemskirk was deserted, but with the approach of summer prospectors hurried back to test the thousands of acres of tin-bearing ground.

There was no rush. Transport was the problem. The overland trail was unfit for pack-horses, and the sea voyage was long and dangerous. In October 1877 two ketches left Hobart with parties of prospectors for Macquarie Harbour, 210 miles away. The *Coral* sailed on the 22nd and spent the next four weeks sheltering from heavy seas in Recherche Bay. Snatching a lull in the weather, she made Port Davey in the south-west, where the other ketch *Priscilla* had been windbound for over a month. After sheltering for eighteen days the *Coral* scudded along the coast and, despite the loss of her main top-mast, reached Macquarie Harbour on the fifty-third day. The *Priscilla,* however, was so tossed about on the swell of the ocean that she returned to Hobart. She set out again, this time sailing around the north of the island. After nearly being dashed ashore by boiling surf near the Arthur River, she finally entered Macquarie Harbour on Christmas Day, seventy-nine days after leaving Hobart. A fast mail steamer leaving Hobart at the same time would have steamed to London and halfway back again in seventy-nine days, even in that era of slow travelling. In these circumstances freight was dear and provisions were scarce on the coast. Some prospectors lived for weeks on mouldy flour, green bacon and damp tea; others were not so fortunate.

The majority of the men came from Victoria or New Zealand where gold was the backbone of mining and the alpha and omega of mineral knowledge. Charles Sprent was amazed to find that few prospectors could identify even the commonest minerals. 'I have over and over again seen prospectors completely puzzled, unable to distinguish tin from iron', he wrote. Even prospectors who carried dog-eared mining guides were sometimes at sea, and they staggered in from the bush with much-prized pack loads of hematite and tourmaline, only to learn that their specimens were worthless.

The first 'tin' shipped from the west coast proved Sprent's criticism. For six months the Great Western Company employed twelve men in cutting tracks, erecting huts, and making dams at Heemskirk. In June 1878 they had sluiced seven or eight tons of tin concentrate. Sixty bags of this tin were shipped to Hobart, and promptly seized at the order of the Minister of Lands. The prospectors of the Corinna Company, T. B. and John Moore, claimed that the tin was mined on their lease, and the commissioner of mines awarded them the tin. But the Great Western Company, which had spent £2,700 raising the tin, had the last laugh—a very forced laugh. The disputed 'tin', on assay at the smelters, contained mostly titanic iron and sand, and was quietly dumped in the Derwent.

Heemskirk survived the shock. There was plenty of genuine

tin on the mountain slopes, and every week of the following summer some rich find excited the public. In 1879 a rich lode was found on the surface at South Heemskirk, and the Montagu Company was floated in Melbourne. Mining promoters seized their chance to boom Heemskirk; 'a mountain of tin', they said. Tin prices were rising, Mt Bischoff was paying amazing dividends, and the island was prosperous. Tasmanians tasted their first mining boom. Hobart and Launceston investors began a wild mania of speculation in which almost fifty companies were floated, many on the strength of doubtful publicity. One smiling prospectus allegedly claimed that its ore had an enormous percentage of tin, and, to cajole gold-mining investors, 56 ounces of gold to the ton. Some 16,000 acres were pegged out as mining leases from the heights of Heemskirk to the swell of the Southern Ocean, where two-thirds of some leases lay beneath the thundering surf.

The boom supplied capital; in two years, companies spent £60,000 exploring the field. At first they had to carry stores and explosives twenty miles on pack-horses from Macquarie Harbour or the Pieman River, where tiny steamers and ketches unloaded supplies. In January 1881, however, four Baltic sailors—Gustav Weber and the Karlson brothers—found a better port. They had sailed to the Pieman in their seven-ton cutter *Trial* with a cargo of provisions when the manager of the Montagu mine persuaded them to search for a landing place nearer the mine. Sailing down the coast, they saw a small bight about seventeen miles north of Macquarie Heads. It was only a hole in the rocks, protected by a reef to the south and a jutting headland to the north, but it held no terrors for the Russian Finns. They steered the *Trial* between the rocks and anchored off shore in barely five feet of water. During the night the wind freshened, and great rollers curled over the reef and dumped the boat on the sand. In the morning, miners unloaded the cargo and dragged the boat back to the water. For six years the *Trial* made scores of trips to the new port and here it finally foundered in the harbour which bears its name, after five day's battering by mountainous seas.

Along the sand dunes the small settlement of Trial Harbour arose, with its stores and hotels partly built of bricks and timber scavenged from the convict ruins on Sarah Island. It drank in all the praise of the mining men. One Victorian engineer said that the lodes were as distinctly marked as squares on a chess board and that Heemskirk would be the Cornwall of the Southern Hemisphere. Even the government mines inspector was amazed at the 'perfect network of tin bearing deposits'. Men naturally thought, in the last months of 1881, that the mines only needed a macadamized road or a tramway to the port to begin exporting their marvellous wealth. The sun shone on Heemskirk that summer.

Tin was the staple but the search for gold went on. Two summers after the Heemskirk field was born, Jack Brown was prospecting along the track from Waratah to Heemskirk when he found gold on the button-grass plains about seven miles northeast of the Pieman River. Brown and an old Chinese won a few ounces, apparently kept the secret, and there was no rush. Two years later four prospectors rowed up the Pieman, a dark mirror of a river with forest lined banks, and found gold in Middleton's Creek, about fifteen miles from Pieman Heads. Harry Middleton and Alex Tengdahl ('Alec the Swede') pegged out claims and turned up in Launceston with the news.

Some Latrobe storekeepers chartered a steamer to rush food and fourteen diggers to the new goldfield. The steamer reached the mouth of the Pieman on 5 April 1879, leaking badly and almost swamped by the surf, and Captain Turner had no alternative but to steer the ship through the bay of foam and over the sand bar. Alec the Swede, who was returning to the new rush, was an experienced sailor and he knew the treacherous entrance; with a young member of the crew he agreed to be lashed to the railings near the tiller and steer the ship through the breakers. The fires were stoked until a full head of steam was raised, the plucky helmsmen were securely bound with rope, and all but two men who adjourned to the cabin scrambled up the rigging. The men who had rushed from the hotel and store at Pieman Heads looked beyond the ten lines of breakers which raced towards the beach, saw the cloud of black smoke swept westward by the gale, and feared that the steamer would be swamped. They held their breath as they watched the ship disappear behind the waves with only the top of the mast visible from ashore.

But the steamer emerged from every trough and kept to her course until, approaching the estuary, she was overtaken by a white mountain of sea and heaved on to the sand bar. There she stuck fast, decks lathered with foam, as wave after wave rose above the ship and swallowed her as they crashed along the decks. For an hour and a half the men clung to the rigging and gazed across the surf to the bare green hills that seemed a mere stone's throw away. Then in the evening gloom, when many feared that the ship might founder, she slid off the bar, and the little engines had just enough power to take her into the choppy waters of the river. The passengers climbed down stiffly from the rigging and released the plucky steersmen; but they were so bruised that they did little digging for many days.

Within a few months four hundred men were washing gold near Middleton's Creek, a large rush considering the nature of the country and the perilous voyage. The rich ground was shallow and narrow; the scrub was almost impenetrable; it rained half the week; and there was not enough gold to go around. The storekeeper advertised in the press that there was room for two thousand men on the field, and more ships steamed up the Pieman in the spring of 1879. The diggers were indignant at the trick. 'The storekeeper's right. There's room for two million', commented one digger, seething behind his whiskers. 'But we want more than b—— room. We want gold.'

The new diggers spread out, and the Pieman goldfield eventually embraced hundreds of square miles between the Donaldson and Whyte Rivers. Five years later the scattered flats and gullies were still giving such profitable returns to 'hatters' and prospectors that one writer estimated that 40,000 ounces had been won from the field. At the Rocky River, a tributary of the Whyte, the largest nugget of gold found in Tasmania was unearthed in 1883. It weighed 243 ounces (about one-ninth of the size of Ballarat's famous 'Welcome Nugget') and yielded almost £1,000 to the lucky Irish discoverers.

Meanwhile, prospectors had gained a third foothold on the west coast. After almost thirty years of futile searching gold was found in the mountains near Macquarie Harbour. Cornelius ('Con') Lynch, the discoverer, had qualities common to the best western prospectors. He was Irish, and he had roughed it on the

New Zealand diggings. To other prospectors Lynch seemed an old man; he had probably passed his fortieth year. He was wiry, red-faced, hot-headed, and usually clean shaven. Though a man of great courage, he had a phobia that native tigers attacked in the night, and he always slept with a loaded revolver, a bill-hook, and a tomahawk by his side.

Lynch, Currie—another former New Zealand digger—and Lenehan had sailed west in the *Priscilla* on her seventy-nine day voyage. Impressed with the old reports of Clarke and Gould, they had scrambled and waded up the King River and through the gorge. Lynch climbed Mt Jukes while his mates washed £1 worth of gold in the Queen River. It wasn't good enough, and the wiry Irishman walked overland to Waratah, where he bought an interest in the 'Catch 'em by the Wool' tailings claim, a syndicate which extracted tin that escaped from the Mt Bischoff mill.

Lynch and Currie, possibly stirred by stories of the rich gullies up the Pieman, returned to Macquarie Harbour at the end of 1881. With the Reverend W. B. Clarke's book as their bible they hacked their way north of Farm Cove, struck up the Queen River and washed coarse, heavy gold in a gully less than five miles from Mt Lyell. Currie continued up the Queen River and climbed the ridge that overlooked the valley of Chamouni, unvisited for twenty years. He collapsed near the summit, less than half a mile from the outcrop of the Mt Lyell mine, and staggered back to Lynch's Creek. He was fossicking at Lynch's thirty years later, old and infirm, a prospector to the end.

News of Lynch's find was carried by word of mouth to the Pieman where a few score diggers left their bush camps, shouldered their swags and rushed to Strahan, the new port that lay on a treeless plain by the shores of Macquarie Harbour. The settlement had a store, huts and a makeshift jetty, and was visited by the occasional ships which carried logs of Huon Pine from the Gordon River or traded with Trial Harbour. At Strahan the diggers hired boats, and rowed across the bay and up the King River to the first rapids. At each of twenty rapids, they splashed into the cold torrent, dragged the boat through to deeper water and rowed or stumbled upstream to the next rapid. 'Only doses of rum made us endure the cold', said Jim

Elliott who made his first trip as a sixteen-year-old, and still survived, at eighty-nine, to tell the story. At the gorge, the diggers slushed up Sailor Jack's Creek, crossed the ridge near the present Mt Lyell railway, and went downhill to the timbered gully where Lynch had pitched his tent. The seven-mile track from the top landing to the diggings soon became the beat of professional packers who carried sixty pound loads to the diggings once a day. They received two guineas a week, with food, tobacco and rum thrown in.

The new goldfield was not a success though two diggers found 120 ounces in Guilfoyle Creek in a month. One by one men packed their swags, until only seventeen remained in March, 1883. Just when the prospect seemed darkest a digger named Howard, who had abandoned his claim at Lynch's, found gold in a creek that ran down from the plains, five miles to the northeast. His mate, Harry Everett, cut his way up the Queen River, and found rich gold due west of Mt Lyell, on the present Comstock tramline. Excitement mounted as prospectors realized the extent of the auriferous country.

To open up the country, the government financed a track from Strahan to Howard's Plains, the scene of Howard's discovery. The track-cutters, George Meredith and Ted Peevor, received the miserly sum of £10 a mile, and the violent oaths of every prospector who dragged heavy pack and leaden feet along the trail. Nevertheless, the track was a gigantic labour. The forest was lined with patches of the dreaded horizontal scrub, a plant consisting of slender shoots which rose to a height of fifteen or twenty feet, collapsed in wild storms, and extended new shoots that toppled again in stormy weather. This tangled mass of interlaced scrub sometimes rose forty feet above the ground, and in one part of the track Meredith and Peevor hacked a tunnel through the scrub for several hundred yards.

Meredith's track proved an alternative route to Lynch's Creek, and the first men to use it were Con Lynch and a group of miners whom he had engaged at Heemskirk. Lynch believed that the coarse gold in the creek was shed from a reef, and he instructed the new men to trench along the hillside. On a frosty spring morning one of the boys was digging a shallow trench in the red clay when he struck white quartz. He cracked it open and his

Trial Harbour, 'a hole in the rocks', about 1890

Pack-horse track on the west coast in the 1890s

eyes almost left his head when he saw the splashes of gold. Lynch hurried up and his broad brogue swore the boy to secrecy. A hundredweight of quartz was rushed to Melbourne where gold worth £830 was extracted. Four thousand ounces to the ton was a sensational average, and shares in the King River Prospecting and Gold Mining Association—the Hobart syndicate that financed Lynch—soared forty-fold in a fortnight. In Hobart and Launceston quartz specimens studded with gold were displayed in jewellers' windows, and drew great crowds by day and night.

Two new companies, Pateena and Mt Owen, were floated in Hobart to explore leases at Lynch's Creek. Pieman diggers hurrying south found that all likely ground had been pegged, and fanned out to prospect the timbered creeks that ran into the Queen River. In October 1883 red-shirted diggers were washing gold in the very shadow of Mt Lyell.

Western miners were now working on four fields, each roughly twenty-five miles apart and lying in a new moon crescent. In the north, at the top of the crescent, lay Mt Bischoff, the richest tin mine in the world, and Waratah, a town of 1,300 people. Twenty-five miles south-west lay the heart of the scattered Pieman diggings, employing several hundred men. Twenty-five miles south, the Heemskirk tin field employed another 150 men. At the foot of the crescent, south-east of Heemskirk, the King River goldfield was begrudging gold to fifty diggers. Down this crescent came the discoverers of Mt Lyell.

3

Poverty Gully

The McDonoughs and Steve Karlson discovered the Mt Lyell mine. The McDonoughs were Tasmanians, born in the years when Gould went west. Their father, Mathew McDonough, was of Irish descent and a rural labourer at Deloraine when that district was the frontier between the north Tasmanian wheat-fields and the sparsely settled, thickly forested north-west coast. William McDonough was born at Deloraine on 6 February 1859. During the next two years the McDonoughs settled on a farm at Black Forest, on the Latrobe road, four miles from Deloraine. Here Michael McDonough was born on 13 April 1861. The father presumably died while the boys were young, for the family shifted to Waratah and for a time took the name of Cooney, the maiden name of Mrs McDonough; the name McDonough was unknown in Waratah. Bill 'Cooney' was tall and well-built and readily found work as a labourer in the slush and rain of the white face at the Bischoff mine. Mick 'Cooney' earned 7s a day as a hopper scratcher in the mill.

The bearded, bowyanged prospector, back from the Pieman with a chamois of gold or fresh from Heemskirk with some fabulous lease, was a common sight in the muddy streets of Waratah; and the McDonoughs decided to take to the track. In January 1883 Mick McDonough and Ted Connors left for the Pieman in search of tin. In three weeks they ran short of food and money, heard that tin was being shipped from Heemskirk and worked there through the winter months. There they were joined by Bill McDonough, who divided his time between the mines in the hills and the pubs on the beach. In fact, all three were out of work and lounging around the port when the bush

24

telegraph brought the sensational news that Lynch had found a rich reef near the Queen River. They packed their swags and hurried down the ocean beach between the breakers and the sand dunes. Crossing the button-grass plains near Macquarie Harbour, they saw the low sheet of water where old Strahan nestled, and in the distance, in well spaced array like a line of bastions, the mountains of the west coast range. And they knew that the massive chalk-white peak of Mt Owen towered above the forest where the creek waters were muddy with the wash dirt from the diggings.

Hearing that Lynch's Creek was thoroughly pegged, they changed their minds and cursed their way up Meredith's track to Howard's Plains where twenty diggers were winning gold. They stayed a month and barely earned 'tucker money'. Then the McDonoughs returned to Strahan for a load of food, intending to cross the Queen River and prospect on the other side of the west coast range. At Strahan the storekeeper persuaded them to take Johannes Stefanus Karlson as a mate. 'Steve' Karlson was a Russian Finn, one of three brothers whose cutter, *Trial,* had charted the port for Heemskirk. He drove a string of pack-horses between the port and the northern mines or served in the bar and billiard room of Weber and Karlson's two-storied hotel at Trial Harbour. He was big and stout with a leonine head and fair bushy whiskers. He was twenty-nine; the McDonoughs were in their early twenties.

With heavy packs the three prospectors returned to Howard's Plains. Storing some of their food in a tent, they carried blankets, tent-fly, tools and nine days' food down the dark forest in the Queen Valley, forded the stream and pushed through tangled undergrowth up the slopes of the west coast range. Here they stumbled across a camp of the Moore brothers, who were prospecting a gossan outcrop near the site of the present Queenstown smelters. The Moores were the sons of a New Norfolk doctor, fine bushmen but inexperienced prospectors. Earlier that year T. B. Moore had come overland from Lake St Clair in search of a track to Heemskirk and Macquarie Harbour. In dense forest he had seen axemarks blazed by the expeditions of Gould twenty years before. He had also found veins of quartz, impregnated with copper and iron pyrite, close to the Mt Lyell mine, but neither he nor the government seemed interested in the discovery.

With the traditional hospitality of bushmen, the Moores boiled a billy for the prospectors and yarned over mugs of tea. 'You won't find much up there', they declared, pointing out Currie's track up the range. But the prospectors were not deterred; they shouldered their swags and began to follow the blazed trail. It was a warm November noon when they reached the top of the saddle and paused to catch their breath. Behind them lay the valley of forest and the hidden tents of scattered diggers, then the grey sea of scrub and range, the glittering ocean and the crisp blue peaks of Heemskirk. Ahead, the ground dipped steeply into Gould's vale of Chamouni and the boulder-strewn course of the Linda Creek. After resting, the prospectors descended a small creek and stumbled on one of Gould's camps, marked by an old shoe, a brandy bottle, and some enamel cooking utensils. They sunk a hole in the gravel, but panned no gold. That night they pitched their tent near the old rotting poles, still standing where Gould had pitched his tents in 1862.

Next morning Bill McDonough cut a track southwards along the steep western face of Mt Owen to prospect the creeks nearer Lynch's, only seven miles away. The others pushed through the wet scrub, prospecting the creeks, when they noticed a massive outcrop of iron on the side of a steep spur. They trudged up the hill, weaving their way around great iron boulders that littered the slopes, and examined the strange formation. It jutted twenty or thirty feet above the surface and was split by deep cracks and crevices as if a great explosion had fractured the rock and flung slabs far down the hill. Small peppermint gums and shrubs sprouted from patches of dirt on the outcrop and a huge eagle, perched on a bare bough, eyed the bushmen with suspicion.

Karlson and McDonough had seen no similar outcrop in their brief mining experience. What lay beneath the ironstone crust? Was it auriferous? Karlson jabbed his shovel into the softer iron grit and Mick clambered down to the creek and washed the sample. Finding no gold, they dismissed the 'iron blow' from their minds. They dug shallow holes in the creek, later called Cooney's, and washed the dirt. There was gold all right this time.

Every dish gleamed with the fine specks, one dish alone yielding two pennyweights. Together with Bill McDonough, who had just rejoined them after a fruitless search in the wild gorge to the south, they pegged three quarter-acre claims in the gully below the Iron Blow, and hurried back to Howard's Plains to collect stores and mining implements.

A dozen diggers followed them back to Chamouni and pegged claims and pitched tents in the valley. They were a cosmopolitan band; two Frenchmen, two Italians and a Finn were in the first group at the 'rush'. The new diggers were soon filling their chamois with fine gold more quickly than the discoverers, who had pegged poorer ground.

One day, digging a hole for drinking water in the gully below the Iron Blow, Karlson found good gold. Suspecting that it might have been washed down from the Iron Blow, he climbed the hill to the massive outcrop, clambered on to the ironstone and shook the dirt from the grass roots into his tin dish. He panned fine gold, similar to the gold in the creek. It strengthened his conviction that the Iron Blow concealed a reef. Sometime later his mates walked around the deposit and found conglomerate rocks —composed of small rocks cemented together—heavily charged with fine gleaming grains. Moving swiftly they hammered in corner pegs to a fifty-acre lease around the outcrop. Karlson and Bill McDonough hurried down to Strahan to secure from the commissioner of mines a protection order, which would confirm their right to the fifty-acre lease while they searched for a reef. They reached the bay in darkness after a thirty-mile tramp.

After Karlson had returned from the coast with a load of food, he and Mick continued to gather the boulders and hide them beneath timber and brushwood in their camp. Inspecting their hoard one morning, Karlson chanced to pick out a grain of 'gold' with his penknife. The yellow grain powdered to dust. It was either wet sand, or iron pyrite, a deceptive mineral commonly called 'fool's gold' on the Victorian diggings.

Karlson later denied this version of the story, for it showed his inexperience. But it must be remembered that Karlson was not yet a good prospector, that many experienced prospectors were tricked more than once by gleaming brass-like pyrite, and that

Mick McDonough publicly admitted the mistake in a newspaper fourteen years later. There was no disgrace in this error, and, as it happened, it turned out well.

Other diggers in the Linda had scorned their chance to peg the Iron Blow. When they saw Karlson's pegs driven in they laughed, safe in the knowledge that they had nothing to learn from a sailor and the 'young Cooneys'. Only one prospector showed interest. In 1897 T. B. Moore informed the *Mount Lyell Standard* that he had intended to peg out the Iron Blow early in November 1883. Of the McDonoughs and Karlson he wrote: 'We took no notice of them at the time, but when we went to do the pegging we were astonished to find that the new chums had more nous than we gave them credit for; they had posted a notice on the ground we wanted'.

But if Moore was genuinely impressed with the Iron Blow, he had had weeks to peg it. He could have pegged it in March. And in November he had been within an hour's walk of it before the discoverers filed past his camp. He could have pegged even then, while the McDonoughs and Karlson sank holes in the creeks. Above all, when the Howard's Plains diggers 'rushed' to Chamouni—men who were not 'new chums', men who had mined on many fields—Moore still did not stir from his camp. He probably thought that the Iron Blow was one of several interesting outcrops in the neighbourhood, maybe worth testing in spare time, but certainly not as good as the valueless gossan outcrop which held his interest near the Queen River.

About Christmas time Bill McDonough returned to the valley after walking 240 miles to secure his protection order from the mines commissioner at Waratah. Having survived the shock of the 'gold' boulders, he began to prospect the ironstone while his mates panned gold in the creek below. In January 1884 they carried explosives to their mine and fired the first shot in the iron crust amid the cheers of the alluvial diggers. They blasted out a trench beneath the spot where gold was first found, but found that the rock was quite barren at a depth of seven feet. They sank shallow holes in the reddish gossan (oxide of iron) and the decomposed pyrites, without finding payable gold. A sample of the pyrites was taken to Strahan and posted to Hobart where the Government Analyst assayed traces of gold, but not in payable quantities. Years later four hundred men would blast this very pyrites in the largest mine in Australia.

On 23 February 1884 the *Tasmanian,* a Launceston weekly, casually reported that 'the Cooneys' had found a reef four feet wide and specked with gold. Three weeks later a roving correspondent, 'The Owl', denied that any reef had been found at Mt Lyell. 'I say I am hopeful—but first wait.' These are the first known newspaper references to the Iron Blow, and they appeared more than three months after its discovery. Similar snippets were written on a thousand mines a year in Australia in the 1880s. Mt Lyell, so far, was just newspaper gossip.

In the first summer of the Linda goldfield (the name 'Shammany' or Chamouni was not popular) less than sixty men worked in the valley; but they were giants. Every pound of food, every tent, crowbar, shovel and stick of dynamite was strapped to the back and carried from Strahan, thirty miles away. A return trip took three days of perspiring toil, and in winter the last miles were covered by candlelight—dim light for a track strewn with fallen trees and thick scrub, and often veiled by mist and rain. Once a fortnight every prospector had to take to the track or pay a professional packer £1 to carry a fifty- or sixty-pound load of bacon, flour, and dried oatmeal from the coast. Probably all but half a dozen diggers would have earned more money driving a waggon or mining for wages at Beaconsfield or Waratah; but they were optimists, sure that they would 'strike it rich' at last. But even optimists cannot live on storekeepers' credit for long, and at the end of the summer perhaps twenty diggers remained in the valley.

One day in March the three prospectors tramped through the bush to the Fifteen Mile, the hill above the present railway siding of Rinadeena, to buy more food. Here the dray road from Strahan to Lynch's diggings thinned into a pack track, and here Henry and Gaffney, the Strahan merchants, stocked supply stores for the diggers. In the evening Harry Turner, the storeman, would cook a hot meal for the visiting diggers for a shilling each and serve it in the shingle-roofed hut.

On this night, after the meal was over, the McDonoughs, Karlson and several other diggers sat around the blazing log fire and mostly listened to Bill Dixon, a powerful Irishman with slightly stooped shoulders and crossed eyes. For a penny a pound Dixon carried stores on his back from the King River gorge up Sailor Jack's Creek to the Fifteen Mile. Fallen logs, thick scrub and patches of deep mud and decayed vegetable matter made the four-mile journey an arduous test of grit and strength. But the lion-hearted Dixon often made his journey twice a day, and on one memorable occasion he hoisted on his shoulders a barrel of New Zealand corned beef which weighed a hundredweight and without bothering to drain off the brine, he staggered up to the store four miles away. For this gigantic labour he earned nine shillings and fourpence and many an oath of amazement from the incredulous diggers as they sucked their old pipes before the fire.

'Bill! How did you get those cross eyes?' asked one blunt digger. 'It was like this', Dixon replied. 'I was sluicing for gold in New Zealand when the nozzle of the hose slipped, and the water hit me fair between the eyes.' The hut almost shook with the laughter. Unperturbed by the merriment, Dixon proceeded to boast of his experiences while sluicing in New Zealand. The McDonoughs were impressed. They were trying to sluice the hillside below the Iron Blow but the grains of gold were so small that most of them were washed away in the swift stream of muddy water. When Dixon paused for breath one of the McDonoughs asked him if he could save fine gold. 'Save anything', said Dixon. The McDonoughs and Dixon went outside and in the darkness they talked quietly. A little later Dixon opened the door of the hut and said to the diggers: 'I'm going back to show them how to save the gold'.

Dixon returned to the Linda with the three discoverers and, although not an experienced digger, he was so impressed with the gold in the creek that he waited for a chance to buy into the claim. Bill McDonough was not so keen and frequently indulged in bouts of drinking at Herr Zeplin's Hotel at Strahan. He was at Strahan and Karlson was at Trial Harbour for weeks, leaving Mick McDonough to work the alluvial claim single-handed. It was during their long absence that Mick admitted Dixon into partnership for a load of food. Then Dixon really set to work. He hollowed a sluice box out of the trunk of a sassafras tree and helped McDonough build the dams and water races in preparation for sluicing the alluvial when the rains came down.

Although Dixon originally owned no share in the Iron Blow, in later years he acclaimed himself as the discoverer of Mt Lyell. 'I am the real discoverer and explorer', he said in 1912, 'I did the work, I did the first prospecting, I fired the first shot; and it is only right that the Tasmanian government and the Mt Lyell Company should vote me a pension.' Dixon eventually bought his share in the Iron Blow about six months after it had been discovered. Like Karlson, he thought that the reef gold on the side of the hill must have been washed down from the Iron Blow, and so he approached Bill McDonough who had always been a lukewarm partner. McDonough agreed to sell his one-third share, possibly on condition that Dixon paid off his debts at Henry's store. Two witnesses alleged years later that Dixon defrauded the discoverer by repudiating his promise to give McDonough an equal share if payable gold was found. When rich gold was found Dixon had legal ownership and laughed at McDonough's protest. Bill McDonough left the mine and wandered over the west coast for years, finally becoming a night-watchman on the field he had found.

His brother, Mick McDonough, bore the brunt of the labour for six months, only to be driven out by poverty. The claim did not yield enough gold to buy all his food and his debt mounted. James Crotty, a Linda digger, paid him half an ounce of gold for his quarter-acre alluvial claim in the creek, and later bought his one-third share in the Iron Blow by paying Mick's bill at Henry's store. For £20 Crotty bought a share which would be worth £1,500,000 in thirteen years time. But the enhanced value of the mine was to be due in large measure to Crotty's faith, energy and guile.

A native of County Clare, Crotty had studied at Trinity College, Dublin, before migrating to Victoria in the early 1860s. At one time he had intended entering the priesthood and when he was prospecting for gold in the forests by the Pieman River he would sometimes walk into Waratah, dressed in the typical digger dress of moleskin trousers and red flannel shirt, and worship at the wooden Catholic Church. He was a charming, eloquent and entertaining Irishman, and an experienced miner and battery man on the Victorian goldfields. He was barely forty years old, but in this land of the young he was called an old digger: his slightly bald head, his goatee beard and his dignified manner imparted that impression. He chanced to be returning from a prospecting trip along the Gordon River at a time when the new-chum miners, struggling to save enough gold to pay for food, were tempted to abandon their promising deposit. The entry of Crotty revived the syndicate, and he soon made the claim pay well with a sluice box.

During 1884 F. O. Henry was given one-tenth of an interest in the Iron Blow. Henry was storekeeper, gold-buyer and timber-buyer at Strahan; thirty-eight years old, portly in build and sandy of beard. His was a hazardous business. For several months he might receive, in return for several hundred pounds worth of stores, a sovereign, a chamois or two of gold and a ledger full of bad debts owed by diggers in the mountains. Diggers often rewarded his trust with a small share in their mine, and Henry must have been laden with interests in leases such as the Iron Blow.

Through the bitter winter of 1884 the prospectors worked on, sheltering in smoky tents only when snow carpeted the valley or storms swept past. The rains filled the dams, and they won good gold sluicing the hillside directly below the Iron Blow. They had found no gold in the ironstone but they lived in hope, for they followed the gold up the hill until they approached the iron knob itself.

At the end of the winter only ten diggers were working at the Linda, but all miners who had worked in quartz mines in other colonies swore they had never seen more promising reef country. Transport was the problem at Mt Lyell, and in all the west, and there was little relief while good pack-horse tracks were impossible. Most tracks churned through peaty soil, sheltered by forest from wind and sun, and they were boggy all the winter and much of the summer. Even a corduroy track, made of young saplings laid along the track, might float, sink, or up-end—cracking the horse and spattering the rider with mud. For a time pack-horses jogged along from Strahan to Lynch's Creek until the track became so impassible that at least one horse was left to die, stuck fast in the mud. In 1885 pack-horses came right to the Linda, but not for long. The diggers returned to the 'wallaby track', crossing the Queen River on felled saplings and climbing slopes by grabbing tree roots and branches. The high cost of provisions almost froze mining activity, but each summer the tracks improved and scores of diggers returned to their old haunts.

In the last months of 1885 the Mt Lyell syndicate employed from two to five wage-earners who carried on two distinct operations. They blasted and excavated the Iron Blow in search of the gold reef; and they sluiced the slopes for the fine reef gold, which sprinkled the surface soils below the Iron Blow. The blasting was a long-term investment; the sluicing earned them bread and butter. Water races wound down the hills from four catchment dams, and steady streams of water washed away the auriferous gravel to a depth of from two to six feet. The diggers used blankets and mercury to attract the gold, but the grains were so fine and the rush of the slush so swift that more than half the gold glided down the tailings race. Nevertheless, one piece of ground fifty feet square, sluiced to a depth of less than four feet, yielded over a hundred ounces of free gold.

The upper face advanced so far up the hill that gold was being sluiced on the fringe of the dark boulder mass. The men were sure—cocksure, in fact—that this gold had been shed from a great gold lode somewhere beneath the ironstone. Accordingly they began to strip the great slabs of ironstone, weighing fifteen or twenty tons, that formed the Iron Blow. They blasted them with dynamite, and levered, swayed and rolled them down the hill with the aid of a screw-jack which Karlson had brought from Trial Harbour. It was a herculean task. Exposed to icy Antarctic winds, pelting rain, hail and snow, drilling the rock with hammer and steel by sheer strength of muscle, heaving with all their weight against firmly wedged boulders, working day after day drenched to the skin, they explored the mine the hard way. By September 1885 the excavation in the ironstone was twenty feet deep and a large deposit of chocolate-coloured gossan—a mushy mineral that might prove rich in gold and silver—was laid bare. The diggers were so confident that rich gold was at hand that when Peter Balstrup, a Danish-born prospector and investor, offered to buy the mine for £5,000 they scorned his offer.

To finance and hasten the exploration of the iron outcrop, the owners had sold equal shares to F. O. Henry, the storekeeper, and to Steve Karlson's brothers, Peter and Karl, for £30 a share. The big fair-headed Finns had lost heavily on their store at Trial Harbour when the Heemskirk mines crashed, and they willingly entered into the partnership. They were as strong as horses, and as old carpenters and shipbuilders they were handy men about the mine. Although four of the proprietors had been sailors, they proved good miners and tore away the ironstone with fanatical vigour.

It was at this stage that the six shareholders formed the Mt Lyell Prospecting Association and agreed that if a shareholder did not work in the mine, he must pay the wages of a miner to take his place. An independent manager was therefore necessary, and it was the selection of a manager that drew the prospectors to Strahan in January 1886. There had been bickering between the Finns and the Celts, but now they split into hostile camps. The Karlsons, mustering only nine of the twenty shares, were in a minority and could not stop the election of Henry as secretary and Tom Strong—young, tall and commanding, a skilful miner from Waratah and a loyal friend to Crotty—as manager.

Strong went to the mine with strict instructions to send sealed reports to Henry, the secretary, who would inform shareholders of developments in the mine. This step was partly justified as Crotty and Peter Karlson no longer worked at the mine and had a right to be informed. But in actual fact this regulation gave the ruling group information which they withheld from the Karlsons and which they cunningly used to drive them from the mine.

No sooner did Strong begin to direct mining than the syndicate fell into debt. The large credit balance was dissipated, and in a few months shareholders paid more than £20 each in calls. By March six wage-earners were working at the Iron Blow while the shareholders were scattered far and wide between Linda and Flannigan's Flat, striving to win enough gold to feed themselves and pay their substitutes at the mine. By April the syndicate was so poor that Strong stopped excavations on the ironstone and once again sluiced the slopes for gold.

4

Karlsons' Hard Luck

In the west a digger had to find gold or get out. Storekeepers might give him five or ten loads of food on credit, but if there was no sign of repayment their generosity ebbed. The credit of the Scandinavian sailors was running low. The loss in working the mine had plunged them into debt, and in April 1886, when a digger named Carroll offered to buy six shares for £250, Peter and Karl accepted the money. Two months later Steve Karlson, having lost his job at the mine and being heavily in debt to storekeepers and publicans, sold his three shares for £120. A few days after he had agreed to sell, he was working in the creek when Fred North, an old digger, approached him, 'I'm sorry you sold out, old man,' said North, 'they've struck it very rich in the face.'

Digging in decomposed ironstone at the bottom of a deep tailings trench, Strong had found rich gold. Crotty gathered a small bag of specimens and set out for Launceston, where his arrival was heralded in the *Examiner* by a telegram from its correspondent at Waratah: 'Some stir has been caused here by the reported discovery of a rich gold bearing reef near Mount Lyell, and about seven miles from the King River [mine]. James Crotty arrived yesterday and applied to-day on behalf of the Mount Lyell Prospecting Company for the usual reward claim ... Crotty left to-day for town and appears very sanguine though somewhat reticent'.

In Launceston, Crotty's imagination ran riot. He referred to Mt Morgan, the wonderful Queensland gold mine, as 'a mere backyard' compared with Mt Lyell, and spoke glibly of erecting

35

a forty-head battery to crush the ore. Excitement soared in stock exchange and miner's camp.

Launceston merchants, shopkeepers and investors financed six prospecting associations and sent men to the new rush. On 24 August, the worst of winter gone, the grimy little steamer *Wakefield* left for Macquarie Harbour, packed with diggers. At Strahan the men rolled their swags, studied the special maps which the *Examiner* had issued to guide them to the diggings, and filed into the bush on their exhausting two-day tramp. They waded in mud almost up to their knees, crossed dangerous sidlings and gullies, heard the roar of unseen mountain streams, and staggered into the goldfield on the second day. In September, at the height of the rush, two hundred diggers—ten times the winter population—had pitched their tents in the valley.

Other prospectors came from Hobart and quickly pegged the remaining ground. Six registered companies—Lightly, New York, Union, Launceston, Queen River and Tasma—employed men to prospect the ridge. Among the wealthy investors who came to inspect the new goldfield was old, white-haired Colonel Powell, who had retired from the Indian Army to farm at the River Don. Powell was a gentleman-farmer who employed ten or twelve labourers and lavished his money in strange ways. As a hunting ground he once carved the 'City of Melbourne' out of virgin forest, employing axemen to cut wide rows of clearings until the forest resembled city blocks, surrounded on all sides by neatly ploughed streets. The old colonel was good sport for the wily prospectors, and William Dixon seized the chance to sell him three shares for £12,000, a hundred times more than Karlson had received only three months previously. The colonel paid a deposit of £1,000 and later cancelled the deal.

Everyone who saw the ironstone, matted with fine gold that glistened after showers of rain, was impressed with the mine; the more so when they saw how much gold had collected in the box after the gossan was sluiced in a powerful stream of water. The miners sank a paddock, ten feet by twelve feet, into the ironstone, but eight feet down the iron became so hard that it had to be smashed into lumps with a pick. Eager to know how much gold lay in the hard iron, the men bagged half a ton and, when the warmth of spring began to cake the mud on the track, sent it on pack-horses to Strahan. The Bendigo School of Mines reported that the gossan (decomposed iron) contained fifteen ounces of gold to the ton; the prospectors were jubilant.

The Tasmanian government sent its geologist, Gustav Thureau, an old German, who issued a glowing report in October. He declared that the gold-bearing gossan was volcanic mud which had originally come to the surface as a hot liquid solution. This 'volcanic mud' had eroded, shedding the alluvial gold which diggers washed in the creeks and hillsides of the valley. Thureau raved about the mine, and placed it amongst the foremost gold discoveries of the age; he called it Tasmania's richest gold mine, fully aware that Beaconfield's famous mine had paid over £400,000 in dividends in less than eight years. 'We may anticipate with every confidence', wrote Thureau, 'that these gold deposits will extend to great depths and be practically inexhaustible.' No wonder Crotty went mad with excitement. 'Begorrah, it's all gold, I tell you', he shouted. 'I'll be that rich I'll buy Ireland and make it a present to Parnell.' He accompanied the geologist to Strahan and made merry at the Long Bay Hotel. On the third day, the local magistrate intervened and ordered the publicans to supply him with no more liquor.

The Karlsons did not celebrate. They suspected that Strong, the manager whose appointment they had opposed, had hidden rich specimens some time before they sold their last share. Although they could not prove this at law, they discovered another method of redressing their grievance. Steve Karlson saw a loophole in the Mining Act, and decided to 'jump' the lease.

Crotty, Henry and Dixon had each pegged out a reward claim of fifteen acres, the reward claim being a form of lease granted at peppercorn rental to discoverers of unique or remote deposits. Now it was a moot point whether each man was entitled to ten or fifteen acres, for under the Goldfields Regulations Act the discoverers were only entitled to fifteen-acre blocks if their mine was more than five miles from any other similar mine. If the new find was less than five miles away, the maximum reward was three ten-acre leases. Karlson believed that the Mt Lyell mine was less than five miles from Lynch's mine and that the discoverers were consequently entitled to thirty, not forty-five acres. He resolved to 'jump' fifteen acres from the lease.

Aided by Tom Jones, a barman and billiard marker from Waratah, and loaded with wooden pegs, Karlson set out in the darkness of early morning to peg the ground. Crotty had wind of their plan. He lay awake in his camp, his revolver loaded and his eyes peering into the gloom. He saw the flickering light and quietly approached the intruders.

'What's your business here?' he asked Jones heatedly.

'I've come to peg the ground.'

'Then why come at night-time', snapped Crotty. 'This is a queer time to mark off a claim.'

'Oh, any time does.'

'What ground do you intend to peg?' said Crotty.

'This ground', said Jones defiantly.

'This is our ground', said Crotty.

'I came here to peg this ground, and I am going to do it.'

'Very well', said Crotty, fingering his revolver, 'I warn you before you do it, to say your prayers, if your mother ever taught you any. It will be your last peg.'

'Is that loaded, Jim?' said Jones tactfully.

Crotty pulled back the breech, revealing cartridges in the chamber. Jones dropped his pegs, returned to his smoky billiard room at Waratah and took legal action. The wild Irishman was bound over to keep the peace for a year.

Although Crotty had intercepted the 'jumpers', they had legally pegged their ground. The case *Jones* v. *Henry* was heard at the Court of Goldfields at Waratah in February 1887. The issue at stake was immense, and all day bearded prospectors and pressmen crowded into the little court house. The evidence of the surveyor favoured the 'jumpers'. Measured in a straight line the mines were $4\frac{1}{2}$ miles apart, less than the legal distance which justified a reward of fifteen acres. Unless Henry could prove that the Iron Blow was a geological formation distinct from Lynch's reef, he must forfeit fifteen acres to the Karlsons. But Gustav Thureau swung the case Henry's way by swearing that the Mt Lyell mine was unique; and Karlson lost the case. Later he appealed to the Supreme Court to issue a writ of mandamus forcing the mines commissioner to reopen the case. The Court refused, and the Finns accepted their lot.

Nine years later, the Karlsons' sense of injustice was drama-

Laying the rack rails on the Mt Lyell railway, 1896

Mt Lyell locomotive climbing above the King River gorge, 1896

tically justified in a celebrated lawsuit in the Supreme Court of Tasmania, where Dixon sued the Henrys for 2,467 Mt Lyell shares, valued at nearly £20,000. Dixon claimed that in 1886 F. O. Henry had promised him part of that interest which Steve Karlson had sold just before the rich discovery. The drunkenness of one arch witness and the feigned illiteracy of the other, the appearance of leading Melbourne barristers, and the issue at stake made the case the event of Hobart's social round for three sensational weeks. The doubtful transactions with the Karlsons were argued at length, though the three judges did not think it relevant to judge whether the Karlsons were defrauded.

Early in 1886, according to the evidence, Crotty and Henry decided that there was only one solution to the ill-feeling that divided the Karlsons and the other shareholders. The Karlsons must be bought out. In April Carroll, the gold-digger, paid the Karlsons £250 for six shares. A little later, Carrol sold half of the shares to Strong, the manager, who obviously believed that the mine was promising. Sometime in April, either before or after the sale, Strong discovered rich specimens which, he believed, came from a lode. Steve Karlson did not learn of the promising discovery; he was dismissed for absenteeism and had to leave the lease. The other shareholders now made a determined effort to buy him out. Early in May Henry instructed Carroll to try and buy the share, and at the same time he warned Dixon, who was digging for gold at Flannigan's Flat, to retain his share and not sell out as he had planned. Secret letters passed between Strong and Henry, showing that plans were in hand. When Karlson asked to see the manager's reports, Henry refused to produce them, alleging that they contained offensive references to foreigners. 'There was unmistakable evidence', said Mr Justice Dodds, 'that Henry, Dixon, Crotty and Carroll were working amicably together and that the Karlsons were excluded from these friendly relations.'

According to plan, Carroll met the big, fair-bearded Finn and offered to buy his share on behalf of a wealthy investor in the north-west of the island. F. O. Henry, making no reference to his own interest in the projected sale, advised Karlson to walk to Mt Lyell and inspect the mine before he sold out. Karlson inspected the mine on 1 June, and saw no sign of any promising lode, though he admitted that the alluvial looked well. Seven days later he agreed to sell.

Henry, Crotty and Dixon were each to receive a quarter of Karlson's interest. They met in Henry's hut at Strahan on 15 June, and Dixon set off with a £90 cheque to the small port of Don, near Devonport, over 150 miles away. Dixon paid the cheque to William Shaw, chief clerk of the River Don Trading Company, a man of integrity who was to share the other quarter of Karlson's interest with his manager, John Henry. As Shaw was the buyer in Karlson's eyes he wrote out a cheque for £120 and gave it to Dixon, who handed it over to Karlson at Strahan on 9 July.

In court F. O. Henry said that he maintained the secrecy so that he could retain control of the mine. He said that if Karlson knew who was really buying the shares, he might mention it 'in his cups' to the Strahan hotel-keeper, who would then outbid Henry for the shares. This excuse did not hold water. Even if the publican had bought Karlson's three shares, the Henry faction would still have retained control of the mine. Moreover, as a discoverer of the mine, Karlson surely had a right to receive the offer of the highest bidder, for the rich ore was on ground which he had cleared of boulders six months earlier and which Strong had refused to prospect.

Henry showed the poverty of this excuse by carrying on the secrecy long after Karlson had pledged to sell. Secrecy was essential, it seems, either because Strong had found the rich gold in the tailings race before Karlson sold out, or because the rich gold was found so soon after Karlson had agreed to sell that he would be full of suspicion if he knew that his fellow-shareholders were buying him out. There is no doubt 'Long Tom' Strong was unscrupulous enough to hide rich specimens; the Chief Justice branded him as a rogue for giving false evidence against the Karlsons at the Waratah 'jumping' case, nine years previously. Moreover, Strong acted very suspiciously when he found the rich gossan in the trench; he quickly ran water down the race and filled in the hole where the gold glittered. It was not surprising that Mr Justice Dodds, who delivered the most penetrating of the three judgments in the 1896 trial, believed that the gold was probably found between 1 June and 8 June, the day on which Steve Karlson sold his shares.

The passing of the years, the absence of records, and the frailty of human memory made it impossible for the court to decide the date of the rich discovery with absolute certainty. Even if it had passed judgment on the Karlson transaction and induced the Finns to take legal action, it is doubtful whether the Karlsons would have recovered their loss, for the disputed shares had been divided into thousands and been sold and re-sold, issued and re-issued many times by three successive companies in the intervening years. And even if luck had smiled on the Karlsons in 1886, they might not have risen to great wealth. Too poor to retain a large interest in a money-burning mine, they would have been forced to sell most of their shares in the dismal period through which the little syndicate was yet to pass.

5

The Mine that Failed

The prospectors returned from the court house at Waratah and continued to mine the rich gossan that had caused the furore. They sluiced it in a swift water race, using mercury, blankets and copper plates to collect the gold, but the grains were so fine that most of the gold rushed down the tailings race with the rubble. Nevertheless, they saved some six hundred ounces and made a good profit before the richer, softer gossan was worked out. Deeper prospecting and efficient treatment methods were now essential. Share interests, subdivided and sold at fantastic prices in 1886, had scattered through the island. The Association needed efficient organization, expert advice, and more capital. During 1887 Crotty went to Launceston, the exchequer of Tasmanian mining.

There is probably no mullock heap or old shaft within twenty miles of Launceston, yet the investors of that small city drew most of the prizes and a fair share of blanks in Tasmanian mining. The heyday of Launceston's mining interest was the 1880s, in which decade its population soared after years of stagnation. In 1888 Launceston was an imposing city of 18,000 people, the centre of trade for the northern mining fields, the site of large tin smelters, and a haven for a fleet of ketches which shipped bagged tin from Burnie, Bridport and Boobyalla. Between 1880 and 1890 the Mt Bischoff mine and the 'Tasmania' Gold Mine were two of Australia's richest mines, and in this decade, on a trifling paid-up capital, they handed out £1,400,000 in dividends to Tasmanian shareholders. This sum was sufficient to explore and equip with crushing battery or plant two hundred average mines, for it was a prosperous mining company that had £7,000 to spend. Both Bischoff and Beaconsfield had been financed with Tasmanian wealth; they were directed from Launceston; and their immense dividends had made Launceston a new Ballarat, a busy hive of mining speculation.

There was significance, then, in moving the office of the Mt Lyell Prospecting Association to this city. Here were mining agents, directors, experts, stockbrokers and enterprising investors with money to spend. A few of their number embraced Mt Lyell. The first board comprised George Horne, general manager of the National Bank of Tasmania; John Henry, a merchant; William Ritchie, a Launceston solicitor; old Colonel Powell; and three of the prospectors, Crotty, Dixon and Carroll. The legal manager was Robert Carter, mayor of the city, an old 'forty-niner' from California, and a professional mining agent with offices in Patterson Street.

The directors acted wisely. They consulted Dr J. R. Robertson, a Sydney geologist, who spent four days at the mine in September. This retired Indian Army surgeon shattered Thureau's much vaunted claim that the mine was a wonder of the golden age. He said that the ore was poor in gold and silver and so difficult to treat that it might not pay the expenses of mining. Even more surprising was his statement that the ore body resembled the Tharsis mine in Spain, which consisted roughly of half sulphur, half iron and a small percentage of copper. In Spain cheap wages, fuel and transport and a market for sulphur and iron made such an ore body highly payable. In Australia, however, all these factors were absent, and Robertson doubted whether it would pay to work the Mt Lyell mine for its 3 per cent copper. Finally, he advised the directors to search for richer ore at depth.

The smiles of anticipation on the faces of the directors must have frozen as Carter read out Robertson's scholarly report at the board meeting. The report, however, so contradicted the advice of the government geologist that the directors were loath to believe it. They decided to raise capital and find out more about this mysterious ore body. Early in 1888 they dissolved the Prospecting Association and formed the Mount Lyell Gold Mining Company, No Liability, issuing 16,400 shares to the old shareholders and reserving the remaining 1,600 shares. In **May,** when the company made its first call of sixpence on each share, it numbered thirty-one shareholders, of whom fifteen were Launceston men. Ten shareholders described themselves as 'gentlemen'. There were eight prospectors and miners, three merchants, two solicitors, a storekeeper, a miller, a broker, a tailor, a mine manager (Kayser of Waratah), and a bank manager.

The directors rejected Robertson's advice, forgot the copper, and turned again to the gold-bearing gossan. Countless centuries of sunshine, rain, frost and ice had leached the copper and sulphur out of the upper oxidized zone of the ore body, leaving a small deposit of reddish gossan enriched with gold and silver. The richest gossan had been sluiced by the prospectors in the exciting months of 1886; the remainder was poorer and harder, and would have to be crushed to release the gold. Eager to learn if there was enough gossan to justify the erection of crushing machinery the manager drove two shallow tunnels from the side of the hill. In the top tunnel the miners drove through sixty feet of rich gossan before they struck the massive copper pyrite. In the second tunnel, amidst intense excitement, they drove into gold-bearing pyrite. The gold soon petered out, but the manager estimated that 1,700 tons of gossan, carrying one and a half ounces of gold and eighteen ounces of silver to the ton, were definitely in sight. The directors were satisfied; they ordered an eight-stamp mill from a Melbourne foundry.

This was a gamble. The ore blocked out for mining might well yield insufficient profit to repay the cost of machinery. Moreover, it carried as much as 50 per cent baryta, a mineral which had wrecked the efficiency of hundreds of Australian batteries since the first one worked at Clunes in 1857. And Thureau and Robertson both warned the company that the stamp mill and amalgamation treatment would lose much of the gold. Their warnings were ignored.

The practice of erecting machinery before testing the ore body was almost a first commandment in Tasmanian mining. Six Heemskirk mines and every western gold-mining company that erected machinery in the eighties made this mistake. Optimistic directors, spurred on by dividend-hungry shareholders, gambled on making enough to finance further exploration or pay a dividend. This practice was encouraged by the system of time-payment of shares which characterized the 'No Liability' mining company. If the mine took too long to pay, many shareholders tended to forfeit their shares and invest in a new mining company rather than pay more calls to the old company. Forfeitures were infectious, and a company which refused to erect machinery might be left with a few shareholders who collectively were too poor to finance the high cost of mining in difficult terrain.

The Mt Lyell directors were probably under pressure from the leading shareholders, for we know that Crotty and Dixon had fallen deeply into debt to pay calls on their large holding of shares. William Dixon, still a director but dabbling in land in Melbourne after the fashion of the times, was so heavily in debt that when the directors visited the mine they had to pay his expenses to enable him to make the journey. Crotty was so poor that he resigned from the board and went to Sydney to look for a remunerative clerical position. His good education was of no avail, and he worked as a miner in the underground sewer at 14s a day, a high wage in those days. At week-ends the dapper Irishman dressed well and mingled with merchants and squatters in the fashionable hotels of Sydney. At one hotel he befriended the barmaid, who introduced him to wealthy country pastoralists; and on at least one occasion he sold several hundred shares in his little-known company at handsome prices. 'Forget all about them', he whispered to the squatter, 'they'll come good in time.' This sale did not keep Crotty solvent, and he was forced to borrow £900 from a pastoralist at heavy interest.

They were anxious days for the shareholders as the machinery lay in the rain on the wharf at Strahan, awaiting transport to the mine. In fact, it would not have reached Mt Lyell but for the efforts of the King River Company to erect a battery at Lynchford two years earlier. This Hobart company had asked the government to make a dray road to their mine, and, after incessant agitation, the track was repaired sufficiently to enable a ten-stamp mill to be sledged to the mine. The roadmakers were about to continue the road another eight miles to Mt Lyell, but they went on strike for 10s a day. The road was not completed until the end of 1888 when Mt Lyell miners took axe, pick and shovel, and built the last rough mile in readiness for carting the machinery.

The 'jackass' steam boiler was eighteen feet long and six feet in diameter; and years later, when it lay rusting at the mine, newcomers used to puzzle how the leviathan was dragged up from the coast. Like all the machinery it came in pieces and was assembled at the mine. Henry's horses dragged the drays from the coast to a spot two miles past the shingle-roofed battery of the King River mine, where the drays were unloaded beside the road. For weeks, the horses ploughed along the track, crawling up razorback slopes, plunging into bogs, and slipping on greasy saplings that formed part of the road. On the steep hills which rise above the Roaring Meg Creek the track narrowed, and mules and horse-drawn sledges replaced the low drays. The sledges wound uphill, past Yankee Dan's sly-grog tent and his craftily hidden still, and round the back of Little Owen. They forded the small creeks which cataract down the sides of Mt Owen and climbed around massive white boulders on the steep foothills until they reached the top of the roaring waterfall, where the waters of the Southern Ocean could be seen above the tree-tops. The next stretch of several hundred yards was the most treacherous part of the track and, according to tradition, the alluvial miners came to the rescue and rolled and skidded and tugged the heaviest iron plates of the boiler to the crown of the hill overlooking the Linda Valley. The cost of carting finally exceeded the cost of the machinery itself.

On the hillside beneath the mine, close to the tents and shingle-roofed huts which nestled among the trees, carpenters built two neat paling sheds with semi-circular roofs and black, iron chimneys. Here a boilermaker and blacksmith assembled the boiler and battery; and on 5 April 1889 the rhythmic roar of the mill echoed down the valley as the clattering stampers crushed their first ore from the mine.

Gold-diggers hurried up the gully to watch the little mill working. In the noisy battery house they watched the man shovel ore into a narrow cast-iron box, filled with water, and the eight long iron stampers crash down sixty to ninety times a minute and smash the ore into pulp. The method of extraction was simple. The impact of the throbbing stampers splashed the pulp through an opening in the box on to sloping tables. As the sludge ran down the tables copper plates coated with mercury attracted the heavy particles of gold, allowing the waste rubble to spill over the tables and run down the tailings race.

The first crushing was a failure. As the experts had prophesied, the baryta and pyrite were so heavy that they covered the amalgamating plates and allowed much of the gold to escape with the tailings. In twenty months of spasmodic crushing the stamp mill treated 1,875 tons of ore and recovered 1,670 ounces of gold and 852 ounces of silver, valued at £6,159. An equal amount of gold escaped from the mill in the thick slimy water and was dammed in tailings ponds on the hillside. These black dams were richer than the average Bendigo and Ballarat mines of the day, and would have been a celestial Paradise had miners allowed Chinamen to fossick in the west.

To visitors, the incompetence of the company was alarming. In the semi-circular quarry, where the ore was being mined, the miners were endangered by huge overhanging boulders. The wheelbarrows, iron trucks and self-acting trams which carried ore down to the mill were primitive and inefficient. The underground tunnel was crooked and unworkmanlike. The battery house was so placed that if the haulage cable broke, the truck would crash through the building. The cost of carting firewood to the boiler house was almost prohibitive, although dense forest lay only a stone's throw away. And the dam was so poorly constructed that, although 115 inches of rain fell in an average year, it frequently dried up and the battery had to close for want of water. Frank Gee Duff, Launceston director and stockbroker, was the most trenchant critic of his company's operations, and roundly declared that 'the mine has been shamefully mismanaged from every standpoint'.

George Lightly, a dignified English gentleman, with bushy whiskers, who succeeded Tom Strong as manager, was chiefly responsible for the inefficiency. He came to Mt Lyell from Heemskirk, where he managed the battery at the West Cumberland mine during the boom; but as his battery had produced about enough metal to make a kerosene tin, the experience was not a good testimonial. Nevertheless most of the directors had faith in him, and shielded him from criticism. Thus, in January

1890, at a meeting of the shareholders the chairman apologized meekly for the financial plight of the company with the lament that the top of the quarry had accidentally caved in, covering the gold-bearing ore with hundreds of tons of rubble. This apology was too much for some of the shareholders. William Dixon leapt to his feet and shouted out that the collapse of the mine was only another instance of Lightly's incompetence. Duff carried on the attack until he and Dixon were ruled out of order. Their protests, however, were effective, for Lightly resigned and became a storekeeper on the banks of the Pieman and later an inspector of mines at Kalgoorlie.

When Lightly resigned, Crotty returned from the mainland to manage the mine. An experienced battery man from Bendigo, Crotty had the necessary technical knowledge and vested interest in making the mine pay. He improved the battery and treated twice the tonnage crushed by Lightly in a similar period. Nevertheless the outlook was not promising. The deafening roar of the mill betrayed the rattling of many worn-out parts; and there was such a heavy loss of gold that the company was struggling to pay the wages of its twelve or fifteen men. At the Launceston stock exchange the market value of the mine was only one-fifth of its 1886 value.

For three years the company's operations had been conducted at a loss. The shareholders who paid 5s 11d in calls on each share received back only 6d in dividends, and this was only the second dividend ever paid by a West Tasmanian mine. It was paid on 27 October 1889, at a time when the battery was not paying its way and when the company urgently needed money for fresh machinery. This amazing financial expedient plunged the company into debt for seven months, and it remained so, on and off, until its liquidation.

Duff strove day and night to enlist more capital. After months of canvassing he interested a wealthy Melbourne syndicate, led by Joseph Clarke, who offered to form a new company if his consultant reported favourably. On 31 January 1891 the shareholders met in Launceston and voted by two to one that the Melbourne men be given an option over the mine; but in March the Clarke group withdrew, possibly on the strength of the expert's report.

All hands had been discharged from the mine in January, and

only the caretaker remained. Rainstorms washed the debris into the mine; the boiler chilled; the stampers were silent, never to clatter again. In May the shareholders paid a call of twopence a share, but this did not discharge the company's debt. On 6 July the directors resolved to wind up the company.

6

A Silver Lining

But for the rise of Zeehan, the Mt Lyell goldfield might have remained as dead as the dinosaur. A year before the prospectors stumbled on the Iron Blow, Frank Long, prospecting in the forest near Mt Zeehan, had struck his pick into an outcrop of gossan and discovered glittering silver. Clothes tattered, a month's stubble on his face, he staggered back to civilization with specimens of galena that contained up to one hundred ounces of silver to the ton. But Zeehan was not the old story of lucky miners digging fortunes in shallow holes. It was essentially a capitalists' field, requiring tramways, pumps and ore-dressing machinery to make it pay. Long could not raise the capital to explore his lease; and sixteen years later, when Zeehan was a town of 8,000 people, he was sleeping on bags on the floor of an engine house, on the very lease where he found the first galena.

The swampy silver-field made little progress until 1888, when Broken Hill boomed. This stunted range in the dry, western outback of New South Wales, pegged by a boundary rider in 1883, inspired the greatest of Australian mining booms. Rising on the crest of Melbourne's land boom, the gamble in silver shares so gripped the humble investor that in March 1888 £1 million a day was said to be changing hands over silver shares in Melbourne. Eighty brokers working day and night won £250,000 in brokerage fees alone. Broken Hill mines were the first fancy; then the craze spread to all the country thirty miles around, to Umberumberka, Thackaringa and a score of other musical names. 'Years after the boom', wrote Randolph Bedford, 'I calculated the market value of mines that never had a

50

chance of paying. The total was £18,000,000 and they are all as forgotten now as if they never were.'

Broken Hill gave Zeehan the breath of life. Tasmania was an economic backwater but it felt the wash of the mainland whirl-pool; Hobart and Launceston investors caught the silver craze and turned to Zeehan. They were fortified by the opinion of Thureau, the geologist, who returned from Broken Hill at the zenith of the silver boom to proclaim its similarity to the Zeehan lodes. In the winter of 1888 the Silver Queen, Silver King, Silver Hills, Silver Harp, Silver Trumpet and twenty more of these silver syndicates were prospecting at Zeehan, and more than 24,000 acres embracing 370 claims, had been pegged as mining leases. A few companies mined rich surface ore and sent it by pack-horse and dray over the bleak granite hills to Trial Harbour, 'that miserable apology for a port', twelve miles to the west. Here the bagged ore lay on the wharf, alongside old machinery salvaged from the dead Heemskirk mines, and awaited shipment to German and Australian smelters. Transport costs stole most profit from Zeehan's early exports.

When Melbourne's silver speculation tapered off and the shouting and the tumult died, mining promoters and stock-brokers from Melbourne, Broken Hill, Ballarat and Adelaide began to trek to Zeehan in search of new mines. Several direc-tors of the Silverton Tramway Company, then beginning its amazing career as one of the richest Broken Hill companies, drew up plans to spend £70,000 on a private railway from Strahan to Zeehan. They spread a prospectus, spiced with superlatives. But the Tasmanians invited to subscribe were not so sure that 'This will be one of the greatest fields in the world', and they refused to buy shares. A year later Zeehan employed only sixty or seventy miners, and most shafts were flooded. Without cheap transport Zeehan grew the hard way. Finally, in 1890, the Tas-manian government began a 3' 6" gauge railway from Strahan to Zeehan after John Provis, manager of the Dry Creek smelters, had issued a favourable report on the field. The railway was the official seal on the prospects of the silver-fields, and before the first earthworks had risen the public grew in confidence. English money, rare enough in Australian mining and altogether absent in any quantity in Tasmanian mining, financed the Mt Zeehan

Silver Lead Mines Ltd, which soon employed seventy men. Colonel North, Chilian nitrate king and millionaire gambler, began to speculate in Zeehan shares in London.

With prolific surface lodes extending over more than thirty square miles, Zeehan was a prospector's paradise. The mining experts, tested on silver at Broken Hill and found wanting, came in the train of the company promoters, praising wherever they went. The mining expert of the Hobart *Mercury*, after touring the field, expressed the feeling of the hour: 'So far, nothing to equal it in extent has yet been discovered in the Australian colonies, and if indications are to be relied on, it bids fair to become a rival to the celebrated silver-fields of the United States, Mexico and Peru'.

When the celebrated H. H. Schlapp, metallurgist of Broken Hill Proprietary, said the Zeehan lodes would live down, the few cautious mining advisers who thought that the lodes might be faulted or too low-grade at greater depths, received few consulting briefs thereafter. But the sceptics were only too right, and no payable ore was found below 600 feet. By 1947 the shallow lodes of Zeehan had produced some £5 million in silver and lead. Broken Hill, in the same time, had yielded £237 million and was still going strong.

Nevertheless, in 1891, when Australian silver mining was in its infancy, who was to say that Zeehan and Dundas might not offer prizes as rich as Broken Hill? Investors who had already earned £2,100,000 from one mine at Broken Hill thought the silver age was dawning and began to rush Zeehan shares in January. Almost every day prospectors and managers slipped quietly into Zeehan with valuable specimens, and telegraphed the news of rich silver strikes to brokers and directors in the cities. The journalists of the *Australian Mining Standard* were almost swept off their feet: 'We cannot remember any period in the history of these colonies when discovery after discovery of undoubted value followed each other so quickly'. By July, 159 companies and syndicates owned leases at Zeehan and Dundas.

Mining fever swept the southern cities. In Hobart the stock exchange was open all night, and people queued outside brokers' offices to order their Zeehan shares. Prices of favourite shares

soared far above their paid-up price; Silver Queen rose from 12s
to £8; Renison Bell from £2 to £24; and Silver King from £19
to £95. Shares in West Adelaide Proprietary rose eightfold in a
week. Most of the capital came from Melbourne where the stock
exchange met four times a day in order to exchange silver shares
for the surging crowd. Zeehan itself boasted a stock exchange
with sixty members and seats worth 75 guineas each. Stockbrokers stood about the main street all day, and hotels held
'open calls' at night in a town which held no more than 3,500
people in 1891. And it was only natural that while the people
craved for Tasmanian silver shares the shareholders of the Mt
Lyell Gold Mining Company should prefer a promised land to
their own disappointing mine. When they met in Launceston
and decided to sell their mine, they were certainly thinking of
the fortunes which were waiting to be mined barely twenty
miles away from their silent stamp mill. But the mania that
hastened the desertion of Mt Lyell was to lead, by chance, to its
revival. In the very week when the miners carried their swags
out of the Linda Valley Broken Hill investors, drawn by the
silver magnet, were crossing the seas to Launceston. Kelly and
Orr were the investors; and at Zeehan they heard of Mt Lyell
and finally bought the mine.

Bowes Kelly was a generous optimist of the Australian outback; thirty-eight years old, sixteen stone in weight, ginger-
bearded, and slow of speech. After a little schooling in Denili-
quin, New South Wales, where his father was police magistrate,
Kelly became a grazier, first in Victoria, and then in the far west
of New South Wales, where he sold out after several good
seasons and came down to Melbourne. Searching for a good
investment, he went to Silverton, in the Barrier Ranges, where a
sharebroker who was acting for an outback cattle dealer offered
him a fourteenth interest in the Broken Hill Proprietary mine. On
the recommendation of a surveyor Kelly bought the interest
without bothering to visit the mine. He rode out of Silverton,
share certificate in his pocket, little knowing that he would soon
be one of Australia's richest men. Within six months his £200
share was worth £70,000; within six years its market value plus
dividends amounted to £1,250,000.

Kelly was in his early thirties when he became a director of the Broken Hill Proprietary mine, but he was not content to retire in luxury for the rest of his days. He had heard of Zeehan from his Broken Hill friends, and stories of its long surface lodes induced him to invest in a Dundas mine in 1889. That was the first mainland capital in Dundas. In the next few years Kelly made plunge after plunge, financing mines, railways and smelters. He spent £20,000, and lost all.

William Orr was older and not as wealthy and well known as Kelly. A grey-whiskered, slightly stooped businessman, 'Willie' Orr had been on the Victorian goldfields as a lad, had run sheep in Queensland, and sold stock and stations in the Victorian district of Wangaratta, where he was small-town mayor. He went to Broken Hill before the boom, and stayed there six years, acquiring mining interests with Kelly.

Balstrup's Manganese Hill was their prize at Zeehan. In 1888 Peter Balstrup, a Danish prospector, had sent samples of green crystals which he found in a trench to W. F. Petterd, a Launceston boot importer and mineral expert, who said they were embolite, 66 per cent silver. Bulk samples from Balstrup's claim yielded 598 ounces of silver to the ton, the richest ore on Zeehan.

William Orr, who was a pacemaker in the Broken Hill march on Zeehan, was so impressed by the manganese boulders which capped Balstrup's lode that he and Kelly formed Balstrup's Manganese Hill Silver Mining Company and bought a controlling interest for £7,500. In the end Manganese Hill yielded only a trifling amount of rich ore and finished its life, like a racehorse turning the whim, mining barren ironstone for the Zeehan smelters. But it was a vital link in reviving Mt Lyell, for it was when Kelly, Orr, and Herman Schlapp, the American metallurgist, came to Zeehan to inspect the promising mine in January 1891 that they heard of the immense and puzzling deposit at Mt Lyell.

In the crowded stock exchange, boisterous bars and long main street of Zeehan everyone talked mining. The three Broken Hill men, their ears alert for any whisper of a large mineral deposit, chanced to meet Frank Duff, a stockbroker and director of Mt Lyell, who had been hawking photographs of the Iron Blow around Zeehan and inviting investors to visit the mine. On Duff's advice Kelly obtained copies of a recent report on the mine written by A. Montgomery, the government geologist. At Strahan the mine was again brought before Kelly's notice by F. O. Henry. the largest shareholder, who urged him to unpack his assaying plant, which was crated on the wharf, and to sample the mine. Kelly rejected the invitation.

Some months later Otto Schlapp, a professional assayer and mining reporter for the *Zeehan and Dundas Herald*, became interested in the Iron Blow. Walking back from South Dundas with a mine manager named Luke Bryant, Schlapp stopped to eat his lunch on the hillside near the Mariposa mine. He was reading the newspaper that had wrapped his sandwiches when he came across a letter entitled 'Canvas Town', written by Bryant. 'Chappy', said the American, 'there's a letter of yours here.' 'That's fine', said Bryant. Schlapp read the last lines: 'To the south of my old haunts is Mt Lyell, awaiting capital to make its wealth known to the world'. 'Where is this Iron Blow?' he asked.

After Bryant had pointed out the mountains in the west, Schlapp mentioned that he was going over that way to inspect a gold mine. Bryant told him to put a dozen sample bags in his kit and, if he had the chance, to sample the Mt Lyell mine. Schlapp took his advice. Some time later, seeing Bryant walk down the main street of Zeehan, he called him over to the assay office and showed him the gold content of the samples, tabulated in chalk on a bench. 'That's pretty good', said Bryant. 'Yes', commented Schlapp with a smile, 'it's better than you said it was.' Schlapp learned the name of the legal manager of the mine and wrote to his uncle, Herman Schlapp, at Broken Hill.

Assays of the ore and Montgomery's favourable report convinced the metallurgist that the mine was worth a close inspection, and he induced Kelly to approach old George Horne with an offer to purchase the mine. No sooner had negotiations begun, however, than the threads were almost snapped. On 3 August 1891 the Bank of Van Diemen's Land closed its doors. The oldest and busiest bank in Zeehan, it had advanced large sums to mining companies on the false security of ore at grass. There was panic in Zeehan. All afternoon hundreds poured into the long main street and waited tensely, shut off from the world by a broken telegraph line. The bank had over-traded. Next day twenty-seven Zeehan mines, their funds locked up in the bank, ceased operations.

Then the Melbourne investors who were the backbone of the silver-fields became anxious as the Victorian banks begun to shut their doors. The year 1891 proved to be 'the most disastrous one in the annals of the Stock Exchange of Melbourne' according to the annual report of that body. During the year shares listed on the exchange declined in market value by an average of 40 per cent. One land bank with £400,000 paid-up capital became so shaky that its shares were offered for nothing with a bonus to those who would take them.

Western mining had stagnated for years through lack of capital, and now blight swept the silver-fields and cut short the harvest. A hundred mines were short of funds for sinking shafts and erecting machinery. Mining investors sold their shares for ready cash or begrudged every 'call' on new shares. Melbourne financiers began to file their insolvencies.

The Zeehan boom collapsed late in 1891 and it marked the end of this extravagant era in Australian history. The 1880s were a decade of tremendous progress, railway expansion, and the ornate skyscrapers of the city called 'Marvellous Melbourne'; an era of unsound finance and mad speculation, led by politicians and backed by the great inflow of English capital. In 1889, Melbourne's land boom was almost over and the silver boom had petered out. For four more years the Australian economy shakily revolved, its gilt edge tarnished and its core propped up by imports of English capital. The silver-fields of Zeehan and Dundas proved to be a last hope for investors working in an economic system already quivering under the impact of its own excesses. Perhaps £1 million of investors' money was flung into this outpost of Melbourne's financial empire before August 1891, and probably another million followed in the next twenty years. Only a fraction of this sum, perhaps £500,000, was returned to shareholders in public companies. The unexpected prize of the Zeehan boom was Mt Lyell, a ghost mining camp when Zeehan swarmed with a battalion of bluey-clad miners. Mt Lyell became Australia's greatest copper-field and in the following sixty years was to yield ten times the wealth mined at Zeehan and Dundas.

7

The Great Gambler

The father of Bowes Kelly gambled away his property in Ireland and came to Australia in the gold rush. The son inherited the gambling spirit. When other investors were sacrificing shares at ridiculous prices and refusing to be tempted into new ventures Kelly was speculating as freely as ever. In the last week of August 1891 he and Orr returned to the west, not to salvage a few fluttering notes from the fortune they had buried in the silver-field, but to visit Mt Lyell, an abandoned field that might prove even more treacherous than Zeehan.

At Strahan they were greeted by James Crotty, the caretaker at the mine, who had horses saddled for the journey to the mountains. All day they rode across the cold hills until, drenched and numbed, they saw the lights of the 'Queen River' hotel twinkling in the valley. In the rough bush shanty, by the light of smelly kerosene lamps, the city investors ate the tough muttcn and drank the post and rail tea served as menu. Then they adjourned to the private lounge, sat around the log fire, filled their pipes and talked of Lyell. The cold air filtered through the warped timber walls, and the rough gold-miners, hearing that wealthy men were passing through, crowded in to stare at the magnates and Irish Jim. And so the evening passed, and the weary men rolled into their plank bunks, half drowsy and half excited for what the morrow might reveal. Next day, 29 August 1891, they led their horses round the side of Mt Owen and saw the peaks of Lyell, veiled by mist and rain.

For several days they chipped samples of ore from every face and tunnel and placed them in little sample bags. The bags were sealed and sent to Broken Hill for Herman Schlapp to examine.

Someone with an interest in the mine sprayed or shot gold fragments on the specimens and resealed the bags. At Broken Hill in boom days 'salting' was common enough to make the experts wary, and Schlapp detected the tampering. He was not perturbed. It was the copper, not the gold that fascinated him. 'I guess this is a metallurgical proposition', he drawled. 'If there's quantity there, I guess it'll pay.' When the American visited the mine a few months later he was just as impressed.

The Mt Lyell Gold Mining Company had offered the Broken Hill men a controlling interest in the mine if they spent £18,750, on the property before fresh calls were made on the present shareholders. Kelly and Orr knew, however, that the company was desperate for capital and that its bargaining power was weak. They whittled down the terms during negotiations or sidestepped them later, paying only £5,000 for an interest in the mine.

Kelly bought a copper mine. The old company sold a gold mine. Although Dr Robertson had told them that the Iron Blow capped a large deposit of copper, the Launceston directors still valued their mine for the rich gold-bearing ore near the surface. There is no evidence that they even bothered to assay the mine for copper. It is significant that when the Ballarat School of Mines tested the final samples for the old company they analysed the oxidized gold ore which fed the battery, not the huge but poorer mass of copper pyrites that fascinated Schlapp. And long after the copper deposit was being explored, mining leaders who gave evidence before a Parliamentary Committee in Hobart, emphasized that the ore contained gold and silver, and did not even mention copper. The legend of the gold mine died slowly.

In January 1892 the Mount Lyell Mining Company (No Liability) was formed in Melbourne and 100,000 £1 shares were issued. The shareholders of the old Launceston company received 45,000 shares and the Broken Hill group received 55,000 shares for their £5,000. Bowes Kelly received 20,000, Orr 15,000, Herman Schlapp 10,000, Alec Kelly 4,000, D. McBryde and W. Knox 2,500 each, while three of their friends took the remaining thousand. These men thus paid less than 2s a share; within six years the same share interest was to rocket to £16.

The first directors were Orr, McBryde, Joseph Clarke and the two Kellys. Every member of this first board had been a sheep pastoralist for most of his working life. Clarke was fifty-six, a former Tasmanian who had acquired a large interest in the gold mining company; from 'Mandeville Hall', his Toorak mansion, he ruled a rich pastoral kingdom. Aloysius Kelly, twenty-nine-year-old brother of the chairman, was a Riverina grazier who had turned to mining. Scotsman Duncan McBryde was a wealthy New South Wales squatter who had come to Melbourne to direct Broken Hill Proprietary. Three of these directors resigned and Clarke died, all in the space of three years, leaving Bowes Kelly as the sole survivor when the first copper was smelted. St John Biggs was the first secretary, but he became insolvent in the troubled times, and gave way to Alfred Mellor who was secretary for the rest of his life.

As the mine had been purchased by six men who had won their fortunes at Broken Hill, it was natural that a procession of Broken Hill managers should file along the mountain trail to Lyell. Among the experts was John Howell, who walked down the steep hill that fell five hundred feet from the iron outcrop to Cooney's Creek, and recommended that three tunnels should explore the ore body at depth. Otto Schlapp, the new manager, recruited miners from Zeehan and employed them in three shifts, seven days a week, in an effort to drive the tunnels as quickly as possible. Large huts were built of palings, sledged from the river flats three miles away. Iron trucks, rails, detonators, dynamite, provisions, chaff and oats were sledged from Lynchford.

In June, after making a wildly inaccurate survey of the ore body, Schlapp estimated that five million tons of ore, averaging 5·8 per cent copper, lay above the tunnel near the battery house. When Kelly told the shareholders that the company would make a profit of £2,500,000 even if it only mined half of the ore above the tunnel, mining men were justifiably sceptical, for the united Wallaroo and Moonta mines, the largest copper mines in Australia, employing several thousand men for thirty years, had paid less than £1,600,000 in dividends. Mt Lyell was just another mine, and investors shunned the shares.

The directors were so certain that their leases held the largest ore body in Australia that they asked Herman Schlapp, who was on holiday in the United States, to select a metallurgist capable of designing cheap and efficient smelters. Schlapp chose Edward Dyer Peters, a doctor of medicine and a high-ranking metallurgist who had built some of the largest copper refineries and smelters in North America. In November the directors cabled Peters, offering him £2,500 for a six months engagement. Peters inspected modern pyritic smelters at Kakorico and Leadville, and boarded the Australian steamer at San Francisco.

At Strahan the arrival of a metallurgist who was said to be receiving the highest fee hitherto paid by an Australian mining company was an event of great interest; and the conversation of the stocky American with the bushy mutton-chop whiskers and thin-rimmed spectacles was followed with awe and reverence. Preceded by crates of whisky and swags of blankets, Peters was led to the mine and set up in the old battery house. Blowflies, snakes, mud, tinned foods, and the deafening noise of blasting from the adjacent tunnel almost unnerved the lonely visitor. 'This is just the uncivilized, uncomfortable, backwoodsy kind of place that I swore off going to', he wrote to his wife, 'but what won't we do for money?'

For several weeks Peters wandered through the workings, chipping samples, examining rocks, and taking notes, while Kelly and Orr sat in the battery shed, draining a crate of Scotch and anxiously awaiting the verdict. Peters sliced the manager's estimates of the value and size of the ore body, but atoned for these corrections by asserting that the chimney of ore probably descended so far into the earth that it would never all be mined. He believed that the $4\frac{1}{2}$ per cent copper ore could probably be mined a mile below the surface—twice as deep as Lansell's 180 Mine at Bendigo—the deepest mine in Australia. The directors celebrated the good news by up-ending another crate.

Near the battery house Peters built a simple roast stall consisting of layers of wood, ore, charcoal, silica and limestone. It rained so heavily that the miners laughed when Peters flooded the pyre with kerosene and said the fire would roast the ore. But the fire burned for days, discharging deep yellow sulphur fumes, which coloured the low-lying clouds and withered the grass that fed the miner's goats. The test proved beyond doubt that the sulphur could be roasted from the pyrite without turning the ore to powder.

The smelting trial was conducted at Argenton, four miles south of Zeehan, on the new railway to Strahan. Today a lofty water tank for the engines, an old railway truck, a shed, and a few lumps of slag and broken bricks mark the site of a smelting town and railway junction that would have been a small city if the silver-field had justified its promoters. In 1893, however, the Broken Hill Ore Dressing and Smelting Company had only recently ceased smelting after a short and sad innings, and the reverberatory furnace was still intact. While G. F. Beardsley, an American metallurgist, prepared the smelters, a former share-broker named Adams, who was ruined by the crash of the Zeehan Bank, plied his teams of mules between the mine and Strahan until a hundred tons of 7 per cent copper ore were loaded on the Zeehan trains. The furnace was lit in May. It worked well until rain blew on the molten metal and exploded the copper matte. The furnace was lit again, but the gold disappeared down the cracks in the bottom of the furnace and was not recovered. 'Even under these ridiculous conditions', said Peters, 'it is probably as cheap as any smelting in the country.' A few tons of rich matte carrying 65 per cent copper were sent to Strahan for shipment to Europe, and Peters crossed to Melbourne to complete his report.

His final report was the company promoter's dream. 'In the past twenty years', he testified, 'I have never seen a mining and metallurgical proposition that promises so certainly to be a great and enduring property as this.' The directors thinking that their mine could stand any inspection, invited T. Alexander Allan, a former manager of the famous Tharsis mine, who chanced to be in Melbourne, to report briefly on their mine. But Allan, though impressed with the prospects, derided Peter's opinion so strongly that his report was given little prominence. After the government geologist had reported on the mine the three reports were handed to the printers in preparation for raising the necessary capital to exploit the mine.

In normal times Peters' report would have sent shares soaring and made shareholders delirious with excitement. On the eve of the greatest financial crisis in Australian history it was received languidly. Even in December 1892, when the share market was far healthier, the shareholders had been reluctant to buy 50,000 new £1 shares at 5s a share. Now, when banks were failing on almost every city corner in Melbourne, and shares in the dividend-paying mines were falling, who would think of investing in a mine that might take five years to pay a dividend or might never raise enough capital to produce one ton of copper? English capital and English capital alone, could save the company.

In March 1893, in preparation for courting the British investor, the directors liquidated the old company and formed the Mount Lyell Mining and Railway Company Limited. They called in the 150,000 £1 shares and issued in exchange 150,000 £3 shares, reserving the same number for sale in Britain. This reconstruction exacted no additional payment from the 164 shareholders; indeed 'watering the stock' was the traditional practice of Australian companies, which wanted to raise capital in England, and yet retain an interest in the mine out of all proportion to the money which they had invested. Since 1888 Australian shareholders had paid £22,000 in return for Mt Lyell shares with a face value of £450,000. The Englishmen would be asked to pay £450,000 for the same number of shares. It was doubtful, however, whether the scheme would succeed, for English investors were hardly likely to pay £3 for shares which were selling on the Australian stock exchanges at 8s each.

The directors were lion-hearted men. They believed that their managing director, William Knox, might raise the capital. He was a big-built and kindly man with long, wavy hair parted in the middle: a former bank clerk who had spent seven years as the dynamic secretary of the Broken Hill Proprietary Company. During the silver boom he and George McCulloch had floated the British Broken Hill mine in London when that city at first was unaware that Australia's premier silver-field even existed. This achievement stamped him as the one man who might accomplish the mission that now lay ahead.

8

A Lucky Bonanza

William Knox arrived in London in June 1893. Never was a time less favourable for raising money for an Australian mine. The collapse of banks in Australia and the United States, the fall in silver and copper prices, a long coal strike, and a depression of trade had so undermined the confidence of investors that scores of dividend-paying investments were yielding 15 per cent interest on their market prices. Bank vaults were stored with investors' money, left there for safety and earning no interest. The dice were loaded against new companies.

There was no news from Australia to rebuild the shattered faith of English investors. Sir Matthew Davies, Melbourne banking magnate and former Speaker of the Legislative Assembly, had been arrested at Colombo on a charge of filing a false balance sheet and been escorted back to Melbourne to face trial. James Munro, millionaire and Victorian Agent-General in England, had returned to Melbourne to file his insolvency, paying creditors 6d in the £ and starting life afresh as overseer on a sheep station. In the winter of 1893 scores of financial leaders went bankrupt; bank after bank fell, burying millions lent by English and Scottish investors. In Britain the name of Australia was dust.

Knox took an office in St Swithin's Lane, in the copper corner of the City of London, opposite the iron gates that guarded Rothschild's Bank. Here he began his publicity and his long interviews with bankers and financial houses. He interviewed editors, who printed good reports of Mt Lyell in the *British Australasian, Financial Times* and *Statist*. He even tried to insert an article in *The Times* through the good office of Miss Shaw, their famous correspondent, just back from Australia.

63

Critics soon found chinks in the company's scheme. Dr Peters carried little prestige in England, and his book on copper smelting, though famous in the United States, was labelled 'outmoded'. Allan, favourably known in London, was critical of the company's plans. Furthermore, potential investors resented the allocation of half the shares to Australians, who in five years had invested only £22,000 in the mine—a valid complaint since these Australians would receive the same dividends as the Englishmen who subscribed £450,000. When Knox allayed this criticism by offering preferential shares to the English investors Australians were offended and share prices fell. Knox was also impeded by the absence of the official estimates of the railway line, for it was London practice to support every claim in a prospectus with signed documents—a practice soon to disappear. Some critics said that the railway might cost £300,000—double the company's estimate.

Knox failed to raise the money in July, and postponed the next attempt because the 'city men' had left for the summer's hunting. 'The man who is in London in August is ashamed of himself, and apologises for it. He fears he may be thought a nobody', Knox lamented. So he followed the grouse shooters into Scotland, home of the Spanish Tharsis company, and for seven years the happy hunting ground of Australian banks and building societies. Millions of pounds in Scottish savings had been lost or frozen in the Australian bank crash of that year and Knox found that 'utter distrust and repugnance of anything Australian was most marked'. 'The Scottish people have suffered terribly over this bank collapse', wrote Knox, as he hurried south.

In October, the summer recess spent and the financiers back in London, Knox circulated a prospectus containing the abridged reports of the experts and inviting private subscriptions for 150,000 8 per cent preference shares at £3 each. The *British Australasian* expected a successful flotation of 'this latest Australian prodigy', but the response was so trifling and the hostility to anything Australian so fierce that the shares were withdrawn from sale. Wealthy companies then offered assistance. The Exploration Company Limited offered a £60,000 loan to test the mine; the Hull and Barnsley Railway Company offered £200,000 for the railway; and the principals of the French Copper Ring made an unscrupulous offer to rig the share market and form a French company. Knox rejected these schemes and approached the directors of Rothschild's Bank. He offered them 50,000 shares at £3 each; he left in half an hour. The Bank had cabled Melbourne to learn that the same shares were selling there at 27s each.

Knox's task had been hopeless from that day when he landed in San Francisco and heard of the Melbourne bank crash. In November, after Kelly had cabled him to break off negotiations, he appointed a London Advisory Committee which included George McCulloch, once owner of the unknown wealth of Broken Hill, and George Meudell, author of the slogan 'Australia for the Australians'—quite a popular slogan in England in that year. Knox left London, suffering from his hectic labours, and down at heart. Friends who saw him off at Victoria railway station wondered if he would reach Melbourne alive.

The company's financial plight was to be redeemed by a lucky discovery. Peters had only been at the mine a week when, standing near the old battery with Otto Schlapp, he noticed a seam of grey, mud-like ore in a truckload of pyrite which a miner was tipping on the dump. It resembled rich silver. Peters inspected the crumbling ore and handed a tinful to the mine manager. 'We'll put that through the pot, boy.' The ore assayed 2,000 ounces of silver to the ton!

About 350 feet from the mouth of the tunnel, on the footwall of the ore body, miners sank a winze (shaft) and followed the silver down. At first Peters was cautious. 'The rich ore', he said, 'is only interesting and not important.' Part of the seam consisted of baryta and oxide of iron, similar in composition but far richer than that mined and crushed by the Launceston company; it averaged 300 to 800 ounces of silver to the ton and 3 per cent to 5 per cent copper. The remaining ore was argentiferous copper pyrites, assaying 26 per cent copper and up to 2,000 ounces of silver a ton. The entire seam averaged over a thousand ounces of silver a ton, and some specimens were more than half silver. The ore showed signs of living down but an inrush of water flooded the winze, and the windlass could not bale the water fast enough. A winding engine was packed to the mine; poppet heads were erected above the shaft in a large underground chamber; and the men began to sink two timbered shafts to explore the wealth below.

While Knox was in London, the early shipments of this ore were being smelted at Swansea, in South Wales, but as the seam might well peter out at any moment, Knox saw little reason for optimism. When he landed in Melbourne at Christmas 1893, however, he learned that phenomenal developments at the mine could modify his entire financial scheme. The new shaft had cut the fringe of the silver fifty feet down, and the vein was now thirty feet wide! The directors began to live in hopes that the silver might supply enough money to carry out the early stages of their construction programme. When the bonanza was exhausted, they might raise £150,000 of debentures and build a shorter railway and two furnaces.

As the Australian economy was still sick, and the company had little chance of selling shares or debentures, the directors decided to see if the Tasmanian government would guarantee the debentures and make them a gilt-edged security. The company would deposit £25,000 with the Treasurer to defray the first six years' interest and would repay the rest out of profits. If the company collapsed, the Treasurer would be burdened with the interest for the remaining sixteen years. The Mt Lyell Debentures Bill, embodying these provisions, was submitted to the Legislative Assembly in June 1894 and was backed by Sir Edward Braddon, the Premier, who had been a member of Mt Lyell's London advisory committee. The government was in a precarious financial position, the great hopes of western mining had only been partly fulfilled, and Parliament refused to take the risk which should rightly be borne by the private company. Without this guarantee the debentures were too risky for investors, and the issue was withdrawn.

By mid-1894 the company was little nearer the end of its construction programme than two years previously. Then the rich silver saved it. Three miners blasted the ore, mining over 10,000 ounces of silver a week. In an area of ten feet square £18,000 worth of ore was mined in a fortnight. A quarter of a million ounces of silver came from a stope barely the size of a suburban dining room. In September 1894, after nearly £84,000 had been won from the vein, there was no sign that the rich ore was exhausted. But a new cross-cut, driven into the vein from 75 feet down the shaft, passed through seventeen feet of good ore and then struck barren conglomerate rock. Underfoot the rich patch lasted four or five feet and suddenly pinched to a mere thread. When the bonanza finally vanished in May 1895, eighty feet below the spot where the deposit was first discovered, 849 tons of ore containing 858,000 ounces of silver and 176 tons of copper had been shipped to smelters in Adelaide and Wales. In two years of silver mining Mt Lyell had raised more silver than any mine on Zeehan, Australia's second silver-field.

Years later William Jamieson, a Mt Lyell director, recalled that if the company had not struck the rich shoot of ore Mt Lyell would have been 'as dead as a doornail'. It yielded a clear £106,000 after paying high shipping freights and smelting costs. It was the company's sole income through two and a half years of sustained efforts to secure capital.

Once the bonanza was mined, the directors resumed their plans to sell £150,000 of debentures. As the London market had revived, and was plunging money in Western Australian gold mines, George Meudell, an energetic Melbourne stockbroker, was sent to London to assist in the sale of the debentures. Offering 6 per cent interest without success, he advised the directors to grant prospective buyers the right to exchange one £100 debenture for 33 Mt Lyell shares at any time in the next two years. Thus if Mt Lyell shares soared, investors could exchange a £100 debenture for shares worth double or treble that sum. If shares did not rise, debenture holders were reasonably assured of 6 per cent interest. Aided by this inducement the London men floated the loan and cabled the good news to the directors. Next day the Melbourne Board withdrew the issue on the grounds that their terms had not been followed, and a day later they floated the loan in Melbourne in a few hours. Twenty-six Melbourne and Adelaide businessmen, many of whom were directors' friends, tendered for the whole issue. Each debenture, being exchangeable for shares, rose from £90 to £405 when Mt Lyell shares soared.

A group of Irish-Australians, led by James Crotty, secured from the Supreme Court of Victoria an injunction restraining the directors from issuing the debentures until the shareholders approved. The shareholders met in Melbourne on 26 July 1895 and accepted Kelly's assurance that no director was pecuniarily interested in the transaction. The debentures turned the tide. They raised £135,000, which, added to silver profits and £60,300 from the sale of shares in April 1896, financed the work until the first pure copper was railed to the port.

9

Smelting in the Forest

During 1892 J. A. Moore had reported on routes for a tramway from Mt Lyell to the sea. He agreed that a tramway could be built across this rugged tract of country and he respected Bowes Kelly's wish that Strahan be the port of shipment. This decision was embodied in the Mt Lyell Tramway Bill and confirmed by the Tasmanian legislature in December 1892. It satisfied Bowes Kelly's prejudice but it fettered the legs of the surveyors who had to select the actual route, and it led, six years later, to the construction of a second railway to Mt Lyell along a route which Bowes Kelly had obstinately damned.

F. A. Cutten, the company's railway engineer, engaged a staff of four surveyors and four assistants in February 1893. They surveyed and rejected the Queen River cart road and then traced the deeply scoured valleys of the Tully and Burgess which flowed west beneath the new Strahan-Zeehan railway. To cross these watersheds the track would require sharp curves and steep grades. It would be costly to maintain because of damp, shifting ground in winter and the danger of bushfires destroying high wooden viaducts in summer. Finally, the surveyors followed the King River to its tributary, the Queen, and upstream to the reduction works site in the Queen Valley. At first sight the King River seemed impossible. A 3′ 6″ gauge railway track might follow the meanderings of the river just above floodwater mark for the first eight and a half miles, but then the river narrowed into a precipitous gorge with cliffs rising five hundred feet above the torrent. It seemed that no railway could penetrate a gorge so steep, narrow and rocky. The only pass out of the King Valley was up Sailor Jack's Creek and over a short dividing range, much

69

steeper than any grade that had hitherto been attempted by Australian railway engineers. Cutten, however, had an answer for the problem—an Abt railway.

The Abt system, named after the German inventor, had been introduced in the eighties to climb the Harz mountains, where giant adhesive locomotives were powerless. The Abt railway employed a middle rail or rack, supporting two parallel rows of overlapping teeth. The steam in the rack cylinder of the locomotive turned a toothed pinion wheel, which hauled the train up by the teeth. The ordinary cylinders in the engine continued to work the wheels on the rails, giving the train a dual means of locomotion and a firm grip of slippery rails in wet weather.

Cutten thought the Abt was ideal for Mt Lyell. A locomotive would take a full load to the beginning of the rack rail, haul half the load to the summit, and return again for the remainder of the trucks. The load had to be split because the gradient of the rack section was one in sixteen for a mile and a half on the Queen River side of the summit, and one in twenty for three miles on the King River side of the summit. Such gradients must have been heresy to orthodox railwaymen, for grades steeper than one in forty were rare in Australia.

Cutten's choice aroused bitter criticism, both from old miners who had come up Sailor Jack's Creek to Lynch's diggings ten years before, and from two of his surveyors who were forthwith dismissed. Critics alleged that Cutten had chosen the Abt system because he would receive a royalty from Rinecker, Abt & Co. of Wurzburg, Germany, for introducing their patent railway into Australia. The directors ignored this allegation and refuted the engineering criticism by quoting the opinion of Napier Bell, an experienced railway engineer. The Tasmanian Parliament promptly sanctioned four and a half miles of Abt railway and decreed that, in the interests of a swift passenger service, trains on the rack section must travel at no less than four miles an hour.

In March 1894 Cutten estimated that the railway, without the rolling stock, would cost at least £200,000. After cutting three hundred miles of foot tracks to survey a route, however, the company found that its bank balance was almost negligible. The money market in the City of London was still too dull to excite the hope that Knox could raise the money if he returned to

England; and it was too much to hope that £125,000 could be raised from the rich ore to finance a shorter railway from the smelter site to Teepookana, the highest navigable reach of the King River.

In June 1894 the outlook was so bleak that the directors seriously considered building a tramline of wooden or steel rails and using eighty draught horses to haul the coke and copper. Next month they revived T. A. Allan's idea of an aerial tramway or ropeway. Allan claimed that the copper, coke and general cargo could be carried cheaply in large buckets on a wire ropeway, suspended from high steel trestles, Electricity from the lake near Mount Sedgwick would work the three stationary engines along the ropeway and haul the endless line of thousands of buckets from the smelters to the wharf; the ropeway could be built in eight months for a mere £36,000.

Again the directors consulted Napier Bell, who recommended a railway along the easy stretch from the smelters site to Hall's Creek, the proposed start of the Abt, and an aerial tramway up to the ridge and down to the lower landing of the King River, where barges could ship the copper to Strahan. When smelting yielded profits, the company could scrap its aerial tram and complete the railway to Strahan.

More engineers were rowed up the river and led through the soggy forest to inspect the railway route. In August James Johnstone, a Melbourne civil engineer, suggested a thirty-chain tunnel from Sailor Jack's Creek to the other side of the King River gorge, thus making an easy grade all the way from the harbour to the smelting site. Johnstone believed that the additional £20,000 expenditure would be repaid in a few years by the cheaper running costs. 'If it had been a Government line,' said Napier Bell, 'I should certainly advise that the line be taken through the gorge.' In the light of later events the gorge route was justified; and if the directors had known that Mt Lyell would still be smelting copper sixty years later they would have tunnelled under the ridge at a very early date.

In the dim light of events in 1894, the aerial tramway was wisest, quickest and cheapest. Allan knew far more about pyritic deposits than Peters or anyone in Australia, and he knew that as such mines deepened the ore grew poorer. His warning that capital expenditure should be curtailed ruthlessly was not heeded by the stout-hearted gamblers who directed Mt Lyell. Fired with wild optimism by their fabulous luck at Broken Hill, they vested that same rugged, illogical faith in Mt Lyell. Having seen the huge profits the Silverton Tramway Company had earned carrying silver-lead from Broken Hill to the South Australian border, they believed that Mt Lyell would become an equally rich mining field, yielding huge profits for a railway that tapped it. They laughed at Allan's reasoned pessimism, but they could not afford Johnstone's optimism. The tunnel was not built, although an expert engineer has re-examined the plan in recent years.

Finally, heartened by the way the rich ore was living down, the directors decided to build fourteen miles of railway from the smelting site to Teepookana, crossing the summit on an Abt track. By the close of September 1894 the company had saved £60,000 from the sale of rich ore. It budgeted this on opening up the mine; constructing a crushing mill, roast stalls, two furnaces, and a haulage railway from mine to smelters; clearing fourteen miles and building four miles of the railway; and buying launches and barges for the King River. This was an ambitious estimate but at least it was a beginning. The directors hoped that rich silver and the sale of shares on a slowly awakening stock exchange might finance the other works.

Gaffney and Harvey, the Strahan storekeepers, tendered to clear the timber from the railway route in October, and in the dry summer their men hacked and burned the forest and undergrowth. In November Garnsworthy and Smith, Melbourne con tractors, began the hazardous four and a half mile stretch from Teepookana to Dubbil Barril, completing it in eleven months for £22,403. As tenders for building the remainder of the railway were too high and as the pace of construction was too slow, the company appointed E. Carus Driffield as railway engineer. An energetic South Australian, who had already supervised the construction of two private railways, Driffield rushed through the last ten miles in ten months, employing day labour.

Deep cuttings and embankments were built with pick, shovel and wheelbarrow; and almost a mile of bridges and viaducts, built of logs hauled upstream over the rapids, took a heavy toll of time. The trestle bridge across the King—eight hundred feet long, and the second longest railway bridge in Tasmania—posed the greatest problem, and months were spent in driving piles sixty feet into the silt before they found firm foundations. Landslides were the second serious problem. A sudden slip at the summit of the Abt killed two men.

The Mt Lyell railway was Tasmania's largest construction job in this time of depression and it became a Mecca for the unemployed from all over the island. The strong in heart tramped overland from Hobart, carrying their swags and hoping for work. Others enrolled for relief work, and if they were lucky received from the government a 10s steerage ticket to Strahan. Steerage passengers supplied their own food and catered liberally, knowing that the voyage might take a day or a week; usually they arrived white of face with tucker bags untouched. Many landed at Strahan without a penny to their names, bought bread, groceries, boots, picks and shovels, billys and pans 'on tick' from the storekeepers, and shouldered their loads to the camps along the railway. Axemen, labourers, butchers, clerks, carters—all engulfed in the depression—they built the Mt Lyell railway. Old pictures show them in their flannel shirts buttoned to the neck, thin-legged trousers, bowyangs, and battered felt hats, sporting ragged beards and drooping moustaches—and toiling before the sharp eye of the foreman.

Bush settlements housing five hundred men trailed the earthworks up the King and Queen Valleys. Starting Creek, Camp Spur, Wire Rope, Rinadeena, and Hall's Creek had their little day, with their cluster of smoky tents, paling huts, stores, boarding-houses, and the inevitable sly-grog shop or 'refreshment tent' for the day of rest.

While the railway advanced, the mine and smelter sites were linked by three quarters of a mile of steam tramway and an equally long haulage line which climbed the high dividing ridge on an average grade of one in three. At the top of the ridge a stationary engine hauled the ore trucks up by cable and lowered them on the counterbalance principle. This, too, was Driffield's work.

At the mine the ore body was explored by a mile of tunnels, drives, and cross-cuts, driven through hard rock with hammer and steel, for there was no compressed air plant at the mine. It was slow work, and the depths of the ore body still remained a mystery. In the upper levels, where thousands of samples of ore had been tested and the ore body was known to be about 560 feet long and 200 feet wide, the overburden was being removed in preparation for the systematic mining of the ore in a huge open cut. Lindesay C. Clark, a young civil engineer from Melbourne's sewerage and water works, who had been appointed engineer-in-charge of mines, directed this operation.

At the smelting site in the Queen Valley the chief metallurgist, Robert Carl Sticht, had been busy since March 1895. A short scholarly American, Sticht (he pronounced his name Stisht) was a native of the German-peopled city of Hoboken just across the river from New York. In 1880, as a young graduate of a German mining academy, he went west to the great mining camps of the Rocky Mountains, where he designed and managed smelters at Pueblo and Great Falls. He became interested in pyritic smelting, the most attractive in theory of all smelting techniques, for it utilized the heat generated by the combustion of the iron and sulphur in the pyritic ore as a fuel in the furnace, thus dispensing with large quantities of expensive coke. But the process was full of practical pitfalls which led to the closing of Sticht's first pyritic smelter at Toston, Montana. Spurred on by failure, Sticht continued to experiment and had become the United States' leading authority on pyritic smelting when William Knox approached him in Montana in 1893. Samples of ore convinced him that the Mt Lyell mine would make pyritic smelting an unqualified success for the first time in the world, and he was delighted at the invitation to erect the Mt Lyell smelters.

Dr Peters had been wary of the prospects of pyritic smelting, and his large sheaf of plans for the new reduction works did not embrace the pyritic technique. Herman Schlapp and Alexander Stewart, eminent men at Broken Hill, had agreed with Dr Peters' insistence that the ore should be roasted in stalls before being smelted in a blast furnace, and Driffield was actually building the stalls when the new American metallurgist arrived at the smelting site. Sticht abandoned the stalls, insisting that pyritic smelting should be the first and main step in treating the ore. 'The Mt Lyell ore is fitted for it in a measure far surpassing any

Miners gathered at the mouth of the bonanza tunnel, Mt Lyell mine, 1894

Queenstown, 1896 and 1954 (from the same position). T

odern town stretches far down the valley to the right

Penghana, the industrial town in a forest clearing, 1896

other ore that I have ever used or seen used.' He suggested, as an initial plant, two blast furnaces, larger than any extant, converter vessels, and a reverberatory furnace. The directors boldly adopted his report in full.

Dr Peters had selected a site for the reduction works, near the Queen River. Two wood-choppers cut a track through the forest to let him inspect the location in the valley. It took Peters two hours to stumble over that track, and when he returned to the mine the cook scraped the mud off his clothes, waist down, with a shovel. Now axemen, carpenters, labourers and tradesmen swarmed to the valley, felled trees, cleared scrub and levelled the ground. By the rising skeleton of the smelters clustered several hundred tents and shacks, the town of Penghana, its roots in the black peat and tree stumps. Blacksmith's forge, stores, lime kilns, and carpenters' shops were built. A sawmill whined; a little locomotive on a two-foot line shuttled between quarries, mills and smelter building; kilns baked hundreds of thousands of red bricks. The long iron smelter building and its huge brick flue and chimney stack, rising 250 feet above the smelter floors, began to dominate the landscape. Crushing plant, storage bins and the long, three-storied smelting shed were built. In the thick of it was Sticht, clad in his long bluey, indistinguishable from the workmen around him. The year was one of the wettest on record, but rain, snow and hail, the work went on.

The railway was still miles away and everything was dragged by horse teams from the coast. From the bay at Strahan the track rose a thousand feet to the undulating scrub country, where the Southern Ocean lay low in the west, and the chiselled peaks from Sedgwick to Jukes were lost in passing mists to the east. Five horses, plodding single file, dragged four-wheeled wagons which rattled over the corduroy or oozed black mud through the wheels. In time the track became three deep ruts, two carved by the iron wheels, one by the horses. Slogging from dawn to dark, a team usually reached the stables and boarding houses near the half-way peg at nightfall.

These wagons rarely hauled more than one and a quarter tons but they dragged up several thousand tons of machinery in eighteen months. Boilers, blast stoves, rails, steel girders, engines, six-ton locomotive, 46,000 firebricks, 116 heavy cast-iron U pipes, thirty tons of galvanized iron and a million bolts were a few of the burdens the old track carried. Travellers on the modern road from Queenstown to Strahan cross the teamsters' track, abandoned in 1896 when the iron horse steamed through.

In June 1896 the two 150-ton furnaces were ready and ore was being hauled across the ridge from the mine. For weeks the horse teams had pulled the small wagon-loads of coke through the winter rains from Strahan, and now the coke bins were filled at last. Thursday, 25 June, was the long awaited day; ten years to the day since Tasmania had heard the news of the rich gold discovery at the Iron Blow. In the afternoon Sticht sent a coded cable to the head office in Melbourne—'Sentery Schurzung'— which being interpreted, read, 'will start to smelt tonight'. While the furnace was being kindled G. F. Beardsley handed out instructions to the furnacemen imported from Lithgow, N.S.W., and briefed the bushmen and labourers who had never seen a furnace in blast. Hitches were all too frequent in blowing in a new furnace, and Sticht prepared for every emergency. He knew that the success of the whole enterprise depended on this delicate smelting technique that had failed so often.

In a nervous, hushed atmosphere, broken only by rain drumming on the iron roof, he lit the furnace, and supervised the charging of coke, ore and white silica into the roaring inferno. Shortly after midnight he tapped the furnace, and a stream of molten orange slag glided into the waiting slag pots. The furnace was working so quickly that six men, constantly wheeling away the glowing pots, could barely cope with the work. In the early hours of the morning the front gate of the furnace was knocked open, releasing the copper matte which hissed into firebrick-lined trucks. Assays revealed that little copper was lost in the smelting. But for singed beards and burnt arms, the smelters were a brilliant success.

Down the valley, the last rails were laid on 18 July. At noon the little locomotive steamed into Queenstown, the new smelters' town, through a cheering crowd which adjourned to the Queenstown Hotel, and in bumpers of champagne toasted 'success to the enterprise and the plucky shareholders'. Until the Abt locomotives arrived from Glasgow in August, an ordinary engine laboured over the steep rack section with trifling loads.

The railway laid, and smoke billowing from the smelter stack, Bowes Kelly celebrated in grand style. He arranged for the Governor of Tasmania, Lord Gormanston, to preside at the official opening of the railway and smelters in March 1897. Two steamers brought the distinguished guests to Strahan. The *Grafton* left Melbourne on a Monday morning, and after calling at Devonport ran into mountainous seas which raked the ship from stem to stern. One giant wave smashed the bulwarks and washed overboard fifty sheep that were penned on deck; another seventy sheep perished the same night. In the storm the propeller shaft jammed, and for a time the ship drifted helplessly towards the shore. She was nearly wrecked again at Macquarie Heads before finally berthing at Strahan, no less than 59 hours after leaving Melbourne.

The *Australia* left Hobart on the Monday evening, sheltered in Port Davey, steamed into the same gale that endangered the *Grafton*, and slipped back to Hobart after a 48-hour voyage. Lord Gormanston staggered ashore, pleaded official business, and the *Australia* steamed to Strahan without him.

Meanwhile, the *Grafton* contingent travelled on a steam launch across the harbour and through a tattoo of hailstones to the river port of Teepookana. They boarded a train that was almost smothered with ferns and bunting, praised the scenery and the remarkable railway almost incessantly, and came into the crowded Queenstown station beneath the flags of all nations and to the strains of a brass band. After quickly touring the smelters they perforce returned to Strahan, for the small Queenstown hotels could not accommodate such a large influx of visitors. Next morning, at half past six, they set off again for Mt Lyell, where they vied with one another in heaping superlatives on the mine, all vowing that the mine must be one of the largest in the world. That evening, at Strahan, they saw the lights of the *Australia* as it steamed up the bay; and the following morning, while Bowes Kelly guided the Hobart visitors to the mine, William Knox took the remaining guests to the old convict settlement down the harbour, the dignitaries amusing themselves on the return journey by firing at a bottle which was towed astern of the launch. At West Strahan that evening, in the splendid sixty-six-roomed Palace Hotel, the guests banqueted on a French menu, served by cooks and waiters specially brought from Melbourne, and to the music of Herr Holm's Zeehan Orchestra. There were seventy guests; every third guest insisted on making a speech, and the others would certainly have done so if they could. More banquets followed in Hobart and Melbourne.

In July 1897 the Mt Lyell Mining and Railway Company paid its first dividend. Other mines may have hoarded their treasures in the face of fourteen years' prospecting and mining, but no Australian mine had absorbed more than £400,000 before paying its first dividend. The immensity of this sum is lost in the inflation of our century, the astronomic budgets of paternal governments, and the great investments of modern overseas corporations. But in the early nineties, when a labourer earned 6s or 7s a day, and government budgets were measured in hundreds of thousands, not tens of millions, £400,000 was a huge expenditure. To the visiting journalists who came along the new railway, Mt Lyell was undoubtedly one of the seven wonders of Australia.

10

The Copper Boom

In October 1896 Macnamara Russell published in London his *Mount Lyell Mines,* a lavish, well bound volume of 170 pages. He analysed the figures of the first four weeks' smelting at Mt Lyell and concluded that ten furnaces would earn an annual profit of £780,750—more than the annual revenue of the Tasmanian government—at ruling metal prices. He thought there was enough ore already in sight in the Iron Blow to feed ten blast furnaces with a thousand tons a day for thirty years.

Five months later the *Zeehan and Dundas Herald* wrote: 'It is the greatest mining property known of to-day in the Australias, and will, ere another year or two, stand pre-eminent as the most profitable copper producer in the world'. Maybe this was boom journalism, for the Mt Lyell Co. had sponsored this special edition of the *Herald* to acquaint its two thousand shareholders of the opening ceremonies. Yet these sentiments thundered through the mining columns of most papers in the land. And when the first quarterly dividend was paid on 1 July 1897 the *Australian Mining Standard* made the bold prophecy that 'this mine will prove one of the world's wonders, and the holder of a hundred shares can consider he is provided with a moderate income for life'.

In January 1895 the £3 shares had been selling at £1 16s on the Melbourne stock exchange. Late in 1896, when smelting had succeeded, they rose to £9 5s in anticipation of prolific dividends. They continued to rise until September 1897 when each of the 250,000 shares cost a miner eight weeks' wages. With shares at £16 10s the market value of the mine exceeded £4 million. Few mines had so taken the Australian mining public by storm.

79

Meanwhile other companies were prospecting at Mt Lyell. Most of their leases were sluiced for gold after the rush of 1896, then abandoned, and re-pegged as copper leases when the Broken Hill men began to work the Iron Blow. In 1894 six companies employed a few miners to tunnel the hillsides in search of copper. Next year at least seventeen companies held leases at Mt Lyell, and their shares were bought and sold each night after the plates were cleared away and the kerosene lamps lit in the new Mt Lyell Hotel. Some companies were mere pawns, awaiting a mining boom. All lacked the lifeblood of western mining—capital and cheap transport; and all lacked payable copper. These mushroom companies depended entirely on the Mt Lyell Mining and Railway Company, and had the smelters failed or the railway been abandoned, these mines would have raised no more capital and closed within a year.

Sticht's smelting success interested a legion of investors in the new copper-field, and the mushroom companies kept the printers busy, issuing millions of new shares. In its review of the year 1896 the Sydney stock exchange lamented that the reputation of the Iron Blow had resulted in 'much rubbish being thrown on this colony'. But, compared with Melbourne and Tasmania, Sydney was spared the bundles of doubtful Lyell shares, and the year 1896 was only a dull prelude to the excitement of 1897. The success of the Iron Blow had set the stage for the West Tasmanian copper boom, the last great mining boom of the century.

The economic atmosphere was favourable for a mining bubble. Australia was slowly recovering from the bank crash and the great depression, and thousands of investors had money to gamble. Melbourne investors envied the fortunes won by Adelaide and Sydney investors who had bought shares in small Western Australian gold mines before the gold boom. They had watched the Western Australian companies refloat in England and their shares soar to mad prices before the companies had even struck gold; and they lamented their restraint in buying those shares. Now they saw a score of speculators each amassing at least £10,000 from their Lyell shares, while hundreds more made smaller sums. Bowes Kelly, the boldest Lyell investor, had paid about £3,500 for 27,000 shares which he held in 1893. After selling more than 7,000 shares at a handsome profit, he and his wife still retained a parcel of shares which, at £9 a share, were worth £178,000 before even the smelters were in blast. 'If the stock sees £20, and many sanguine Southern scrippers swear it will,' wrote the *Bulletin*, 'Kelly will—well, what would you do if you had £400,000 in one parcel?' This was one of the success stories of the age and when cheap shares in a host of new Lyell mines were offered to the public its influence was infectious.

More important, English money was pouring down Australian mines in unprecedented volume. Kalgoorlie and Coolgardie gold mines absorbed at least £10 million in 1895-6-7 and became the golden Samarkand of the English investor. When the desert bubble burst British investors bought shares in other Australian mines. In 1895, when the Mt Lyell railway was advancing through the forest, shrewd Englishmen began to buy cheap Mt Lyell Mining and Railway shares. Next year the writings of Macnamara Russell and London financial journalists had swelled the trickle of Lyell shares crossing the ocean to a swift river. In January 1898 there was more than idle boasting in the claim that 'there is no dividend-paying mining stock on the London market that can be named in the same breath as Mt Lyell'.

If one great copper deposit was buried at Mt Lyell, there might be—no, there *must* be more! Kalgoorlie, Broken Hill, Ballarat and Bendigo were not one-mine fields. Why should the copper of Mt Lyell be confined to the one 82-acre lease? To gold and silver speculators whose knowledge of mineral formations ended at reefs, lodes and leads these analogies came instinctively; and they were willing to believe any expert who described a copper lode stretching north and south of the Iron Blow. Many promoters and bush experts, inexperienced in copper mining, had the same lode prejudice, and in their prospectuses they swore, hinted or suggested that their particular lease embraced the 'Mt Lyell lode', and that splashes or veins of copper in their tunnels were derived from that lode. And so it was that the mad gamble we call 'mining boom' centred on Mt Lyell in 1897 and 1898.

We know today that the ore bodies buried in different parts of the Lyell field are separated by millions of tons of barren rock, and that these deposits vary in chemical composition and richness. Even in 1895, before most companies were re-floated on the wave of prosperity, only one independent and accredited expert had suggested that they were joined in one lode. He was Gustav Thureau, the retired government geologist, whose prediction that there was an inexhaustible lode of gold at Mt Lyell had caused so great a sensation in 1886 and such great disillusionment in the following years. He reappeared in 1895, when the field was little explored, and predicted that one great copper lode stretched across the field. In the next few years no evidence of this lode was found in scores of trenches and tunnels, but as late as 1899 unscrupulous promoters still raised capital by publicizing Thureau's misleading and outdated report.

Mere possession of the mythical lode, however, was no password to wealth. The copper ore body had to be large enough, and it had to be rich enough, to yield a profit. Until a company proved this by shafts and drives lode talk was meaningless. After April 1898 it was known that much deep ore in the Iron Blow was unpayable, and that if this ore formed a deep lode across the ridge, underground mining costs would far exceed the value of the copper. The Mt Lyell lode was a myth, but it picked at least £200,000 from English pockets.

A glance at a few Lyell prospectuses reveals the promoters' guile. The prospectus of the Mt Lyell Copper Estates Ltd, issued in London in August 1899, included a map of its lease liberally strewn with lodes, and a report written in 1895 by Thureau, the promoters' favourite geologist. 'The continuance of the celebrated Mt Lyell "Iron Blow" has been proved during the half mile or less to your ground by means of open cuts and shafts,' wrote Thureau. This was a brazen assertion even in 1895. Four years later the Mt Lyell mine had been contoured with drives and showed no tendency to dip half a mile to the south, but Mt Lyell Copper Estates did not hesitate to publish this deceptive report. British investors rushed 'THIS SAFE AND LUCRATIVE INVESTMENT' and subscribed £25,000. They were shocked to learn, a few years later, that the company had abandoned its Copper Estates without selling a pound of copper.

The Great Mt Lyell Copper Co., which had been launched in London in 1899, owned a square-mile lease, the size of a farm and adjoining a far flung lease of the Mt Lyell Co. on a frontage of a few yards. Its glib English prospectus announced that 'the well-known copper mines of the Mt Lyell Mining and Railway Company adjoin this property. The shares of that company, at their present market price, show a value of more than £2,500,000. The property of this company is nearly double in area and is believed will prove equally valuable'. The Great Mt Lyell claimed 'every reasonable expectation' that a southern extension of the Mt Lyell lode would dip deep into its ground, 'at which great richness of ore may be expected'. The prospectus went on to describe the 'temperate and salubrious climate', a 330′ lode assaying 7.5 per cent copper, and a probable annual profit of £350,000. Pasted to the prospectus was a white slip of paper which announced in bright red lettering a last-minute cable from the mine: 'The tunnel is now in one hundred and forty feet. Is opening up splendidly; payable concentrate ore throughout.' Forty years later systematic sampling of this tunnel revealed that the richest ore in the first 140 feet carried only 0.3 per cent copper. English investors were not to know this. They subscribed £25,000 and lined the pockets of the promoters.

The Mt Lyell Comstock Copper Co. unearthed a deposit of copper on the northern slopes of Mt Lyell. It was an isolated ore body, differing from the Iron Blow in chemical composition and too poor to be mined at a profit. To raise money for a railway and to explore this deposit the company printed a glowing English prospectus and a gaily-coloured map which showed the blue 'line of lode' tortuously wending its way north of the Iron Blow, across five leases and through the middle of the mountain, to arrive safe and sound at the Comstock mine, a mile and a half away. This bold lie drew £50,000 from gullible English and Scottish investors.

Each of these companies raised a large sum in London on the strength of assertions which would have been laughed to scorn by Melbourne investors; assertions which were feasible in 1896 but which had been exposed as lies in the intervening three years. Not every company distorted its prospects, but the companies which raised the largest sums certainly deceived the British investors.

Admittedly, the few companies which adjoined the Iron Blow had genuine hopes that the pyritic ore body might enter their lease, for it dipped into the hill at an angle of 30° from the vertical. Of the three companies which shared this hope, Central Lyell had the best chance. In 1896 it carried the first diamond drill to the field and erected a high derrick on the slope of the hill above the open cut. It sank several vertical holes on the boundary of its lease, and in one hole the round core of rock which was hauled to the surface contained shining specks of pyrite. The excited manager rushed the sample to an assayer and deep was his disappointment when he learned that the ore carried less than 1 per cent of copper. To add to his worries, the drillers could not retrieve an £800 diamond-drill bit from the hole and his company had to bear the loss. Work ceased and the lease passed into the hands of the Mt Lyell Co. Years later some miners who were shooting rock in the side of the Mt Lyell open cut found the drill hole, but not the diamond—unless they kept the secret. Apparently the hole had deflected across the boundary and penetrated the ore body in the Mt Lyell lease. Nevertheless, the theory that led to the drilling was ultimately justified, for the ore body entered the old Central lease at great depth and was mined in the underground workings of the Mt Lyell mine.

While the scaffolding of the diamond drill hovered near the busy benches of the Mt Lyell mine, the manager of the South Lyell mine announced that his company was also heir to the riches of the Iron Blow. He began to sink a shaft in a narrow gully, hidden from the top benches of the Mt Lyell mine by a small spur. Down went the shaft, deeper than any on the field, and still there was no sign of copper. The shareholders grew restless and they were not reassured when a leading director announced in London that South Lyell had the main ore body of the field and that the famous Mt Lyell was a mere offshoot. But there proved to be a grain of truth in this unscrupulous boast, for when the shaft was over five hundred feet deep it struck ore. Miners lowered down the shaft after a charge had been fired were surprised to see massive ore that was identical with the ore being mined in the open cut, less than 150 yards away. They loaded the bucket with wet ore and signalled the engine driver to haul it up the shaft. Once the ore reached daylight, the news spread like wildfire, and all day the Gormanston post office sent cables to Melbourne with coded orders for the sharebrokers. South Lyell shares soared until they had a total value of £330,000. Even Robert Sticht thought that South Lyell had intercepted his company's ore body until subsequent exploration disclosed that the new ore body was isolated and unpayable.

A third company, the West Lyell Co., exploring ground to the north-west of the Blow, did not have the excitement which befell the blind stabs of its two neighbours. But it had the satisfaction of raising more than £30,000 from the wily publicity of Macnamara Russell, who published a map showing the 'assumed position of the pyrite lode', twisting across the West Lyell lease like a mammoth python.

The shrewd promoters named their companies with ingenuity rather than imagination. Of the forty-two companies which had been floated by October 1898, all but four had 'Lyell' in their pompous titles, and many included some point of the compass to press home the pretence that they adjoined the Iron Blow, and shared in its wealth. There was a North Mt Lyell, South Mt Lyell, Central Mt Lyell, and Copper Mines of Mt Lyell West; Great Mt Lyell, Great Mt Lyell South, Mt Lyell Blocks, Mt Lyell Peaks, Mt Lyell Extended, Mt Lyell Consols, and Lyell Pioneers; King Lyell, Queen Lyell, Prince Lyell, Duke Lyell, Empress Lyell, Kaiser Lyell, and Crown Lyell—and so through the points of the compass again—North King Lyell, North Queen Lyell, North Prince Lyell and North Crown Lyell. To woo overseas investors, directors borrowed the names of the world's great copper mines: Mt Lyell Anaconda, Mt Lyell Tinto, Mt Lyell Tharsis (which bred five sons, three of whom renounced the family name of Lyell), Mt Lyell Comstock, and most northerly of all mines, North Mt Lyell Tasman Comstock Silver, Lead and Copper Mining Company.

The name 'Lyell' was carried long distances. A mine near Strahan was called Lyell Strahan Proprietary and a mine near Dundas was called Lyell Dundas. Later, a Victorian Lyell, a Wallaroo Lyell, a Chillagoe Lyell, and a Ballarat Lyell, mining in widely scattered parts of Australia, cashed in on a name that was magic to investors in 1897-8. Like the Pied Piper the name of Lyell led many to their doom.

The wide dispersion of copper at Mt Lyell ensnared investors.

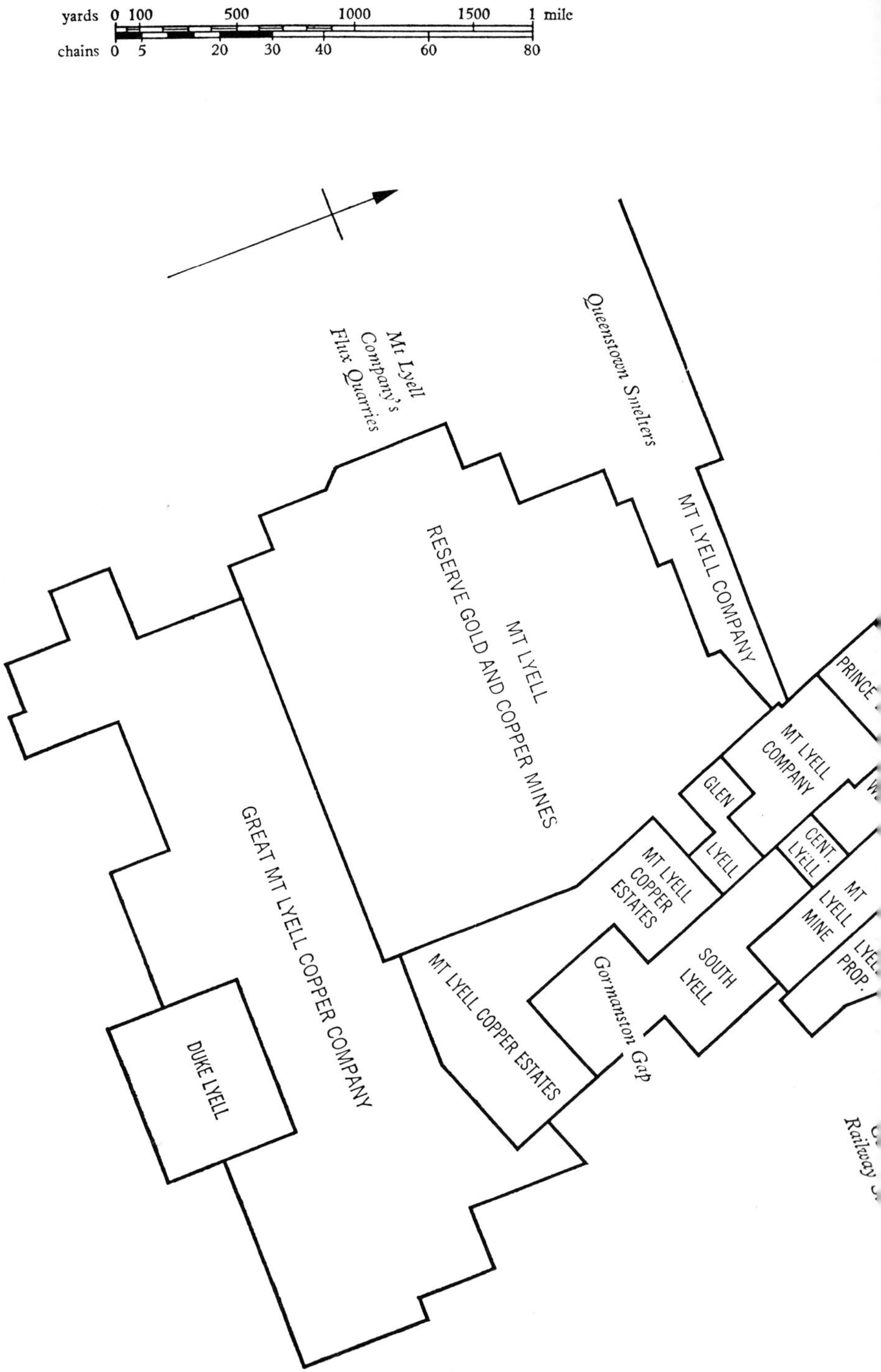

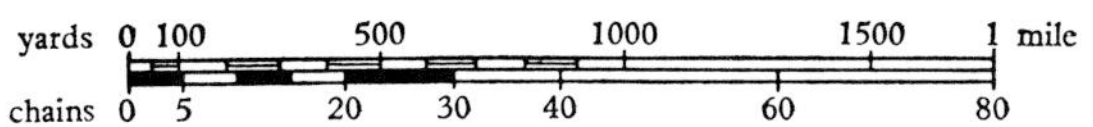

yards 0 100 500 1000 1500 1 mile
chains 0 5 20 30 40 60 80

Queenstown Smelters
Mt Lyell Company's Flux Quarries
MT LYELL COMPANY
MT LYELL RESERVE GOLD AND COPPER MINES
GREAT MT LYELL COPPER COMPANY
DUKE LYELL
MT LYELL COPPER ESTATES
Gormanston Gap
GLEN LYELL
MT LYELL COMPANY
CENT. LYELL
MT LYELL COPPER ESTATES
SOUTH LYELL
MT LYELL MINE
LYELL PROP.
PRINCE
Railway

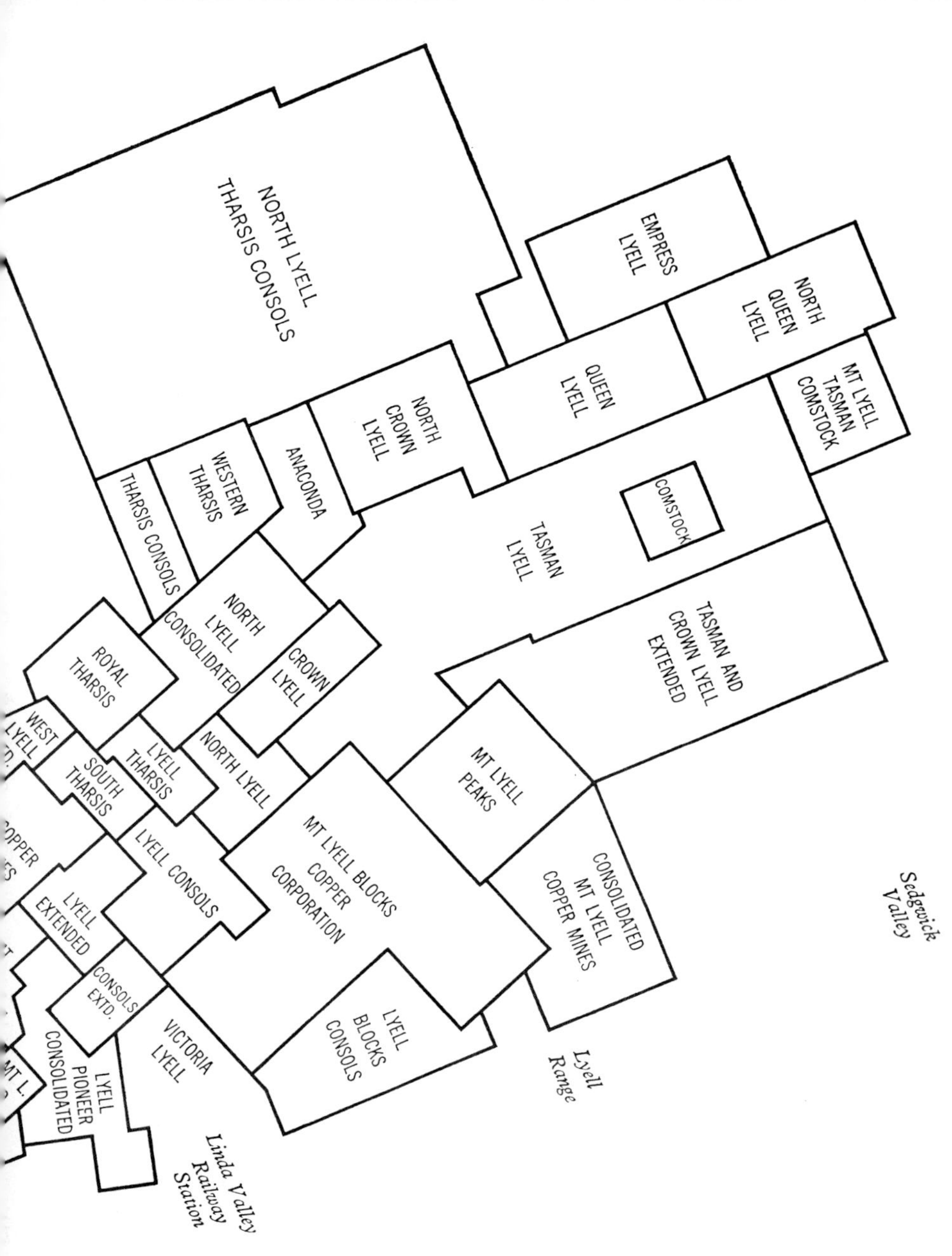

Lyell leases during the boom, about 1900

Almost every company discovered small splashes of bornite, native copper, copper pyrite or peacock ore. In the space of a few months newspapers recorded discoveries of amazingly rich ore carrying 12 per cent copper in Queen Lyell and Tasman Lyell, 23 per cent in North Crown Lyell, and 35 per cent in Crown Lyell, while Prince Lyell found beautiful bunches of yellow pyrite carrying 35 per cent copper, and North Lyell Consolidated found veins of black copper oxide, 20 per cent pure. The ore of the famous Iron Blow seemed like road-metal compared with these rich ores, but not one of these six companies paid a dividend. Investors forgot that copper must be in large quantities, not in small veins, to be mined at a profit; that many samples were handpicked; and that assays were faked.

By March 1898, when twenty-eight companies were busily working on the field, the mines stretched as far south as the spurs of Mt Owen and the rugged, timbered gorge of Conglomerate Creek; while to the north they had crossed the peaks of Mt Lyell and reached the sheer rock wall in the Sedgwick Valley. Although the copper belt was four miles long, and in parts almost a mile wide, the important mines were scattered along the western spurs and gullies of the Linda Valley amidst a dreary waste of black peat and stumps. Here the landscape was dotted with small tunnels and mullock dumps, boiler houses and smiths' forges, shafts surmounted by tall poppet heads or windlasses, managers' houses and primitive iron offices, tents and miners' huts by the hundred, and wandering pack tracks.

No week passed without some mine reporting a new discovery in shaft, trench or adit. More sensational were the chance discoveries, the valuable ore body which roadmakers discovered when blasting a cutting for a road through the North Lyell lease, and the yellow copper which miners found on the Crown Lyell lease while levelling the ground to pitch their tents. Lucky discoveries excited speculators, and shares soared or slumped in a day. In five months Lyell Tharsis shares leapt from 3s 6d to 90s and Tasman Lyell jumped from 2s to 63s. Melbourne investors, speculating more freely than at any time in the previous eight years, transacted a huge volume of business in Lyell shares, while stockbrokers in Hobart and Launceston worked day and night to cope with orders. Such was the popularity of Lyell shares in Melbourne that Victorian and Western Australian gold shares and Broken Hill shares fell under the 'cold shade of neglect', according to the *Annual Review* of the stock exchange in 1897. 'The year had closed with a movement in progress which may eventuate in dazzling success or disastrous failure.'

Pegging day typified the excitement of the Lyell boom, which had its greatest and maddest hours in the summer of 1897-8 when acres of scrub and rock were valued as highly as city blocks, and one mine alone was worth £80,000 an acre. The government decided to throw open 2,305 acres of land east of the smelters and along the lower reaches of Conglomerate Creek, land hitherto reserved from mining operations. This huge reserve was known to contain gold and copper, and moreover it adjoined leases in which the original peggers held bundles of free shares, worth thousands of pounds. Noon on 15 February 1898 was the chosen hour. On the eve of pegging day Queenstown was invaded by trainloads of strangers who had come from as far afield as Melbourne and Hobart. Orr Street was packed with people, all discussing the great event. Ironmongers sold out of axes, toma-hawks, and nails. Hotels were packed to the billiard-room floor.

Before the summer sun had risen next morning prospectors were clambering up the hillsides from Queenstown and Gor-manston, and by mid-morning the streets of the towns were silent. At noon the smelter's whistle shrieked and suddenly slope and gully rang to the sound of axe and hammer as hundreds of promoters, miners and prospectors hammered in pegs, dug trenches, blazed trees or built stone cairns to mark their claims.

The maximum lease allowed by law was eighty acres, but 450 leases, totalling almost forty square miles, were pegged. Overlapping claims and triple pegging made such a jig-saw that the applicants amalgamated their claims in one great lease as large as a sheep-run and called it the Mt Lyell Reserve Copper and Gold mine. Shareholders subscribed £7,500 to test their lease, and returned home to await news of a 'copper lode'.

Meanwhile prospectors had hacked south of Queenstown to the valleys at the foot of Mt Jukes and Mt Darwin, and climbed the massive multi-peaked mountains in search of fresh Iron Blows. Others had trekked to Mt Read, Rosebery and the Pieman where early gold and copper mines had stagnated for lack of capital. New discoveries were reported almost daily—always copper, the glamour metal. Even the honourable members caught the fever. Stafford Bird, venerable and bearded Speaker of the House of Assembly, splashed through the mud at Rosebery, while others searched the wilderness of Port Davey. Small wonder that the Treasurer, in his financial report, believed that the discoveries on the west coast read like the romance of King Solomon's Mines. He knew, for in 1898 he collected £40,000 rent from 160,000 acres of mineral lease—the most pegged mineral district in Australia.

Of the copper-fields near Lyell, the Dora field caused most excitement in the summer of the boom. Prospectors wore a rough track from Lyell to the back of Mt Sedgwick, where shallow trenches had revealed green carbonate of copper, yellow copper ore, and even bornite. In the ensuing craze on the Launceston stock exchange was born the large family of Dora companies—Royal, Lake, Lady, North, South, Mount, Extended, and plain Dora. Miners sank many shafts and sent scores of glowing telegrams from the new telegraph hut until winter snowstorms drove them down the mountain.

Mt Jukes was first pegged in February 1897, and Mt Darwin late in the same year. Almost every morning in the summer of the boom, prospectors and businessmen walked stealthily out of Queenstown and Gormanston towards the coral-coloured peaks of Mt Jukes, where they pegged every inch of available ground until the rugged ranges became a chess-board of several hundred leases. A few pack-horses and many men carried stores, explosives and anvils up the steep mountain tracks, and soon huts and the proverbial blacksmith's shop sprang up beside a score of new tunnels. At least thirty companies were floated, many with Melbourne money. For long the most favoured mine was Lake Jukes, which stood on a bleak mountain beside a lake that was often encrusted with inches of ice in the dead of winter.

Prospectors, financiers, swindlers, investors, clairvoyants and carpet-bag speculators congregated in Queenstown. The Tasmanian press called it 'Copperopolis', the copper city. In January 1898 the Queenstown stock exchange began its brief life, and here most Jukes and Darwin mines were formed into small companies to prospect their ground. Here they gained a footing in the investment world and awaited the next step in the upward path, the longed-for Melbourne or London flotation that mostly never came.

In Queenstown, in December 1897, it was said that you could not meet a businessman who was not dabbling in mining shares; and in Hobart it was said to be just as rare to meet anyone from Lyell who did not own a lease as good as the Mt Lyell mine. Who remembers 'Beau's lode' at Mt Jukes? The *Mount Lyell Standard* whispered that 'many who know what they are talking about, say Beau's lode is richer than even the magnificent North Lyell'. In those years 'Beau's lodes' were a dollar a dozen. Many a west coaster knew of, or knew someone who knew of, 'another Iron Blow'.

If we winnow the grain from the chaff and the comments of independent engineers from the loud boasts of stockbrokers, it is reasonable to assume that most Tasmanians thought that their west was one of the richest mineral regions in the world. Cautious men thought that Queenstown might hold 40,000 people within a few years; others pictured a great city stretching from Queenstown to Gormanston, down the Linda Valley and across the King River; and the sober man, who pictured Gormanston as a beautiful city with tramcars running down streets lined with skyscrapers, was not howled down. One Lyell company was employing two thousand men, and another forty mines might become as large and as rich. One journalist, writing in hundreds of British newspapers in November 1897, when six giant furnaces had just been ordered for the Queenstown smelters, even claimed that 'Mount Lyell has been endowed with a golden history without parallel in the annals of the world'.

11

Land of Fire and Brimstone

Penghana, the industrial town in a forest clearing, rose with the smelters. In February 1896 it numbered five hundred men, mostly navvies, axemen, builders and teamsters. When smelting began, perhaps a thousand people lived in small houses, tents, and iron huts, packed tight where the offices, slag dump, and sub-station stand today. But Penghana was doomed from birth; it squatted on the company's lease almost in the morning shadow of the chimney stack that smoked sulphur day and night. Every resident knew that sooner or later he would have to remove his shack or shop.

On 12 December 1896, a blustery Saturday morning, a bush-fire roared down the hill, spared the smelters, but destroyed butchers' and grocers' shops, skittle alley, billiard room. Ali Baba's Assyrian Haberdashery, and 140 other buildings. While some men were throwing their possessions into the shallows of the Queen River, others were rolling barrels of beer from a blazing house, and soon the upturned barrels were surrounded by bushmen, 'SNARLING AND FIGHTING' (so the *Zeehan and Dundas Herald* alleged in bold capitals!) in the smoke haze. One wood-cutter perished in the flames.

No new Penghana rose from the ashes. Within three years the town was only a memory, and its eastern arm was buried beneath the black slag from the furnaces.

Queenstown, a mile down the railway line, had already been surveyed by Selby Wilson as the official smelters' town. It was hewn out of dark swamp-forest, so treacherous that gold-diggers rarely ventured into the valley. In the winter of 1896 Queens-town was just a suburb of Penghana, comprising railway station,

92

hotel and cluster of huts. In May 1897 it held 200 dwellings and Penghana was the suburb. In May 1899 it had 1,300 dwellings and 5,000 people. No Tasmanian town had grown so rapidly. It spread down the valley, climbed the steep foothills, and twisted up the gullies to new suburbs called 'Piggery', 'Raggedy', and South Queenstown.

From the Queenstown railway station drays and coaches crawled up a steep corduroyed road—a death trapeze for poorly-shod horses—and over the ridge to Gormanston, four miles away. The Mt Lyell Co. ran a small steam train from Queenstown past the smelters to the foot of the haulage, where the trucks were hauled by cable over the hill to the Mt Lyell mine, a quarter of a mile from Gormanston. This was the company's private line, and it carried only ore, mining supplies and the few miners and officials who could produce an official permit.

Gormanston, the miners' town, was named after Lord Gormanston, Governor of Tasmania, and like Queenstown the name was not popular with many a radical miner. Early in 1898 Gormanston seemed likely to become a serious rival to Queenstown, with four large hotels, miners' hall, band hall, churches and a wide main street that rapidly filled with shops. As the northern mines developed, new mining settlements sprang up to disperse the population and slacken Gormanston's progress. In August 1898, when Gormanston had 160 dwellings, another 130 dwellings lay around the Lyell Tharsis and North Lyell mines. This town of North Lyell was inhabited by miners who built huts on the mining leases, near the smithies, stables and charcoal kilns of the mines. Hotel, stores, boarding house, iron and paling huts formed a straggling settlement which was threatened by bush-fires every summer, was a snowfield in the depth of winter, and lay exposed to sulphur and wind the seasons round.

In 1900 a fifth town, Linda Valley—popularly called Linda—expanded rapidly along the valley below Gormanston; and with 600 people, two hotels and billiard saloons, it began to rival Gormanston, though not in amenities. The three towns of the mining valley now held over 2,000 people and were growing every day until the slump in the price of copper closed fourteen mines and reduced the population to 1,760 in April 1901.

These five towns on the field were so compact that the most

distant two were less than three miles apart. The mountain ridge, however, tended to isolate miners and smelter hands, making the small communities independent of one another. Queenstown was a town of smelter hands, woodcutters, quarrymen and railwaymen, with a handful of miners who walked long distances to work at the mines. Every day some fifty would walk the three miles from Queenstown to the 'Blow', and back again when work was done.

At first most men lived in small hillside huts, erected by their mates in Sunday working bees. Even in 1901, when houses were rapidly replacing huts, 1,100 of the 2,900 habitations in the district were single-roomed huts, and another 700 houses had only two rooms. In the same year, males predominated by almost two to one, and by an even higher ratio in Gormanston, where gales and rain and creeping mist made miserable the days of the housewife. As the women increased, the shanty suburbs gave way to small houses with red or tarred roofs. The main street of Queenstown, already packed with solid shops and two-storied hotels, wore an impressive façade when the three-storied brick hotels—the 'Empire' and the 'Imperial'—sprang up by the railway station to greet wealthy investors.

In the first years they were insanitary towns, scourged by typhoid and dependent on frequent rains to wash away the refuse. As there were few acres of arable land on the west coast fresh vegetables and fresh milk were luxuries. In 1898 two cows grazed in the district, and tinned milk was the vogue. Despite the high rainfall water was often scarce. At Gormanston running water was often impregnated with copper, and miners complained that sulphur fumes contaminated tank water.

The miners did not thirst. Many drank their hard-earned wages, and pay-night in early Queenstown was often a drunken carnival, with streets and hotel bars noisy with brawling drunks until midnight sent them staggering to their huts. That was the pattern of the large company mining towns of the eighties and nineties—Broken Hill, Zeehan and Coolgardie—during the first boom months. By February 1898 the town had sobered down, and visitors were openly amazed that pay-night should provoke so few brawls. The hotels lagged behind the influx of people. Queenstown had two hotels in 1897, eight in 1899, and fourteen in 1901. Across the ridge at Mt Lyell the miners patronized another ten. Every Sunday the little village of Lynchford, long depressed by the failure of the local gold mines, found its feet again, catering for the scores of bona fide travellers who strolled three miles down the railway line from Queenstown.

But the social life of Lyell did not centre long in hotel bars, though they were rarely silent in a field of shift-workers. Old sportsmen still sigh for the old meets when axemen, runners and pit sawyers came to Lyell from every corner of the island. They recall the immense popularity of wood-chopping contests, and the platforms propped outside hotels where axemen chopped for a wager. They recall Australia Day 1898, when a large crowd gathered to watch foot-running down the main street of Queenstown.

Almost every week in the late nineties some travelling troupe of minstrels sang and played in Cairns Hall, Queenstown. Heralded by exaggerated publicity bills, announcing 'Great Clavier Virtuoso', 'Great Solo Violinist', and 'Refined Balladist', they farewelled their audience with a 'sacred and sentimental' concert on the Sunday. Travelling actors strutted the boards and played the popular melodramas of the day. Nellie Stewart came to Queenstown, and here in 1899 old Grattan Riggs, beloved of Australian playgoers, saw his last curtain fall and was buried by the bay at Strahan.

When Zeehan's huge Gaiety Theatre was opened in February 1899, J. C. Williamson sent over a Melbourne company of sixty to play the current hits, *The Sign of the Cross* and *The Royal Divorce*. Each night for a week a thousand packed the theatre, and at 2 p.m. on Saturday a special train packed with playgoers steamed out of Queenstown on the first stage of the long journey to Zeehan. They reached the Gaiety just before 8 o'clock, watched the drama unfold, and returned to Queenstown next day, completing the round journey in twenty-four hours. Zeehan that year was a dignified town of eight thousand; a third as large as Hobart. A trip to Zeehan was like a visit to the city for the young bloods of Lyell.

The 'open calls' in the hotels, quadrille assemblies and political meetings drew workmen down muddy hillsides, with lantern or bottled candle in hand. Their mongrel dogs followed them into the halls and sat beneath the forms. Bendigo men who saw Orr Street on a Saturday night, when shops were open to 10 p.m. and hotels until after midnight, when the street was thronged with people and gay with the music of the brass band, called it a 'new Pall Mall'.

The field was spiced with picturesque characters. Gormanston's first boarding house was kept by 'Old Properly', a fiery old soldier who had marched under Havelock to the relief of Lucknow. With his frothy whiskers, peak cap, stern toothless face, and white apron, he crouched over his stews morning and night, and greeted the miners coming off shift with the gruff shout, 'Come and get it'. To those who complained of the same old fare the crusty veteran would clench his first and bellow the evergreen threat; 'Get it into you or get out. If I hear from you again, I'll give you a sou-wester under the jaw; I will properly, old soldier, I will'. A much feared man was 'Old Properly'.

At Queenstown a cockney tended a glowing brazier on the road outside the Imperial Hotel and hailed the returning smelter hands at midnight with a piercing cry that was heard far down the valley. ' 'Ot dogs, 'ot dogs', he shouted. 'All 'ot and tasty. Warm your 'ands and fill your belly.' Equally notorious was 'Nugget' Reid, an eighty-year-old vagrant who was rarely seen without a dog-eared copy of a Dickens' novel and a bottle of the blood-curdling brew known locally as tanglefoot. And then there was 'Hot Stuff', a small, bearded old man who was the butt of the larrikins as he shuffled down the streets. When the old fellow was barracked, he would wheel slowly around, neck stiff, and spit out a morsel of profanity that sent respectable ladies hurrying for shelter. And who could forget the town bellman? He paraded the streets at night, roaring out the merits of the evening's entertainment in a laboured voice that kept rhythm with the swinging of the bell. 'Oyez, oyez', he would shout, 'Now staging . . . at the Acamady of Moozic . . . the great melodrama' and his voice would mount a crescendo as he shouted the name *East Lynne,* or *The Silver King,* or one of the moving melodramas of the day.

The best-loved of all was 'Jack the Savage', a prematurely aged prospector who spent his last years vacillating between the hotels at Queenstown and the gaol at Strahan. A hopeless drunkard, the Savage won fame for his patriotism during the Boer War. In his sober hours he would earnestly harangue the laughing crowds on the merits of the British generals, calling again and again for three more cheers for 'our brave boys'. At night, he was always the last to withdraw from the window of the *Mount Lyell Standard,* and sometimes sat by the editor's fire until the last cable was received in the early hours of the morning. If, by chance, his vigil was rewarded by a British victory, he would cheer himself hoarse in the streets; and if nobody was there to support him, his indignation was intense.

No entertainment seemed complete without the Savage. In the last year of his life he was dragged aboard a picnic train and taken to Strahan. Late in the day, when he had loyally toasted every British victory from Talana Hill to Mafeking, a wag pointed out to sea and exclaimed that a pennant which fluttered on a buoy was a Boer flag. The Savage was so incensed that he splashed into the water and waded toward the flag until only his grizzly beard and tanned face could be seen bobbing above the water. He appeared in public for the last time one Saturday in November 1900 when he proudly strutted the streets as a sand-wich man for the early closing movement. On Sunday he was the worse for liquor and was placed in the cells for safe keeping. He died on the Monday, aged forty-seven, his passing mourned by all the town. 'The army has had millions of supporters during the war', wrote the *Standard,* 'but there was not one more de-voted than the Savage.'

The Boer War aroused fanatical enthusiasm at Mt Lyell, and inspired patriotic processions and mass jubilations that far ex-ceeded any celebration during the two world wars. The fervour reached its height in 1900 when the news that Mafeking had been relieved was posted in the window of the *Standard.* All morning a cheering crowd jostled around the window, and on every verandah a Union Jack floated in the fog. In the after-noon the band marched through the sunshine to the smelters, and at the changing of the shift seven hundred men fell in behind the band and marched to the town where they were absorbed by a milling crowd. At night five thousand people crushed into Orr Street and cheered to the echo as Jack the Savage, riding a white horse, led a procession around and around the town. Effigies of Kruger, the Boer President, were stoned and burned again and again; an ancient cannon fired crackers into the crowd from a hotel balcony; the Savage rocked the bars with patriotic speeches; a crowd surged past the Commercial Hotel to the shop of a German jeweller and hurled stones on the roof and taunted him for his Boer sympathies; and another group staggered up Spion Kop, a conical hill overlooking the town, and set fire to a barrel of tar which flared like Vesuvius. Over at Gormanston the miners formed a torchlight procession behind the band and marched up and down the rough streets, singing rousing airs until the night was far spent.

Marching had a strange fascination in those days. Men marched through the streets on the least provocation. In 1900, when the Fitzroy football team—the leading Victorian team—came to play three matches against Lyell, the two teams donned their uniforms and marched to the oval. One engineer, a German named Jason, even marched his men to work. He worked for Pohligs of Cologne and came to the west coast to erect an aerial ropeway between the Mt Lyell mine and the smelters. It was his custom to collect his men at the smelters, form them into a squad and march them briskly over the hills to the sites of the steel towers. He always marched like an old sergeant, shouting orders in a guttural voice: 'Lep, right, lep . . . Pick zie feet up . . . Lep, right, lep'. Few resented the military German.

This mania for marching stimulated the bands. In 1897 Queenstown achieved the ambition of every Australian city when its brass band, led by the Partington brothers, won the national championship in Sydney. Thereafter, while brass bands were the craze, the band was famous throughout Australia. In 1900 Queenstown sponsored a second band, a large drum and fife band, but Gormanston was even more musical and boasted the Mt Lyell Brass Band and a first class military band; the latter was a civilian band which blended wind and percussion instruments after the style of European army bands.

The churches flourished in the first years and possibly claimed the active support of a third of the population. Before the smelters were in blast, the Salvation Army mustered a small band in their barracks at Penghana, an Anglican priest regularly carried his swag overland from Strahan and preached in the blacksmith's forge at Penghana, and the Wesleyans had a small church in Gormanston. By 1900 Queenstown had Roman Catholic, Anglican, Presbyterian, Salvation Army and two Wesleyan churches. In the mining valley were another two Wesleyan churches and good Catholic and Anglican buildings.

The vigorous life of the mining fields is not hard to explain. When most people lived in tiny huts or two-roomed houses, when there was no cinema (except a magic vitascope that depicted such breath-taking subjects as 'Railway Train' and 'Angry Sea'), when 'five distinct selections from Edison's Marvellous Gramophone' was an absorbing item at any concert, when newspapers had only four pages—half news and half advertisements, when the wireless was unknown, when railway fares were exorbitant and gardens were impossible, the people obviously had to make their own entertainment. Hence no day passed without some crowd-pleasing event, be it a political meeting, band recital, procession, concert, sports meeting, boxing match, wood-chop or stage show.

The *Mount Lyell Standard* found its first news when the long line of refugees straggled down the track from the smouldering ruins of Penghana. After January 1899 it was published daily under the editorship of E. H. C. Oliphant, Shakespearian scholar and pegger of mining leases. The *Standard* specialized in mining; so did the lawyers. There were eight lawyers at Queenstown and seventeen in the west. They rose and fell with the mines, and today there is not a lawyer on the west coast.

Sulphur was the curse of Mt Lyell. When the big company smelted its pyrite in ten or eleven large furnaces Queenstown found its climate changing. In still weather sulphur from the smelters thickened fogs into pea-soupers, choked Queenstown, and blanketed the valley. For days on end men working in the flux quarries on the hills above the town basked in the winter sun, and looked down on the creamy waste of cotton wool in the valley. Men who set out with hurricane lamps for the smelters in the morning were sometimes found miles away at evening. Sulphur was in every breath of air; even tobacco lost its taste. One holiday procession became hopelessly confused when marchers split in different directions at a fogbound corner.

On clear days passengers on ships sailing into Macquarie Harbour could see the sulphur pall of the Mt Lyell smelters, hovering over the rugged mountains, fifteen to twenty miles away. The few travellers who walked overland from Hobart saw the corroded iron telegraph poles, ten miles before they reached Linda. At the Mt Jukes mines, seven miles from the smelters, miners tasted the sulphur when the wind was northerly. The prevailing sou'westerlies blew the fumes to Gormanston, but Queenstown fared worst in fogs or northerly winds.

The second curse was rain. In fifty-seven years of recording rainfall, Gormanston recorded only four years when less than a hundred inches of rain had fallen. In 1906, $56\frac{1}{2}$ inches fell in three months; seventy-nine of these ninety-one days were wet, with an average fall of some 70 points a day. The next winter it rained for thirty-three consecutive days. 'There is a legend at Queenstown', wrote one Melbourne journalist, 'that in the dim past it did not rain for ten whole days and nights.' Most of the large mines were open cuts, and rain, sleet and snow often retarded work. In no other part of Australia was open-cut mining carried on in such a climate. The 'bluey'—a loose, grey flannel overcoat, worn by navvies, metallurgists, miners and parsons—became the national dress in the west.

Every summer bushfires scorched the hills, thick with undergrowth as dry as tinder. The fires roared through the forest and burned the black peat so fiercely that the townsmen invented the myth that the sulphur was actually coating the bush and making it inflammable. Even the mountain slopes caught fire and glowed red in the night sky. In five summers more than four hundred huts and houses were destroyed; and some men were burned out three times, losing all they owned. Several mining leases were burned and blackened fifteen times until it seemed that they could burn no more. House fires were frequent, though rarely so devastating as the bushfires. But one winter night in 1898 the two storied, wooden Criterion Hotel caught fire at Gormanston, and a charcoal burner, two Assyrian hawkers, and three miners were burned to death.

Sulphur, rain and fire swiftly painted a new landscape. Fogs heavily charged with sulphur made green grass and plants yellow in a day. Bushfires raced through the scrub in successive summers and left blackened hillsides. No fresh vegetation grew, for the sulphur fumes killed almost all the plant life within miles of the smelters. Heavy rain began to erode the top soil. Early in this century the landscape was black and desolate, a cemetery of black stumps. Two beautiful valleys had become as ugly as battlefields.

12

The Feud of the Irishmen

In 1892 Crotty, the prospector, quarrelled with Bowes Kelly, the investor. Rightly or wrongly Crotty was indignant at Kelly's tactics in bartering down the price of the mine from £18,750 to £5,000. More than any man Crotty had kept faith in the Iron Blow, and the cheap sale of the mine on which he had poured the sweat of seven years and the savings of a lifetime made him downhearted and resentful. His enmity mounted when his ambition to be a director of Mt Lyell was thwarted by the Articles of Association of the new company, which ensured Kelly's dominance of the board with the decree that no election of directors be held for three and a half years. But the seal on his hatred was fixed by Kelly's obstinate refusal to sanction a trial survey of a railway along the gently sloping country between Mt Lyell and Kelly Basin, a sheltered bay at the south-eastern end of Macquarie Harbour. And the quarrel of the Irishmen became the costliest feud in Australian mining.

Crotty had his cards, though he did not know he held the ace of trumps. North Mount Lyell was his prize lease. Jimmy Watson, an old Queensland digger from the Palmer, had originally sluiced the ground for gold, and in the leases later called the 'Blocks' his mates found the heaviest nugget unearthed on the diggings. It weighed $6\frac{1}{2}$ ounces and won high praise from Thureau who called it 'an exquisite specimen fit for a museum'. After the rush of 1886, Watson's six leases were floated into the North Mount Lyell Prospecting Association. The syndicate searched for Thureau's gigantic lode of gold and found nothing.

Jimmy Watson was a shrewd digger. He often washed lumps of native copper in his tin dish, and wondered if they came

102

from a copper lode. His syndicate consulted an Adelaide copper-mining expert who reported that even a rich lode of copper would not pay without cheap transport to the coast. The plucky syndicate died, and Watson crossed the Queen to find the Madam Howard mine, which he named after a Hobart publican's wife.

Shortly before Kelly first rode to Mt Lyell, Crotty pegged out the mile of ground between Watson's deserted lease and the Iron Blow in the belief that the irregular outcrop of barytic hematite which passed through the leases indicated the presence of a large mineral formation. A few years later he floated these leases into small copper-mining companies in which he held enough shares to paper the walls of the stock exchange. As the Mt Lyell field attracted speculators the poor Irish prospector repaid his debts. He acquired 'Yallambee', a large residence in the fashionable Melbourne suburb of Auburn, and became a gentleman of leisure, well spoken, immaculately dressed, his beard neatly trimmed. He became a celebrity in the Melbourne law courts, where his persistent attempts to increase his holding of 3,000 Mt Lyell Mining and Railway shares involved him in seven major civil lawsuits in the space of a few years.

In 1895 he bitterly attacked the Mt Lyell Co.'s method of issuing debentures and invoked the Supreme Court of Victoria to uphold his contention; but the directors were victorious. Crotty gained some satisfaction, however, by inducing 'Bertie' Langford, who was Kelly's confidential clerk, to become his private secretary. He rewarded Langford with loads of shares, and when Lyall boomed, the former lift-boy was worth £40,000.

November 1896 was the long awaited month when Crotty could stand for election as a director of his old company. For months he flooded shareholders and newspapers with printed circulars urging them to elect himself and his nominee, David Stratton, a New South Wales flour-miller, to the two vacant seats on the board. His allegations that fourteen miles of railway had cost £290,000, 'an outrageous and extravagant price', and that the debenture scheme was corrupt, gave promise of a stormy general meeting when the shareholders met on the seventh floor of Broken Hill Chambers, the land-boom skyscraper in Queen Street, Melbourne. The promise was fulfilled. In one of several heated clashes Crotty accused the directors of misappropriating 608 tons of rich ore which had been put through the smelters. Big Bowes Kelly jumped to his feet and said: 'I didn't eat it, I know, and neither did the board'. There was uproar, interjections and bitter exchanges. In the election of directors Stratton lost to William Jamieson, one of Kelly's Broken Hill friends, by a substantial margin. Crotty had previously withdrawn from the contest. In the new year he sailed for England.

Bold plans were fermenting in his mind. He knew that his companies needed at least £150,000, far more than he could raise in Australia, to explore their leases. And if his mines proved rich, he would require double that sum to carry out his cherished scheme for his own railway and his own copper smelters. But these two ambitions did not weaken his over-ruling desire to govern his old mine, the Iron Blow. He hoped that he could enlist the aid of the British shareholders, who already owned 40 per cent of the shares in the Mt Lyell Co. and whose interest in the mine was increasing daily. He thought that the day was not distant when he could muster their votes and defeat Kelly at the annual election.

Crotty had chosen good friends to guard his interests in his small Lyell mines. His nephew, James Patrick Lonergan, a smiling generous optimist who resigned as suburban station-master at Glenferrie to become a professional mining investor, became acting chairman of Crotty's companies. When Crotty left Melbourne, Lonergan carried on the vendetta with the company across the valley.

The English investors had been sour when Knox spent his fruitless year in Britain. In 1896, however, many had swung to the wildest extreme, and would have almost offered capital to mine ingots in the Islands of the Blest. Australia's prodigal sons, having wasted the substance of British investors in the land boom, returned impenitent with the leases of more than three hundred Western Australian gold mines. They were welcomed with open arms and showered with sovereigns. It was the golden age of the Australian promoter. Crotty saw the sun-tanned promoters and prospectors board the mail steamer at Albany, the port of the goldfields, with glad tidings for the English investor, and he knew that while Western Australian gold mines were the

craze and while the shareholders of the Mt Lyell Mining and
Railway Company had months to wait for their first dividend,
the task of floating his barren leases would demand all his energy
and ingenuity.

In London, Crotty set out to educate the public. He spent
thousands of pounds of his own money, publishing and dis-
tributing literature on his mines in every daily, weekly and provincial newspaper in Great Britain. He published a French trans-
lation in the Paris press. He paid journalists to interview him
and these long interviews were published verbatim as subtle
advertisements in leading London papers.

'Hearing that Mr James Crotty, pioneer of the Great Mount
Lyell, is in London with good news for the English investor, we
journeyed round to the Strand where we found Mr Crotty busy
in his offices. He graciously consented to answer our questions',
'We understand, Mr Crotty, that you are practically the pioneer
of the Mt Lyell field.' 'Well, that title has been applied to me by
others but not by myself.' And so the interview turned to
Crotty's mines, and Crotty whispered his secrets. 'When the
adjoining mines to the south and north of the Mt Lyell Mining
and Railway Company are in active operation, the field undoubtedly will be the greatest in the world. The formation is the
richest of its kind that has ever been known to exist and its
extent and magnitude are marvellous . . . When twenty furnaces are in blast, the Iron Blow will yield £1,000,000 in dividends for 45 years', confided Crotty.

Crotty lost no chance to inform the journalists that the 'Mt
Lyell lode' ran through his own leases, especially North Lyell
which was his first prize for the British investors. He boasted
that there was already £1 million of ore in sight in the North
Lyell mine, including large quantities of the richest ore in the
world, when, in reality, the mine consisted of the small, unpayable eastern ore body. His praise of the South Lyell mine was
equally unscrupulous. 'South Mt Lyell', said Crotty, 'has by far
the largest and most continuous extension of the pyrites body
in the Mt Lyell field'; in fact, the shaft had barely found enough
copper to mint a penny.

Back in Melbourne, Lonergan kept the home fires burning. He
took the chair at the half-yearly meeting of North Lyell, de-

plored the company's poverty, and reiterated that Crotty would raise the money when the Graeco-Turkish war scare subsided. He announced that samples of copper from the mine assayed between 25 per cent and 66 per cent copper at the Gippsland School of Mines. These samples were peacocked; they were no more typical of the ore that the company must mine than the sea-sands at Strahan.

Forty tons of this rich copper ore had been hand picked and shipped to Liverpool to assist Crotty in raising capital. Analysed in a laboratory at Liverpool, the richest ore carried 23.9 per cent copper. This fraudulent sample interested Scottish financiers, who consulted J. S. MacArthur, a famous Glasgow metallurgist. He said that the ore could be smelted cheaply. The syndicate then bought £45,000 of shares in a new London company, of which Crotty would be chairman.

The North Mount Lyell Copper Company was registered in September 1897 to acquire and work the mine of the North Mt Lyell Mining Company and erect railway, wharf and smelters. Less than a seventh of the nominal capital of 500,000 £1 shares was working capital; 300,000 fully-paid shares were distributed to old shareholders in the ratio of two new shares for one old share; 95,000 shares apparently rewarded Crotty, stockbrokers, financial newspapers and new directors for their services in floating the company; 45,000 shares were bought at £1 each by the directors and their Scottish friends; 25,000 shares were offered to the public at £1 a share; and the remaining 35,000 were reserved. When the shares were offered to the public a prospectus anticipating an annual profit of £250,000 per annum was widely publicized in the English press. The shares were rushed, though the chances were that the British shareholders would not see their £70,000 again. Within a month, however, a gang of road-makers had handed them a fortune.

The North Lyell mine stood on a steep ridge, a thousand feet above the Queen Valley. To reach the mine cases of explosives were loaded into drays at the Queenstown railway station, hauled up the slippery road past the Gormanston Gap, and strapped to pack-horses for the last muddy stretch across the ridge. Rails for the mine tramways had to be carried a mile on men's shoulders. Without a good road across the ridge, the

North Lyell Company could neither secure cheap supplies nor erect the boilers and air compressing machinery to work mechanical rock drills. Working with hammer and steel, miners often had to drill in conglomerate rock so tough that one miner was reputed to have blunted seventy pieces of steel to drill a seven-inch hole.

After protesting for months, the North Lyell Co. persuaded the government to share the cost of constructing a narrow road to its mine. On the crisp, sunny afternoon of 20 October 1897 a gang of men who were cutting the road along the side of a steep hill within the North Lyell lease began to blast away a large outcrop of white quartzite that ran across the track. After the smoke had drifted away they were surprised to see a glittering blue and purple mineral embedded in the quartz over a length of nearly thirty feet. It was bornite, one of the richest of copper ores. While the labourers worked on for their six shillings a day, a shrewd spectator ran down to Queenstown, cabled his sharebroker to buy up North Lyell shares, and reputedly cut the telegraph line to give his broker time to buy before the rush set in.

The company forgot its old ore body. The manager, hurrying back from his honeymoon, ordered three shifts of miners to blast a trench along the outcrop while other men drove new tunnels and cross-cuts to explore this discovery at depth. The roadmakers had discovered the richest mine in Tasmania, a mine which would yield more than three times as much copper as the famous Iron Blow. Neither Crotty nor the mine manager had the faintest idea that the main ore body lay only three feet below the rocks. In his last will and testament, made shortly before the discovery, Crotty had directed his executors to sell all but his shares in the Mt Lyell Co., after his death. He believed that only the Iron Blow was certain of yielding regular dividends. If he had known what lay beneath the quartz, he would not have floated the mine in London. As one of the new London directors remarked, the unexpected wealth found by the roadmakers was a disappointment to the original Australian shareholders, who had just sold, for £70,000, shares that rocketed to £900,000 in less than three months. The Australians had been hit by their own boomerang. Even so, they made a substantial profit from the mine. All the shareholders who bought a hundred new shares in the North Lyell Mining Co. for £10 in June 1896, and later paid calls probably amounting to no more than £25, held shares worth £1,020 at Christmas 1897.

In London, early in 1898, when the North Lyell shareholders met for the first time, Mr James Crotty stroked his beard and raved about the sensational discovery. 'There it was, shining with all the colours of the rainbow. It was astonishing. It was a revelation . . . Such an ore body has never been seen by the eye of man before.' John S. MacArthur, world-renowned metallurgist, echoed Crotty's amazement. 'I have never heard of such a thing in the course of all my reading or travels through the world.'

Meanwhile Crotty was preparing his bold plan to capture a majority of seats on the board of the Mt Lyell Co. His coup required subtle publicity in the British Isles. He must continue to praise the enormous wealth of the Mt Lyell mine so that British investors would retain the majority of shares in the Mt Lyell Co. He must convince the British shareholders that he himself, and not Bowes Kelly, was the man to direct this great mine. Above all, he must conduct his campaign in a manner that would convince shareholders that his advice was not only impartial, but backed by Australian opinion.

Crotty was equal to the task. He had prepared a secret weapon, the *Mount Lyell Standard,* whose presses first clattered in Queenstown on the day Crotty and Kelly clashed at the Melbourne meeting. The first edition of the 3d weekly carried a proud caption—'Circulating in the leading Australasian, New Zealand, South African and Great Britain mining circles'—which amply foretold Crotty's designs. Before Crotty could use the newspaper for his own ends, however, the Mt Lyell Co. had distributed several thousand copies of a photographic supplement of the other west coast newspaper, the *Zeehan and Dundas Herald,* to its Australian shareholders. This edition, published in March 1897, boomed the Mt Lyell mine, described the official banquet at Strahan, and recorded a brief history of the Lyell field in which the McDonoughs' discovery was belittled and Crotty was not mentioned. Crotty resented this, but reserved his reply until his newspaper was ready for the fray.

In November the *Standard* entered the attack with two editions that probably surpassed any Tasmanian newspaper of the century in journalistic style and quality of paper. The highlights of these editions were two long articles, entitled 'The True History of Mt Lyell . . . the Mineral Wonder of the World'. A clever Melbourne journalist had read a copy of Crotty's impartial reminiscences and rewritten them in polished style, adding sentence after sentence glorifying Crotty, deriding Kelly and marvelling at the treasures of Mt Lyell. To make the articles ring true, Mick McDonough, the easy-going, barely-literate discoverer of the Iron Blow, whose association with Crotty had lasted only a few months, lent his name to a long, polished panegyric of the North Lyell chairman. A gift of shares apparently placated Mick, for judging by the style and content of the passage attributed to his pen he did not see the articles until they were already in print.

Although these articles admirably promoted Crotty's cause, describing 'the halo of glory which belongs to James Crotty alone', they amused countless readers on the west coast. The history of the mine was distorted to fantastic lengths to praise Crotty. Thus the Karlsons were condemned for trying to defraud Crotty in 1886, when, in fact, it was the Karlsons who were defrauded by Crotty. More amusing was the claim that Crotty had sometimes fed on button-grass while developing the mine. In fairness to Crotty, however, this was a timely if exaggerated comparison with the great banquet at Strahan when city investors congratulated each other on their achievements, forgetful that not far away the real pioneers were eating johnny cake and bacon in the flickering light of their camp-fires.

In December the *Standard* published a sarcastic, 1200-word editorial castigating Kelly for making an indiscreet estimate of the ore reserves in his mine. A man of Kelly's ignorance, low intelligence, elephantine humour and irresponsibility, was unfit to be the chairman of a great company, sneered the *Standard*. 'With a stockwhip in his fist scouring the plains of the Riverina on horseback . . . [that is] an occupation for which nature and training had so admirably fitted him.' No sooner was the controversial paper selling in the streets of Queenstown than W. H. Taylour, the editor, resigned. He told Bowes Kelly, who later gave him a lucrative position in the Mt Lyell Co.'s office, that the editorial had been written in Melbourne and sent to the paper's business manager with strict orders to be published. Despite Kelly's exposure of these tactics, the *Standard* continued the attack. On New Year's Day 1898 the new editor criticized the inefficiency of the Mt Lyell Co. in not damming sufficient water to keep the furnaces in blast in time of drought. Sticht quickly retaliated. He instructed his staff to give the *Standard* no information, banned its reporters from entering the works, and withdrew the company's advertisements. When the editor came to the company's office to protest, Sticht forcibly evicted him.

Meanwhile five hundred copies of the contentious issues of the *Standard* had been rushed to Melbourne and loaded on the mail steamer. Before long Crotty was handing out copies to unsuspecting British journalists who naturally believed the paper was a genuine expression of Australian opinion. Long quotations from the *Standard* began to appear as well-disguised advertisements in the *British Australasian*, the *Financier*, and even the respectable Liberal paper, the London *Daily News*. Armed with his unassailable propaganda, Crotty demanded that Kelly should resign. 'I have data which would convince the most sceptical that a change of administration is urgently required', he told journalists as he waved his newspaper in his hand.

It was easy for Crotty to shape the columns of the *Mount Lyell Standard*. It was more expensive to penetrate the editorial columns of London financial journals; but it could be done. During the Transvaal and Western Australian gold booms, Horatio Bottomley, Whittaker Wright, and Hooley became millionaires by using trusted mining journals to swindle investors. They entered the inner sanctums of newspaper offices with a full purse and a bundle of shares. The newspapers boomed the mine, shares soared, the promoters sold both their own and the newspapers' shares at high prices, and floated some new company to repeat the trick.

In the last months of 1897, Crotty's propaganda began to permeate the editorial columns of the journals on which the British owners of nearly £5,000,000 of Lyell shares depended for reliable news of their investment. The loudest of Crotty's new fanfare of

Queenstown smelters with eleven furnaces in blast, 1899

The main street of Crotty looking towards the North Lyell smelters, 1902

trumpets was the *British Australasian,* an authoritative journal on Australian affairs which published a large supplement on Tasmanian mining on 2 December 1897. The edition slavishly echoed Crotty's views. It said that Mt Lyell was perhaps the largest and richest deposit of copper ore the world had even seen, containing some hundreds of millions of tons of copper. It described a 10 per cent copper lode, a mile and three quarters long, three hundred feet wide and a mile deep, just eight times deeper than the deepest working on the field. The lode, of course, passed through Crotty's main leases. The paper went on to ridicule the engineering works of the Mt Lyell Co., attributing absurd costs to all its operations and computing the terrific financial loss caused by the blindness of the early directors. This tirade of abuse was so vicious and unfair that Sticht, on reading the journal, wrote thirty concise, typewritten pages in which he exposed forty-nine major errors and distortions in this one edition. Before Sticht's overwhelming rebuttal reached the British press, however, three months had elapsed, and the damage was done.

Kelly was worried, and his anxiety was strikingly indicated by the anxious cable which he sent to the office in London, asking if Crotty and Stratton were organizing proxy votes for an assault on the board at the forthcoming election. But Crotty did not nominate for the board; the dazzling wealth in the North Lyell mine made him hesitate. It might become the greatest mine of all, a mine that would outlive the Iron Blow and every other gilded mine. He began to see that his own railway and smelters —mere blueprints as yet—might dominate the field and crush every company into subjection. He postponed his assault on the rival board, and marshalled his forces for the railway war.

13

The Railway War

Twice a day, at eight in the morning and two in the afternoon, the steam ferries *Pioneer* and *Eagle* drew away from the busy wharf at Strahan and sailed with passengers and mails for the copper-field. At the mouth of the King River the captains steered their ships across the shallow sand bar, past loaded lighters that sometimes grounded there, and up the deep, winding stream. With rich green forest rising up precipitous cliffs on both banks of the river and the reflections in the dark water, it was a picturesque journey which moved even the dullest cigar-smoking sharebrokers. 'The famous picture gallery at Madrid', wrote one shrewd broker, 'scarce afforded me more pleasure last Christmas day than the trip from Strahan up the King River to the budding city of Teepookana.'

This 'budding city' had two hundred people, police barracks, school, stores, goods sheds, and two-storied hotel, but only two fettlers' houses and the rotting piles of the wharf remain today. Between 1896 and 1899, when thirteen barges were in the river trade, the black smoke of locomotives, launches, tugs and steam cranes always hovered above the port; and whenever three or four lighters came up the river together, a night shift of labourers had to be employed to unload coal, coke, timber, beer and stores and pack them on the Queenstown train. In wealth shipped Teepookana probably ranked as the fourth Tasmanian port, and in its last year the copper which it shipped to refineries in the United States and Germany did not fall far short of the value of the city of Hobart's entire exports.

Investors and financiers who boarded the train at Teepookana quickly saw the limitations of the Mt Lyell railway. They patiently watched the engine labouring up the clattering cogs at walking pace, hauling only four or five loaded trucks at a time. They travelled fourteen miles in one and three-quarter hours, only to see that the railway was cut off from all the mines by a steep ridge. They thought the railway was slow, costly and inefficient, and incapable of handling the enormous wealth of the field.

But expensive railway freight and the heavy cost of carting goods from Queenstown to the mines mattered little compared with the exorbitant cost of shipping the goods to Strahan. Ships entering Macquarie Harbour had to cross a long sand bar, deposited in countless storms by breakers rolling in from the southwest. At low tide this bar lay less than nine feet under water, and at high tide the water was barely two feet deeper. Inside the bar the main shipping lane was a narrow mill-race, barely a hundred yards from shore to shore and scoured eighty feet deep by the ebb and flood of tides. When there was a lull in the northerly gales which bottled floodwaters inside the harbour and the tide ebbed, the channel became a wild cataract of water, thick with sand swirled from shoals in the harbour. Napier Bell, world-renowned harbour expert, called it 'the most furious ebb tide' he had ever seen. Often ships rode the swell outside the heads for ten or twelve hours before venturing across the bar; and sometimes, after their long vigil, they had to steam south to Port Davey for shelter. As five ships had been wrecked at Hell's Gates in seven years, and as the entrance was only navigable to small vessels of less than six hundred tons, high freight and insurance rates were inevitable. The sea freight from Burnie to Strahan was six times as dear, per ton-mile, as the freight from Burnie to Sydney.

Strahan was the natural west coast port, but so long as the sand bar clogged its entrance and inflated shipping charges the deeper Tasmanian ports might snatch the western trade by building long overland railways to the mining fields. Burnie, Hobart and Launceston had been interested in the west since the silver boom, when Parliament authorized railways surveys from those ports to Zeehan. Frozen by the depression, the plans were thawed by the copper boom, which made Mt Lyell the goal of the fiercest railway war in Australian history.

The Mt Lyell railway, the most profitable line in Tasmania,

already served the field, but many wild schemes had their backers. Eight railways, all hoping to haul away the inexhaustible wealth of the copper mountains, were planned during the boom. Syndicates petitioned Parliament and appeared before parliamentary select committees, sent surveyors and axemen into forests and mountains, and fought in the local press, the lobbies, the public halls and the English newspapers. They issued glowing prospectuses and colourful maps. Their eyes were tinted by the dividends which the Silverton Tramway Company had won from Broken Hill mines. Tasmania's 'wonderful west', they boasted, would yield a dozen fortunes to railway promoters; and English investors, they thought, would willingly subscribe the capital.

Hobart was the first port which threatened to wrest the trade of the copper-field from Strahan. In 1896 two rival companies lobbied for permission to build railways from Hobart to the west. The Great Western Railway Company, promoted in Melbourne, planned an electric railway from Glenora to Mt Lyell and Zeehan. It proposed to rail 450,000 tons of ore a year to Hobart, and smelt it by the Ashcroft process. There were two flaws in the blueprint. Electricity was unproved for long-distance railways, and the Ashcroft process was still in the experimental stage. A London syndicate proposed an equally grandiose scheme.

The theoretical plans of the rival syndicates passed as genuine currency in Hobart, where the *Mercury* printed a huge red and black map, showing the respective land grants which the syndicates demanded. But the outspoken manager of the government railways ridiculed these schemes. He deemed it absurd to spend almost £1 million in building more than 120 miles of mountain railway and hauling low grade ore to Hobart, there to extract a twentieth of its content and dump the rest by the Derwent. As the west coast was the economic smelting site, he urged the government to deepen the sand bar and encourage its own western railway system.

The politicians ignored his wise advice. Like the politicians of Transvaal and Western Australia, they treated the western miners as interlopers and foreigners, sent to restore the gangrenous commerce of the island. Although cheap transport was the lifeblood of western mining, they were so desperate to share in the wealth of the west that they were willing to keep western transport expensive if it brought greater profits to Tasmanian merchants. They feared that if the bar was deepened their overland railway plans would evaporate over-night, and Melbourne, which was only 316 sea miles from Strahan, would dominate the west coast trade. The intentions of Melbourne merchants were clear. 'When Macquarie Harbour is rendered accessible to large sea-going vessels by a breakwater', said a writer in the Melbourne *Herald*, 'the west coast of Tasmania will be merely another province added to Victoria, another tributary to our national wealth, and another home for our restless mining population.'

Like those pillars which, as ancient legend relates, Hercules flung together near Gibraltar to keep the ocean monsters out of the Mediterranean, so Hell's Gates became a sacred barrier against those ocean monsters, the ships of Melbourne. C. D. Hoggins, a Hobart politician and the apostle of a western railway, who waged a successful parliamentary campaign with the motto, 'Tasmania for the Tasmanians', expressed this view in strong terms. 'The removal of Macquarie Harbour bar,' he warned, 'would be one of the rashest undertakings that could be proposed by any man who had the interest of Tasmania at heart. It would be throwing trade into the hands of Victoria.'

The mining companies and the mining population bitterly resented the refusal of the government to deepen the bar at Hell's Gates, for high shipping freights cut the profits of the mines and made food dearer for the miners. In August 1897 they decided to make a concerted protest. Leading businessmen from all the towns formed the 'Facts and Figures' deputation, sailed to Hobart and assailed Parliament with statistics which showed that the west employed the breadwinners of 19,000 people, and that the government, after paying all expenses, had raised £106,000 in revenue from the west in the previous year. The government, possibly playing for time in the hope that the overland railways might begin, promised to engage Napier Bell to inspect Hell's Gates. As Bell had already recommended that £150,000 be spent on two breakwaters, a second report was superfluous.

While the Great Western Company dawdled and the boom in copper shares grew louder, Hobart merchants were awakened by activity at the north-western port of Burnie, a small town on Emu

Bay. The nearest port to Melbourne and the nearest deep-water port to the west coast, Burnie had a third advantage in the forty-eight miles of railway which ran to the tin mine at Mt Bischoff, half way towards the fringe of the copper belt. Shrewd promoters realized that so long as the sand bar guarded Macquarie Harbour a branch railway to Mt Lyell might become a gilded lifeline between Melbourne and the copper-fields. They secured a ninety-nine year lease of the private railway to Mt Bischoff and formed the Emu Bay Railway Company.

J. S. Reid promoted the new company. He was at Silverton in 1885, editing his newspaper the *Silver Age,* when he saw the opening for a short railway between Silverton and the terminus of the South Australian railway. Formed with the blessing of the New South Wales government, the Silverton Tramway Company built a 3′ 6″ gauge railway across the plains to the dying town of Silverton and on to the booming town of Broken Hill, which saved the company from bankruptcy. It became Australia's most profitable railway and paid £4 on every £1 share in its first nine years. Its chance success fired Reid with an incurable optimism for mining railways; and he promoted the Tarrawingee line at Broken Hill, and then Chillagoe and Emu Bay, two of Australia's most ambitious companies which spent nearly £1 million on long railways that, alas, never reached the golden shore. Reid, John Grice, William Jamieson and Bowes Kelly became directors of this new Melbourne company.

Reid watched the 'Facts and Figures' deputation return to Strahan with only a pawn to disguise the stalemate, and seized his chance to float the company. Late in September 1897 the Emu Bay Railway Company offered to sell 150,000 £1 shares to finance thirty-three miles of railway from Guildford to Rosebery. In a widely advertised prospectus, the company claimed that the dangerous entrance to Macquarie Harbour would ensure them a monopoly of the whole mineral belt from Mt Bischoff to Mt Lyell and an annual dividend of 30 per cent. The prospectus, except copies published in Tasmanian papers, contained a large map of the mining fields, showing only one railway, the proposed Emu Bay line, stretching south through Rosebery to Mt Lyell. Three existing railways, the Mt Lyell, Zeehan-Dundas, and Zeehan-Williamsford, were neither marked on the map nor mentioned in the prospectus, although they were steaming into the very fields which the Emu Bay would allegedly monopolize. Nevertheless the map was successful, for investors subscribed £400,000 in one of the most hectic shares rushes of the decade. The directors retained £150,000, rejected applications for the other 250,000 shares, and began to ship rails and fishplates to Burnie.

Their dishonest publicity provoked an outcry. As directors of rival companies which must compete for the same traffic, Kelly and Jamieson were accused of dividing their loyalty and abusing the trust of the Mt Lyell shareholders. Kelly calmly replied that he was not told about the distorted map. He merely echoed Reid's remark that the main line would go to Zeehan, with a branch line to Mt Lyell if traffic warranted it. The investors had been tricked. They offered £400,000 in the belief that the railway would go straight to the mountain of copper, but when the ink on their cheques was dry they were calmly told that Zeehan, which was already served by a short government railway, would be the destination.

The Great Western Company was up in arms on the day the prospectus was published. Its chairman, Sir Richard Baker, a South Australian politician, wrote to the Premier, Sir Edward Braddon, challenging the right of the Emu Bay Company to build a line to Mt Lyell. Braddon, in reply, said that he had privately given the rival company permission, and that it was not infringing the rights of the Great Western. Packed meetings of Hobart residents rallied behind Sir Richard Baker and hurled abuse at Braddon. Angry speakers inferred that it was the duty of Parliament to ensure that the Hobart railway received a mono- poly of the wealth of the west. They forgot that the Emu Bay was the enterprising company which had begun its railway, and that it was not an idle land grant company which wanted a slice of Tasmania as large as an English county. In Parliament the Premier faced a hostile block of Hobart members who seemed certain to overthrow his Ministry, but he survived the crisis and lost only the Attorney-General, who crossed to lead the Opposi- tion. Supported by public meetings in Zeehan, Devonport, Launceston, Burnie and Penguin, the Ministry tried to pacify the citizens of Hobart by suggesting that wooden rails be laid across the mountains and teams of horses be yoked to haul away the wealth of Mt Lyell. The men of Hobart were incensed.

Meanwhile, rival Launceston syndicates, carrying the high-sounding names of the Tasmanian Central & West Coast Railway Comapny and the Great Midland & West Coast Railway Company, asked Parliament for permission to construct railways across the mountains by way of Mole Creek. The Great Midland, led by the mayor of Launceston, promised to spend £500,000 on a hundred miles of railway and to build smelters at Devonport or Launceston in return for a grant of half a million acres. It would smelt ore from the northern copper-fields—Cutty Sark, Colebrook, Rosebery, and, above all, Lake Dora, 'where mineral discoveries have been made that almost equal Mt Lyell', whispered the promoter. Critics who pointed out that the syndicates had not yet surveyed a route across the mountains were scorned by those who had the honour of the northern city at heart. 'There are hidden gaps and valleys', said the apologists knowingly, as they eyed the ranges.

While the Emu Bay was full of energy, the Great Western full of fight, Launceston's syndicates at loggerheads, and Mt Lyell quietly running its profitable trains, the manager of the government railways insisted that the government should monopolize the copper-fields with its own lines. He urged his Minister to halt the Emu Bay railway at Rosebery before it began to compete with the government railway. He even suggested that the government should build a railway from Devonport to Rosebery and perhaps a branch line to Mt Lyell. His memoranda were duly tabled, shelved and dusted, and no government railway corkscrewed into Mt Lyell to share in the spoils. The government did not enter the fray; it simply dictated the terms of the combat.

Back in London, Crotty stayed his hand until the time was opportune. In August, after a Victorian railway engineer had made a trial survey of the route from Linda Valley to Kelly Basin, he announced that the North Lyell Co. would build a thirty-mile tramway on a gauge of 2′ 6″. Two months later, when his advisers heard of the roadmakers' discovery and rich strikes of copper all along the western range, they drew up ambitious plans for a 3′ 6″ railway. Running on easy gradients, it would be far cheaper to operate than the Mt Lyell railway. Moreover it would run close to every good mine on Lyell and pass by the foot of the new copper-field on Mt Jukes and Mt Darwin.

Although geography suggested that the North Lyell railway would wrest most of the traffic from the rival railway across the range, Crotty left nothing to chance. In the *British Australasian* and in London's *Mining Journal* he blasted his two serious competitors off the map. Lieutenant-Colonel E. M. Tudor-Boddam, who retired as captain of the Hobart shore batteries when Mt Lyell was a little-known goldfield, was Crotty's eloquent spokesman in these journals. As an old Tasmanian, a high military officer, and a man recommended by Crotty to the British investors, the Colonel was able to pose as an oracle on Western Tasmania. He feigned an intimate knowledge of the Mt Lyell Co.'s workings. 'It is well known', he lied, 'that the company is hindered because the railway does not reach the smelters.' He pretended that the entire railway, not four and a half miles, ran on the slow, expensive Abt system. He multiplied by ten the true cost of hauling ore across the ridge from mine to smelters, and multiplied by thirty-four the cost of carrying the copper from the mine to Strahan. He advised the company to use the North Lyell railway and smelters, and increase its profits by the astonishing sum of £675,000. The Colonel dropped one last bombshell. He said that 'in the opinion of the engineer who surveyed the line and the very capable contractor who built it' the Mt Lyell railway would soon disappear into the river. He would have been galled to learn that the railway still runs on dry land nearly sixty years later.

The Colonel prided himself on his engineering prowess. He published a gay map showing in loud hues of yellow, crimson and fawn the seven lucky companies which shared the Mt Lyell lode and in bright blue the route of the North Lyell railway running along the 'accurately surveyed line of lode'. The blue line curved around from Gormanston, passed the bottom tunnel of the Mt Lyell mine, went straight up and down two razor-back ridges and up the steep gully to the North Lyell mine. Such a railway consisting entirely of long tunnels and high bridges would surely rank as the maddest engineering feat of the age.

The editor of the *Zeehan and Dundas Herald* was certainly on safe ground, the century being almost over, in branding the Colonel as the 'champion liar of the century'.

The *Mining Journal* tore to pieces the Emu Bay Company's proposed branch to Mt Lyell in the same ruthless manner. A journalist produced this mockery of west Tasmanian geography from a London newspaper office: 'The only practicable route for a line, in the opinion of experienced bushmen who have spent a lifetime in the locality, is to follow the Pieman river to the coast and travel along it until the Henty is reached, when a road might be found over Misery Flat to the western side of Mt Lyell. This means a line several hundred miles in length and millions of money spent on tunnelling and bridges, and absolutely useless when constructed, to serve any of the existing mining fields'. The surveyors of the Emu Bay Company quickly disproved this distortion by surveying a practical route which squeezed down a branch of the Queen River to the slag dump of the Queenstown smelters. If Lyell became a field of thirty thousand people and the sand bar still blocked the entrance to Macquarie Harbour, the Emu Bay Company would build a railway to Mt Lyell.

In the winter of 1898 there was great activity amongst the four companies which still had visions of building railways to the copper-fields. The Great Western surveyors slashed through bauera, cutting grass and myrtle forest in search of a route to Rosebery, while the directors wandered the streets of London in search of £1,500,000. A Launceston syndicate had surveyors out near Mt Pelion, where they proposed to break the gauge of their ninety-eight mile line to Rosebery. The Emu Bay Company employed eight hundred men in August, and at the Pieman River, where the high bridge was being built, a canvas town called Brookville with three stores, two butchers and a commodious hotel sprang up to cater for the advancing battalion of railway navvies. At Kelly Basin on the evening of 11 August the *Orowaiti* brought the first shipment of rails and fishplates to the partly built jetty and was unloaded by a gang of men from the new brickyards. That month the sale of eighty-four allotments in the new town raised £4,000, of which £157 was paid for one small block. The keen bidding reflected the confidence of everyone who made the twenty-three mile trip from Strahan.

Kelly Basin seemed certain to become a wealthy port of the copper-fields, even if the sand bar choked the entrance to the harbour, for Crotty was unlocking Hell's Gates on his own initiative. He ordered Tyneside shipyards to design a shallow-draught steamer to trade between Kelly Basin and Melbourne. They designed a ship of 2,027 tons, 310 feet long, drawing barely ten feet of water, and capable of carrying a cargo of 800 tons at high speeds. Three times as large as any ship that had entered the harbour, the new steamer would slash freight charges and draw commerce to the North Lyell port.

Two shipwrecks strengthened Kelly Basin's position. In June 1898 the 584-ton steamer *Grafton*, carrying Robert Sticht and the most valuable shipment of cargo ever made by his company, grounded on the sand bar, a quarter of a mile off shore. The Mt Lyell Co. bought the cargo at auction and salvaged part of a furnace and two locomotives before the ship became awash. Two months later the *Anne McDougall*, a new three-masted schooner carrying hardwood for the wharves at Kelly Basin, foundered at the heads, a few cable lengths away from the battered hull of the *Grafton*.

These wrecks aroused the wrath of the western towns and inspired a second 'Facts and Figures' deputation, which hurried to Hobart in August. Cabinet ministers were sympathetic. They were anxious that no lives be lost on the treacherous bar; they knew that mining revenue would enable them to finance expensive harbour works; and, as the colonies would soon federate, they were resigned to the supremacy of Melbourne shipping in Macquarie Harbour. In October they formed the Strahan Marine Board to direct the spending of the first loan of £60,000, and only Hoggins, with his hoarse cry of 'Tasmania for the Tasmanians', and a few bearded die-hards tottered across the floor of the House to oppose the measure.

The decision to deepen the sand bar killed the Hobart and Launceston railways, though death was not sudden, and it crushed the hopes of Emu Bay. John Grice, chairman of Emu Bay, announced his company's withdrawal from the combat and fired a last shot at the North Lyell Co. with the statement that the Mt Lyell Co.'s railway could carry all the copper mined at Mt Lyell. What a far cry from his optimism of fifteen months before when he had raised his capital on the assumption that Mt Lyell could hand fortunes to two railways!

The rival companies, North Lyell and Mt Lyell, were left to fight out the railway war. In November newspapers advertised for three hundred axemen to clear the route of the North Lyell railway. Navvies poured into Kelly Basin, bought pick and shovel, and carried their swags along the formation to the long string of advancing tents. Frequent landslides in the cuttings and the slow construction of trestle bridges retarded the progress of the railway. Meanwhile the Mt Lyell Co., complying with an Act of Parliament which obliged it to complete the line to Strahan by 1901, began to extend its railway downstream from Teepookana. This was abundant proof to Colonel Boddam that the line had neither slid into the rushing river nor had been abandoned.

In June 1899 navvies building the railway along the shores of the harbour saw the graceful steamship *North Lyell* make her maiden voyage to Kelly Basin with locomotives and wagons for the new railway. It was her one and only voyage under the North Lyell flag. As rock was already being quarried for the break-water a fleet of shallow-draught steamers was superfluous. The Union Steamship Company bought the ship for £60,000, re-named her the *Moura*, and took her off the west coast run.

As summer approached, nearly two thousand men worked desperately to complete the railways. The Mt Lyell Co., with little more than seven miles to go, easily won the race. The first train squeezed through the narrow cuttings between Teepookana and the company's wharf at Regatta Point on 19 October 1899, but the official opening was reserved until 1 November when a passenger train from Queenstown, moving at a speed which still commands respect from local railwaymen, travelled the twenty-one miles in two and a half hours. Mrs Sticht declared the railway open, punched the first ticket, and hammered in a last spike of pure Lyell copper. Another year passed before the first bronze-green North Lyell locomotive steamed from Kelly Basin to Linda Valley. And one month later the directors of the Emu Bay Company, having watched their shares fall from £1 to 5s after £363,000 had been spent on fifty miles of railway, had the doubtful pleasure of seeing their railway join the old Dundas line near Zeehan.

When the three railways were completed, the high hopes of the copper boom had melted. 'Much has been written in the Australian press about the marvellous richness of the West Coast', wrote the London *Economist* on 11 August 1900, 'but it is usually the mere hysterical gush which, in Australia, passes current for mining criticism.' The plucky railway investors learned this truth the hard way. Mt Lyell and Zeehan could each keep one railway and port busy, but when each field had two rival ports and two rival railways, then a mighty sum in capital equipment was likely to be wasted.

In 1900 and 1901 Strahan exported more wealth than any other port in the island, and in the following two years it lagged little behind the two Tasmanian cities. At Hell's Gates the breakwater increased the depth of water on the bar to fifteen feet and enabled larger ships to enter the harbour, but they often left with holds half-filled. The passing of the great era of construction—of new town, smelters and railways—reduced Strahan's imports, but the Emu Bay railway was the chief enemy. It captured most of the passenger traffic and much of Zeehan's freight, and its trucks of coke and coal often passed the very wharves of Strahan on their 138-mile journey to Queenstown. For a time it made a small profit but, as Zeehan, Dundas, Rosebery, Waratah and Magnet declined, it could not even pay interest to the English debenture holders, owing them £270,000 in arrears of interest in 1953. One of the largest and most glamorous of Australian companies at birth, it paid not one dividend to the thousands who had rushed the shares in 1897.

The Emu Bay railway made—and still makes—mining possible in a wild, mountainous region where railways were essential. It saved the people of the west from the dangers of the ocean voyage and the long wait on the swell outside Hell's Gates. Through competition with the government line from Strahan, it gave Zeehan cheaper freights. The reward for all these services did not reach the holders of the ordinary shares until nearly seventy years later, at the very time when to some observers the railway seemed doomed to die.

14

The Reign of Extravagance

Meanwhile Crotty was in England, directing his publicity, making plans for the North Lyell railway and biding his time to float his mines on a favourable market. 'I am not done with Mt Lyell by any means', he said. 'My projects are vast projects and they will all be carried out.' He had toured Scotland and the north of England on business and pleasure. He had summered in the Alps and wintered on the Riviera—a prospector taking his ease. Now he was living in Piccadilly, the silk-hatted man-about-town, guiding many interests, and proudly displaying his peacock ore.

But the old prospector did not live to see the mine that had brought him new riches. He suddenly became ill and lingered only a few days. He died on 16 April 1898, in his fifty-fourth year. The news of his death was cabled to Melbourne, and spread like wildfire down Queen Street, the home of every company in which he owned a vital interest. In Queenstown the *Mount Lyell Standard* came out in black mourning bands and devoted most of its columns to a panegyric of the pioneer. And while Crotty was being laid to rest at Kensal Green, the last boulders of purple and black ironstone, the remains of the outcrop to which he gave the best years of his life, were being blasted from the top of the open cut and trucked to the mullock tip.

All Lyell shares were falling fast when Crotty died, and within a few months the value of his estate was probably halved. In July, when shares were nearly at their lowest, his Victorian estate was valued at £160,000, a huge sum in the late nineties. Crotty had once told the parish priest at Queenstown: 'In my uphill fight for Mt Lyell I know there was a supernatural power

124

which assisted me, and to that power which is God, I owe my extraordinary human success'. It was not surprising, then, that he should bequeath all but a few thousand pounds to the Roman Catholic Church in Melbourne. To his widow, however, he willed a £300 legacy, £100 a year for life, and another £500 a year if she agreed to enter a convent. As inmates of a convent can own neither goods nor chattels, this clause was denounced as a 'refinement of cruelty' by the Melbourne *Age*, which led the nation-wide criticism of the will. It was certainly true that Crotty had violated the convention whereby rich men willed their estates to their descendants and gave little or nothing to charity. And by trying to persuade the widow to enter a convent and to deprive her of the luxury to which she had recently been accustomed, he seemed to be demanding a sacrifice which he himself was not willing to make. But the indignant protest that the whole will was a mockery of Christianity was not valid. In simple apportionment of wealth, few wills have conformed more to the spirit of the New Testament; it gave the widow enough to live on in comfort and dedicated the remainder to the service of God. The widow, however, preferred the joys of Paris and London to the simple life of the convent and contested the will with success, receiving an income of £1,000 a year for the rest of her life. The last of James Crotty's Lyell shares, a parcel valued at £20,000, were not sold until 1937.

Crotty, the prospector who became a mining magnate, was almost a unique figure in Australian mining. What is more he wrested his fortune from adversity enough to crush nine out of ten stout hearts. He had faith, perseverance, mining knowledge, and cunning, that rare mixture of qualities which, spiced with luck, brings mining success. Unlike many shy bushmen he did not shudder at the sight of a cable tram or a crowded street. He was equally at ease cooking bacon on a camp-fire or mingling with the silk hats and frock-coats in fashionable London hotels. He could sink a shaft or write a prospectus with the same skill and energy.

One Melbourne industrialist described Crotty as 'a blather-skite'; so he was. Journalists had facetiously called the Iron Blow 'Crotty's Blow' in earlier days. But Crotty was also courteous and charming, brimful of kindness, and a fine mate in miners' camps.

When he directed sluicing on the slopes of the Iron Blow, he frequently had hot stew and dry clothes ready for the drenched miners and packers at nightfall. His English publicity was the blot on his career. He conformed to the unscrupulous standards of most English mining promoters of his day but he was no Horatio Bottomley, for he believed that time would prove his leases rich. The chance North Lyell discovery saved his reputation, but his five other mines paid no dividend in the next decade.

After Crotty died the North Lyell Co. drifted. Crotty carried in his hands threads of important negotiations, threads which were not woven together after his death. He was the practical man on a board of directors who knew little of Australian mining and less of Mt Lyell. His vast plans were taken up by less practised hands.

William Jacks, D. J. Mackay, J. S. MacArthur and L. Higgins were the London directors of North Lyell. MacArthur, a brilliant metallurgist, and Mackay, a London financier who dominated the counsels of the company, did not see the mine until they had been directing it for two and a half years. They valued their time too much to gallivant year after year on a three-months' journey merely to spend a breathless fortnight in the Australian bush. Instead, they spent thousands of pounds a year, cabling coded messages, which were often mutilated in transmission. In eight months, when the organization was still small, the company spent £12,838 on directors' fees, cablegrams, printing, travelling fees and expenses of administration—more than its entire expenditure on mining from 1892 to 1897. The London board was obviously too far away to exert effective control.

The advisory Melbourne board which supervised the execution of orders from London had no real power and tended to be irresponsible. Lonergan and Madden, the chairman and secretary of the Melbourne board, resented losing control of the property to London only a month before the rich ore was discovered. The resentment was mutual, for when the first London director visited the mine in 1898 and saw the poor eastern ore body which he and his Scottish friends had bought at a high price the previous year, he knew that Crotty and his friends were no better than bushrangers. The London directors naturally trusted the colonial board as little as possible.

Bowes Kelly

Robert Carl Sticht

The old Mt Lyell open cut, nearing exhaustion, 1917

In 1899 Captain J. F. Anderson, a grey-bearded, well-groomed skipper of the Orient Line, was appointed captain of the North Lyell fleet on a five-year contract. When the company sold its steamship Anderson was appointed chief superintendent, and given a large white house on the shores of Kelly Basin. North Lyell would have fared better if it had paid him his £600 a year, let him fish off the Kelly Basin pier and paid five times this sum to an experienced general manager of the calibre of Robert Sticht. Anderson was as straight as a rush, but knowing nothing of mines he was at the mercy of his extravagant staff.

The superintending engineer was content to sit in his magnificent Melbourne office while numerous engineering blunders were committed at the mine, tramways, sawmill and brickworks. His expensive sawmill at Kelly Basin drew from one expert the comment: 'I did not suppose that any modern English-speaking nation contained a sawmill so awkward or antiquated'. The railway engineer and chief assayer were equally unreliable, indulging in long drunken sprees during working hours. The foremen in the mine employed any men who either belonged to their own religious sect or came from the Victorian town of Malmsbury, where Crotty and Lonergan had lived. The answer to the query, 'Have you ridden on Ben Leach's coach?' was often the password into the North Lyell mine, those who answered 'yes' were acknowledged as Malmsbury men and given work. The mine naturally became an asylum for the inefficient and worthless, and was riddled with miners who were paid to cable every new development to shareholders in Melbourne or London.

Captain Anderson was also betrayed by his legal advisers. His company, requiring cheap timber for the mine, built a tramway two miles along the timbered slope of Mt Lyell only to learn that the Blocks Company, which owned the timber rights, refused to lease the land. Likewise, a director who was the solicitor for both the company and the railway contractor was allegedly party to a deal whereby the railway contractors secured the contract without competition, and he drew up a contract which imposed no penalty for infringements. The contractors calmly took twice the promised time to build the line.

The railway reflected the optimism and extravagance of the

company. The thirty-three miles of railway cost £316,638—three and a half times the first official estimate—and were equipped with superb rolling stock, including two travelling cranes, a hundred trucks, and some luxurious Pullman passenger carriages which had originally been ordered by an Argentine railway. Although cheap to work, the railway was costly to maintain. It was blocked for days on end by landslides in the cuttings, and in some months a sum equal to the wages of eighty men was devoted simply to keeping the railway open. At the port, the crossings and switches were so defective that locomotives ran off the rails a dozen times in five months.

As the terminus of the railway was at Linda, a mile downhill from the North Lyell mine, the directors decided to build the branch line, which, according to their advertisements in the London press, would pass within a stone's throw of every important mine on the field. The surveyors planned a fantastic railway that slowly climbed around the foothills of Mt Owen, leapt the loop past Gormanston to the Gap, rolled along the ridge past the South Lyell shaft and crossed over the Mt Lyell Co.'s haulage to the North Lyell hotel. Here one branch would curve around the western cliffs of Mt Lyell to the Comstock, three miles away, while the main branch would run on half a mile to the North Lyell mine. In 1900 the tents of the navvies sprang up at the eastern end of the Linda Valley, where the five and a half mile branch line would leave the main line. The railway, however, did not reach the mine. After winding for nearly three miles through deep cuttings and along high earthworks, the railway was approaching the outskirts of Gormanston when the directors, alarmed at the cost of the work, built a station and abandoned work. The impressive two-storied hotel that was erected near the station was a bad investment, for the Gormanston station was so close to Linda that the company found it cheaper to use the main line. The £26,000 branch line was dismantled in 1904.

If the London directors had adhered to the original survey and built a narrow-gauge railway from Kelly Basin, a branch could have well reached the mine for less than £26,000. But the broader-gauged railway demanded such heavy earthworks and such gentle curves and gradients on the steep slopes of the valley that the company might well have spent £65,000 before the branch line reached the North Lyell mine.

This blunder embarrassed the directors. Having spent over £300,000 on a railway which came no nearer their mine than the much abused Mt Lyell railway, they built a narrow tramway from the tunnel mouth to the ore bins, and a £10,000 aerial tramway down the hill to the Linda station. Even the aerial tram was unsatisfactory, for the last steel tower was so far from the railway line at Linda that the ore had to be unloaded from the buckets and carted to the railway trucks. Moreover, the buckets were too small to carry timber and machinery, and so all heavy material had to be carted by horse and dray from the station to the mine at higher freight than the twenty-eight mile journey from the wharves. No wonder shrewd critics began to say that if the North Lyell Co. had built the same aerial tram to the Queenstown smelters, it would have saved half a million pounds and paid regular dividends since the year of Crotty's death.

As soon as the North Lyell railway reached Linda and even before the branch to Gormanston was built, the Queenstown-Strahan railway lost nearly all the traffic from the Linda Valley. Worried at the substantial loss of revenue, the Mt Lyell Co. despatched an official to investigate how the traffic could be recovered. The investigator spoke to merchants and storekeepers in the Linda Valley and walked to Kelly Basin, gleaning information on freights from woodcutters, prospectors, and storekeepers all along the way; but the North Lyell Company's method of charging and weighing goods was so slapdash and inconsistent that he could not compare their tariff with the charges of the rival railway. His experience was common amongst those who carried on business with the North Lyell Co.

Like the railway the North Lyell port was built on the grand scale. Visitors to Kelly Basin,* who saw from down the bay the smoke-ringed hills where the charcoal-burners worked, and the straggling settlement of huts, stores, hotels, Waxman's Hall, Catholic Church, library, railway station, and the North Lyell Co.'s offices and dwellings, were invariably surprised on reach-

---

*This port, sometimes called Pillinger, was named after James Kelly, the mariner who discovered Macquarie Harbour, and not after Bowes Kelly.

ing the waterfront to hear the noise and bustle of the little
port; the sound of the ore crusher, the shunting of trains, the
throb of steamers and launches, the noise of the steam crane and
the whine of the sawmill. In some weeks four interstate steamers
berthed in twenty-five feet of water at the company's ocean pier
and unloaded stores, rails, and machinery on to railway trucks
that stood in three parallel lines on the pier. At the 400-ft wharf
the rich ore for Germany was mechanically crushed and bagged
in a long shed and loaded on the steamers by a travelling crane.
And across the bay a 900-ft jetty served the large brickworks
and sawmill, on which the company had spent nearly £24,000.

One of the best equipped of the smaller Australian ports, Kelly
Basin not only reflected lofty ambitions but also sheer extravagance. The company had lavished its money with such a prodigal
hand that it was viewed locally as 'a sort of philanthropic institution where everything but mining is carried on regardless
of cost', wrote the Hobart *Clipper*. The boom psychology had
run amok. The company's policy was well expressed by J. P.
Lonergan when he told a Tasmanian Parliamentary Committee:
'Money is no object whatever, as long as we develop the
property'. Nemesis dealt firmly with that policy.

The mine was the spring whence flowed the optimism and
extravagance of the North Lyell Co. Its ore was exceptionally
rich for a primary ore, and some of the weekly reports which the
manager posted to the secretary in London read like a fantasy
to modern engineers. Thus on 19 January 1901, miners were
breaking 15.9 per cent copper ore in No. 1 tunnel, 18·6 per cent
copper in a cross-cut off No. 2 tunnel, and 27.9 per cent copper
in No. 3 tunnel. In reports to the press the manager and directors
wildly exaggerated the wealth of their mine, neglecting to mention that most of the ore carried only 6 or 7 per cent copper.
In 1898 the chairman said the North Lyell ore carried 25 to 40
per cent copper. In 1899 the *Mount Lyell Standard* announced
that the 'marvellous mine can without the slightest exaggera-
tion be termed the richest copper mine in the world'. In 1900
Lonergan restrained this claim to 'one of the richest copper
mines in the world', but eighteen months later the chairman
recovered lost ground and called it 'the richest copper producing
mine in the world'. North Lyell's richest consignment consisted

of 512 tons of 29.6 per cent copper, and was sent to Europe during three months of 1898. The 19,000 tons of ore shipped in the following four years averaged only 18 per cent copper, but it was more than five times as rich as the ore being mined at the Iron Blow, and rich enough to convince the mining world that the mine was one massive bonanza.

Like many of the mining brethren, the manager who estimated the value of the mine was an optimist and an unconventional statistician who made no allowance for the unpredictable nature of the ore bodies. In July 1899 he computed that the value of the 'ore in sight' was £5,700,000, reckoning the price of copper at £50 a ton. In March 1903, however, after only £700,000 of ore had been mined in the preceding forty-four months and after new workings had disclosed fresh reserves of ore, the 'ore in sight' was worth only £635,000, taking copper at £50 a ton. Where was the other £4,365,000 worth of ore? It vanished as mysteriously as it came. When Crotty accused Bowes Kelly of losing some £2,000 worth of Mt Lyell ore he little thought that one of his own companies would lose sight of more than £4,000,000.

The directors, beguiled by enthusiastic reports from the mine, in turn beguiled the shareholders into subscribing £332,000 to the company in three years. When, year after year, the payment of dividends was postponed, and the annual meeting was months overdue, wealthy Scottish shareholders began to suspect that all was not well at the mine. Experts whom they sent to Tasmania at great expense found so much evidence of extravagance that there were belated protest meetings in Scotland and London. 'Fellow-shareholders', said one Scotsman at the annual meeting in London, 'I have visited this property and stayed for about a fortnight . . . The whole place was conducted like a free park. Nobody expected to do any work . . . They were tumbling over each other in the mine, (laughter and interruption).' Before the angry murmurs had died on the shareholders' lips, the enraged chairman leaped to his feet and told the gathering that this very Scotsman had appeared at the company's office, posed as a director's friend and requested and received free transport from London to the mine. No indictment of the company's laxity could have been so crushing. So the shareholders thought, until they learned of the smelting fiasco.

To the North Lyell directors smelting seemed the easiest of their problems. In January 1900, when J. S. MacArthur, director and metallurgical adviser, made his first visit to Tasmania, he favoured pyritic smelting. Twelve days later he said North Lyell could adopt pyritic smelting one day and common smelting the next day, varying the technique for the different ore. His inspection of the South Lyell mine, the only mine which would sell pyrite to his smelters, was so disappointing that he spoke no more of pyritic smelting. He recommended twelve large reverberatory furnaces and returned to England to select a metallurgist.

The North Lyell ore contained 60 to 70 per cent silica and 15 to 20 per cent alumina, a chemical compound that was common in the most refractory fireclay. To smelt such ore a furnace consumed large quantities of coal, iron, and limestone, and literally burnt up the profits of smelting. L. C. Trent, the company's new metallurgist, discussing the smelting technique with MacArthur in London, questioned his decision on raw smelting. He believed it would be cheaper to crush the ore, wash away as much silica as possible in a concentration mill, and smelt the copper concentrate in the furnaces. 'I will produce copper cheaper than any other mining company in the world', said Trent. Again MacArthur changed his mind. He bowed to the deluge of twenty-four letters which flowed from Trent's pen in the following months, and agreed that a concentrator would assist in treating the poorer copper ores.

Lamartine Cavaignac Trent came from Salt Lake City, Utah. He had been a machinery salesman, designer of reduction works, and one-time director of Fraser and Chalmers, a wealthy Chicago firm which sold mining machinery throughout the world. He was a powerful, aggressive man with the flat nose of a prize-fighter, the nasal drawl of a Yankee, the cloth cap and spotted dogs of an English squire, and the complexion of a Red Indian; he once admitted, in reply to a blunt query of an old bushman, that he had Red Indian blood in his veins. He reached Tasmania in February 1901, and within two months his tremendous energy, drive and foresight had won for him the position of first general manager at £2,000 a year. The faithful sea captain was deposed and the first era of extravagance came to an end.

Whereas Robert Sticht had smelted his first copper before the railway reached Queenstown, the North Lyell Company did not even begin to build its smelters until a year after the first train reached its smelting site. Dissatisfied with the site which MacArthur had selected near the railway bridge across the King River, Trent selected a plateau which nestled beneath the evening shadow of Mt Jukes, a mile south of that immense gorge where the King River foams through the mountains. A new brick hotel, built to await the legion of parched throats, was thereby stranded in the bush so far from the rising smelters that five sly-grog tents flourished until licensed houses were built in the new settlement. The smelting town was to be called Crotty. If Trent's plans for furnaces, concentrating mill, converters, electrolytic refinery, explosives factory and a mill to make copper sheets, wire and wire bars were completed, Crotty would become the industrial hub of Tasmania.

Along a two-mile branch line from the south heavy locomotives 'J. P. Lonergan', D. J. Mackay' and 'James Crotty' hauled in loads of bricks, timber and crated machinery from Kelly Basin, seventeen miles away. Electric motors, Roots blowers, iron-work for furnaces, steam engines, boilers, generators, condensers, fly-wheels with a diameter of eighteen feet, and thousands of smaller parts were assembled on the site and installed in the power station, sampling mill, boiler house, assay office and workshops that clustered to the west of the lofty smelting shed. In a locality notorious for thunder and lightning and storms that brought 114 inches of rain in an average year, carpenters, bricklayers and mechanics laboured throughout the winter, working by night when the weather was fine.

In the last days of August 1901, two furnaces, thirty-three feet by nineteen feet outside the hearth, each with a square brick chimney ninety feet high, were ready for the fires to be kindled, and two more chimneys were rising within the wooden scaffolding. An electric travelling crane weighing forty tons was ready to feed the furnaces from ore bins that were being stocked daily by long ore trains rumbling down from Linda. The great day was near, and thousands of British shareholders breathed with relief, confident that the long-promised dividends would soon be in the mail.

15

The Deceptive Mine

While the North Lyell Co. celebrated the completion of its ultra-modern smelters, its rival was dazzling the mining world. In 1899 the Mt Lyell Co. made a net profit of £294,000 and in the next two years the profit was steady at £248,000. By August 1901, when the first furnace was aglow at Crotty, the Mt Lyell Co. had already earned £1,107,000 in profits and paid £794,000 in dividends. Victoria, the richest mining colony, had seen only four more profitable mines in fifty golden years, and by 1905 Mt Lyell had passed them all.

In 1898 the Mt Lyell Co. led Australian copper mining for the first time and railed away 4,787 tons of blister copper. Two years later, eleven furnaces had doubled output to 9,455 tons, a record which stood until 1930. The old Iron Blow became the largest copper producer in the British Empire and the largest in the southern hemisphere. In the seven years to 1903 it produced 44,000 tons of copper, more than four million ounces of silver and almost 147,000 ounces of gold. In one year, 1897, it was yielding more silver than any mine on the Zeehan field and more gold than any mine in Victoria, the leading gold-mining colony. And although in the last four years of the century the 2.78 pennyweights of gold which lay in the average ton of copper pyrite was in itself unpayable, the scale of operations was so large that the company extracted as much gold in two months as the prospectors and stamp mill won in seven heart-breaking years. While the income from gold and silver was valuable, copper was really the precious metal in the eyes of the company.

For several years the Mt Lyell Co. mined more ore than any other mining company with the exception of Broken Hill

134

Proprietary. The pay-roll reached its peak in the September quarter of 1889 when it averaged 2,621 men.

Mining engineers and politicians marvelled at Mt Lyell's immense works; the smelters almost smothered in their own smoke cloud; mine, quarries, workshops, wharves, railway, aerial tram and a hundred miles of wooden tramlines disappearing into the forest to fetch timber. The Sydney *Bulletin* called Mt Lyell 'a colossal mining and industrial concern, the biggest in Australia and one of the biggest in the world'. The Adelaide *Critic* described it as a 'marvel unequalled in the industrial history of the Southern Hemisphere'; and even the London *Economist*, bitter foe of the mine booster, called it 'a little kingdom in itself'.

But behind this façade of wealth lurked doubts and fears. In 1893, when Dr Peters saw the walls of the ore body dipping further apart, he predicted that the pyrite would probably descend so far into the earth that the deep copper would never be mined. Peters' explanation of the origin of the copper strengthened this idea in the public mind. He thought copper water had filled a long swamp in prehistoric times and that over the years the swamp had solidified and been buried beneath sand and pebbles. When the mountains were thrust up, the swamp was tipped on its side. 'The Mt Lyell Mine', said Peters, 'was an upturned, solidified swamp and therefore it was far deeper than it was wide.' He claimed that the bottom of similar deposits, which had been worked since the days of the Romans, was still unplumbed. Even in 1893 this explanation was so antiquated that Alexander Allan was indignant at the learned American's ignorance. He had managed an old Roman mine, the famous Tharsis mine in Spain, and he knew that most pyritic deposits suddenly grew poorer at depth. Allan was not enthusiastic about the mine, and the directors were not enthusiastic about Allan. They honoured Peters and accepted his predictions.

Peters' theory soon exploded. In 1896 the ore mined at the Iron Blow averaged 6.04 per cent copper. In 1897, the first year of full production, the copper fell to 4.96 per cent. There was no alarm, for experts had predicted that the bulk of the ore would yield 4 per cent copper. But the copper content declined so much that in April 1898 the directors asked their general manager.

Robert Sticht, to write a special report on the ore body. Sticht admitted that below No. 4 tunnel much of the deposit was poor in copper, and that insufficient work had been done to compute the ore in sight. He expressed the hope, however, that copper pyrite could be mined 250 feet below the deepest workings. Above No. 4 tunnel, there were 2,460,000 tons of ore, of which three-quarters could be quarried at a profit at the ruling price of copper.

Although Sticht had not been a disciple of Dr Peters' theory, he once believed that the mine might last half a century; and at a banquet in 1897 he had said, in light vein, that $22\frac{1}{2}$ million tons of ore were in sight. Later that evening, explaining to a journalist that he did not wish the phrase 'ore in sight' to be taken literally, he modified his jest with the comment that, although no one could say for certain what lay beyond the point of a pick, the mine probably contained 20 million tons of ore, maybe even 220 million tons.

In 1898 Sticht's thorough inspection suggested that the mine held far less ore and alarmingly less copper than he had suspected. His cautious report undermined the value of shares, dragging them down from £13 13s in April to £5 18s in August. The market value of the mine fell almost £2,000,000 in seven months, although in this period the price of copper rose. To mining investors it was the blackest event since the Barrier collapse in 1888. All other Lyell shares bowed in sympathy. South Lyell's dropped from 22s 6d to 2s 3d, North's from 70s to 28s, and Tasman Lyell's from 93s to 28s.

The Mt Lyell shareholders had not heard the worst. The grade of ore that was mined in their mine continued to decline, falling from 3.83 per cent in 1898 to 3.31 per cent in 1899, and tumbling down to 2.59 per cent in the following year. In 1900 the company had to mine and smelt a hundred tons of ore to yield as much copper as forty tons were yielding when smelting commenced. The spectre of an abandoned mine, railway and smelting works began to loom large in the minds of the directors at the turn of the century.

The Mt Lyell Co. faced a second crisis, the same crisis which would threaten the smelters at Crotty. In 1899 it had to mine one ton of barren silica for every three tons of ore in order to separate the iron from the copper inside the blast furnace. Dr Peters had neglected the problem of finding a supply of silica and assumed that the old gold mines of the district could provide gold-bearing quartz. Thus, when Sticht reached Penghana in 1895, he immediately sent out men to search the hills for a large deposit of quartz that might contain enough gold to pay the cost of mining. In thick forest above the Queen River, sixty chains south of the smelting site, they found a large hilltop of barren, white rock that eventually became the company's flux quarry.

In the meantime old bewhiskered prospectors, hearing of the search, hurried to Penghana with tales of quartz reefs carrying one, five and ten ounces of gold to the ton, and led Sticht through the bush to inspect reefs that were incapable of filling one sugar bag with quartz of the promised richness. A fortnight before the smelters were fired, Sticht walked six miles along the Strahan track in the hope of finding a large reef in the Macquarie gold mine. The journey was futile, and he was forced to mine silica for the furnaces in a large quarry overlooking Queenstown. Such was the public interest in his search for a payable flux mine that a 'wild cat company', the Mount Lyell Golden Flux Supply Company, was floated in Melbourne with the express purpose of selling to the Queenstown smelters gold-bearing quartz from a valueless reef at Hall's Creek.

In six years, the Mt Lyell Co. spent almost £93,000 in mining and smelting white silica that was no richer than road metal. Between 1898 and 1902 the Queenstown quarry produced 332,389 tons of silica, more than two and a half times the ore mined at the North Lyell mine in the same period. Several hundred men laboured in the flux quarries and visitors who came to Queenstown and saw a terraced quarry on the white cliffs above the town craned their heads from train windows to snatch a first glance at the famous Iron Blow. When they learned that this was a flux mine which yielded neither copper nor gold, they were astonished.

There was a common answer to the scarcity of silica and to the decline of copper in the Mt Lyell ore. If the Mt Lyell Company purchased from neighbouring mines ore that was rich in both silica and copper, it could abandon its expensive silica quarry, check the rapid depletion of ore reserves in its mine, and expect longer life and larger dividends. This policy was adopted in 1898, and Sticht began to construct a new nest of five furnaces in the large three-storied building which holds the present furnace. The new furnaces were rectangular, cast-iron columns, 17′ 6″ high and 3′ 6″ wide, and each furnace was crowned by high iron stacks, and connected with the main flue that led to a lofty chimney on the hill. The increased height of the new furnaces, 3′ 6″ higher than the original nest, quickened smelting beyond expectations, and enabled the new furnaces to smelt all the ore into a matte of 15 per cent copper, leaving the old furnaces to concentrate the matte into 50 per cent copper. To treat the higher output of matte the converter building, which stood on the site of the present coarse-crushing mill, was enlarged to hold two remelting furnaces and six Bessemer converter vessels. By the end of 1899 the converters were despatching to the refinery at Baltimore, U.S.A., eight thousand cakes of copper a month, each cake weighing two hundredweight and containing 98.93 per cent copper, 8 ounces of silver, and 6 pennyweights of gold.

On 29 June 1899 the eleventh blast furnace was blown in; and Sticht assured the directors that after minor repairs were made, his smelters could treat a thousand tons of ore a day. To smelt this huge tonnage, even under the fuel-saving pyritic method, the company would possibly consume more coke than any other company in Australia. The directors, foreseeing the profits which large coke ovens would yield, therefore contracted with the Mt Kembla Coal Co. to buy coal and a building site at Port Kembla, N.S.W., and sent E. Tuxworth, the brickyard foreman at Queenstown, to build the new works. By 1901 the company's sixty-two ovens were producing 25,000 tons of coke a year, about a fifth of the total production in New South Wales; and their success had inspired Broken Hill Proprietary to borrow the services of Tuxworth and build its own ovens at Bulli.

In March 1899, seven months before the coke ovens were completed, the first large consignment of purchased ore was tipped in the new furnaces at Queenstown. The Lyell Tharsis Mining Co. contracted to sell a hundred tons of siliceous ore a day, and

·spent £9,000 on a long aerial ropeway between their mine and the Mt Lyell tram, a quarter of a mile from the smelters. The 60,000 tons of 4.64 per cent copper ore which were hauled in buckets down the ropeway gave the Mt Lyell Co. a large profit and made Lyell Tharsis the second dividend-payer on the field. Down the same ropeway came 18,000 tons of 7.5 per cent copper from the Blocks mine; across the haulage came thousands of bags of native copper from the King Lyell puddler; and loads of copper concentrate came in a horse-drawn tram from the South Tharsis mill. In 1900 the sampling mill in the smelters presented a busy scene as umpires, representing each company, watched the weighing and sampling of their ore.

Ironically, the North Mount Lyell Copper Co.'s ore kept the Queenstown furnaces in blast longer than the ore from any other outside mine. A month after Crotty died, the directors of North Lyell, realizing the futility of cherishing a grudge that reduced the profits of their company, reviewed their policy of sending thousands of dray loads of rich ore past the new chimney stack of the Queenstown smelters and on, by train and ship, another 12,000 miles to smelters in Wales and Europe. Enquiries revealed that the Mt Lyell Co. exacted heavy charges for smelting, and the two companies bartered over the smelting tariff until September 1899 when a contract for the smelting of 14,000 tons of rich ore was signed in Melbourne.

The first hissing stream of orange slag that poured out of the furnaces convinced Sticht that the ores from the North Lyell and Mount Lyell mines were an ideal smelting combination, ordained by nature to be smelted together. The North Lyell ore was deficient in iron and sulphur—the very minerals which Mt Lyell ore had in abundance—and rich in silica, the mineral which was sadly lacking in the Iron Blow. A united company, smelting ore from both mines at the one smelting works, might earn twice the profit that both companies could earn independently. The directors of Mt Lyell, tempted by these profits and perturbed by the news that their mine was yielding them less profit than the purchased ores, sought their salvation in unity. As the North Lyell railway was only half built and as the Crotty smelters were mere blueprints, they thought that there might yet be time to befriend the enemy. So they approached their old Broken Hill friend, W. R. Wilson, wealthy Melbourne racehorse owner and chairman of Lyell Blocks, who publicly suggested in February 1900 that every large mine on the Lyell field should amalgamate into one huge company. 'If it matures', wrote the Melbourne *Argus,* 'it will be the most ambitious financial project yet achieved in Australia.'

William Knox, acting chairman of Mt Lyell, had no sooner applauded Wilson's plan than the North Lyell Co. scorned the white flag of the peacemakers. J. P. Lonergan ridiculed the scheme and denied Wilson's statement that he had previously approved it in private conversation. Wilson indignantly repeated his assertion. Lonergan denied it again. When Wilson died, in May, his scheme was buried with him.

In September the London *Economist* published a series of brilliant articles in which it warned North Lyell that it made a 'grave economic mistake in planning its own smelters'. The cost of mining fluxes might eat away the profits; moreover, unless fresh reserves of copper ore were discovered below the 300' level, the North Lyell Co. would last only six and a half years, and mine in all no more ore than the Mt Lyell Co. was mining each fourteen months. The *Economist* was promptly rebuked by Lonergan who, breathing that airy optimism of old, thought his mine was as deep as the seas.

North Lyell derived confidence for the coming struggle from its satellites, 'the affiliated mines'. In 1899, when the Mt Lyell Co. had one mine, North Lyell had twenty or more satellite mines which extended from the northern slopes of Mt Lyell to the scrubby spurs of Mt Darwin, in sight of the piers of Kelly Basin. These mines were linked with North Lyell by interlocking directorates, shareholdings, or financial agreements and were mostly managed from the new offices of the North Lyell Co. in the Equitable Buildings, Collins Street, Melbourne. Any ore that these companies mined would be smelted at Crotty. 'It is of vital importance to us that we should have control of these companies that are likely to be producers', said D. J. Mackay at the annual meeting in London. 'Our mine is centrally situated to control the field.' This long-term strategy of dominating all the mines on the field and encircling the Iron Blow fascinated the chairman of North Lyell. He predicted that, before long, the Mt Lyell mine would be unpayable, and that the Mt Lyell Co. would have to absorb new mines or surrender to its rival.

In the winter of 1900 the directors of Mt Lyell adopted a similar strategy through desperation, not foresight. In May they learned that a further decline in the copper content of the ore had reduced the half-yearly profit from £182,000 to £134,000. They learned that the ore body was far poorer even than Sticht had predicted in his alarming report of April 1898, and that if price of copper ruling in that month had remained the same the mine would be 'practically unremunerative'. Three weeks later the directors were shocked to learn that the average grade of ore smelted in the previous month was even poorer. Terse cables passed between Sticht and Mellor, the secretary.

Realizing that the company would make more profit if it bought and worked one of the siliceous copper mines on the field, the directors ordered Sticht to inspect the Lyell Tharsis mine and assess its value. Sticht found a pretext to visit the mine when a huge fall of rock killed two miners and disrupted the supply of ore to his smelters; but the news that he was interested in the mine reached the newspapers and compelled him to act with extreme caution. The directors then decided to buy the South Tharsis, Prince Lyell and Royal Tharsis mines. Four days later they received a cable that the average grade of ore for the month had fallen again, and that the mine manager had been forced to disrupt the systematic working of the open cut in order to mine payable ore. The directors summoned Sticht to Melbourne. After hurried consultations, they resolved to capture the South Tharsis mine by force.

South Tharsis was a plucky Melbourne company, which numbered among its directors old Con Lynch, the gold-digger of 1881, who made his fortune on the goldfields of Western Australia. Just below the peat, gravel, and tree stumps this company had uncovered an extensive deposit of siliceous ore of such promise that it erected an £8,000 concentration mill to treat a hundred tons of ore a day. On the last day of November 1899 the clatter of crusher and jigs had risen above the speeches in the rambling iron mill on the hillside, and in the following month the first sample of copper concentrate was railed down the winding gully which is followed today by the new West Lyell highway. In seven months, however, so much copper was lost in the tailings that treatment was unprofitable. The directors did not lose heart, believing that if they raised £15,000 Captain Hancock of the Moonta copper mines in South Australia would be able to make their mill as successful as his own. But these plans were not to be fulfilled.

On 9 July 1900 two sharebrokers attended a meeting of the Mt Lyell directors and received instructions to buy quietly a majority of South Tharsis shares, which were selling at 4s 1d each. Next day the Mt Lyell Co. made an official offer to buy the South Tharsis mine for £45,000, or 10s a share. While the directors pondered the offer the sharebrokers raked the stock exchange for South Tharsis script, and had bought two-thirds of the shares by the end of the month.

On 16 August the few remaining shareholders of South Tharsis met in Melbourne to discuss the offer. The chairman rightly resented the Mt Lyell Co.'s 'stand and deliver tactics', while the minority of shareholders who, several years before, had bought shares at the peak of 25s said the tactics were immoral even if legal. These protests were futile. A delegate of the Mt Lyell Co. sat calmly in the room with his 64,436 shares, and when the motion was put to the vote he voted the company out of existence. The Mt Lyell Co. had paid shareholders £30,651 on the stock exchange and paid the company £46,500, but £29,000 came back as a liquidation dividend on its own newly acquired shares. The tactics of the Mt Lyell Co. were desperate rather than unethical. It offered a good price for the mine and the great majority of South Tharsis shareholders approved of the sale.

This desperate measure was ineffective. In August 1900, at the height of the controversy, the South Tharsis mine manager had reckoned that 206,600 tons of ore were 'in sight'; but the Mt Lyell Co. mined only 88,863 tons. The manager had claimed that the ore averaged 2.4 per cent copper a ton; but the Mt Lyell Co. mined only 1.6 per cent copper ore. He had inflamed an indignant public with the claim that, after deducting mining and smelting costs, the Mt Lyell Co. would make £265,000 profit on the deal. If the Mt Lyell directors cherished that hope they were soon disillusioned; for they made a profit of only £9,187 from the mine. The indignant shareholders had the better bargain.

The failure of the South Tharsis mine was offset by two heartening developments. In January 1901 North Lyell agreed to send 50,000 tons of 6 per cent copper ore to the Queenstown smelters, an arrangement dictated solely by the need to raise £70,000 to complete its own smelters. The Mt Lyell Co. also made handsome profit in smelting 6,000 tons of rich ore which, unknown to all but a few officials of the Blocks Company, had been looted from one of the richest ore bodies in the North Lyell mine.

Working on the eastern boundary of the North Lyell lease, the Blocks miners worked rich ore right to the underground boundary of the lease. There the glittering wall of copper was so tempting that the manager let his miners drill into the adjoining lease. He allowed no stranger to enter his mine, and as he knew that the nearest North Lyell workings were hundreds of feet away he had no fear of detection. The Blocks miners accordingly followed the ore body fourteen feet into the North Lyell lease and stoped this ore to a height of eighty feet. They tore out copper worth £33,000, filled the stope with barren mullock, and reluctantly abandoned the mine. Three years later some North Lyell miners drove a cross-cut towards the deserted Blocks workings and penetrated a pocket of rich ore. About fifteen feet from the boundary they fired their charge, and were amazed to find that the ore had disappeared, and in its place— timber and mullock. They informed the manager, who surveyed the boundary and swore vengeance against the Blocks. Six weeks earlier the Lyell Blocks Copper Corporation had shrewdly liquidated and re-formed as the Lyell Blocks Mining Co. This subterfuge absolved the directors from legal responsibility, for the old company, being defunct, could not be sued.

The guile of the Blocks' manager had strengthened the Mt Lyell Co. by increasing the profits of its smelters and by looting North Lyell's diminishing hoard of rich ore. But the Blocks mine closed before the end of 1901, about the same time as the Lyell Tharsis mine, and the profitable supply of ore that went down their aerial ropeway to the smelters came to an end. There were no new mines to take their place. Although the Mt Lyell Co. employed Lindesay Clark and two secret representatives to inspect every working mine on the field in the hope of locating other payable ore bodies, their reports confirmed Sticht's belief that Mt Lyell was essentially a low grade copper-field, and that the fabulous deposits of copper in North Lyell's satellite mines were invariably the gifts of their manager's imagination and certainly not the gifts of Nature. During the inspection the company bought two promising mines—King Lyell for £2,600, and Royal Tharsis for £13,000—but they yielded little ore.

The future became so uncertain that Bowes Kelly, leviathan shareholder who had loyally clung to his shares through good times and bad, sold over 10,000 shares—half his holding—in the three years to December 1901. The Mt Lyell Co.'s days seemed numbered. So long as Amalgamated Copper, the giant American monopoly, flooded the market and kept copper prices low, the Mt Lyell Co. could not expect to mine at a profit after 1904.

At dusk, in the quiet winter evenings of 1901, Lamartine Trent, watching the brick chimney stacks rising on the bare flanks of Mt Jukes, would hear dull thunder in the north as sixty or seventy shots rang out from the Iron Blow and cannon-aded down the Linda Valley. He smiled. He knew that every ton of ore blasted from the Mt Lyell mine brought its company nearer extinction. The day seemed near when he would govern two mines, two railways, two smelters. The evening blast was his ally, breaking down the enemy's walls.

16

The Toy Smelters

There was excitement at Crotty when people standing in the main street first saw smoke and steam hovering above the smelters. Across the gully, in the draughty, barn-like smelter building stood Trent, his forehead beaded with sweat, his tired eyes watching the men rake molten slag off the furnace. When the furnace was tapped he examined the lumps of ore that studded the molten metal, wired the directors that all was well and went to bed. He was confident that once he crushed the ore and used dry wood, the furnace would work efficiently.

Three weeks later, after a second furnace had failed to melt large lumps of ore, Trent cracked beneath the strain and wanted to draw the fires until the crushing machinery arrived. When rumours of failure filtered through the veil of secrecy, journalists came down the railway to inspect the smelters. They were heartened to see smoke rising from the chimneys, the bustle of workmen, and a pile of rich copper matte lying near the furnace. Again there was secrecy beneath the rising pall of smoke. The smoke stacks were the barometer of Crotty's fortunes and as the weeks passed by travellers reported that the barometer was very low; rarely more than one chimney was smoking. The brick arches that crowned the furnaces collapsed with alarming frequency; the grates were so small that expensive coal had to be used in place of wood. Shortly before Christmas the smelters closed, re-opened, closed and opened again. In fifteen weeks they smelted as much ore as Sticht smelted in two days. Their sluggishnesss was equalled by their inefficiency, for they lost 45 per cent of the copper in the slag. So far, smelting at Crotty had failed.

Trent spent Christmas at Menzies Hotel, Melbourne, hiding from angry shareholders. When finally cornered he said that his smelters would be a brilliant success as soon as the rest of the concentrating mill, then on the high seas, arrived at Crotty. But the *Mount Lyell Standard*, which circulated extensively among Melbourne's wealthy mining investors, had already decided that Trent's smelting would fail. Having spent November refuting adverse rumours from Crotty, it spent December blessing and spreading rumours. 'If the North Lyell ore can be smelted in Wales, Germany and Queenstown', thundered the *Standard*, 'why can't it be smelted at Crotty?'

As the *Standard* was directed from Melbourne by J. P. Madden, a colonial director of the North Lyell Co., Trent was indignant. He refused to carry bundles of newspapers down his railway and thereby banned the penny daily in the growing towns of Crotty, Darwin and Kelly Basin. He cancelled the *Standard*'s free railway pass and ordered his staff to give no information to the paper. These edicts provoked fresh streams of roundshot and the *Standard* peppered the 'toy smelters' with ridicule. As Trent could no longer buy his *Standard* at the Crotty newsagents, a special locomotive rushed to Linda each morning and returned to Crotty with the day's copy straight from the press.

Trent did not lose the intiative in his feud with Madden. He informed newspapers in Hobart and Melbourne of blunders which Madden had made while secretary of the company. He observed that a more favourable contract for the sale of the company's ore could have been drawn up by an escaped lunatic, and condemned the railway to Gormanston with the scathing remark, 'We have no more use of a line to Gormanston than to Jericho'. When F. D. Mitchell, the financial director of the company, supported Madden, he was accused of 'obstructionism and Iago-like treachery'.

The helplessness of the London directors was never more apparent. The dispute had raged for three months; the smelting results were shocking; the company's bank overdraft exceeded £60,000; and still the directors refused to intervene. Instead, they issued a complacent report which anticipated a profit of £180,000 in the forthcoming year. But the British shareholders had been deceived so often that they were not easily consoled by glib promises. Wealthy Scottish shareholders met in Glasgow, denounced the company's inefficiency and voted that two of their number should represent east and west Scotland on the board. In London, at the annual meeting, an eminent accountant said that the directors had promised dividends years ago, and yet no profit was in sight. He complained that everything exceeded the estimates except the actual profit, which fell short by hundreds of thousands. Another critic said the cost of the steamer appeared as a debit in the accounts, but the money from its sale was not credited to revenue. The chairman tried to pacify the gathering with the assurance that North Lyell was 'the richest copper-producing mine in the world'. Whereupon a shareholder replied that it was obviously not the directors but simply the wonderful mine that had saved the company from bankruptcy.

Back in Tasmania, on the very day when the chairman was trying to calm the shareholders, the internal strife became open war. Herbert Muir, a popular, easy-going prospector who had managed the North Lyell mine since the days when it consisted of a few shallow trenches, was the cause of trouble. The mine grew beyond his capacity to manage it. He made so few sections of the ore bodies available for mining that he was repeatedly unable to break the quota of rich ore which his directors contracted to sell to foreign smelters. This deficiency could not be attributed to a shortage of labour, for 280 men were employed in the mine in some months. Poor management caused the trouble. When Trent walked through the mine one night shift, he found seventy men working without a foreman or shift boss. 'The labour performed could easily have been done by six or eight men', said Trent.

The directors sanctioned the dismissal of Muir, but Trent was loath to act, knowing that Mitchell and Madden would show their resentment in no uncertain manner. Finally, in the heat of the feud, Trent attempted to entice over the manager (and also the surface foreman) of the Mt Lyell mine to take Muir's place. When they refused to cross to the camp of the enemy, Trent advertised throughout Australia for a competent underground manager to take over 'a mine somewhere in New South Wales'. From 160 applicants he selected two Broken Hill men and told them to come to Tasmania. On the afternoon of 17 February 1902 Trent led them to the mine and dismissed the astonished Muir. On the following morning F. D. Mitchell, the financial director, was cutting an aristocratic figure in his cloth cap, long socks, and plus-fours on the other side of Mt Lyell when he received a message that Trent had taken over the mine. He hurried up the steep track, and over the mountain. To quote Trent's colourful narrative: 'Mitchell came down the mountain from the Comstock mine like a raging lion, waving his arms and singing out, "I am coming, I am coming. Stop it, stop it!" He harangued the men, told them to stick by Muir, and actually raised a howling mob who took possession of the mine'.

Mitchell, of course, had a more dignified version of the incident. He said he met Trent in the mine office and told him that Muir would be reinstated. 'Trent used very strong epithets and came at me with his clenched firsts', wrote Mitchell, 'but luckily for himself and myself he did not attack me.' Late in the afternoon, Trent withdrew his managers and rang for the police. Mitchell shifted from his small residence to Muir's house; 'I did not wish to sleep alone so near to your general manager', he confided to the London Board.

Next day Trent returned to the mine, determined to reinstate his men. He warned Muir that unless he left the mine he would prosecute him for trespassing and for inciting violence. Finding that Muir was defiant, Trent toured the open cut, warning miners that they would not be paid while Muir was manager. Meanwhile it was rumoured that Trent had ordered two hundred men to come from Crotty and seize the mine. When surface miners saw, far down the misty valley, black smoke rising from the flanks of Mt Owen and a fast train come round the bend, there was high excitement. They warned the men who stood guard at the mouth of each tunnel and watched the train race along the straight to Linda. Loud was the miners' mirth when they learned that the midday special carried Trent's lunch from Crotty!

Fortified by his lunch, armed with a pistol holster, and accompanied by his sons and dogs, Trent tried to force his way past the pickets at the mouth of the tunnel. The burly miners jostled him and forced him back. Trent was furious. He cut the telephone wires at the mine office, stalked down the hill to the Linda station, and ordered another special train to take him to Crotty. He despatched an hysterical telegram to the Melbourne *Age:* 'Myself and managers were forcibly prevented from entering North Lyell mine at the incitation of F. D. Mitchell who is without authority. —L. C. Trent'.

The huge company was split asunder. Men dismissed at Crotty found work at the mine, and men dismissed from the mine were greeted as old friends at Crotty. When the Broken Hill men left the field, Trent refused to acknowledge Muir, and insisted that the manager of the Lyell Tharsis mine was lawfully in charge. Mitchell refused to acknowledge Trent as general manager and instructed the bank not to honour his cheques. Trent then appropriated the railway revenue to pay for the bulging sheaf of letters and cables which he sent to the directors in London. 'I can say this', Trent said of Mitchell, 'if you had raked all the madhouses in Europe, you could not have sent me a more excitable and less competent man.' Mitchell's abuse was more gentlemanly: 'Trent has not only abused me before the men, but used disgusting language of me through the telephone'.

Armed with such testimonials and accompanied by two Welsh smelting foremen, two London directors, J. S. MacArthur and D. J. Mackay, sailed from Marseilles to intercede in the dispute. At Crotty they summoned the contending factions to a conference. On the second day of the hearing Trent and some of the smelters and railway staff were suspended. On the fourth day Trent was found guilty of 'violation of trust and abuse of the powers vested in him' and he left Crotty within twenty-four hours, forfeiting three months' salary and £700 in expenses. The rough Australian democracy had shocked the American, and as his ship swung away from the wharf he thrust out his fist and called, 'Farewell Australia! I leave you to the working man and the servant girl!'

But the last scene of this melodrama, watched with curiosity throughout Australia, was not yet played. In his club at Salt Lake City Trent composed long indictments of North Lyell's corruption and bungling, and showered the English and Australian papers with copies. He recalled with some truth that in his

reports to London he had charged enough crime and corruption to fill Newgate with scoundrels. He offered to meet any
responsible committee of shareholders or the cream of
Britain's engineers and metallurgists in order to clear his reputation. People were not interested in past bungling, which
was obvious to all who could read, but in their fast receding
chance of receiving a dividend. Trent's offer was not accepted. And so he vanished from the scene, a man more wronged
than he deserved, a fearless, colourful and arrogant American.
Let this be remembered in his favour. He predicted Mt Lyell's
two great developments of the next thirty years: the North
Lyell tunnel, and the West Lyell open cut.

Bad luck shadowed him to Utah where later in the same year,
1902, he was given the option of buying a small copper mine at
Bingham for no large sum. He declined it. He let slip from his
grasp the wonderful Utah mine which became the greatest
copper mine in the United States—a mine that was greater than
twenty North Lyells.

Back at Crotty twelve men picketed the works while Mac-
Arthur analysed the failure of the furnaces. Believing that
Trent's decision to enlarge the furnaces on the pattern of those
used by Dr Carpenter at Deadwood, U.S.A., was the cause of
the trouble, he re-erected smaller furnaces with larger fuel grates
and safer arches. But the three reconstructed furnaces suffered
the same fate. In a tedious trial of twenty-five days they produced
$94\frac{1}{2}$ tons of copper at a loss.

MacArthur had selected reverberatory furnaces partly because
these furnaces used less fuel and less flux. He had selected Crotty
as the smelter site with the proud claim that it abounded in
natural fluxes and cheap timber. Ironically, it was the very
absence of these two requirements—cheap fuel and cheap flux
—that ruined smelting at Crotty. Ironstone had to be railed and
shipped at exorbitant cost from Penguin, on Bass Strait, or carried on a roundabout journey of seventy miles from Zeehan.
Coal imported from New South Wales was devoured so greedily
by the furnaces during MacArthur's trial run that it became
a greater item of expense than both ore and fluxes.

The failure of MacArthur's furnaces did not wreck the North
Lyell Co. For months F. D. Mitchell, the new managing director,

had urged directors to copy the Mt Lyell example and smelt the ore in blast furnaces with pyrite from the South Lyell mine as flux. His campaign had been intensified after a visit to the Queenstown smelters where the sight of copper pouring out of a long row of furnaces made him envious of Sticht and ashamed of his own smelters. For long enough, MacArthur scoffed at Mitchell's plan; then he bowed reluctantly to the clamour. He bought four second-hand blast furnaces at Dry Creek, near Adelaide, and sailed for England before they were lit.

Again the mists closed on Crotty as the small blast furnaces were assembled on the northern edge of the plateau. The first furnace was lit on 2 September, and beer flowed more freely than copper. When the metallurgist increased the pressure of the blast, the overhead flue became so hot that the rafters caught alight, and the smelter hands had to drop their frothy tankards and chop away the blazing timber. No sooner was the second furnace in blast than the first one cooled and clinkered. A third furnace was blown in and, alas, the second furnace immediately became sluggish. For one happy day all three furnaces produced copper matte. At the end of September, however, no smoke drifted from the new chimney on the hill, and old rumours revived. Muir, who knew nothing about smelting, rushed to Cobar to inspect new blast furnaces, while Mitchell quietly approached the metallurgist at Queenstown, and then his assistant, with offers of handsome salaries if they came to Crotty.

The small blast furnaces were better than the monster reverberatory furnaces but they had many defects. They were only 9' 3" high—barely half the height of Sticht's—and too small to allow rapid smelting; the brickwork between the water jacket and the hood tended to collapse beneath the heat; and the peculiar construction made the feed floor an inferno for the workmen. Nevertheless Mitchell believed that the four furnaces would yield a profit of £14,000 a month as soon as copper pyrite from the South Lyell mine was available. So the South Lyell shaft was pumped dry while fifty navvies extended the Gormanston railway westwards towards a new self-acting tram that ran up to the mine. Eighty men began to mine pyrite at the 600 level of the mine, and ore trains sped down to Crotty twice a week.

While Mitchell was priding himself that his furnaces were now using only fourteen tons of coke to smelt a hundred tons of ore and flux, Sticht was smelting without coke at all. On 13 November 1902, a day famous in the history of metallurgy, he staged the first absolutely successful pyritic smelting in the world. The age-old dream of metallurgists—the smelting of ore without fuel—had come true. Sticht had perfected his furnaces by blowing a cold blast of air instead of a hot blast into the furnace, and then increasing the pressure of the blast to a revolutionary degree. The result was astonishing; the experimental furnace used no coke, required no large stoves to heat the blast, and smelted at such a pace that more labourers had to be employed to drag carts of silica and ore from the bins to the licking flames at the mouth of the furnace.

Sticht hoped that he would be able to dispense with coke permanently in the primary smelting and generate the required heat from the iron and sulphur in the copper ore. But ideal pyritic smelting was a delicate technique which imposed such a strain on the furnacemen that, after several weeks, up to 1 per cent of coke was again tipped into the furnace. Even so, the saving in coke was enormous; within a year the annual consumption of coke had fallen from 15,300 to 6,300 tons.

In the last months of 1902 the smelting practice of two companies desperately struggling for mastery on opposite sides of the same mountain range captured the interest of scientific men throughout the world. At one smelters Robert Sticht was winning world renown. At the other smelters, nine miles away, J. S. MacArthur, whose skill had won millions of ounces of gold from mines and tailings dumps since he and the Forrest brothers invented the cyanide process at Edinburgh, was ruining a worldwide reputation. Fourteen months after the first furnace had been lit he was still cabling futile instructions from America. MacArthur, it seems, was a brilliant water metallurgist, but a poor fire metallurgist. Scotland's capital in the North Lyell Co. was gathered through his prestige and lost through his folly.

17

The Fall of an Empire

Robert Nivison, better known as Lord Glendyne, saved the day for the North Lyell shareholders. One of the most influential financiers in the world, he conducted the affairs of Mackay, the chairman, and held the company together in the face of a huge bank overdraft. Believing that a merger was essential, he secretly sounded out William Knox, learned that his views were favourable, and forced the resignation of those four North Lyell directors who were tainted with the traditional enmity. After conferring with a representative of wealthy Scottish shareholders, he appointed a new board of seven trusted financiers. In this new regime Nivison played a strange role. He held no office, but he negotiated with the Mt Lyell Co. in such secrecy that neither the old nor the new London directors knew of his manœuvres. At the close of 1902 Edwin Habben, London secretary of the Mt Lyell Co., met Nivison and discussed difficulties that beset the merger. In a letter to William Knox, Habben confided, 'Our policy is to show no anxiety to Nivison'.

Both companies had cause to be anxious. In the last twelve months North Lyell, mining one of the world's richest ore bodies, had made a working loss of £24,000 with nothing written off for depreciation. Liabilities exceeded liquid assets by £230,000; the company owed the bank more than £80,000; its blast furnaces had yielded little or nothing; the Mt Lyell ore contract, which yielded £148,000, had ended; and there remained little ore that was rich enough to ship to Europe at even a modest profit.

The Mt Lyell Co. faced an equally serious crisis, and it required ruthless retrenchment and all the ingenuity of the com-

153

pany's staff to make less than half of the profit of a few years past. The Mt Lyell ore body was not only becoming perilously poor, but was also narrowing at depth until finally it would be cut off by barren rock. The company mined its best ore and left the low grade ore in a desperate effort to make a profit and conceal its real plight. To show the extent of this selection, ore mined in the year ended September 1903 averaged 2.17 per cent copper, but in the next twelve months it averaged only 1.12 per cent. The company knew that by 1904 it would be working the mine at a heavy loss.

Meanwhile, the new North Lyell board decided to send out an independent expert to report on the mine and smelters. The company was so poor, however, that it had to borrow £4,000 from Nivison to pay William Rich, a former manager of the Rio Tinto mine, to inspect the property. Jonathan Angus, one of the new directors, was chosen to accompany Rich, and he was secretly briefed by Nivison to discuss the terms of a merger in Australia.

At Burnie pier the visitors were greeted by William Knox, who escorted them to Queenstown in a private rail motor. The Mt Lyell directors, having debated whether they should let Angus and Rich inspect the depleted workings of the Iron Blow, finally warned Sticht not to divulge any information unless it led to satisfactory results. Sticht led the visitors through the mine, confident that they could not discern that only the poorer ore remained. The North Lyell Company allowed Batchelor, the rival manager, two days to inspect its mine, but Herbert Muir was as shrewd as Sticht. He promised to meet Batchelor at various parts of the mine and guide him through the stopes. Through unforeseen circumstances he was usually missing at the appointed times and Batchelor was left to wander unaccompanied through the maze of workings.

Angus and Rich then caught the train to Crotty, where they saw the leaning chimney that reflected the company's financial despair. On the last Sunday morning of the year Mitchell had been sitting in his dining-room, worrying over the failure of the furnaces, when there was a clap of thunder and a flash of lightning. He went outside and saw, on the side of the hill, the jagged remains of the main blast-furnace stack surrounded by seventy thousand bricks. He closed the furnaces and erected arc lights on the hill to enable bricklayers to work day and night on the chimney. The cessation of smelting had so strained the financial resources of the company that he ordered the men to complete the stack without waiting for the mortar to set. In consequence the chimney developed a dangerous lean at seventy feet.

Rich was disappointed with the smelters. The four blast furnaces, known locally as coffee pots, made a small profit on rich ore and lost on anything poorer than 7 per cent. He estimated that if they smelted all the ore that remained in the mine they would lose £119,000 in two years. But although these furnaces were hopeless while the price of copper was low, Rich saw no reason why carefully designed blast furnaces should not succeed; and he entered with zest the game that had made the town of Crotty famous, the game of designing smelters.

Before Angus and Rich left Tasmania they agreed to meet the Mt Lyell directors in Launceston, the city where the two companies had found their first capital. They met at the Brisbane Hotel on 12 February 1903, and, after a two-day discussion, drew up a secret agreement whereby half of the shares in an amalgamated company would go to Mt Lyell and half to the North Lyell shareholders. They agreed also that William Knox should sail for London to discuss the scheme with the North Lyell board. He was the free-trade member for Kooyong in the Commonwealth Parliament, and as director of Mt Lyell, Chillagoe and Broken Hill Proprietary, three of Australia's largest mining enterprises, he was favourably known in London.

Knox and Angus left Melbourne on 25 February 1903, and as the mail steamer tossed about in the Indian Ocean Angus compiled a voluminous report to the London board. Frequently he and Knox would pace the decks and discuss their problems. Angus was troubled lest the price of copper might so fall that the Mt Lyell ore would become unpayable, but he regarded unity as so urgent that he deleted these fears from his report. On the other hand, William Rich was not convinced that North Lyell should surrender, and he had told Angus that a competent metallurgist might improve the Crotty works beyond recognition. Whether his hopes were genuine or stated merely to hide North Lyell's predicament, Knox could not tell. He took the pessimistic view.

Meanwhile, in the Lyell district, rumours of amalgamation were rife. If the two companies united, then only one smelter, one railway and one port would survive. Several thousand men would be thrown out of work and scores of businesses and hundreds of properties would be ruined. Either Crotty or Queenstown, Kelly Basin or Strahan would decay, and even the Lyell miners scented unemployment. Throughout February, March, and April suspense and rumour were rife; one day Crotty despaired, next day Queenstown despaired.

It was not easy to predict which town would perish. Crotty was served by the better railway, but her smelters were inefficient. Queenstown had magnificent smelters, but her railway was far from adequate. The difference between the North Lyell and the Mt Lyell railway was most marked in 1902, the first and only year of full competition, when the decade-old quarrel between Kelly and Crotty resolved itself in a hollow victory for Crotty's ghost. The North Lyell railway was seven miles longer than the Mt Lyell railway, but the large North Lyell locomotives could haul loads almost three times as heavy as the Abt engines could haul. They could haul a load from Linda to the wharves at a little more than a third of the cost of hauling the same load on the shorter Mt Lyell railway.

The alternatives were clear: would the united company smelt at Queenstown and use the steep Mt Lyell railway or would it shift the smelters to Crotty and use the gently graded North Lyell railway? In the autumn of 1903, when this question agitated the minds of ten thousand people, shrewd businessmen reasoned that the cost of dismantling and re-erecting Sticht's smelters in the opposite valley would be repaid in full by the saving in rail freights in the following five years. They little knew that there was not enough ore in sight in the large mines of the field to keep the smelters in blast for five years. And they forgot that Queenstown had two other advantages; it was five times as large as the town of Crotty, and it had direct rail communication with Zeehan, Burnie and Hobart.

The *Zeehan and Dundas Herald* distorted this truth. It had enjoyed a monopoly of the west coast since the demise of the Strahan *Banner* and the *Mount Lyell Standard,* and it strove to dissuade a new firm from publishing a paper at Mt Lyell by inferring that Kelly Basin was the best port, that the Mt Lyell railway was inefficient, and that soon the Queenstown smelters would have nowhere to dump their slag. The fourteen Queenstown publicans drank this in and would have sold their hotels for a fraction of their former value if any buyers had come forward. This fear was shared by the working men of the town. It was the practice to work the converters until all the copper matte was treated and then close the plant and dismiss the men until enough matte had accumulated to feed the converters for another fortnight's run. The foreman of the converters was so taken in by the rumours of merger which were galloping through the town that, one evening, when he was about to close the plant for the usual spell, he went around the building, saying: 'Put your tools away, boys, there'll be no work here again'. The men walked through the fog to the town that night, certain that Queenstown was doomed.

While Queenstown imagined itself in the trough of the wave, Crotty rode on the crest and little thought that the wave would break. Ever since Trent had led his dogs across the button-grass and found a new smelter site, a mile and a half from the original town, Crotty had periodically writhed with uncertainty and pulsated with hope. Late in 1902, when the blast furnaces poured out copper matte and half of the company's eleven hundred men were working at the smelters, Crotty gave promise of becoming another Queenstown. A large hall and the scaffolding of two brick two-storied hotels, both of them as large as Queenstown's new 'Metropole', symbolized the confidence; brick hotels were rare in the west and were regarded as the hallmark of optimism. Land in the main street was bought and sold at high prices, the smoke and noise of the smelters spurring on the bidders. In February 1903, during the first amalgamation scare, work ceased on the new copper converters, several hundred people left the town, and confidence waned. In March the people drifted back and the Zeehan *Herald* instilled a spurious sense of security into the heart of the town.

Back in London, Knox and Nivison discussed the terms before they met the full board of the North Lyell Co. While negotiations proceded, the price of copper rose and redeemed the fortunes of both companies. No longer so desperate for amalgamation, they tended to draw apart. At the North Lyell mine, crafty officials who knew that they would be unemployed if the companies merged, sent cable after cable to their directors in London, announcing that rich ore had been discovered in different parts of the mine. They refused to let Sticht visit their mine to see the new, glittering ore bodies, though by the Launceston agreement Sticht was entitled to enter the mine. Sticht knew, moreover, that Mitchell was gutting the mine and smelting the rare pockets of rich ore. He angrily advised Knox to threaten to call off negotiations if these practices continued.

The North Lyell directors were either deceived by the ruses of their Tasmanian staff or else they tried to bluff Knox, for they demanded 650,000 shares for their shareholders and 550,000 for Mt Lyell's. Twice they made the demand and twice Knox refused. Negotiations broke down and Knox booked his passage to Australia. Then North Lyell agreed to accept an equal number of shares in the new company, but refused to sanction a clause whereby the Mt Lyell shareholders would receive an additional dividend of £68,500 as compensation for the profits which they had sacrificed in order to buy the Tharsis mines. Knox cabled this new offer to Melbourne and received the blunt reply. 'Launceston terms or nothing.' Negotiations collapsed again. Francis Webster, who represented 200,000 shares, denounced the Launceston terms, for he believed that the Mt Lyell Co. would cease to smelt within a year and that the North Lyell mine would provide 80 per cent of the copper for the new company. He reasoned that if North Lyell battled on for one more year, it would be in a position to demand a majority of the shares in the new company. The directors agreed with Webster and spoke of reconstructing the company, issuing 100,000 new shares and engaging an American metallurgist at £4,000 a year.

Then Nivison intervened—and wrecked the Webster scheme. His influence with the banks and his £20,000 loan to the North Lyell Co. made him all powerful. He spoke and North Lyell yielded. On 22 May 1903 the companies signed a provisional agreement on the basis of the Launceston terms. That same day Knox sailed for Australia, and Sticht took over the two mines, two railways and two smelters.

Diamond drill, boring for zinc at Rosebery, 1917

The *Kakariki*, steaming through Hell's Gates into the open sea

There were light hearts that morning when the news of the impending merger was cabled around the British Isles. The North Mt Lyell Copper Co. was more than a union of rich financiers and merchants. It represented the hopes and savings of perhaps five thousand people, of whom barely one in ten lived in Australia. There survives one London register listing 2,350 shareholders who held about 40 per cent of the issued capital. It would seem that the Scottish cities—Glasgow, Edinburgh, Aberdeen, Paisley, Leith and Inverness—held the greatest share in the North Lyell mine, Glasgow alone claiming several hundred shareholders. Many shareholders were humble working people who owned £5, £10 or £20 of shares and worked in foundries, meat-markets, ironworks, shipyards, breweries, warehouses and roller mills. At the other end of the social scale stood Scottish merchants and brokers, London solicitors and industrial magnates, country gentry, doctors, bankers, clergymen and Oxford dons. They were the North Lyell Company; they had financed its blunders, and had waited in vain for the dividends.

The news that all the ore would henceforth be smelted at Queenstown was hailed with excitement in the 'copper city'. But at Crotty, where carpenters and bricklayers had completed villas, shops, a church, a school, and a thirty-room hotel that very month, the first tidings were taken quietly. But on the Saturday night the confirmation of the rumour hushed the crowded street and silenced the hammers forever. Businessmen gathered beneath the verandahs and discussed the calamity while the single men—and there were hundreds at Crotty— adjourned to the hotels and celebrated, for they had nothing to lose. £20,000 of private property and a huge fortune in company property was practically worthless.

The last buckets of ore slid down the aerial ropeway to the busy railway yards at Linda, and the last long ore train left for Crotty. The smelters shut down on the last morning of May, a Sunday, and three hundred men were paid off on the following day. The great exodus began. People left the doors of their huts and houses wide open and poured into Gormanston and Zeehan where they roamed the streets and tramped hopelessly from mine to mine in search of work. Buildings were chopped down for firewood or auctioned at mock prices; twelve huts sold for

£13 10s the lot; a cottage and a church sold for £26; the mansion-like offices of the North Lyell Co. sold for £85; a two-storied brick hotel, complete except for verandah, was apparently abandoned before it had sold a pint of beer. Within three weeks, a town of nine hundred people was almost deserted and grass was sprouting in the streets.

Darwin, described as a 'Zeehan in the making' by one optimistic journalist, lay near the limestone quarries, four miles south of Crotty. It had a hotel, stores, sawmill, workingmen's club, railway refreshment room and the luxury of a metalled street. The quarries were now abandoned, and eighty men removed their families and chattels in a week.

Kelly Basin was almost as large as Crotty, a thriving port and railway town with four hotels and the busy wharves where coastal steamers had loaded six thousand tons of copper matte and hundreds of thousands of bags of ore. The crack of doom had sounded so suddenly that the steamer *Kamona* was on its way to Kelly Basin with five hundred tons of coke for the smelters, while hundreds of tons of Zeehan ironstone lay on lighters at Strahan, waiting to be towed down the harbour. Shortly before the fateful cable arrived, a steamer had unloaded four large converter vessels designed to smelt the matte into blister copper, 99 per cent pure. The iron bowls were left to redden with rust on the wharf of a derelict port.

On 16 July, when less than thirty people remained at Crotty and 'watchman' was the chief occupation of the silent town, a crowd of North Lyell shareholders gathered in London to confirm the amalgamation proposals. Halfway through the meeting, they learned that the Mt Lyell shareholders had voted unanimously for the united company in Melbourne. Thereafter, the London meeting became a lengthy vendetta in which the enraged shareholders bitterly abused the old directorate. One expert summed up the tragedy thus: if the North Lyell Co. had merged five years earlier, it would have saved £500,000 in capital expenditure and have earned £250,000 in dividends instead of making a large loss. After hours of bickering the motion was submitted to the shareholders, who voted overwhelmingly for amalgamation. Next day engineers began to dismantle the Crotty smelters.

The new Mount Lyell Mining and Railway Company Limited

was registered in Melbourne in August 1903, with a share capital of £1,200,000. Half the new shares went to North shareholders and half to Mt Lyell shareholders. The Mt Lyell shareholders shared a bonus of £68,500; the North shareholders received a liquidation dividend of twopence per share, the first and last dividend of their ill-fated company. The old Mt Lyell organization—railway, mine, smelters, Melbourne offices, and staff—remained intact; and Robert Sticht, probably the greatest figure in the huge Australian mining industry of that day, became general manager at the princely sum of £5,000 a year. A London board of five, four of whom were North Lyell directors, was set up to guard the interests of the British shareholders, inform them of the company's affairs and cable their votes to Melbourne. The real administrative power lay, however, with the old board of the Mt Lyell Co.: Kelly, Knox, Jamieson, J. C. Syme, and Tulloch. They made the policy; the Londoners gave advice.

And so it was that the greatest merger in Australian mining history was sealed. The largest and the fourth-largest copper producers in the British Empire, long sundered by two dynamic and dogmatic Irishmen, were one; and new prosperity came to Mt Lyell.

18

Counting the Cost

In 1893 Dr Peters had told Bowes Kelly that he had not yet seen an English engineer who had learned the meaning of cheap construction. He insisted that the Englishman learned and practised his profession under conditions which were as silk to sackcloth compared to the crude but enterprising methods practised in the colonies. To prove his point, Dr Peters recalled his own experiences:

> Not many years ago, in an out-of-the-way district in British America, where either corrugated iron or lumber were almost worth their weight in copper, an American and an English company began building works at the same time on adjacent mines. The Englishman ordered iron columns, beams and corrugated iron from England, and then waited seven months for it to get there.
>
> I used the slightly hewn trunks of straight pines for my frame, and finding plenty of birch trees about, covered the entire plant with large sheets of birch-bark, good for thirty years in that climate. Our works were running before his iron left Liverpool, and our buildings cost actually less than one eighth of his, and in that cold climate were much more comfortable. The American mine has paid a dividend ever since its second year. The British mine, which is equally good, closed down and wound up in eight months, but was leased by its American neighbours and they regard it as the more valuable of the two properties today. That all came from management.

This incident was strangely prophetic of events to come. Ten years to the month after Peters had related this parable it was re-enacted at Mt Lyell. The Australian company's mine, the Mt Lyell mine, was brilliantly managed and paid large dividends. The British company's mine, the richer North Lyell mine, was shamefully mismanaged and suffered heavy losses.

Why did one company succeed and the other fail? Was it simply the luck of mining? The fates did interfere, but they favoured North Lyell, for its mine was unexpectedly rich and large while the rival mine was unexpectedly poor and much smaller than predicted. The essential difference lay in management. Even in this sphere North Lyell seemed better endowed, because it was directed from the financial capital of the world by some of Britain's greatest financial and metallurgical minds, while the Mt Lyell Co. was directed by self-made men in Melbourne, a city notorious in the early nineties for its unsound financial methods. But the proximity of Melbourne was a great advantage. On at least twelve occasions between 1893 and the lighting of the first furnace Bowes Kelly crossed to Macquarie Harbour; and, often accompanied by technical experts from Broken Hill, he inspected progress at the mine, railway and smelters. The periodic visits of Kelly and other directors created a close liaison between the financial and technical leaders of the company, and cultivated that spirit of impartial criticism and consultation, which is as essential to the efficient management of large companies as it is to the system of parliamentary government.

The North Lyell Co. did not achieve this liaison. Its directors were busy London magnates who could not spare three months of each year to hurry half-way across the world; and it was not until February 1902, when two new directors were appointed, that the chairman was able to announce that the London directorate 'has the singular distinction of having all been to Tasmania, and four of them are familiar by personal knowledge with local conditions on the field'. Despite this pathetic boast, and the hundreds of pounds which the company spent each month on cables, the London board always leaned heavily on its Tasmanian managers who, unfortunately, were not equal to the responsibility. When the directors departed from this practice and made vital decisions, their ignorance of local conditions often ruined their policies. Thus their preference for an expensive broad-gauged railway instead of a cheap tramway plunged the company into lasting debt; and their metallurgical policy, dictated by MacArthur, ultimately wrecked the company. James P. Lonergan, who sat on the first Melbourne and the last London board of the company, spoke from bitter experience when he farewelled the shareholders in 1903: 'I have got no confidence whatever in the management in London of Australian companies'.

George Meudell, a bustling little company promoter of the nineties, shared Lonergan's views. He laid down the rule in his autobiography, *The Pleasant Career of a Spendthrift*, that if directors were not in close touch with their mine and manager, their company tended to be inefficient. Not only North Lyell, but also Chillagoe Railway and Mines, a group of North Queensland mines directed from Melbourne, were shining examples of this truth; so were some of the British companies at Mt Lyell. The directors of Copper Mines of Mount Lyell West sent out from England two six-ton boilers which were so heavy that the steam crane on the wharf at Teepookana could not lift them from the barge and so large that they could not pass through the narrow tram cuttings between Queenstown and the mine. Six months later the boilers still lay on the wharf at Hobart. For many months the directors retained a high-salaried English staff, comprising mine manager, metallurgist and accountant, to direct the work of one shift boss and four miners. To crown these blunders, the directors, apparently believing that all branches of chemistry were the same, employed a pharmaceutical chemist instead of a metallurgical chemist, and provided him with an elaborate assay office more complete than even the Mt Lyell Co. assay laboratory, which hitherto had coped with all the ores of the field.

The Mt Lyell Comstock Copper Company, directed by five Scotsmen domiciled in London, decided to build a railway from its mine to Linda and send its ore to Crotty. In 1901 a hundred navvies began to build the railway along the rugged slopes of Mt Lyell. It was a difficult feat of engineering, especially in the north-east of the mountain where workmen had to blast a narrow ledge along a sheer precipice of quartzite rock which overhung the button-grass flats on the King River, hundreds of feet below. The company built six miles of the formation and laid three and a half miles of rails before the sudden cessation of smelting at Crotty forced it to abandon plate-laying within sight of the mine. The loss of £13,361, four-fifths of the sum which the North Lyell Co. spent on the railway, was a harsh judgment on the plucky shareholders, but it saved them from heavier loss. The railway, authorized after the manager had estimated that the ore bodies carried 6 to 7 per cent copper, would have been utterly useless, because systematic sampling later revealed that the ore was only half as rich and certainly not worth the cost of mining. Even if the mine had fulfilled expectations, and even if the furnaces at Crotty had continued to glow, the company would still have merited censure, for the curves of the completed section of the railway were so sharp that the little 'Shay' locomotives frequently jumped the rails and crashed into trees and boulders.

Some British directors must have pictured Australia as a vast wilderness to which every machine and brick had to be exported from England almost regardless of cost. In their eagerness to secure lucrative contracts for supplying their mine with boilers, rails, locomotives and bricks they were possibly happy to retain that primitive idea. Scattered down the gullies of the Linda Valley and along the desolate plateau at Crotty are thousands of yellow Scottish bricks, all shipped to Melbourne, transhipped to Strahan and Kelly Basin, and railed to the building sites at a time when there were three efficient brickworks on the west coast, and numerous makers of firebricks in Melbourne.

It must have been a premonition of this kind of bungling that curbed the natural temptation of the directors of the Mt Lyell Proprietary Mines to harness their local manager with detailed instructions. Instead, they vested full power in their manager and stayed in London to await the dividends which the tricky Italian promoter had promised them. Their trust was brazenly betrayed.

In England their first manager had been told that his company's lease merely awaited the sinking of the main shaft to yield its buried hoard of copper. He alighted from the coach at Gormanston, scoured his lease in vain for a sign of copper and eventually resigned in disgust. The new manager was a dapper Cornishman who resembled the black-bearded villain of the popular melodramas of the day. He had spent eleven years in Chile as an engineer in the copper mines, and such was his experience and popularity that he was soon chosen to preside over that august body, the Mt Lyell Mine Managers' Association.

In Gormanston he lived like a fighting cock; and a growing pile of empty bottles and *pâté de fois gras* tins began to surround his residence at the top of Peters Street. In the hotels his parties were just as extravagant, and during one drunken spree he delighted his cronies by trying to purchase the Federation Hotel. To recuperate from the revelry of the previous night and to prepare, perhaps, for the evening carousal, he often slept in the mine office after lunch; and he made it a strict rule that no miner should ring for the cage during his siesta. In consequence, work down the shaft was often impaired.

He loved cricket. In choosing workmen, it was said that he preferred a good batsman to a good miner; and it was certainly true that on some sunny afternoons, the only driving performed by his miners was the straight drive on the local cricket pitch. The Mt Lyell Proprietary cricket eleven, thriving on frequent practice, became the most formidable team on the west coast and challenged the best eleven cricketers in Queenstown to a two-day match for a £100 wager. A town of five thousand people did not allow a challenge from a company employing only seventy miners to remain unanswered, and it agreed to play the match on the Queenstown cricket ground. The Proprietary team batted last, and in its second innings had to score 101 runs to defeat the town. They reached 96 and, with five wickets in hand, victory seemed assured. Then, to the delight of the large crowd, the remaining five batsmen added only four runs, and Queenstown won by a run. The manager had quietly backed the Queenstown team for a heavy wager and instructed his miners to lose. This transpired in a subsequent lawsuit.

The site of the Proprietary's main shaft can still be seen on the Gormanston oval just north of the cricket pitch. Through faulty timbering, or pressure of ground, the shaft became so badly out of plumb that it was condemned by the inspector of mines. The manager then drove two long tunnels near the foothills of Mt Owen and told the world that one of the tunnels was heading for an 'extensive lode'. A Queenstown wag wrote to the *Mount Lyell Standard* and pointed out that if the manager continued the tunnel for a mile and quarter he would certainly strike a large lode—the Gormanston sanitary depot. As soon as the manager read the letter he dressed himself immaculately, gathered his gold chain, walking stick and terriers, and caught the coach to Queenstown. At the *Standard* office, where the Queenstown Club stands today, he brandished his stick at the counter and roared for the blood of the 'infamous blackguard'. No blackguard stepped forward, but a burly compositor accepted the challenge and wrestled with the Cornishman until the shafts of sunlight were grey with rising dust.

Finding no copper in his three main workings, the manager sank a shaft on Mt Owen, a little above the waterfall. When the shaft had descended a hundred feet he informed the directors that a crushing battery and cyanide plant were necessary to extract the £50,000 of gold that lay in sight. The directors, however, realizing that the seemingly inexhaustible funds of the company were nearly exhausted, offered to sell this new gold mine to Mt Lyell Copper Estates, which sent out a Mr Black to inspect the mine. Black tested the conglomerate gravel in the shaft and found that it carried barely a trace of gold.

Black found that cricket was the most harmless of the manager's activities. Apparently he had grown wealthy by adding fictitious names to the pay-roll and collecting their pay; the barman at the Federation Hotel was one who admitted that his name was on the company's pay sheet. It was also alleged that the manager had recorded the cost of driving imaginary tunnels in his monthly balance sheet, and been paid for his labours accordingly.

Before Black could complete his report, he was stricken with typhoid and died in the Queenstown hospital. The mine fell into the hands of its creditors; and its wealthy manager, the dandy of Gormanston, vanished from the field and is said to have ended his working days cleaning boots in an Adelaide hotel. If, somewhere in England, a few former shareholders of the company are still alive, they will surely appreciate the predicament of British companies that directed mines on the other side of the world, and the difficulty of steering a safe course between the twin dangers of giving unbridled power to the local manager or choking him with ridiculous instructions and machinery.

The British mines at Mt Lyell could not claim a monopoly

of inefficiency. Small Melbourne and Launceston companies often explored their leases in such a haphazard way that their workings resembled rabbit warrens. Their managers were often working miners whose chief virtues were physical strength, skill with hammer, steel, and blacksmith bellows, and ability to let a favourable contract for driving a hundred feet of tunnel. The poverty of these companies forced their managers to search for quick profits and explore their lease short-sightedly in the same way that the wealth of the large London companies encouraged extravagance.

Rumours of extravagance, inefficiency, and corruption in the management of many mines and the fact that only four of forty Lyell companies—namely Blocks, Lyell Tharsis, Mt Lyell and North Lyell—had found payable ore bodies naturally prompted investors to ask themselves the question: 'Does mining pay?' About the turn of the century, when the death-roll of British mining companies in Australia contained thousands of names, Sir Henry Wrixon made the outspoken statement that, on the whole, it had cost more to produce the mineral wealth of Australia than that wealth was worth. This opinion seemed logical to English investors, whose eyes were coloured because their purses were empty, and it aroused widespread discussion amongst journalists and financiers. While the argument was raging, the North Lyell Co. came to its ignominious end, a débâcle which armed the contestants with high explosives.

The North Mount Lyell Copper Company, in six years, had spent about £1,250,000, or the equivalent of about £8,000,000 in present-day currency when the costs of modern construction in the outback are considered. Slightly less than half of this amount came from working operations; the remainder came from shares, debentures, banks and financiers. In May 1903 the company owed banks, financiers and debenture-holders £284,000, and had paid no dividend on the £247,894 which it collected from more than five thousand shareholders. It had thus lost almost £532,000 of borrowed money and squandered at least another £250,000 of mining profits. It was left with a valueless railway, port, smelting works, machine shops, offices, villas, aerial tram, sawmills, brickworks, tramways, and a mine so badly timbered and worked that the Mt Lyell Co. had to spend £20,000 in re-timbering and repairing it. At the three settlements along the railway hundreds of houses and huts, numerous stores and halls and public buildings, and nine hotels were left derelict and barely worth the cost of removing. Some of the machinery at Crotty and Kelly Basin was sold to companies as far afield as Chillagoe and Broken Hill but the sale of liquid assets probably did not recoup 15 per cent of the total capital expenditure.

The critics who believed that mining was unprofitable gleaned telling evidence from the North Lyell farce but confused the evidence which existed in the fragmentary records of many other companies. The Mt Lyell Comstock Copper Co., for example, which had issued 450,000 £1 shares to its shareholders, received a working capital of only £49,925. In 1904, when shares had little market value and the balance sheet appeared in the press. it was natural that many readers should infer that shareholders had lost £450,000—the total face value of the fully-paid shares. The traditional formality of the balance sheets obscured from the layman the true story that when the company was floated in England, 400,000 fully paid £1 shares were divided amongst promoters, new directors, and shareholders in the original Melbourne company in payment of the money they had previously spent in developing the mine and floating a new company in London. In fact the shareholders of the two Comstock companies had subscribed no more than £65,000, of which £2,572 was still available. What was true of the Comstock was true of other companies. Balance sheets showed that fifteen different companies had issued more than 100,000 fully-paid £1 shares by 1903, whereas only the two leading companies on the field had actually raised more than £70,000 from shareholders. And while more than £5,000,000 was listed as 'paid-up capital' in all the Lyell companies, less than a third of this huge sum had actually been invested in the mines of the field. This is clear once the mask of paid-up capital is torn away.

On a careful reckoning, investors and banks subscribed about £1,600,000 to all the Lyell companies in the decade 1893–1903. About a third of this sum went to the North Lyell Co., a third went to the Mt Lyell Co., and the remainder was invested in the forty or more smaller companies. How much of this money was repaid in dividends? By 1903 Mt Lyell had paid £996,574 in dividends or a return of 188 per cent on the money invested. Four companies which had been absorbed by the Mt Lyell Co. had paid dividends of more than £65,000 in liquidation, while Lyell Tharsis had paid £30,750 from working profits. At the time of the great merger the Lyell field had yielded nearly £1,100,000 in dividends—about £500,000 less than the money which had been invested in its mines. So far the field as a whole had been worked at a loss.

It was premature in 1903 to draw definite conclusions whether the field would ultimately prove payable, for the dividends going out far exceeded the capital still rippling in and steadily brightened the ledger. Nevertheless the end of the field seemed near and the legion of Lyell investors, which may have numbered 20,000 people, seemed likely to receive back little more than its capital outlay, let alone interest on the sum invested or the fantastic profits which promoters had promised.

The men who bewailed the financial failure of the Australian mining industry were correct, therefore, in thinking that the long death-roll of Lyell mines supported their contention. But their assumption that the days of Mt Lyell were numbered was wrong. The unexpected discovery of the 'New Development Ore Body' at the 500' level of the North Lyell mine reprieved the field from the sentence of death, and made Mt Lyell a highly profitable field of investment. By 1906 the field had repaid the total sum of money it had absorbed, and by 1920 the field had repaid the investment at least twice over.

Who paid for the early losses on the field? The directors and legal managers were often the largest shareholders but they did not necessarily fare worst. They often received free 'promoter's shares' and lucrative contracts as well as annual fees that would make a modern director envious. Some companies spent almost as much on administration as on mining: in thirty months the Comstock Co. spent £6,900 on directors' fees and office expenses but only £8,900 on wages, stores, explosives, timber, and salaries. Directors who received high fees for attending occasional meetings of the board had a vested interest in keeping their company going even after it had abandoned its original mine. The directors of Mt Lyell Copper Estates prolonged their sinecures by tin scratching near Renison Bell; Copper Mines of Mt Lyell West abandoned their leases at Mt Lyell and acquired gold leases in New Zealand; Mt Lyell Consols abandoned their mine and worked a copper mine at Wallaroo, S.A.; Mt Lyell Comstock acquired an interest in the Oonah mine and smelters at Zeehan; and the Great Mt Lyell Copper Co. was reformed into the Ballarat and Lyell Mines, Limited, and acquired the old Woah Hawp gold mine at Ballarat. The London chairman of this new 'wild cat' company received £300 a year, and his fellow-directors received £150, preferential shares, and a special fee if they decided to visit Australia. These five companies all failed in their new enterprise and replenished the pockets of the directors with money that should have been returned to shareholders.

The dice were heavily loaded against the British investor. When Crotty floated North Lyell in London the Australian shareholders who had spent less than £15,000 in exploring the lease received 64 per cent of the shares; the promoters, new directors and their friends paid £45,000 for 30 per cent of the shares; the British investing public paid £25,000 for 5.3 per cent of the shares. For the same money the Australians received twenty shares, the British financial clique three shares, and the British investing public one share. In theory the Australians deserved the cheapest shares, for they had taken the greatest risk in spending money on undeveloped ground. In fact the British shareholders unknowingly took an almost equal risk, for most of the mines in which they invested were as worthless as the day the first trench was dug.

The Australian gain did not end here. In 1897-8, when John Bull began to fancy Lyell as the coming copper-field, the price of Lyell shares soared and thousands of Australians were enticed into selling their shares to British buyers. Eventually these transactions gave Britain a majority of shares in all the principal mines at Mt Lyell, including the Mt Lyell Mining and Railway Co. At least £2,000,000 was transferred from Britain to Australia to pay for Mt Lyell and North Lyell shares alone, while perhaps another £500,000 was paid for shares in other Lyell companies in deals on the stock exchange.

In 1902 R. L. Nash, financial editor of the Sydney *Daily Telegraph* made a close study of British capital in Australia and implied that Mt Lyell had attracted more British capital than any Australian mining field, with the exception of the Western Australian goldfields. British investors held an overwhelming majority of shares in the good mines, and for long they received most of the profits of the field. But the Australians monopolized the more attractive profits of share speculating, selling out early and generally wisely, though ignorant of the unexpected profits which the richest mine would yield to its British owners.

The Mt Lyell mines may have smiled treacherously on the majority of their investors, but they certainly revived the fortunes of the stagnant colony. The Mt Lyell field, in its first twenty-five years of smelting, produced £18,000,000 of copper, gold and silver—more than the combined production of Zeehan, Mt Bischoff, Beaconsfield, Mathinna, Rosebery, Renison Bell, Derby and all the other Tasmanian fields in this period.

In 1891 mining became the most valuable of the Tasmanian export industries; and from 1894 to 1909, minerals never provided less than 40 per cent of the island's export revenue. In 1897, when the first bars of Mt Lyell blister copper were lowered into the ships moored along the crowded waterfront at Strahan, the mines provided 52.5 per cent of the island's export and gave Tasmania its highest income from exports since 1853, the height of the Victorian gold rushes. By 1901 more than 60 per cent of the island's export revenue was coming from metal-buyers in Germany, the United States and Great Britain, and in that year Mt Lyell produced more than £1,000,000 of copper and made Tasmania's mining exports worth £1,767,000—more than the total export income of the island in any year before 1897. In the years 1896-1910 the mines always contributed more than a quarter, and sometimes a third, of the total wealth produced in the state.

Even in comparison with the Tasmanian government the expenditure of the Mt Lyell Co. was formidable. When the company declared its first dividend in 1897 it had already spent as much money as the government had spent on education, customs, civil service, law, defence, the post office and all the expenses of construction and administration in the last financial year. In one year the Mt Lyell Co.'s revenue exceeded the revenue of the Tasmanian government, and frequently the company's revenue was almost as large. The *Australian Mining Standard*, surveying the colony in 1898, passed sound judgment with these words: 'Mt Lyell has, in short, been of talismanic virtue to Tasmania, and it is the centre whence radiates all its present hope of progress'.

Probably a seventh of the island's population earned their daily bread between Mt Bischoff and Macquarie Harbour at the end of the last century. In August 1897 the west coast held 16,000 people, of whom half lived on Zeehan. In the following two years Mt Lyell came to the front, and thereafter its various mining and smelting towns always supported a greater population than the Zeehan field. Late in 1899, when about 2,500 railway navvies were camping in the bush, and mines were working energetically during a phase of high metal prices, the coast probably had its peak population of 25,000. When the census was taken in March 1901 metal prices had slumped, scores of mines had closed, the great construction projects were completed, and the population had fallen to 19,000—a ninth of Tasmania's population. At this census Queenstown (population 5,051) and Zeehan (population 5,014) were the third and fourth largest towns in Tasmania, Gormanston was seventh, Strahan was ninth, and Waratah was eleventh. Thus four of the eleven largest towns and cities were western mining towns, while another two—Burnie and Strahan—were the ports of these towns.

The Mt Lyell field was probably most populous in the summer of 1902-3 when the two great companies fought their last round and directly supported a population of more than 11,000 people. Queenstown held about 5,000, the Linda Valley towns 2,500, Strahan 1,300, Crotty 900, Kelly Basin 800, Lynchford 200, Darwin 150, while scattered camps of woodcutters and prospectors held several hundred more. In 1911, when the next census was held, more than 4,000 of these people had moved on, leaving slightly less than 7,000 people at Mt Lyell and Strahan.

In the Tasmania of 1899 there was no Labor Party, no working man in Parliament, only one strong union—the Amalgamated Miners' Association—and little radical or democratic legislation compared with the other Australian colonies. The western miners, using the manhood suffrage which federation introduced into Tasmania, revolutionized the politics of the island. They founded a Labor Party, which, over the years, made the smallest, least industrialized and most conservative state into the most advanced social-service state in Australia. The Mt Lyell mines and the Gormanston branch of the miners' union were the political schools in which most of the early Labor politicians were prepared for office. John Earle (Premier of Tasmania), J. J. Long, M.H.A., M. O'Keefe, M.H.A., and J. J. McDonald, M.H.A. (later Attorney-General) worked in the mines at Gormanston while George Burns and Ben Watkins were young working men whom Queenstown sent to the Tasmanian Assembly of thirty-five members.

King O'Malley, reputed founder of the Commonwealth Bank, was Mt Lyell's gift to Australian politics. At the first election for the new House of Representatives, when all Tasmania voted as one five-member electorate, he outbid eight other candidates for the votes of Lyell and received 1,906 of the 2,484 votes cast on the field—more than the total vote he received in the remainder of the island. He represented the west until 1917 and died in 1953, in his hundredth year, with £70,000 to his name and a national institution as his memorial.

William Jamieson

G. S. Swinburne

Colin Templeton

P. C. Holmeš Hunt

K. M. Niall

Sir Walter Bassett

Chairmen of the Mt Lyell Company

Russell M. Murray

A. H. P. Moline

Hugh M. Murray

General Managers of the Mt Lyell Company

19

Widening Horizons

Although the North Lyell mine had saved the Mt Lyell Co. from bankruptcy, the ore reserves of this rich mine were small. When W. T. Batchelor took over the mine from the old company the deepest working was a winze at the 400′ level, where the ore body was unexpectedly small. In April 1904, after the new company had mined 54,000 tons of North Lyell ore, only 170,494 tons remained—enough to keep the smelters in blast for eighteen months. This ore averaged 6.25 per cent copper, and was poorer than Sticht had assumed when evaluating the mine before the merger.

The Iron Blow now averaged 1.12 per cent copper and was simply a huge flux quarry, indispensable for smelting North Lyell ore but by itself unpayable. Unless a new ore body was discovered in the North Lyell lease, the field would close about 1907. William Knox was pessimistic, admitting in confidence that the results of the amalgamation had not been favourable. Investors had so lost confidence that shares were selling for 10s each in November 1904 and the market value of the two mines, estimated at £7,000,000 at the peak of the boom, had fallen to £650,000.

The pessimism of the directors was revealed in an incident that took place in 1904. W. T. Batchelor, writing notes to assist Professor J. W. Gregory in compiling a study on the geology of Mt Lyell, remarked that 'in the North Lyell mine, as in all other instances on the field, the most noticeable characteristics of the ore occurrences is their diminution in area as depth is attained, and in some instances their peculiarity of splitting up into one or more legs, with entirely barren material separating

175

them'. A company official, fearing that the publication of this statement would lower the value of shares even more, carefully censored it in Gregory's book.

During this crisis the directors initiated a vigorous expansion policy which, though lasting only three years, was probably the most energetic search for mines yet made in Australia. This policy sprang, not from the ambitious desire for a national network of mines like those directed by the United States copper companies, but from the fear that in a few years, when all payable ore had been torn from the mines, the smelters and railway would be valueless. The company, moreover, was well equipped for the search. It had brilliant metallurgists; it employed competent engineers and miners who could inspect, explore and sample promising mines; it had large, efficient smelting works and two long railways to haul in ores from western mines; it had large reserve funds to finance an expensive mining venture.

On 5 May 1904 Sticht agreed to inspect those Tasmanian and Australian mines which could stand heavy capitalization and be worked on a large scale. He did not seek the small gold reef or silver lode, even if it did offer a good short-term investment; and many such came his way. He wanted a mine as large and complex as the Iron Blow, a mine worked and abandoned by some small company that lacked money and technical skill.

In the following month William Jamieson, a Mt Lyell director, was sent to Cobar in the far west of New South Wales to negotiate for the purchase of the Great Cobar mine. The owners asked for £1,000,000 and another £100,000 to sink a new main shaft. Although the hope of an annual profit of £450,000 made Cobar an attractive mine, Jamieson admitted that the price was enormous and 'almost too much to tackle'. In July he broke off negotiations.

Robert Sticht thought that the stagnant mines at Mt Read and Rosebery were the most promising undeveloped mines in Tasmania, and he sent Luke Williams to inspect them. A native of Bendigo and a pioneer of Heemskirk, Williams had managed the Curtain-Davis Proprietary and Mt Read mines near Williamsford, the town which honours his name. The Mt Lyell Co. took elaborate precautions to conceal its interest in his tour. It addressed all its correspondence to William through John

Moyle, manager of the Ring River mine, and Williams despatched his letters and cables to Knox Schlapp & Co. Pty Ltd, Melbourne mining agents. When Sticht wanted to experiment with a hundred tons of ore from the Primrose mine he made his request to Alfred Mellor, the secretary, in Melbourne. Mellor informed Knox Schlapp, which wired the request in code to Luke Williams. Williams then approached the Primrose tribute miners and asked that a sample of their ore be bagged and shipped to Sydney. When the cargo of ore reached Sydney it was shipped back to Strahan and railed to Queenstown, only seventy rail miles from the Primrose mine. Although Sticht experimented with the zinc-lead sulphide from Rosebery and was impressed with the possibilities of the field, he made no effort to buy the mines.

Williams then went north to Mt Bischoff and began to inspect the small silver and copper mines between Waratah and the Pieman. Three years later Herbert Muir, the old North Lyell manager, inspected the same country without success. Meanwhile, W. H. Cundy had climbed Mt Jukes and Mt Darwin and inspected scores of mines which had been dead or dormant since the liquidation of the great sponsor of the field, the North Mount Lyell Copper Company. Cundy found nothing in this field of no dividends and heavy losses.

In 1905 the Mt Lyell Co. was interested in a large copper mine near Northampton, W.A., and the Blinman mine in South Australia. In February of the same year A. E. Savage begin to inspect Chillagoe, Many Peaks, Cloncurry and scores of small North Queensland copper deposits for copper ores which could be smelted at Queenstown. In the following summers T. B. Moore and a party of men explored the country between Macquarie Harbour and Port Davey, finding few minerals except unpayable gold, iron and copper pyrites. In these journeys Moore travelled across valleys and mountains which no man had previously traversed. He once remarked that anyone could draw an imaginary coast line of south-western Tasmania and be as correct as the official government charts.

From 1904 to 1907 the company's prospectors and engineers inspected hundreds of mines but they found only four properties which merited large-scale prospecting: Blue Tier, Red

Hills, Balfour and Chester. All were Tasmanian mines and all failed.

The Blue Tier was a high range in the north-east of the island and the watershed of the George and Ringarooma Rivers, where several million pounds worth of alluvial tin had been washed since the 1870s. Luke Williams inspected old alluvial workings that scarred the Tier and thought they indicated an extensive low-grade tin deposit. He pegged 858 acres. The Mt Lyell Co. agreed to prospect the leases of other syndicates and, if they showed good ore, to finance a united company in which Mt Lyell would hold a majority of shares.

In January 1906, when Mt Lyell directors and officials visited the Blue Tier, Launceston and the north-east simmered with rumours. Most mining men swore that the Mt Lyell Co. would make the village of Lottah another Queenstown, and newspapers christened the bush valley 'Tinopolis'. In May fifty men began to trench the hillside, and in August diamond drills were secured. The miners dug eleven miles of trenches, sank 57 diamond drill holes and 209 alluvial test holes, made two dams, formed twelve miles of road and pack track, and assayed three thousand samples. The Mt Lyell Co. spent £10,000 on this extensive prospecting programme but found no large payable deposit. In May 1907 it abandoned the field.

Meanwhile the company had leased 485 acres some ten miles north of Mt Lyell, at Red Hills, a pyrites deposit which had been floated as a copper mine in the 1897 boom. It drove several tunnels, prospected the surface, and abandoned the mine after finding only traces of copper.

In December 1907 T. B. Moore returned from the bush north of the Pieman with fine specimens of copper pyrites. He pegged and prospected four hundred acres in the Norfolk Range, transferring his men to Frankland River, Hazelton and South Balfour in 1909. Balfour, a shallow copper-field, boomed and collapsed in 1910 and 1911, four or five hundred men rushing to this last of the western mining booms. The ore bodies in Moore's leases were either too poor or too small to be mined at a profit in this inaccessible region, and Moore returned to Queenstown in 1912.

Moore had prospected at Balfour long after the company had lost the stimulus to expand. Even when he was chipping specimens in the Norfolk Range in 1907 the directors decided to curtail their nation-wide search. For in the previous three years the North Lyell mine had opened out in an amazing manner and dispelled the gloom which had scattered prospectors to every point of the compass. The need to find new mines had vanished.

The more they mined at North Lyell the greater the unsuspected reserves they discovered at deep levels. Ore reserves increased from 170,000 tons in April 1904 to 438,020 tons in September 1907. The main shaft was then sunk from the 1000′ to 1100′ level and ore reserves reached 710,000 tons in September 1908. At the 850′, 1000′ and 1100′ levels of the mine, the ore body extended an astonishing distance. Between April 1904 and April 1913 the company mined or discovered twelve times the tonnage of ore known to exist at the beginning of that period. The Iron Blow did not live up to expectations, but the hidden wealth of the North Lyell mine would have astounded even the most brazen speculator of the nineties.

Before this crisis in the life of the Lyell field had passed the company entered the superphosphate industry. In 1904, when the Mt Lyell mines had two years' payable ore in sight, the directors decided to utilize their huge deposit of poor pyrites, containing 48 per cent sulphur and less than 1 per cent copper.

Dr Robertson, the first expert to realize the value of the copper in the little gold mine, saw the potential sulphur value of the pyrites in the Iron Blow. Likewise the government geologist had predicted in 1893 that some day Mt Lyell might become the centre of the Australian superphosphate industry. Sticht's pyritic smelters thwarted this plan, using sulphur as fuel to smelt the copper. The waste sulphur floated up the furnace chimneys, blackening the landscape in summer and brewing grimy, yellow fogs in winter. In 1900, when seven or eight furnaces were in continuous blast, the sulphur that issued from the tall brick chimney stacks and the short furnace stacks would have made 120,000 tons of sulphuric acid annually—more than Australia would consume for years. Deputations of suffering townsmen who waited on Sticht were told that sulphuric acid could not be made profitably from smelter fumes. And so the sulphur cloud drifted above Mt Lyell for twenty-five years.

Although the sulphur could not be extracted from the furnace gases, the sulphur in the pyrites in the Mt Lyell mine had commercial possibilities which Australia's thriving bone-dust factories and fertilizer works were not slow to assess. These factories had flourished since the late 1890s, when the practice of fertilizing worn-out wheat lands with superphosphate—a compound made from sulphuric acid and phosphate rock—had grown tremendously in Victoria and South Australia. After 1902 Australian fertilizer factories received a cheap supply of phosphate rock from Ocean Island, a German colony in the Pacific Ocean, but they still lacked a local source of sulphuric acid, being dependent on sulphur imported from the volcanoes of Sicity.

In 1903 an enterprising manufacturer of artificial fertilizers, Cuming Smith & Co. of Melbourne, realized that the Mt Lyell mine held millions of tons of unpayable copper pyrites which would never be needed as flux for the North Lyell ore, and sounded out the prospects of buying the surplus ore. Joseph C. Syme, a director of the Mt Lyell Co. and formerly part-owner of the influential Australian newspaper, the Melbourne *Age*, immediately sensed that the Mt Lyell Co. was well endowed to enter the profitable fertilizer trade. In February 1904, after Syme had investigated the question, the directors asked Sticht to report on the cost of roasting the sulhpur from the ore.

Five days later Sticht chanced to meet Philip Mackay, young metallurgist from the Sulphide Corporation, Newcastle, N.S.W., who was inspecting the Mt Lyell smelters before returning to Illinois. Sticht was surprised to learn that his compatriot had worked in American chemical works, and in the hope that Mackay's knowledge might assist the directors Sticht asked him to call at the head office in Melbourne. As a result of his chance visit to Queenstown, Mackay cancelled his passage to the United States and agreed to report on the prospect of the Mt Lyell Co. entering the fertilizer trade. He reported favourably. In June 1904 the directors decided to erect chemical and fertilizer works in Melbourne.

The deserted buildings, machinery, tramway and acid chambers of Thomson's pyrites smelting works, an early venture to treat the refractory ores from the goldfields, stood on the swampy foreshore where the river Maribyrnong joins the Yarra at West Melbourne. The Mt Lyell Co. purchased these derelict works for £7,500 and assembled the modern steam and electrical plant from Crotty in extensive new buildings. At the wharf steamers unloaded ore from Strahan, yellow phosphate from Ocean Island and coke from the company's ovens at Port Kembla; and a horse tram carried the raw material to a long storage shed. The manufacturing process was simple; the ore was roasted in parallel rows of cylindrical tanks; the sulphur fumes were condensed into sulphuric acid in a large lead-lined chamber; the acid was mixed with the phosphate and bagged and marketed as the 'ML' brand of superphosphate. The sulphur which had blackened the Queen Valley began to bronze the exhausted Victorian wheatlands. Henceforth the Mt Lyell Co.'s half-yearly report always listed, amidst voluminous descriptions of the mines, harvest prospects for the coming season.

In the sowing season of 1906 the output of the Mt Lyell Fertilizer Works at Yarraville sold so rapidly that Mackay duplicated the plant, increasing capital expenditure to £75,000 and the pay-roll to 150 men. At Port Adelaide, in 1907, the company purchased the smelting works of the Broken Hill Junction Company, spent £60,000 in the construction of a modern factory, and captured the market in the New Mallee, Adelaide Hills, Port Lincoln and the gulf ports. In the following year the company began to erect works at North Fremantle in Western Australia, the rising wheat state.

The company built these works because it had pyrites to burn. By 1908, however, the Mt Lyell open cut was taxed to the utmost each week supplying the smelters with 5,000 tons of ore to flux the increasing quantities of rich ore that the new Ilgner electric hoist was hauling up the shaft from the 850′ and 1000′ levels of the North Lyell mine. The reserves of open cut pyrites were being depleted so rapidly that the underground workings of the Blow would soon have to be prepared for mining and at the higher cost of mining underground it would not pay to make Mt Lyell pyrites into sulphuric acid. The unexpected developments in the North Lyell mine had absorbed as smelting fuel that surplus of cheap pyrites which had led to the establishment of the fertilizer works. These works now urgently needed a new pyritic ore body, capable of being mined in a large open cut.

Anyone who stands in the grassy main street of Tullah, the little galena mining town where the dark, boulder-strewn rivers of Mackintosh and Murchinson form the mighty Pieman, and looks west into the blue-grey ranges, will see a scar of yellow, white and brown rock, surrounded by forest. This was the Chester mine, a large deposit of iron pyrites discovered by Kershaw and Sanderson in 1896, when every large outcrop of pyrites was hailed hysterically as another Mt Lyell. Three different syndicates felled the forest, prospected the huge lode and reluctantly decided that it was rich in iron and sulphur but barren in copper. In 1908 Luke Williams inspected the abandoned tunnels and concluded that the mine could supply the acid works with cheap sulphur. On his advice the Mt Lyell Co. bought the mine for £500.

Williams laid out a large open cut and built ore bins, a steep haulage tram and a mile of horse tramline through the forest to the Emu Bay Railway. Boarding house, hall, store, stables, blacksmith's shop, assay office and the huts and camps of sixty or seventy men sprang up at the foot of the steep hill. Every month or so the men trekked seven miles down the railway to Tullah or Rosebery and then staggered back to the mine to earn another large cheque.

The three trains of ore wagons that steamed out of the Chester siding for Burnie each week in 1911 gave the mine a flourishing air that deceived. High sea and rail freight and the declining sulphur content of the ore devoured any profit and made it cheaper for the Yarraville works to roast Spanish pyrites. In the hope that the sulphur in the ore could be cheaply concentrated, loads of ore were sent to mills at Tullah and West Bischoff but these experiments were not conclusive. Early in 1913, after 37,000 tons of ore averaging 37.2 per cent sulphur had been sent to Yarraville, the mine ceased work. In the same year the company merged its Adelaide factory with that of the chief competitor, the Wallaroo Phosphate Co., which roasted copper sulphides from the Moonta mines in the largest acid plant in the state. The Mt Lyell Co. received £136,900 of the £336,900 shares in Wallaroo—Mount Lyell Fertilisers Ltd, the first of many companies which Mt Lyell had assisted in forming.

During the Mt Lyell Co.'s first eight years in the fertilizer industry the Australian production of fertilizer increased more than tenfold. Whereas Australian factories supplied farmers with some 14 per cent of their superphosphate requirements in 1905, more than eighty factories were supplying 70 per cent of the local market in 1913. The Mt Lyell Co. played a dominant role in the rise of this valuable industry, manufacturing almost a third of the Australian output by 1911.

With its expanding chemical works, its huge Tasmanian mines, its railways and smelters, its coke works and its mine crusade, Mt Lyell was probably one of the nation's five great industrial companies in 1906 or 1907. This brief phase of industrial and mining expansion had its seed in the threat of extinction, and when the unsuspected riches in the North Lyell mine dispelled that threat the ambition to expand naturally wilted. The Broken Hill board of 1911, which included three of the five Mt Lyell directors, was haunted by the same spectre, a gutted silver mine, and fired by the same will to survive when it converted its ironstone quarries from a source of flux for the Port Pirie smelters into the basis of the mightiest industry in the Commonwealth.

20

Death of the 'Wild Cats'

When the North Lyell Co. collapsed and the bewildered people poured out of Crotty, a shadow of gloom descended on the mining valley. The noisy railway yards at Linda were silenced. The South Lyell mine filled with water. The smaller mines closed so quickly that at the end of the year only seventy men were employed outside the leases of the all-powerful company. Five companies worked where once there were forty, and only one of these produced copper. Most shopkeepers and publicans smiled bravely, though in their hearts they thought Lyell was doomed.

But the price of copper rose in 1905 and soared in 1906. Old mines re-opened; prosperity returned. Seven times a day coaches rattled uphill from Queenstown, often with loads of miners from Victoria. The Gormanston hotels, reduced by fire from seven to four after the expectations of the boom had gone astray, rocketed in value. At Linda, where only the Royal and Linda Valley hotels were in business, the two proprietors of the burnt-down hotel at North Lyell entered the trade. Sidler demolished the two-storied general office at Crotty, known as the 'white house', and re-erected it near the Linda station. Paddy Long built a new hotel and called it the 'Democrat'.

Linda fared better than Gormanston in the revival of mining. It was nearer the northern mines and its huts and small houses straggled along the lower slopes of Mt Lyell and up the gully to the North Lyell mine. Eventually Linda and North Lyell held over twenty business premises, six boarding houses, four hotels, two public halls, grimy locomotive sheds and the one-train-a-week station on which the town had once fastened its hopes. Linda was far livelier and wilder than Gormanston, and looked on its more respectable rival with scorn. Saturday evening, when the main block was thronged with people, the four-in-hand rattled downhill with the evening mail, the sound of singing and boisterous laughter drifted out of the packed bars, and the brass band played lively airs, was the gay time at Linda.

The Linda Valley became famous for its sportsmen. On a Saturday afternoon or evening, outside the hotels, the sight of seventy axemen chopping through logs for a valuable purse, or sinewy old-time miners striving to hammer a steel drill farthest into a great conglomerate boulder was commonplace; and the prize money often equalled four months' wages. At Easter, in fine weather, the celebrated athletic carnival attracted 1,500 or 2,000 people to the oval on the flat, while in winter the footballers of the valley, playing on rough gravel, proved themselves the champions of the west coast on more than one occasion. The valley was also noted for its tough fighters. Tom Dunn trained a school of boxers at Gormanston while Malley Jackson, burly miner and reigning heavyweight champion of Tasmania, trained his prize fighters in the disused Methodist church at Linda in preparation for frequent bouts in Waxman's Hall. The same church on Sunday mornings was the venue of a popular two-up school.

Although only a small mountain ridge and four miles of road separated the mining valley from the smelting valley, there was surprisingly little contact between the two communities. Perhaps a hundred miners thought the cheaper cost of living and brighter lights of Queenstown were worth the two hours spent in walking to and from work each day, but the other nine hundred did not. Most Queenstown people who had seen Linda thought it was the end of the world, and scores of smelter hands who lived in Queenstown for five or ten years never once set eyes on the mines that gave them copper. This isolation was clearly reflected in one journalist's description of a miner's funeral at Queenstown: 'Work at the mines was suspended at noon, and shortly after 2 p.m., the streets began to fill with men whose faces were not familiar to Queenstown, but who unmistakably were miners'.

The mining valley had seventeen inches more rain than

Queenstown, immeasurably more wind, and a bleaker landscape. While Queenstown lay low in a hill-ringed valley, Gormanston was higher, more open, and exposed to wild storms. Near the Gap, where the mountains on both sides acted as a wind funnel, heavy coaches were sometimes blown off the road. And down in the valley telegraph poles and chimneys toppled, windows were smashed, verandahs and huts and outhouses were tossed bodily into the air, and houses swayed and creaked in the moaning wind. When the wind whistled, hail thundered on the roofs, or snow lay thick on the benches of the open cut, nomadic miners thought of warmer climes; and each fortnight there was an exodus of twenty or thirty men to Cobar, Broken Hill or North Queensland. The windswept landscape provoked from King O'Malley the wise-crack: 'If I had two properties, and one was Linda and one was Hell and I decided to live in one, it wouldn't be Linda'. But the valley had its beauty. To stand in the main street of Gormanstown after midnight and look across the valley to the dark, treeless mountain, its bare peaks softened and silhouetted by the moonlight, and see a moving file of several hundred flickering lanterns held by miners walking down the track from the northern mines was an unforgettable sight.

In 1907 more than 2,200 people lived in the mining valley, and almost half the men employed on the field worked on that side of the ridge. The Mt Lyell mine was still the showplace; and the visitor who came over the haulage from Queenstown was amazed to see ten long benches or terraces hewn in the rock and stretching down the hillside into a growing crater at the bottom, a score of horse-drawn trucks, the steam overburden crane, tiny figures drilling and shovelling, great wooden ore bins, and truckloads of boulders rolling down steep mullock dumps that lay to the north. In 1907, when the top benches were being pushed back into overburden to deepen the open cut, two thousand tons of waste rock and a thousand tons of ore were being mined daily.

By 1909 the Mt Lyell mine was not only the largest mine in Australia, it was also the lowest-grade copper mine in the world, carrying only 0.55 per cent copper. The American *Copper Handbook* attributed this creditable though unenviable distinction partly to the technical skill and 'financial courage and sanity of the general management' but more to the metallurgical requirements of the North Lyell ore, which demanded sulphur and iron to separate the gangue from the copper in the furnaces. The Blow was a flux mine, earning enough copper to pay the expenses of mining. Strangely, as the copper declined the percentage of lead and zinc slowly increased until in 1910 the ore contained seven times as much zinc and twice as much lead as copper. Over the years the whole ore body probably carried far more zinc than copper, but neither the zinc nor the lead was recovered. In fact their increased presence in the ore wrecked pyritic smelting, forcing Sticht to tip more coke in the furnace to drive them out.

The Blocks more than any mine revived the valley. In its peak quarter it employed an average of 284 men, only twenty less than the Blow which had temporarily slumped. Having pirated the rich North Lyell ore, the Blocks Company lay low until the favourable price of copper directed its attention to a large deposit of copper-bearing clay. Most of the clay contained about 2 per cent native copper, though there were rich patches in which nuggets of native copper weighing up to $1\frac{1}{2}$ hundredweight were embedded. Finding that 70 per cent of the copper could be recovered cheaply by water concentration, the company built a large and rambling mill, consisting of battery, puddlers, and Wilfley tables, on the slopes of the North Lyell creek. The mill concentrated its first clay in August 1904 but did not attain peak output and efficiency until two years later.

In 1906 the company mined 70,000 tons of ore, and in the last quarter of the year mined more ore than came from the twenty-seven producing mines between Zeehan and Farrell. The mill, visited by metallurgists from all over the Commonwealth and pronounced first class, produced a rich copper concentrate that was railed to sleepy Kelly Basin and shipped to the Wallaroo smelters. Anticipating good dividends, French investors pounced on the shares and with British investors acquired a 93 per cent interest in the mine. Their surmise was correct, for in 1906 the Blocks paid £15,000 in dividends and earmarked additional thousands for driving tunnels at Mt Darwin and Zeehan.

The clay in the mine was treacherous and tended to swell and smash the heavy timbers that supported the workings. By dint of careful mining and costly timbering, the company mined more than 150,000 tons of clay before the first fatal accident occurred. One morning in July 1907 the timber, clay and slurry caved in over a wide area and buried two men. One man was quickly extricated but the body of his mate was only found after shifts of miners, working heroically for more than two days, had driven through 46 feet of debris. Three months later, after the clay had yielded 1,834 tons of pure copper, the exhaustion of payable ore above the tunnel level and the slump in the price of copper forced the Melbourne directors to close the mine. When the notices were posted in the mill and at the tunnel mouth there was consternation on the faces of the men, for the adjoining Consols mine, which seemed likely to employ a hundred men, had just closed its brand-new mill after a brief trial run. The Blocks manager hired a caretaker to guard the mill, and removed all the trucks and rails from the mine. The creek of yellow mill-tailings that flowed past the main street of Linda for two years had already regained its iron-stained colour when the first coaches packed with miners for Victoria rolled out of Linda.

While dripping water echoed through the eerie Blocks mine the North Lyell mine poured out more and more copper. Since early 1903 the labour force had doubled to over five hundred, output had almost trebled, mining costs had been slashed. This last achievement was all the more praiseworthy as the old company had mined half of its ore—the richer half—in two open cuts at cheap cost, whereas almost all the ore was mined underground and hauled up the shaft in 1907.

There were three copper ores in the North Lyell mine: bornite, popularly known as purple ore; chalcocite or copper glance, a soft dark lead-grey ore; and the common chalcopyrite which turned from golden yellow, when broken, into a peacock ore with splashes of carmine, purple, blue and gold as rich as Joseph's coat. The ore lay in some ten minor pockets and two main ore bodies and was invariably found where the soft, flaky, schistose rock had jutted against the pink conglomerate, a tough rock consisting of small pebbles cemented together. The largest ore bodies resembled a channel of copper embedded in grey quartzite and walled in by barren schist on the one side and barren conglomerate on the other. As the conglomerate was tortuous and unpredictable, twisting around in a most remarkable manner, it was impossible to predict accurately where new deposits of copper would be found. And so the four remaining companies which surrounded the thirty-acre North Lyell lease prowled their boundary like wolves in the hope that the rich ore might enter their lease. In 1907 the North Lyell ore bodies at different depths and directions approached within forty yards of the leases of the four adjoining companies.

The richest deposit of copper in the North Lyell mine was known as the 'New Development Ore Body' and its vagaries fascinated the manager of every adjacent mine. At its highest point, more than four hundred feet below the surface of the ground, the ore body lay far to the west of the main shaft. At the 700′ level men struck the ore body while excavating a plat chamber alongside the shaft. At 760′ the shaft passed into poorer rock and the ore body dipped away with a pronounced pitch to the east. At the 1000′ level miners had to drive over a hundred yards towards the Blocks boundary before they broke into the ore body again.

The dip in the ore body awakened the Blocks Company. Robert Ferguson, their elderly manager, who had spent the years of the Blocks idleness in charge of a gold mine at Heathcote, Victoria, studied the Mt Lyell Co.'s published reports and concluded that the ore body would pass into the Blocks lease at the 1100′ level. He returned to Queenstown on the evening train of 26 June 1909. At the North Lyell mine the manager suspected the reasons for Ferguson's return and posted a foreman at the brace to see that he did not go down the shaft during the changing of shifts. Ferguson caused no trouble, being content to renew old acquaintances and inspect his mine. The decision to exclude Ferguson from the North Lyell mine made the Blocks directors contrive other means of finding the desired information, and they engaged F. Danvers Power, one of Australia's foremost engineers, to report on their prospects. Power crossed to Tasmania, and was escorted through the North Lyell mine by the manager who carefully withheld all vital information. Satisfied that the ore body had changed its pitch between the 1000′ and 1100′ levels, Power condemned Ferguson's idea of sinking a deep shaft to search for the ore body. He received for his wisdom a volley of abuse from the astonished Blocks directors.

Two months later a fatal accident on the 1100′ level of the North Lyell mine gave Ferguson a wonderful chance to inspect this crucial part of the mine. One evening a young miner engaged in erecting square set timbers was killed by a boulder which fell from the working face and rolled on top of him. Elected foreman of the jury at the enquiry Ferguson assured the coroner that it was essential that the jury visit the scene of the accident. The visit was arranged. At the 1100′ level Ferguson took a small compass from his pocket and concealed it behind the candle in the cup of his hand. A foreman detected the trick and snatched the compass. When the jurymen returned to the cage the compass was handed back to its embarrassed owner. Nevertheless these security measures convinced the Blocks Company that its neighbour had something to hide; it drained the long tunnel which led to its clays and excavated a large chamber, thirty-six feet from the boundary of the North Lyell lease. It erected winding machinery and began to sink the shaft.

The ore body eventually left the North Lyell lease, but it dipped north into the Comstock and not east to the Blocks. Before Ferguson had begun to sink his shaft, R. M. Murray, the manager of the Mt Lyell Co.'s mines, found that the ore body at the 850′ level was only ninety feet from the Comstock lease. He suggested to Sticht that the adjoining lease, marked 1839/91M on the mining charts, should be quietly acquired. Meanwhile he kept the secret.

In the boom days this lease had been explored by the Tasman Lyell Company which sank shallow shafts and drove tunnels in the hope of intercepting the North Lyell ore body. In 1903 Tasman Lyell amalgamated with the Mt Lyell Comstock Copper Company, forgot its old leases, and concentrated on exploring and diamond drilling the Comstock mine on the other side of the Mt Lyell range. The Comstock ore body, containing several hundred thousand tons of 3 per cent ore, and the new Oonah smelters at Zeehan so strained the financial resources of the company that its manager paid no attention to the vagaries of the North Lyell ore body across the mountain.

This apathy heartened Murray, the more so when his miners continued to stope good ore as they worked towards the boundary at the 850′ level. But Murray was anxious that his company should buy the neighbouring lease without delay, for he knew that in Gormanston and Queenstown residents who speculated in mining shares questioned miners about current developments and could easily learn that the North Lyell ore body was approaching the Comstock boundary. On 10 December 1910 Murray heard such a rumour. He was told that the Comstock Co. intended to diamond drill the southern boundary of its lease in the hope of intercepting the North Lyell ore channel at depth. He sent an urgent cable in code to Sticht, who was at Burnie. Two days later the directors instructed William Jamieson to ascertain the financial position of the Comstock Co. while visiting England. But the enthusiasm of the directors quickly cooled, for they ignored Jamieson's cable that the Comstock lease might be bought for £15,000.

Murray was determined to convince the directors that the ore body was leaving the lease at the 850′ level, and he told his diamond drillers to bore a hole to within a few feet of the boundary. The ore was still rich. He hushed up this development and advised the directors to publish no plans of the mine in their half-yearly report to shareholders. The directors adopted his advice, but not the recommendation to buy the mine.

In June 1911 Jamieson was conversing with a Comstock director in England when he chanced to hear that the Minerals Separation Co., the Australian patentees of the flotation process, would probably erect a concentration mill at the Comstock mine. If this process concentrated copper ore as efficiently as it concentrated zinc and lead at Broken Hill, the Comstock directors could work their low grade mine at a profit. And eventually they would investigate the rumour that the North Lyell ore was heading straight for a far-flung corner of their lease.

At last, after ten months of dallying, the Mt Lyell directors realized that the North Lyell ore was definitely crossing the border, and they forthwith drew up secret plans to 'jump' the adjoining lease. The Mining Amendment Act of 1904 stipulated that in each six months a company must spend £2 on wages or machinery for each acre of its lease; otherwise the lease would be liable to forfeiture. When the Comstock Co. applied to the warden of mines for an exemption from this clause of the act the Mt Lyell Co. instructed its solicitor to oppose the application.

The solicitor contacted witnesses who swore that no work had been done on the lease for eight years. The warden of mines heard the appeal at Zeehan. He decreed that the lease had been amalgamated with other leases on which the required money had been spent, and therefore it was not forfeitable.

This unexpected decision and the news that an expert from the Minerals Separation Co. had visited the Comstock mine shocked the Mt Lyell directors. Although they had carefully concealed their interest in this lease, the court case at Zeehan had strengthened the rumours that the North Lyell ore was crossing the border. How these rumours escaped the serious attention of the Comstock Co. is a mystery. In February 1912 the London secretary of the Mt Lyell Co. actually heard the rumour at the stock exchange and wired it back to the head office in Melbourne. Fortunately at this very time W. L. Baillieu, the Melbourne mining magnate, was negotiating to buy the Comstock mine and treat the ore with the new flotation process. He bought the mine for £15,000 and immediately sold it to Mt Lyell Co. for £16,500. Including liabilities and expenses of liquidation, the Mt Lyell Co. paid £18,176.

The North Lyell ore body extended six hundred feet across the boundary and finally pinched out almost beneath the crags of Mt Lyell. At least a millon tons of copper ore, roughly a quarter of the total output of the North Lyell mine, were torn from the adjacent Comstock lease. And across the mountain the poorer Comstock ore body yielded almost half as much copper as the Mt Lyell mine produced. The title to this wealth was acquired for little more than the sum which the old Comstock Co. had spent on its unfinished railway.

If the Comstock directors had suspected the trend of the North Lyell ore body, they would have bored along their southern boundary, found rich ore, and refused to sell their mine except at a high price. By sinking a deep shaft and selling the ore to the Queenstown smelters they would have made a good profit in the war years, only to be ruined by the post-war slump in the price of copper. In 1920 they would have faced the stark alternative of either liquidating the company or suspending mining for at least a decade. In the light of both past and future events the Comstock shareholders received a fair price. After all, they were absentee landlords who had ignored their southern lease for ten years, believing it was not worth the cost of a drill hole. On the other hand the Mt Lyell directors were willing to take the risk, knowing that a wall of barren conglomerate might cut off the ore before it had repaid the price of the mine. The huge reserve of ore that lay in the adjacent lease exceeded their wildest expectations.

Four of the most enterprising companies on the field ceased their labours in the years 1911-13. The Lyell Consols Copper Corporation, mining copper-clay fifty feet beneath the North Lyell creek, spent £15,000 in opening the mine and erecting a mill above the Linda station. It employed ninety men to treat more than six hundred tons of clay a week until that day in August 1910 when miners heard the ground creeping and the timbers groaning, and quickly left the mine. The warning saved them, for a few hours later the creek water broke into the workings. The mine was damaged so badly that it had to be abandoned. After diamond drills had failed to locate extensions of the North Lyell and Lyell Tharsis ore bodies, the company sold the mill and disbanded. Further up the hill the Crown Lyell Co. had failed to find rich ore in its boring campaign. It lingered on in the hope that its deposits of half a million tons of low-grade ore might become payable. The machinery house collapsed on the rusty boilers; the cage rusted in the shaft; the manager's house was old and dilapidated. In 1913 the company sold the mine on which it had spent £36,000 in the easy-money days for £2,840. The English company, Copper Mines of Mt Lyell West, abandoned its lease in the same year.

Two of the legion of companies which once worked the field still eluded the grasp of the Mt Lyell Co. but in truth their leases were mortgaged. The Blocks continued to sink its shaft until 1915 when it was 1,357 feet below the surface and the deepest shaft on the west coast. The company then flew its old pennant —the skull and crossbones—from the poppet head, drove some fifty feet into the North Lyell mine, pirated about a thousand tons of rich ore, and filled the cavity with barren mullock. In 1919, thirty years after shipping its first native copper to Newcastle, the company approached the Mt Lyell directors and sold out for £5,000. In thirty years it had been refloated six times and renamed five times; it had called £100,000 from shareholders and returned £20,000 in dividends. A courageous and enterprising company, it deserved a better fate.

The Tasman and Crown Lyell Extended, the silver-lead mine in the Comstock valley and the most northerly mine on the field, was the sole survivor of the 'wild cat' mines. In 1910 the company had shifted the rattling Colonel North Mill from Zeehan and hauled the twenty-five-year-old white pine water-wheel from the old King River Co.'s battery to its tunnel mouth on the banks of Gap Creek. The mill produced silver-lead concentrate for the Zeehan smelters, made little profit, and ceased work. In the late 1920s the mine fell into the hands of the Horseshoe Syndicate which sent away several thousand tons of ore before giving a Broken Hill company an option over the lease. Finally, a prospector named Jimmy Cornish fossicked about the workings, occasionally bringing in specimens to be assayed at Queenstown or waylaying engineers to describe the pitch and foibles of his lode. Then some old workings at the back of Zeehan or Dundas gripped his imagination, and the Horseshoe Syndicate sold the mine to the Mt Lyell Co. for £500. Since 1933, one company has operated at Mt Lyell.

In a field of low-grade mines survival of the fittest is the rule, and the Mt Lyell Co. slowly absorbed the forty smaller companies which either had no ore to mine, or which had ore that only the Mt Lyell Co. could smelt at a profit.

21

The Rise of the Miners' Union

While the companies grappled with one another and disappeared, how fared the men who drove their tunnels and mined and smelted their copper? In 1900 the Queenstown smelters were the largest industrial enterprise in Tasmania, providing work for 1,300 men. Most men worked eight hours a day, seven days a week. Once in three weeks, when they changed from night shift to afternoon shift, they enjoyed a 32-hour holiday from eight o'clock on Sunday morning until four o'clock on Monday afternoon. For Saturday and Sunday work, overtime and night work, they received no additional rate of pay. Furnacemen received 9s a day, furnace feeders 8s 6d, slag-pot wheelers 7s 6d, and all other smelter hands 7s a day, but they could board in a hotel for £1 a week or live in a hut for 12s or less. At the start of each shift, be it midnight or foggy morning, a crowd of unemployed men known locally as 'followers-up' gathered round the gate of the smelters, crib in hand and eager to fill any vacancy at the summons of the foreman. If a man arrived at work five minutes late he often found that a 'follower-up' had taken his place.

Most smelter hands were Tasmanians—farm labourers, axemen, road-menders and carters who revelled in hard work and knew nothing of trade unions. An eight-hour day was almost a luxury, and they enjoyed their lot. 'A very happy crowd in here in those days gone by', mused George Eaves, one of many smelter hands who were still robust after working more than fifty years in the smelters.

In the converters, where the copper matte was smelted into blister copper, men worked twelve-hour shifts until 1912. Sometimes they worked 84 hours a week for several weeks on end. A shilling an hour was the flat rate of pay. When the matte bins were almost empty, the four or five converter vessels shut down for days or even weeks and the men had a holiday until word went around that work would resume.

At the reduction works men always had the taste of sulphur in their mouths. When the sulphur cloud was thick and low, new men coughed and gasped and knelt down to catch a breath of less polluted air. Sometimes arms were singed, and clothes, hair and beards were burned by splashing slag or matte. Several men died of burns while others were shockingly scarred with molten slag. Working conditions in the smelters, however, were superior to the open cut. There were fewer accidents, more shelter and warmth at the smelters; and in the first fifteen years there were no strikes and few unionists.

At the mines industrial relations were not so cordial. Miners in the open cut were soaked to the skin day after day, and lacking a change house they walked home in their sopping, sweaty clothes. They worked harder than underground miners since they were under the constant supervision of foremen who could survey the whole open cut from the top bench. Open-cut men worked eight hours a day and 48 hours a week, three more hours than the underground men. At all mines ore-breaking ceased at midnight on Saturday and was not resumed until Monday morning.

The first strike at Mt Lyell was quelled with ease and there was little trouble for another six years. In July 1896 the open-cut navvies struck for an extra 1s 6d a day. To relief workers in Hobart who earned 4s and 5s a day, 7s was not to be despised; so the Mt Lyell Co. booked passages for thirty men and resumed mining.

Most of the skilled miners—the men who bored the rock with pneumatic drills or hand steels—came from the gold mines of Victoria. They knew the value of unionism and they sensed their bargaining power as efficient workmen. They liked to work beneath a roof of rock rather than in the rain, mud, heat and dust of the open cuts and they made the underground mines the early strongholds of unionism at Mt Lyell. A branch of the Amalgamated Miners' Association was formed at Gormanston in 1896, and a hundred men were enrolled. By 1898 the union branch had three hundred members and owned a large hall; Zeehan had the only other miners' hall in Australia.

In February 1898 Ben Tillett, the famous London dockers' leader, a powerful, broad-chested little orator, stirred up unionism at Queenstown where he roused a large gathering in Cairn's Hall. That night the first fifty-seven members, most of whom were smelter hands and quarrymen, joined the Queenstown A.M.A. Twelve months later more than three hundred men belonged to the union.

In 1899 perhaps 650 of the 3,000 wage earners at Mt Lyell were unionists. While the memories of the bank crash, of the great depression, and of bands of men carrying swags along some hot or muddy bush track were fresh in the minds of most men, unionism was likely to remain a weak, defensive minority movement. And while 'followers-up' still lounged at the gateway to the smelters, and each train brought in someone who knew his way about a mine, the A.M.A. did not attempt to strike. It rarely suggested, let alone demanded, higher wages. It tried to defend existing wages and perform the functions of a friendly society, and for this purpose it levied a shilling a fortnight from each member. A financial member of the A.M.A. was entitled to £1 a week if disabled by accident, £1 a week when on strike, and at death his relatives could collect £50. These benefits were the equivalent of half-pay to most men, and they induced Queenstown shopkeepers to join the union. Between 1892 and 1900 the Victorian and Tasmanian branches of the A.M.A. paid £121,000 in benefit money to less than 10,000 members.

The Queenstown and Mt Lyell Medical Unions competed against and weakened the A.M.A. The Queenstown Medical Union was formed in 1896 and gave its members free medical aid and hospital treatment for 6d a week. Over at the mines the Mt Lyell Medical Union collected 9d a week from single men and 1s from married men. It paid hospital fees, sick and accident pay, and the full salary of Dr G. A. Walpole, a fine surgeon who resided at Gormanston. The mining companies astutely fostered this rival of the A.M.A., collecting subscriptions from the men's pay envelopes and, through their mine managers, dominating the committee of management. In 1900 the medical union at Gormanston numbered seven hundred to nine hundred miners and ten or twelve townsmen—more than twice the membership of the Gormanston A.M.A.

At the mining camps of North Lyell and Linda a rival medical union was sponsored by the North Lyell Co. and its affiliated mines. This was known as the North Mt Lyell Mines Medical Union and it employed Dr Hodgkinson who lived at North Lyell. It amalgamated with the Mt Lyell Medical Union when the big companies united in 1903.

Three medical unions, seven or eight friendly societies, and two branches of the A.M.A. gave to almost every working man of Lyell health and hospital benefits as substantial as those introduced by the Commonwealth government half a century later. These societies existed largely on the contributions of the working men, not the donations of companies or governments. They reflect the communal spirit and the sturdy independence of the men who toiled on Lyell fifty and sixty years ago.

The main bias of the miners was against the Chinese rather than the companies. Many north-eastern tin mines had fallen into Chinese hands but the A.M.A. made sure that no Chinaman worked in western mines. In 1896, when two Chinamen planted a market garden in Queenstown, the *Mount Lyell Standard* raised a hue and cry against these 'wily Celestials'. A few days later the editor announced with pride that he 'was accosted in the street by an insolent Chinese, who was promptly told to make himself scarce'.

Two years later, after the sulphur had shrivelled the gardens, the A.M.A. convened a monster rally at Queenstown to consider a rumour that Chinese were swarming into Strahan. The president of the A.M.A., supported by shopkeepers and clergymen, mounted the platform and asked the huge audience if lives were sacrificed at Eureka that Chinamen might be the gainers? He added: 'Wherever the Chinaman went, there also went his vices, and the men of Tasmania owed it to their manhood, to their women and to their children to arise and proclaim that the pestiferous John should not defile a race who were as yet happily pure'. If there were old convicts in the crowd, no doubt they swelled the thunder of applause that greeted this oratory.

Needless to say, the Chinese did not swarm into Strahan, but the fear of an invasion was enough to arouse for the first time a militant spirit in the working men of Lyell.

Most union leaders were reasonable men; J. C. Whitelaw, secretary of the Zeehan A.M.A., of which Gormanston was at first a sub-branch, believed in a 'fair day's work for a fair day's pay'. If there were shirkers in the A.M.A., said Whitelaw, he would side with the mine managers against them. The barrier which separates the attitude of the modern shareholders and miners was probably less rigid fifty years ago. Union leaders not only encouraged hard work, they also encouraged miners to speculate in shares or work their own mines. They knew that miners who bought shares provided capital for new mines and therefore more work for miners; share-buying was a national service while tens of thousands of men were unemployed. Ben Tillett said that miners, with luck, might acquire mines as rich as the Mt Lyell mine. He told the men of Queenstown that he 'did not begrudge any man his glass of beer, but he did begrudge him his waste of money'. Other union leaders condemned the sixty hotels on the west coast as makers of unemployment and enemies of thrift and mining.

The Victorian gold-miners, and there were hundreds at Mt Lyell, were often buyers of mining shares. Many Victorian mining towns—Maldon, Walhalla, Ballarat, Bendigo, Stawell—had professional sharebrokers or busy stock exchanges. Old miners at Lyell could remember the time when the co-operative party of twenty-four to seventy-two working miners, each one of whom owned transferable shares, was the common form of mining organization. In Victoria miners who saw the reef widen or grow richer in the mine in which they worked frequently bought or sold shares or passed on the information to their townsmen. The local miner, in fact, was in a better position to speculate than the city investor, and he frequently did invest.

At Lyell several hundred wage-earners owned shares in the small mines at Jukes, Darwin, Dora and Lyell. They speculated on the Queenstown stock exchange, questioned prospectors in the streets and bars of the town, and eagerly read articles by mining seers in the daily press. They knew that a £5 investment in an obscure mountain copper mine might win them £1,000 if their mine was boomed in London or became a second North Lyell.*

Miners who bought shares or who went prospecting were rarely interested in aggressive unionism. Looking into the future, they fancied themselves as wealthy shareholders, not as poor ageing miners. They believed that they deserved a full reward for risking their savings in untried mines, and therefore they did not support the agitation for higher wages.

Most mines on the mountains of Jukes and Darwin, the Eldorado of the working man, had collapsed by 1901. The Queenstown stock exchange shut its doors and invested its last few pounds in Tattersall's Sweep, and when Revenue won the Melbourne Cup the twenty official members shared £13,000. That was an evil portent for mining, and in the next decade the mining gambler was becoming a racing gambler. Miners who once dreamed that they would become as rich as Crotty now idolized Nat Gould's heroes of the turf. Mining suffered through lack of capital. Industrial relations also suffered. Miners who realized that they were condemned to a life of wage-earning or contract mining began to trust unionism to secure better conditions from the mining companies. Likewise, the end of the Broken Hill boom had braced unionism on that field.

In 1900 King O'Malley, the 'Canadian Yank', cast his spell on Lyell. On many an afternoon he put on his ten-gallon hat and stood at Evans' Corner, Queenstown, and drawled a greeting to the men returning from the smelters: 'Are you on the roll, brother; are you on the roll?' He induced a thousand men to add their names to the voters' roll and so acquire the franchise for the first time. He spoke on the hotel balconies, then graduated to the Academy of Music and the Metropole Hall where he addressed a thousand cheering people in the most popular political meetings in the history of Queenstown. There was magic in his cheap-jack oratory. He could speak for two and a half hours and still grip the feelings and laughter of eight hundred men as they stood in the cold night, rugged in their blueys.

---

*A working man who invested £5 in Mt Bischoff when the company was floated would have received the equivalent of six years' wages in dividends in the next quarter-century.

King O'Malley called Mt Lyell 'the Gibraltar of Democracy', and the miners gloried in the banner. He stirred up working-class consciousness, and the timid unions grew bolder. The army of wandering unemployed who could break a strike in a month had faded to a mere regiment. The bargaining power of unskilled men had strengthened. In 1902, a year of falling copper prices, the truckers at the Lyell Blocks mine came out on strike after the company had tried to reduce their wages by 6d a day. The company gave in and the truckers kept their 6d. For the union, however, it was a pyrrhic victory. The Blocks mine could not afford to pay these wages and it soon dismissed all hands. But this first union victory on the field increased the strength of the Gormanston A.M.A. from 310 to 700.

In May 1903 the A.M.A. petitioned the Mt Lyell Co. to increase the wages of certain open-cut labourers by 6d a day. Sticht ignored the petition on the grounds that the A.M.A. did not represent the majority of his company's miners. Moreover, the three men who signed the petition did not work for the Mt Lyell Co.; James Mahoney, the president of the union, was a timber man in the South Lyell mine; J. B. Wood, the secretary, was a Gormanston barber; and the senior committee-man, John Earle, was a blacksmith at the South Lyell mine. In Sticht's opinion these outsiders had no right to interfere in the internal workings of his company. He also implied, in line with the American tradition, that men employed by his company had little right to interfere, for he dismissed several employees who were firebrands in the union on the grounds that they were poor workmen. Thus the president of the Gormanston union had been dismissed from the Mt Lyell mine and the president of the Queenstown union had been sacked from the smelters.

When Sticht ignored the petition and refused to recognize the A.M.A., the leaders of the union became indignant. While their tempers were still hot, the South Lyell mine closed and the North Lyell Co. collapsed, thus endangering the very existence of the union. These companies so blessed and shielded unionism that their mines had become two of the strongest union mines in Australia. Almost every leader of the Gormanston union had left those mines where unionists were liable to be victimized and had taken refuge in the North and South Lyell mines. In the

North Lyell stopes the miners often interrupted work and mounted a rock to make fiery speeches on unionism and politics, a practice which even today would earn instant dismissal from a mine. The North Lyell miners did less work for more pay than probably any other miners in the land, and they realized that when the Mt Lyell Co. ran the mine their paradise would vanish. In June and July they met secretly at Gormanston to plan resistance to the certain assault on their wages.

As expected, the new company ironed out the disparity between wages at the North Lyell and Mt Lyell mines and announced a common wage scale, similar to that in force at the Blow, but involving more decreases than increases for the different jobs at North Lyell. The A.M.A. thereupon advertised in the *Sydney Morning Herald* and Melbourne *Age*, warning miners to stay away from Lyell as a strike was imminent. Officials of the Amalgamated Miners' Association hurried across from Victoria. They told the miners that the new wages were the highest in Tasmania and that the union should have secured uniform wages years ago for those who performed the same work in different Lyell mines. The union chiefs admitted that working conditions in the open cuts were bad, and that some men had lost four days' pay a fortnight because of bad weather, but they warned the men that a strike was suicidal as the company owned the two railways, the only entrances to the field. This advice was either bluff or ignorance, for the company's railways were public carriers and could not legally refuse to convey food or passengers. The executive council of the A.M.A. then met at Ballarat and refused to grant strike relief. The North Lyell miners remained at work, at the new scale of wages.

Forsaken by the mainland unions, the Lyell union was crippled by the Mt Lyell Co. As soon as W. T. Batchelor, the new manager, took charge of the North Lyell mine he expelled every agitator and shirker in the mine. He expelled most of the leading unionists, no matter whether they were industrious miners or mere slovens. He expelled J. J. Long, a miner and union organizer, who had recently been elected to the Lyell seat in the House of Assembly. Long and George Burns (a Queenstown socialist) were the first working men to sit in the Tasmanian Parliament, and when Parliament was in recess

Long supplemented his income by working in the North Lyell mine.

Long was working underground when he heard of his dismissal. Tall, broad-shouldered, with fierce eyes beneath bushy brows and a face full of strength, he stood in the light of a candle, his muscular arms bulging beneath his flannel shirt as he hammered a sharp steel drill into the rock. Hearing Batchelor call to him, he dropped his hammer and walked across the stope.

'You'd better get out', said Batchelor. 'You're not satisfactory to the company.'

Long was nonplussed. 'What for?' he asked.

'So long as you are taking a leading part in politics', replied Batchelor. 'The two things don't work well together.'

Long protested. 'Don't you think you had better put it off for a while? I shall be attending the House directly.'

'No. Your services are not wanted', replied Batchelor emphatically.

Long completed the shift, collected his pay and left the mine for the last time.

The dismissal of a man whose only alleged fault was that he represented the working men in Parliament provoked protests throughout Australia. Labor politicians alleged that William Knox, who was the foremost critic of their party in the Commonwealth Parliament, had persuaded Sticht to expel Long. This was false; the directors themselves wanted to know why Long had been dismissed. In a confidential letter Sticht answered their query: 'The North Lyell mine is a hotbed of disloyal, intemperate and perniciously inclined influences. We are simply sweeping the place clean of bad characters . . . Long is an undesirable character of bad repute'.

These sweeping charges were doubtless true, but they concealed Sticht's real motive, his determination to clean up the mine and so secure industrial peace and greater production. Admittedly Long was a good miner, but as a Labor politician and militant unionist he frequently derided the company and fomented trouble among its miners. Therefore Sticht thought it was foolish to give him work and keep him in the district.

A gold medal was struck and presented to Long. It bore on one side this inscription: 'Presented to J. J. Long, Esq. M.H.A.

from the North Lyell Miners'. On the other side were the words: 'To commemorate his dismissal from the mine for being a Labour M.P.'

The other unionists whom Batchelor dismissed were banished from the field. No mine would employ them, and only a few men who found work in the hotels remained in the district to vex the all-powerful company. Many of the exiles were black-balled from mines outside the field; at the request of the manager of the Magnet silver mine, Batchelor compiled a secret list of twenty-eight 'disloyal and treacherous men' whom the Magnet Company would be foolish to employ. This black list was headed by John Earle and J. J. Long. Earle became the first Labor Premier of Tasmania; Long became a stormy Commonwealth senator.

Shorn of its fiery leaders, the Gormanston union lost five hundred of its seven hundred members in the space of months. John Joseph Long, surveying the wreck of his union, complained bitterly that the company had used its victory to outlaw the trade unions and crush the employees into serfdom; but there was more thunder than fact in this outburst, for Batchelor believed that all men should belong to a union. The A.M.A. was so reassured by Batchelor's sympathy that in 1906 it sponsored a recruiting tour of the field by Alex Hunter, a seventy-four-year-old orator revered in Victoria as 'the grand old man of unionism'. Hunter tramped the hills of Lyell for ten weeks, kindling interest in the union but enlisting few new members. So long as wages were high and miners plentiful, so long as contract work offered excellent pay to the skilled miners, and so long as the Mt Lyell Co.'s medical union was a wealthier and better benefits society than the Amalgamated Miners' Association, the task of the union organizer seemed hopeless.

The old unionist had the misfortune to visit the field when the standard of living was higher than at any other time in the decade. In 1906 the Mt Lyell Co. announced its sensational profit of £495,000 for the preceding financial year, and from this profit it paid a weekly bonus of 3s to each employee and generous wages which, even allowing for the high cost of good clothing, had no equal on the west coast. Thus while Mt Lyell enjoyed eight years of industrial peace, small towns across the mountains were crippled by some of the longest strikes in the history of Tasmania. In 1905 the Hercules miners began a strike which lasted more than a year and in 1908 the Magnet men struck for twenty-eight weeks.

In 1908 the Mt Lyell Co. began to feel the labour shortage which was afflicting mines all over the southern states. The alarming incidence of miner's disease in the deep quartz mines and the growth of tariff-protected industries in the cities turned men from mining to safer and better-paid jobs. Mt Lyell still attracted scores of skilled miners from dying Victorian towns but they rarely stayed long. At Zeehan wages were lower than at Lyell and unemployment was increasing, but few miners made the fifty-mile journey to secure work. 'Apparently weather and surroundings have given Lyell an unenviable reputation', wrote the Zeehan *Herald*.

The shortage of labour made men sense their power to bargain effectively for higher wages, and the gradual increase in the cost of living made them eager to use that power. In the summer of 1910-11 these favourable portents induced the unions at Queenstown and Gormanston to acknowledge the existence of one another and form a united Lyell union. J. E. Ogden, an energetic politician from Zeehan, succeeded where Hunter had failed and signed up nearly five hundred men in the new union, making it one of the strongest branches in the miners' con-ference—second only to the powerful union in the Victorian city of Bendigo. Ogden's task was made easier by the influx of union delegates to Queenstown for the annual conference of the Amalgamated Mining Employees' Association of Victoria and Tasmania* in March 1911. The spirited speeches of the many delegates were heard far beyond the walls of the Masonic Hall, and were eagerly discussed and debated around the doors, bars and firesides of every hotel on the field.

The union soon came to grips with the Mt Lyell Co. In May 1911 it demanded that miners be allowed to smoke while work-ing underground. The company refused the request, and the North Lyell miners struck for one shift. The bickering grew louder and erupted in September when a small incident led to serious consequences.

*This union had absorbed the old A.M.A. earlier in the year.

Most miners worked eight hours a day and received £3 3s a week, but 240 skilled miners worked irregular hours on contract rates and averaged half as much again. At the Mt Lyell mine, F. Regan, P. Sullivan, W. Lyden, and G. Quill banded together to mine ore underground at contract rate, and worked twelve hours a day on five occasions in August. The A.M.E.A., however, believed that no man should work more than eight hours a day, and on 23 August it sent a deputation to R. M. Murray asking him to enforce the eight-hour day. Murray refused. He told the deputation that his company made no miner work more than eight hours a day, but if an employee wanted to earn more money he could work as long as he liked. Murray said that it was the duty of the union to enforce its own rules among its members, and he would not interfere. The union then interviewed the men in Sullivan's party, and as three of the four were unionists the party agreed to respect the eight-hour day.

On 5 September, Lyden and Quill had to fire a charge of gelignite in a drive off No. 5 tunnel. As gelignite gave off dangerous fumes, it was never used while men were working underground. Therefore Lydon obtained permission to start work at 6 p.m. and so light his fuses in the early hours of the morning when the mine was empty. At midnight, when the other miners ceased work, a union official named Norman White passed the drive and chanced to hear the throb of Lyden's pneumatic drill. White went to the change house at the mouth of the tunnel, changed his clothes and, seeing no sign of Lyden and Quill, gathered a few mates and re-entered the tunnel. He saw the light of candles at the end of a dark drive and found the two miners still at work.

'What's the game here?' said White. 'I thought you fellows were not working overtime.'

'We're not', said Quill. 'We never came on till six o'clock here, and our time isn't up till two o'clock.'

Lyden joined in the argument: 'Look here, White, we came in here to fire out tonight. We came on late for our own convenience and the safety of you fellows'.

'You shut up', said White, 'you aren't a union man.'

'If that's so, you mind your own —— business', Lyden replied.

The site of North Lyell town, blasted away to form the modern open cut

A steep grade on the Mt Lyell railway, 1958

White was a nuggety man with a reputation as a boxer on the mainland and he challenged Lyden to go outside and fight. Lyden refused. White left the mine, muttering vengeance.

Next afternoon, at the changing of the shifts, Lyden confronted White at the bottom of the open cut and told him to repeat his taunts of the previous evening. Both men were eager to fight. The news was shouted round the open cut and the mine was deserted to a man as foremen, navvies, and miners downed tools and rushed out to the ringside on the flat ground near the mouth of the tunnel. The fight was brief. Lyden out-punched White, and to complete the rout White was dismissed for entering the mine after hours and interfering with the workmen.

The committee of the union realized that White had acted foolishly and pleaded with the company to reinstate him. Sticht replied that White had committed 'a gross breach of discipline' and could be prosecuted for trespassing. This last threat was bluff, for White had as much chance of gaining legal redress against the company as the company had of prosecuting him.

By refusing to re-employ White the company invited the unions to a trial of strength, for it was an inflexible rule of the union that if any member was dismissed for performing the union's business, all members must stand by him until he regained his job. Since a strike was inevitable, the A.M.E.A. widened the issue at stake. On Thursday, 21 September, it handed the company a log of claims and insisted that they be answered by Saturday. The union demanded that two men should work each rock drill, that the eight-hour day be sacred, that the company discard inferior candles and explosives, that the miners be allowed to smoke in working hours, that the wage for first-class miners be 15s 6d instead of 10s 6d a day, that the company recognize union officials on its leases, and that White be re-employed.

At the Mt Lyell mine on the Saturday, the afternoon shift gathered at the change house to collect their candles. At seven minutes to four, W. J. Craig, a union official, strode up to the mine manager and said: 'I wish to know if Norman White is to be reinstated'. 'No', replied Murray. 'Well then', declared Craig, 'I refuse to work until he is', and he flung his candles back in the box. The other miners copied his gesture. At the North

Lyell mine the same question was asked and the same answer was given. The news spread to the smelters, and the men stopped work and formed a straggling procession down the railway line to Queenstown where a large crowd witnessed their arrival. That night, at a mass meeting under the street lights, the leaders expressed their determination to hold out until they won their claims.

The union prepared for a long strike. It issued a manifesto appealing to the workers of Australasia for funds to sustain the strikers. 'We earnestly appeal to every worker for immediate assistance to enable us to successfully repel the encroachment of unscrupulous employers who would dare introduce the twelve-hour shifts.' Having re-enthroned the eight-hour day as the issue at stake and having distorted the circumstances which led to the strike, the A.M.E.A. was able to raise money from Tasmanian and Victorian miners whose working conditions were generally far worse than those at Mt Lyell. Thus every unionist in the poor goldmines at Steiglitz, Victoria, paid two days' wages, and other unionists paid substantial strike levies. From all sources £5,918 was subscribed. To feed the strikers and their families the Lyell union issued its own coloured coupons, ranging from 15s a week for each single man to 30s for married men with seven children. Shopkeepers and hotelkeepers accepted coupons as payment and cashed them at the union office as funds came to hand.

As there was no sign that the company would yield, families began to pack their possessions and leave the district. Furniture and houses were sold for a fraction of their previous value. One Queenstown man offered to sell a furnished five-roomed house for £40 and found no buyer. Boards were nailed over the windows of scores of houses at Linda. Half the unionists at Gormanston, Linda and North Lyell left the field and many did not return. On some mornings three horse-drawn coaches packed with passengers and piled high with trunks and cases left Gormanston for Queenstown where the station was always crowded with sightseers farewelling friends on the eight o'clock train to Strahan. In a few weeks over a thousand people left by train, while others carried their swags overland to Zeehan and Hobart.

At a compulsory conference in Melbourne, Mr Justice Higgins, President of the Commonwealth Arbitration Court, failed to break the deadlock. Day after day union leaders and Mt Lyell directors met in futile conference. The directors offered to compel contract miners to work the bare eight hours a day but they bluntly refused to re-employ White. On 8 October, the sixteenth day of the strike, the striking miners met at Queenstown and Gormanston and only one man out of 1,010 voted that White be forgotten.

By day the main streets of Queenstown, Linda and Gormanston were strangely deserted. The midday blast of the Blocks mine whistle was a lonesome sound from hills where the thunder of blasting, the rattle of shunting trains and the whistles of mines and smelters had been constant music. On some days a hundred and fifty miners prospected the impoverished creeks where few tin dishes had swirled since Crotty's day, while scores of men cut timber on the blackened hills. At night the streets came to life; union chiefs mounted the hotel balconies and upheld the morale of the men with fiery speeches.

While Norman White was being fêted and cheered at Mt Lyell the four miners who had worked the twelve-hour shift were hounded the length and breadth of Tasmania. When the strike began, Regan had slipped quietly away to find work elsewhere. He signed on with a gang on the Flowerdale-Burnie railway but after half a day the men discovered who he was and refused to work with him. He went to the Magnet mine where unionists gave him two hours to leave the town. He was hounded out of Waratah, Renison Bell, and the Hercules mine, and within a month of leaving had returned to Mt Lyell where the company gave him half pay and told him to remain quiet. The three other miners were hunted like criminals flying from justice. Sullivan was driven from Balfour and, with Quill, reduced to poverty in Launceston. Lyden was boycotted in Hobart, where the Employers' Federation finally paid him compensation of two guineas a week.

The five thousand people who remained at Lyell began to realize that the company would close the mine rather than employ White. As October ended, fiery speeches and defiant slogans paled and the majority of men were willing to return to work and forget White. The union was desperate for money to feed the striking men and their families and, ironically, nearly half of the money which outside miners had promised did not arrive until the strikers had resumed work.

On 11 November 1911 the Mt Lyell directors, the A.M.E.A., and the Federated Enginedrivers' and Firemen's Association signed a provisional agreement that all men except Norman White should return to work. The company agreed to insert a clause in all miners' contracts that they work no more than eight hours a day, and it promised to discuss the other grievances when work was resumed. On 18 November, after fifty-six days of idleness, the first men returned to work, and a fortnight before Christmas the smoke rose again from the smelters' stacks.

The Mt Lyell Co. and the A.M.E.A. signed a thirty-month truce. The company granted a 25 per cent increase in pay for overtime and Sunday work, paid a higher daily wage, and affirmed in black and white the principle of an eight-hour day for miners. But Norman White had to leave the field; in New South Wales no mine would employ him; in New Zealand he was a marked man. Lyden returned to Mt Lyell, a marked man in the union's eyes. His life was threatened by desperate men and every day for six months he carried a revolver from Queenstown to the mine.

The A.M.E.A. had fought for the sanctity of the eight-hour day, and won the concession of overtime pay to deter the company from asking its men to work long hours. By the late 1940s this deterrent had become an incentive. The rate of pay for overtime work so increased that a man who worked ten hours on Saturday and Sunday received as much money for two days as he received for the five week-days. Since overtime and week-end work became so lucrative, the majority of employees at Mt Lyell decided to forsake the principle for which their fathers fought in the great strike of 1911—the principle of a shorter working week. For years, hundreds of men at Mt Lyell worked 56 hours a week and some of the union leaders set the pace and worked 60 hours or more. At the end of 1951, when the company decided to stop mining at the open cut on Sunday, there was a loud protest from men who wanted their 48- or

56-hour week. And maybe a smile played on the lips of Bill Lyden who, at the age of seventy, could still be seen in gum boots and bluey, directing his gang in the mud of the open cut.

Several hundred old and trusty miners who had served the company for years did not return after the strike. Short of good miners, the company engaged Sampson Bray, an Eaglehawk miner, who toured the dying Victorian fields and recruited seventy-two miners on a three-months' contract. All but nine men left Mt Lyell as soon as their contracts expired. In four months, 358 men were recruited from the mainland, but only a handful stayed more than the allotted term. Many were inefficient and some were useless. An Adelaide labour bureau sent as navvies for the open cut an unemployed lightweight jockey weighing less than six stone and a grand old man who appeared to have a wooden leg. This shortage of good miners and the concessions won after the long strike sustained a powerful union.

In September 1912 an accident in the underground workings of the Mt Lyell mine awakened the old strife. One Saturday evening, at half past eight, a dozen or more men had eaten their crib and were sitting on the ground when a few rocks fell from the roof. Without further warning the roof suddenly collapsed and buried the men. The air mains and the light cable were dislocated, and the darkness and the rush of escaping air added to the confusion. Those men on the fringe of the fall carried out the hazardous task of freeing their mates, but the fallen rock was so extensive and the danger of another fall was so great that they did not recover the third lifeless body until after daybreak. At the inquest a jury of miners found that the company had taken all reasonable precautions to make the ground secure, and recorded a verdict of accidental death.

The accident shook the confidence of the men, especially in the North Lyell mine. No man had been killed by falling rock in this mine for eighteen months, and statistics suggested that it was safer than most mines. But North Lyell was a stronghold of labourers who had not previously worked in a mine, and of Victorian gold-miners who felt safer in cramped, heavily timbered quartz mines than in the high-roofed and lightly timbered stopes of Lyell. The feelings of these men carried the day, and at a mass meeting they complained that the roof of one stope was fifty feet above the floor, that the system of timbering was unsound, and that there was danger of a complete collapse in the North Lyell mine. They could not be blamed for fearing some of the North Lyell workings, because two years earlier shifting ground had crushed the timber in a deep winze that served as an auxiliary shaft. And only a few months previously men who began to repair the timbering heard the ground rumble and refused to continue working.

The North Lyell men insisted that two experienced miners, A. Gadd and F. Simon, should investigate allegations that the mine was unsafe, but Murray demanded evidence that they represented the majority of the men. The North Lyell miners promptly came out on strike and met in their hall at Gormanston. 'We are absolutely afraid to continue work while the mine is in its present condition', declared four hundred men. 'We say that the preservation of life and limb is of more importance to us than daily wages, and that we have lost all confidence in the Government inspector.' Finally Murray agreed that Gadd and Simon, accompanied by Cox and Aaron White, the company's foremen, should inspect the mine and that no man need work in those places which the four inspectors condemned. On 7 October, after five days of idleness, the miners resumed work. Gadd and Simon toured the mine, suggested that more timber or filling be used in certain stopes, and concluded their report with this warning: 'We find there is only one means of exit from the mine at present. We also consider the practice of leaving ore passes open when not in use is dangerous. We find there are no jets in use on rock drills and consider they should be supplied'. The North Lyell men, convinced that their fears were exaggerated, continued to work.

In the Tasmanian Parliament the Labor Party was on the verge of power and used the accident at Mt Lyell as a weapon against the government. The Labor members, most of whom had worked in the company's mines, condemned the government's inspection of mines as an 'absolute farce'. In answer to these charges the Minister for Mines acted briskly and wisely. He invited the chief inspectors of mines in Victoria, New South

Wales and Tasmania to form a commission of inspection and report immediately on the mining methods and safety of the Mt Lyell Co.'s mines.

On the very day when the commission reached Queenstown the North Lyell mine caught fire.

22

The Disaster

On the morning of Saturday, 12 October 1912, shortly after eight o'clock, a hundred and seventy miners descended the North Lyell shaft and began to work on six underground levels of the mine. Two and a half hours later, in scattered parts of the mine, men detected the smell of smoke. Perhaps a candle had singed the hessian padding on the air pipes; perhaps someone was burning paper. These thoughts flashed through the miners' minds as they went about their work. Although smoke drifted along the workings near the main shaft, the chattering roar of the rock drills indicated that no one was alarmed.

Between 11.15 and 11.30 five men rang for the cage. Weakened by fumes, they were vomiting when they reached the top tunnel. They said the pump house on the 700′ level was on fire, and that the smoke was so dense and suffocating that the pump attendant could not reach a hose that lay near the blazing building.

There was no emergency warning system in the mine. To warn the miners below men would have to descend the shaft and run along the tricky maze of drives and cross-cuts to where the men were at work. This slow and tedious method was not even considered. The men who escaped from the 700′ level thought that once the King Billy pine which lined the pump house was destroyed, the fire would burn itself out. As they believed that the fire would not spread to the wet, heavy timbers which supported the roof of the drives, the time-keeper merely sent an urgent message to the mine manager at Gormanston. When Murray reached the mine at midday he learned that no one had come up the shaft for nearly thirty minutes.

Down below, a thick cloud of smoke billowed down the shaft to the lower levels and drifted along the drives to where the miners were working. The mine was so rambling and extensive that miners in remote stopes did not see smoke until the fire had been burning for more than an hour. At the 850' level, after shift bosses had climbed ladders to the 700' level and returned with the news that there was a bank of smoke near the pump house, many miners calmly stopped work and sat down to eat their crib. They knew the fire would not spread.

A few miners and truckers who worked nearer the shaft were frightened by the increasing volume of smoke, and ran along the drives and galleries to warn their mates. At the 850' level, the hub of the mine, more than sixty men retreated into No. 20 stope. Two men, Cox and Gadd, fixed hoses to the compressed air pipes and for half an hour tried to repel the smoke. At noon Cox realized the peril and led fifty-seven men through the darkness to the steel house, a wooden building in which mining tools were stored fifty feet from the shaft. Several men preferred to stay in the stope. They were not seen alive again.

While Symmons groped his way to the plat and rang for the cage, Cox summoned the men from the steel house, eight at a time, and stood in stifling smoke and darkness signalling away successive cage-loads. Although the winding engine hauled the cage at twice the normal speed, the journey of thirty seconds was a nightmare. As the cage ascended smoke gushed up in the draught and when the cage stopped at the 200' level the smoke belched out of the shaft and into the tunnel which led to the hillside. Shortly after the cage had raised its last load from the 850' level, the smoke in the tunnels became so thick that the men who had gathered round the shaft to assist up-coming miners to safety had to retreat to fresh air.

The cage returned to the 850' level and remained there for some time, but if any men entered it they gave no sign. The cage was then lowered to the 1000' level. It stayed awhile, but again the engine driver at the surface heard no signal. Murray, who now directed the rescue operations, thought that the miners might have staggered into the cage and been too stupified to give the signal. With the braceman he entered the smoky tunnel and crawled slowly to avoid tumbling down the shaft. The cage was rushed to the top, and two rescuers groped in the darkness in a vain search for limp bodies. Drowsy with fumes they hurried back to the entrance.

It was now one o'clock in the afternoon, and Murray and the foreman realized the danger. Even if the fire did not spread beyond the pump house, it was burning with insufficient oxygen and generating deadly carbon monoxide fumes a danger which no one had previously suspected. If rescue parties tried to search for miners or extinguish the fire, they would rapidly succumb to the fumes. The men at the surface could only pray that the fire would soon be quenched and that the fumes would rise up the shaft.

Meanwhile the air compressors which worked the rock drills in the mine were pumping fresh air to the large stopes, hundreds of feet from the main shaft, where it was hoped that miners would gather in safety. The empty cage was whisked up and down the shaft in an effort to drive out the smoke; the two hillside tunnels were bratticed to confine the up-cast smoke within the shaft; the shed which covered the shaft was torn apart to allow the smoke to escape; and a surface stream of water was diverted down the pump compartment. At sunset the water was turned off, lest it should drown any miner who might be sheltering in the bottom of the mine.

In the afternoon seventy men who had escaped from the mine returned to their homes at Linda and Gormanston. A special train carried three sick miners to Queenstown. They were dazed and could only mutter, 'The smoke is frightful', in answer to the anxious queries of bystanders. Although the spectators who stood at the railway station could see a white spiral of smoke rising above the North Lyell mine and silhouetted against the dark mountain, there was no panic for everyone knew that the mine was too wet for the fire to spread. The afternoon shift of miners entered the Mt Lyell mine, confident that at midnight the fire would be extinguished.

At half past six the train from Burnie steamed into Queenstown and three distinguished gentlemen, members of the secret Commission of Inspection, alighted on the crowded platform. They were astonished to hear that the mine which they had come to inspect was an inferno of smoke and fumes. They hurried off to the mine.

Darkness came and tension tightened as the smoke continued to eddy up the shaft. At 11 p.m. the lamps of two hundred miners from the Mt Lyell mine flickered through the snowdrifts along the track to the North mine, where a large crowd stood around the entrance and peered down the smoky tunnel, dimly lit by scattered globes. Behind them, in the valley below, were the lights of Linda shining on streets that were packed with people every Saturday night, but strangely deserted on this bleak night.

Sometimes the waiting people would grow excited as a miner emerged from the tunnel but each time they recognized the hurrying man as one of the band of men which was desperately searching for a way to the 700' level, the scene of the fire. Inside the mine several men lowered chain ladders down a mullock pass to the 400' level, a hundred feet below the bottom tunnel, but the smoke became so thick that they retreated to the surface in the early hours of Sunday morning. Another party tried to reach the next level by excavating mullock from an abandoned stope, but smoke drifted up as soon as they made an opening. At midnight on Saturday a third team began to repair the engine winze, a small shaft which descended from the 300' level to the bottom of the mine. For several months men had been repairing the crushed timbers, and in another two weeks the winze would have been sound.

Sunday dawned, bleak and wet. All night a pathetic group of wives and mothers had waited around coal fires at the change house, longing for news. Inside the tunnel, near the top of the shaft, Murray, Sticht, mine staff, mine inspectors and union officials had spent the long hours of the night, poring over maps of the mine. Shortly after dawn, they were overjoyed to hear a voice at the level below, shouting for the cage. The cage brought up a miner, who was just able to gasp that three men were at the 500' level before he fainted. The cage hauled up his three companions; and they appeared to be in good condition. These men had sheltered from the smoke in a remote dead end, where compressed air and an air current up an adjacent ore pass had kept the smoke away. Several times they had crawled along the rails towards the shaft, but each time thick smoke drove them back. In the morning, however, the fumes receded and the men dashed to the shaft, shouting for an hour before they were heard. This was the first news of the imprisoned miners, and hope surged high that all would be saved.

During the morning it was decided to test the air down the mine, and Albert Gadd volunteered to climb down the shaft ladders to the 400′ level. He tied a rope around his waist and disappeared into the steamy mist, while occasionally a bucket of water was poured down the ladder to clear the air. At the 400′ level Gadd saw that there was little smoke near the ore pass which descended to the next level, though smoke obscured the ladder way. Eight men then descended in the cage to the 400′ level and spent an hour erecting a chain ladder way down the narrow ore pass. As six feet of broken ore blocked the bottom of the pass, Gadd and Paterson volunteered to go by cage to the 500′ level and release the ore. They dashed along to the pass, released the ore, and the men then came down the chain ladder way and joined them on the 500′ level. Groping along the tramline, they stumbled over the body of a miner. They carried him to the ladder way but the fumes began to overpower them, and they dropped him and rushed to the ladder. This journey proved that the fire was still smouldering and that the fumes would be deadly in the middle of the mine. Until smoke helmets or diving suits arrived, rescue work was suicide.

Meanwhile a rail motor had rushed a diving suit and apparatus from Devonport, a hundred and seventy miles away. On Sunday afternoon the crowd which stood in teeming rain at the tunnel mouth saw the equipment arrive and clamoured that someone should don it. A former admiralty diver named Chambers, who was working at the mines, volunteered to see if the fire was burning at the 700′ level, and to search for men at the 850′ level. He put on the heavy diving suit, mounted the top of the cage and slowly disappeared into the smoke, while five men paid out the life line and air pipes. A hundred feet down, the air hose began to coil around the cage and entangle the diver. He went close to death in those swirling mists, for the rubber hose was joined by string in ten sections, and the strain could have broken the hose and cut off the supply of air. The cage was hauled to the surface and the hose disentangled.

Again Chambers stood astride the cage and went down slowly into the danger zone. Some feared that the hot steam might have damaged or swelled the shaft, but the timbers were firm. The cage halted at the 700′ level, and Chambers felt his way along the dark drive towards the pump house where he saw that the shell of the building was aglow. He returned to the cage and was lowered to the 850′ level, where he entered the plat for some distance. He knocked on the iron pipe lines and banged the trucks, but no shout or answering sign broke the silence.

After several hours in the mine, Chambers was hauled to the surface. He said he could quench the fire with a water hose. Pipe fitters began to instal water pipes down the shaft, but they could not fit them past the 600′ level, where one compartment of a cage had jammed on Saturday afternoon while being whisked up and down to clear the air. The engine driver now tried to drag the cage clear of obstruction. The cage lurched up six feet and stuck. The cage in the other compartment was lowered to see the damage but it could no longer pass the jammed cage. Below the 600′ level the shaft was now useless. The miners were cut off from the surface and were at the mercy of a fire which could not be extinguished. The ladders were the only passage-ways to the lowest levels where the men, dead or alive, were entombed; but without a smoke helmet no man could survive the journey down hundreds of feet of slippery ladders.

The last miner had left the deep workings at noon on Saturday. It was now Sunday evening and no message had come from the depths. As the telephone line down the shaft was not working, the men at the surface tied lamp, messages, board and pencil to a long rope and lowered it to the 850′ and 1000′ levels. The lamp remained at each level for 25 minutes, and could be seen burning brightly far down the shaft. There was no sign that any miners had seen the light.

The news of the disaster was slow to travel. It reached Zeehan on Saturday evening and Dundas on Sunday evening. In Melbourne there had been rumours that the North Lyell mine was afire, but few heard the news until the bold headlines of the Monday morning papers announced, 'Mining Disaster at Mount

Lyell'. When the trains carried the morning papers to Daylesford, Malmsbury, Eaglehawk and those mining towns where many of the entombed miners were well known, the list of ninety-five missing men caused great alarm. Urgent telegrams pleading for news jammed the Tasmanian cable line.

Meanwhile, at sunrise on Monday morning, the men who had been repairing the engine winze for the last thirty hours forced an opening. A current of air blew down the winze and opened a safer passage way to the lower levels. Twelve men descended 240′ in buckets and climbed down 160′ of ladder way, parts of which were showered by a heavy stream of water. At the 700′ level, Murray, Pearton and H. Williams walked to within eighty feet of the pump house, but smoke and fumes forced them to retreat. Other men rattled the cages and tapped the pipes with spanners in the hope that miners sheltering in some distant drive might hear them. But they heard no reply. Instead, they saw in the dim light five dead bodies, four of which they identified. Pinned to the timber was a pathetic note, addressed to a miner's wife:

> I will say goodbye, sure that I will not see you again any more . . . My mate Lou Burke is done, and so is Poor Old V. and the driver too. Goodbye.

A rumour had swept round the ever-changing crowd at the tunnel mouth that the search party had heard voices at the 700′ level. Cheered by this hope they sank back into the depths of despair when the names of the four dead men were announced at midday. They learned too that fumes had forced the search party to return to the surface and that two men, Gadd and Kinsella, had been almost overpowered by fumes. They began to doubt whether any men would be found alive, for a lamp, board and pencil were again lowered into the depths of the mine and hauled up untouched.

A rail motor had rushed smoke jackets from Launceston, 250 miles away, but when tested, these jackets supplied oxygen for a mere twenty minutes. This was not sufficient to allow a man to descend the ladder way to the 850′ or 1000′ levels but it enabled men to be lowered in a large bucket to repair the broken skids of the shaft. A rope was lowered down the shaft as a knocker-line, and when the man in the bucket felt exhausted he pulled the rope and it rattled a small bucket at the top of the shaft. The rope entangled the workman and was replaced by a longer, weighted rope which hung taut to the bottom of the shaft.

Late in the afternoon, when no one was working in the hanging bucket, the men at the surface heard the knocker rap out the signal, 'Men to go to the surface'. With thumping hearts they acknowledged the signal. Then came a second message, 'Men at the 1000' level'. There followed a long tense silence as the men below obviously waited for the cage to rush down the shaft. Finally the knocker-line at the surface clanged out the signal, 'Haul to the surface'. Quickly the rope was hauled up. At the end of the rope was a handkerchief wrapped around a tobacco tin that contained a pencilled message:

> 40 men in 40 stope. Send food and candles at once. No time to lose. J. Ryan.

Food, beef tea, tobacco, blankets, and candles were lowered down the shaft. Outside the mine there was great excitement when the note was read to the waiting crowd. The excitement mounted when it was learned that fifty-one, not forty men, were alive in the stope.

The previous evening urgent wires had been sent to Melbourne and Hobart asking that smoke jackets and helmets be rushed to the mine. At midnight on Sunday a locomotive and one carriage, carrying Superintendent Trousselot of the Hobart Fire Brigade and special diving equipment, steamed out of Hobart. A few hours later the Victorian government steamer, *Lady Loch*, left Melbourne with helmets and oxygen appliances. Thus when the knocker suddenly clanged at the top of the shaft the special train was steaming into Zeehan, the *Lady Loch* was battling through mountainous seas in Bass Strait, and the *Loongana*, carrying firemen and rescue gear from Bendigo and Ballarat, was racing down Port Phillip Bay to the heads. It was fortunate that assistance was at hand, for every hour was precious.

The train reached the mine at ten o'clock on Monday evening. During the night an air pipe was laid down the winze to the 700' level, and flexible hosing was hung down the shaft. In the early hours of Tuesday, Trousselot donned the helmet, went down the winze to the 700′ level, and walked through the smoky working towards the shaft, where a water hose was ready to be carried to the fire. He saw that the fire had burnt the legs of mine timbering, and that hundreds of tons of rock blocked part of the level. He crawled through a small gap and noticed that the air became clearer. To ease the burden of the heavy air pipes he removed his helmet. Slowly his legs weakened and he wanted to lie down. John Pearton, who had guided Trousselot to the plat, saw the big fellow collapse. Although he had no helmet, he rushed along the level and assisted Trousselot to the winze.

As Trousselot's air-proof armour was too cumbersome for the confined spaces of a mine, the rescuers waited for the efficient Draeger helmets which the *Lady Loch* was carrying from Melbourne. Heavy seas, however, had pounded open the foredecks of the little steamer, reducing her speed to eight knots, and she did not steam into the shelter of the breakwater at Burnie until five o'clock on Tuesday morning. A few minutes later, in the dim light before sunrise, the crew of the *Lady Loch* saw a crescent of foam and a black streak of smoke as the *Loongana* sped towards the port on her record smashing journey.

A special train, fires aglow, had been waiting on the wharf at Burnie since midnight. As soon as the equipment was loaded, it climbed to the uplands and roared through the forest with every ounce of steam the fireman could raise. All along the railway, at every town and fettler's camp, people waited to catch a glimpse of the train as it rushed by on its dramatic mission. At Zeehan an Abt engine took over the carriage, and with sparks shooting high above the funnel raced into Queenstown shortly after midday, five hours ahead of the normal time from Burnie.

The suspense outside the mine was not as cruel as in the prison below, where fifty-one men sat and wondered why the cage had not come down the shaft. On Monday evening they sent up a terse note: 'We have had enough. Losing confidence'. On Tuesday morning, seventeen hours after they had first made contact with the outside world, Ryan sent another urgent note up the shaft: 'Try and get us as soon as possible. The cold is terrible and there is none of us well. We are depending entirely on the compressed air. If that fails we are done'. Four hours

The denuded hills of Queenstown

The Linda Valley

later some of the miners were beginning to despair. 'Don't keep anything from us', pleaded one message. 'How is main shaft at 700'?' The imprisoned men had not been told that the cages could not go down the shaft, and that buckets could not be lowered down the engine winze because men would be over-powered before they reached the surface. The fumes were obviously strong, for chickens lowered down the shaft were dead when hauled to the surface.

As soon as the rescue equipment reached the mine, men wearing helmets were lowered down the winze to the 850' level to search for the miners who had decided to stay in 20 stope on the day of the fire. They climbed a ladder into the overhead stope, and by candle light saw seven men clinging stiffly to the air vent of a rock drill. The searchers moved forward and then turned silently away.

At dusk, Moore, a fireman from Melbourne experienced in the use of smoke helmets, was lowered down the winze to the 1000' level to contact the men who were anxiously waiting in the stope. Escorted by a miner named Peasnell, Moore walked along the tramline and stumbled over three bodies: men who had lost their reason and left the safety of the stope in a hope-less attempt to shout up the shaft. As they approached the stope, the helmeted men heard the sound of singing and saw the miners sitting against the wall amongst the boulders. 'They were as happy as Larry', said Moore. Some laughed, others cried. They kept asking about their mates. 'Are the blokes at the 700' safe?' 'Did you see old Joe?' The two searchers concealed the truth that fifteen bodies had been found, and that twenty-seven men were missing: 'Everyone's right, we think'. After reassuring the men that they would soon be safe, Moore and Peasnell returned to the surface with the welcome news that the men were in good fettle, and capable of climbing the long, slippery ladders in the winze.

Throughout the night, parties of men installed telephone and ladders, and fixed a large bucket to the winding engine in pre-paration for the rescue of the men. Brattices were erected to concentrate the rush of air down the winze to the 1000' level, where it would sweep along the drive and up the main shaft.

They increased the rush of air so much that little smoke remained in the workings through which the man must pass.

On Wednesday morning all was ready for the ascent. The men left their prison and walked along the drive past the obstructed main shaft to the small engine winze. Then, one at a time, and assisted by willing hands, they slowly climbed 160' of ladder way to a staging, where they were strapped into a bucket and hauled to the main tunnel. On this beautiful spring day nearly two thousand people had gathered on the bare slopes at the mouth of the tunnel to see the rescued miners emerge. The first drenched miners came out of the tunnel soon after 1 p.m. and walked through the silent, sympathetic throng to the change house. All afternoon, at short intervals, the approaching light of the miners' candles was seen along the dark tunnel, and the spectators were hushed. Some miners laughed, some cried; some walked briskly, some had to be assisted to the change house. The sun had set when the last man left his prison. One hundred and nine hours had passed since he had casually entered the cage on that fateful Saturday morning.

As soon as the last man was rescued, Trousselot and Brown wore helmets down to the 850' level to learn the fate of those men who were known to have assembled in 22 stope when the smoke became thick. In the most distant end of the level they saw ten bodies, huddled together in a small drive. This was the last journey in search of the living, for it was known that the seventeen remaining men were trapped in the 600' and 700' levels, where the smoke and fumes were thickest. When Trousselot and Brown returned from their search, wet and exhausted, only a few women remained by the coal fires near the tunnel mouth. The news was broken gently and they were led down the mountain side.

On Friday horse wagons, loaded with forty-two coffins, rattled through the silent streets of Linda Valley and up the rough track to the North Lyell mine. But no bodies were brought to the surface. The rush of air through the bratticed part of the mine had fanned the fire and made the fumes so dense that even men with helmets were endangering their lives in the mine. On the tenth day of the fire, the company reluctantly decided to seal the mine. A small mountain torrent was channelled down the shaft, and only the hollow sound of running dripping water echoed through the mine.

A month later thirty million gallons had flooded miles of deep workings and risen to within a few feet of the 700' level. In the upper workings the air was pure, and no smoke and fumes filtered up the shaft. The fire had died before the water reached it. Men descended the mine and found remains of a fire, far fiercer and more extensive than they had imagined. The pump house, a building 35 feet by 14 feet, was a heap of ashes. Heavy logs which strengthened the roof of the drive had been burnt to charcoal, and a timbered ore pass was charred. Nevertheless the fire had burnt only a tiny section of the mine: pump house, steel house, part of the pump compartment of the main shaft, and the timber in the mullock pass between the 600' and 700' levels.

On 5 December the first two bodies were taken from the dry part of the mine. After the inquest the funeral wound down the hill from the mine to the cemetery in Linda Valley, where three hundred miners, heads bare and dressed in rough working clothes, cast a long shadow down the sunlit valley.

As the pumps reduced the level of water in the mine, the bodies were recovered and buried in the Queenstown cemetery amidst the muffled drums of the band and the wail of the bagpipes. Eighteen bodies were buried one warm March day after several thousand people had marched down the railway line in front of the long funeral train. The last body was laid to rest on 8 June 1913, the day on which those buried at Linda were re-interred. The forty-two men lie side by side, mostly in unnamed graves.

The fumes in the mine had killed the bacteria and preserved the bodies, and men who walked along the muddy drives recognized dead miners sitting against the wall as if in idle conversation or lying down in a calm sleep. Carbon monoxide gas induces a feeling of drowsy inertia, and the relaxed postures of most of the men suggested that in the last moments they were content to lie down and sleep. The searchers found many drives red with high grade copper. The copper water had corroded trucks, rails, rock drills, shovels, iron plates and pipes precipitating copper in place of the iron. As the mine was pumped dry the copper water was precipitated into copper in wooden flumes, filled with scrap iron. In all, the flooded mine yielded 135 tons of copper.

The Tasmanian government appointed a Royal Commission to investigate the cause of the fire. This commission of Zeehan men examined fifty-four witnesses and found that as nobody had believed that the mine could catch fire no emergency warning system was thought necessary. In fact not one of the experienced miners who gave evidence knew of a mine where a warning system existed. The Royal Commission considered and, in turn, rejected the three possible causes of fire—incendiarism, carelessness of the men, and an electrical defect in the pump house. The experts, one of whom examined the ruined machinery, emphasized that the fire was not caused by a defect in the pumping machinery; but on the other two theories the evidence was inconclusive. The report of the Royal Commission was essentially negative: 'We regret that, from lack of convincing evidence on several matters arising in the course of the enquiry, we cannot report with that degree of certainty which we should desire. Forty-two men are said to have lost their lives in various parts of the mine; and, with so many voices lost to us in the silence of death, the evidence is necessarily incomplete, and we can only deplore the fate of those whose testimony concerning the happenings in the mine on the fatal 12th of October will never be given before an earthly tribunal.'

The counsel for the company presented evidence suggesting that there was more than one fire in the mine and hinting that the suspicious conduct of several men might explain the fires, but when pressed by the union's advocate he refused to divulge all the evidence and make a blunt charge of incendiarism. He realized that the case for incendiarism rested on circumstantial evidence, which would not convince a jury. Nevertheless, the evidence that did not come before the Royal Commission offers the only feasible explanation of the fire.

Three weeks before the disaster a young miner was killed by a fall of rock in the Mt Lyell mine. His brother heatedly alleged at the inquest that the company had been criminally negligent in not timbering the roof. He accused Con Curtain, the government mines inspector, of incompetence: 'Were you ever bluffed by anyone?' he jeered. The jury rejected these insinuations, and the brother became a sworn enemy of the company. Not only did he protest that the North Lyell mine was a death trap, he also said that the North Lyell workings might collapse and trap the men, there being only one exit from the mine. When the hysteria spread and the North Lyell miners came out on strike, he sponsored the resolution that the men were 'absolutely afraid' to go down the mine. But his campaign against the company was seriously weakened when the two unionists who reported on the mine refuted his wildest allegations and left intact only one charge, that the mine had no emergency shaft.

Three days later, on the afternoon of 11 October, Robert Sticht and the secretary of the Federated Mine Employees' Association at Gormanston received word that the Commission of Inspection would arrive at the mines on the following day. No announcement was made in the press. On the day of the fire only a few union officials and a few of the company's staff knew that the inspectors were coming. It is likely, however, that the embittered brother, as the chief agitator in the North Lyell mine, knew of the government's unexpected decision.

Imagine his feelings on the eve of the inspectors' visit. Knowing that few deep mines had more than one shaft and that the North Lyell mine would have an emergency shaft within a week, he probably thought that the visiting inspectors would exonerate the company from his allegations. As a radical unionist and reputedly a member of the International Workers of the World, he probably suspected that the inspectors would be the lackeys of the mine owners. He probably knew that his feud against the company was defeated, unless he proved his argument in the following twenty-four hours.

He worked at the 700' level, only seventy yards along the drive from the pump house. As the pump attendant often spent several hours at the lower pump house and as few men worked on the 700' level he could easily set fire to the wooden building without fear of being detected. Once the pump house was ablaze and the pumps ceased to work, water would rise slowly in the bottom of the mine, cause some anxiety, but give the men time to climb up the ladders out of danger. Meanwhile smoke would fill the shaft and block the only means of escape until the pump house was burnt to the ground or the fire was quenched. Such an incident would fortify the fears and agitations that the mine was unsafe, provoke more industrial trouble, and convince the miners, if not the visiting inspectors, that an emergency shaft was essential.

Shortly before ten o'clock on the morning of the fire the underground foreman noticed that the agitator and his mate were absent from their working place in the drive, though their tools lay near the bulkheads which they were repairing. At the Royal Commission the two men denied that they had left their working place and even claimed that the foreman had seen them and spoken to them. The agitator also contradicted the sworn testimony of other men who worked on the 700' level on the fateful morning. More suspicious, however, was his conduct after he had come up in the first cage at 11.15. He walked along the tunnel to the mine office, told the timekeeper that the fire was serious, and ordered him to summon a doctor. His advice contrasted strongly with his subsequent conduct. Although he was a leader of the men, he did not return to the mine to try and warn the men below, or even stand at the brace to assist from the cage any weak miners who might come out as the smoke grew thicker. He went, instead, to the North Lyell post office and communicated with union officials. Although this bare fabric of evidence can never indicate with any certainty that an incendiarist lit the fire, several powerful coincidences also point to this fact. Firstly, nearly a month after the fire, a large heap of oily, cotton waste was found beneath splintered timber in the underground workings of the Mt Lyell mine. It could not have been thrown down carelessly because it was arranged beneath the timber, nor dropped in the course of duty because cotton waste was not used on that level. And it was unlikely that any mechanic was trying to smuggle ten pounds of bulky waste out of the mine. Officials of the mine were satisfied that the waste was deliberately placed there to kindle a fire. Secondly, it is a remarkable coincidence that the only fire in the mine's fifty working years should occur on the day that the secret Commission of Inspection arrived to prepare a report on a contentious, emotional subject of great political importance to Tasmania and great industrial importance to the field.

Although the evidence suggests that the fire may have been deliberately lit, the guilt of the suspect should not be magnified. He could not foresee the fatal consequences of a small fire; he did not suspect that the fire would give off deadly fumes. He believed that his brother had been killed through the carelessness of the company and the government's mine inspector, and in his hatred the burning of the pump house and the creation of panic seemed a just reprisal. Perhaps he justified his action with the thought that it might force the government to make all mines safer, or perhaps he was mad with malice. This last explanation is fortified by the epitaph which was carved on his brother's headstone in the Queenstown cemetery: 'A human life sacrificed on the altar of dividends'.

The visiting inspectors who arrived on the day of the fire did not report on the disaster or the mine. Basil Sawyer, acting chief inspector of mines in New South Wales and the only member of the Commission who entered the mine, resigned to become Robert Sticht's right-hand man. The directors appointed him without even consulting Sticht and placed him over both Murray and Dean, the metallurgist, who promptly resigned and returned to Canada. Although this foolish decision reflected the directors' lack of confidence in their own staff and their suspicion that some of the charges against the safety of the mine were correct, its folly did not lie so much in the ill-feeling and inefficiency which it created as in the rumours which began to circle the field. People inferred that Sawyer had 'seen too much' in his brief journey into the mine, and was bribed to keep his mouth shut. This erroneous idea is still common at Mt Lyell today.

The directors' fears were dispelled by A. Montgomery, state mining engineer of Western Australia, who inspected the unwatered mine and found no evidence that the mine or shaft was likely to collapse. During the long flooding of the lower workings only a few sections of rock had fallen and there was no sign of abnormal pressure on the timbers. Montgomery, however, warned the company that some parts of the mine were treacherous, and that the ground had fallen suddenly and unexpectedly in both mines. He recommended certain improvements in working and ventilating the mine, but his whole report strongly justified the mining methods of the company.

The North Lyell fire inspired many heroic deeds. Some are told in these pages; some will never be known. The Royal Humane Society awarded thirty-two medals and certificates to the men who had risked their lives in rescue work, and recorded in its archives the names of Treverton and Bray, the two shift bosses who died in the mine while trying to warn their men. But two of the bravest men did not receive their honours. Albert Gadd, the miners' hero, was already stricken with miner's disease when he ventured down the shaft; four months later, he was dead. Robert Cox, the elderly foreman, who did not leave his post until he had signalled away the last cage, was weakened by the fumes and died within a year. And there were others who seemingly survived the ordeal and went away to other fields, there to die, weak and broken men.

23

Axemen, Miners and Prospectors

Mt Lyell had no sooner recovered from the fire than it was threatened by World War I. As Germany had been the chief buyer of Australian copper, there were strong rumours that the mines would be closed until a new market for copper was found. The British Munitions Department eventually purchased the company's copper, and although 360 men enlisted in the Australian forces the field worked steadily throughout the war.

Soon after the outbreak of hostilities the company generated its first hydro-electricity at Lake Margaret. The lake had originally been surveyed when Dr Peters was camping in the battery house at the Blow, but year after year the cheap cost of firewood and the mine's short expectation of life had deferred the building of a power station. In 1911, however, the cost of cutting wood to feed the boilers at the mine and smelters was so expensive that Sticht had estimated that hydro-electricity would save the company £50,000 a year. If the price of copper did not slump, reserves of ore in the two large mines would last ten years, repaying the cost of the works twice over. A. G. M. Michell, a Melbourne engineer, reported favourably on Lake Margaret, and the directors, after long hesitation, sanctioned the scheme.

Lake Margaret, lying in the mountains five miles north of the smelters, was the second wettest locality in Australia; only a small strip of coast around Innisfail in tropical North Queensland had a higher rainfall. In an average year nearly thirteen feet of rain cascaded down the mountains into the deep, small lake and overflowed a bar of rock to form the Yolande River in the rocky ravine below.* Margaret was a glacial lake, sur-

*In 1948, Lake Margaret had its record rainfall of 177.32 inches.

rounded by steep green hills, studded with thousands of white conglomerate boulders so smoothed and flattened by prehistoric glaciers that they resembled the ruins of an ancient Roman city.

In 1912 several hundred Maltese migrants extended a fire-wood tramline across Howard's Plains and began to clear a site for the power house on the banks of the Yolande River. A haulage tram was built up the steep spur, and a wooden pipe-line was laid around the cliffs to the lake. Concrete dam, pipe-line, power house, transmission lines and all the necessary machinery were erected at an overall cost of £164,000 under the supervision of George Wright. On 28 November 1914 the first hydro-electricity was transmitted to the smelters. Henceforth only two air compressors at the Blow and some machinery in the copper converters continued to burn wood; and the army of hundreds of axemen who had laid waste mile after mile of forest vanished forever.

Lynchford, three miles from Queenstown, was the centre of the woodcutting industry. Railway passengers who passed through the little town at nightfall saw a hundred or more cutters, axe in hand, returning to their huts and tents, and saw the curving wooden flumes in which a swift flow of water carried timber down the gullies to high wood stacks beside the railway. Alongside the railway station stood a delicensed bush shanty and the two-storied Railway Hotel, where the rough wood-cutters made merry far into the night. This impressive hotel reflected the rosy hopes, born of the gold mining revival at the turn of the century when Lynchford was expected to become a town of importance. In five years, five companies erected stamp mills and crushed a few hundred tons of quartz from reefs which invariably petered out at depth. A twenty-two bucket gold dredge was launched on the river between Lynch-ford and the Queenstown cemetery, but the Sydney company which worked the dredge was less successful than the wily fossickers who picked up little nuggets in the piles of discarded screenings. Rusting iron screens and mounds of rubble still mark the site of this disappointing venture. And so Lynchford, founded by gold-miners and long sustained by woodcutters, fell into decay, its axes silenced by the rushing waters from the lake.

The new power station generated 5000 horsepower. It was the largest hydro-electric station in Tasmania, and possibly in Australia, and it perhaps had some part in influencing politicians from the west coast to sponsor the large hydro-electric schemes which have become Tasmania's great achievement of a later generation. 'If the Mt Lyell Company can implement this scheme', argued the Minister for Mines, 'then surely the Government, with its greater resources, can harness the highland lakes.' Two years later, the government station at Waddamana generated its first power.

The power station at Lake Margaret was proof in concrete and steel that the field would be working at high pressure for another decade. This was some consolation to hundreds of miners who knew from experience, whether at Beaconsfield, Walhalla or hundreds of other towns, that every mine must eventually close. But real security sprang from the company's own welfare policy which had its seed in the industrial strife of the times. While many bodies still lay in the flooded mine, R. M. Murray had outlined to Sticht a plan which did more than anything else to cultivate harmonious relations between the company and its employees.

Like every manager in Australia, Murray lacked good miners. Before the mines could be worked efficiently, he had to recruit three hundred underground men and fifty open cut men. Strike and fire had scattered one of the best teams of underground miners that had assembled on any field in the Commonwealth, and Murray knew that he would neither recruit nor retain new men until those conditions which gave Lyell a gloomy reputation were removed. The treeless valley of boulders and black peat in a bastion of rocky, mist-clad mountains gave Linda and Gormanston the reputation of being the most depressing mining towns in Australia. Without better sporting facilities, lively entertainment and cheaper cost of living, nomadic miners would remain just long enough to earn their fare back to the mainland. Murray therefore suggested that the company should renovate untenanted houses at Gormanston and rent them cheaply, supply firewood at cost price, regrade the Linda and Gormanston ovals, grant cheap fares to Kelly Basin, and finance the merging of the Gormanston and Linda brass bands into one large band to liven up the streets on pay night.

Although Murray's plan resembled the new welfare schemes that were evolving in the South Australian smelting towns of Port Pirie and Wallaroo, it was a radical departure from the policy of his own directors. They believed that a mining company owed its first and last obligation to the shareholders who risked their money; and they were loath to spend much of the company's in acts of philanthropy. Sometimes, they generously compensated men who were injured in their employ, irrespective of legal obligations, but they rarely donated money to local institutions. The directors, in fact, gave more freely from their own pockets than from the profits of the company. In 1902, for example, when the Queenstown band returned from the Ballarat contests, Bowes-Kelly invited the bandsmen to a garden party at his Melbourne mansion where they played on the lawns, drank champagne and smoked long cigars in the marquee. He personally gave the band £25, but next year, when the band asked the company to grant £100 for new instruments, the board stipulated that the company would only subsidize the band when it played at functions which attracted custom to the Mt Lyell railway. 'Music', said Mellor, 'does not come within the scope of the company's operations.'

The directors sanctioned Murray's plan but the war delayed its fulfilment. A hundred houses were built or renovated at Gormanston; two Queenstown hotels became company boarding houses; three splendid social clubs each with library, billiard table and buffet were built and handed to the men; the bands, school of mines, soldier's club and local institutions received generous subsidies; holiday cottages were erected at Strahan, and free passes were provided on the company's railways. Electricity was sold at such trifling cost that the homes of Mt Lyell were reputed to be more electrified than those of any other district in Australia.

In 1919 the company established butcheries at Gormanston and Linda, and in 1920, after overtures had been made by unions and friendly societies, the company opened a butcher's shop in Queenstown and a general store in Gormanston. A year before the company began its 'cheap food' campaign the cost of living in Queenstown was higher than in any other town in Tasmania. Two years later Queenstown had the cheapest cost of living of the large Tasmanian towns. And a judge of the Arbitration Court, on studying the statistics, remarked that 'it was difficult to believe that the cost of living in a remote district like Queenstown, away from shipping and inland on the west coast of Tasmania, should be less than in Melbourne'.

Murray's plan harmonised industrial relations. While the bodies lay in the mine, the tension and the pent-up enmity which had flared up against the company could have gouged an irreparable gulf between the company and its men just as the less tragic Bellbird disaster left a permanent scar on the minds of the miners of Cessnock. Instead, the Mt Lyell field had an amazing record of industrial harmony after 1912. There were logs of claims, disputes, and sectional stop-work meetings, but for more than fifty years there was no general strike.

The welfare policy not only sweetened the bitter; it enabled the company to survive several crises. If the price of copper fell drastically a mining company had to cut its cost of production or close its mine. In the last analysis wages constituted the great cost of making copper, and the company that could reduce its wages without reducing the standard of living cut its expenditure to the core. Some of the leading men at Broken Hill scoffed at the Mt Lyell Co.'s new policy and regarded it as a philanthropic scheme which the unions would exploit and extend. Although Murray had the interest of the miners genuinely at heart, he resented the phrase 'welfare scheme'. 'It's not welfare', he used to say, 'it's self-preservation.'

Murray chose Gormanston as the site for the company's re-housing programme, and from that day Linda was doomed. Gormanston had certain advantages. It had good building allotments, untenanted houses and a good water supply. It had a better shopping centre, better streets, churches, and a leavening of professional men—mining engineers, surveyors and clerks. It was the administrative centre with council chambers, court house, police, miner's hall, residential bank and the mine offices of the Mt Lyell Co. It was on sloping ground and, therefore, better drained and healthier than the town in the hollow. One other reason tipped the scales heavily in Gormanston's favour. Linda was a rough, insanitary shanty town, and Murray is said to have expressed his determination to wipe it off the map.

The miners, however, were reluctant to leave Linda, for it was nearer the mines and sheltered from the gales which have rent asunder most buildings in Gormanston. Even in 1917, when good houses at Gormanston could be rented cheaply, twice as many miners lived at Linda as at Gormanston. As cheap food, cheap rent and superior social facilities slowly enticed the people from Linda, the shops closed and the last hotel, the Royal, closed its doors at the end of 1952. Within a few years, the gaunt, concrete hotel, a crumbling concrete hall roofed with rust, a rocky graveyard, some lonely chimneys and a few cottages were all that remained.

Bill McDonough, one of the discoverers of Mt Lyell, lived to see Linda Valley in its prime. He had wandered the coast for thirty years, a lost spirit condemned to roam by his own restless nature and the dream that his Eldorado lay just across the range. When he sojourned in the towns he drank heavily or grew tired of the jobs which sympathetic men gave him. He was night watchman in Queenstown, then vanished for years, returning late in life to Gormanston where sentimental investors paid him to prospect near the Eldon Ranges.

Too old for the arduous life of the prospector, he asked Sticht for work and was appointed night watchman at the North Lyell mine. When the lanterns of the night shift had flickered away into the darkness, old Bill took up his light and wandered around the deserted buildings. He saw forest where stood the valley of desolation, and heard the sound of pick and axe, and in his mind the rushing torrent in the sluice box drowned the throb of the mine pumps. This flood of memories ceased one morning when he was awakened and warned for the last time. He clutched his bottle of wine and made his way to Queenstown. Knowing his own weakness, he asked Sticht for a job at the Chester mine, which was seven miles from the nearest hotel and managed by Luke Williams, an old-fashioned Wesleyan and a sworn enemy of the 'demon'. Sticht was sympathetic. 'Away from the daily temptation of the public houses at Linda

Valley', wrote Sticht, 'he may last a few months before he falls from grace again.'

And so McDonough caught the train to the Pieman and tramped through the forest to the Chester mine, a haven for many old prospectors whose names were once magic to the mining promoters of Australia. Working in mist and rain, he caught pneumonia. He was taken on the little train to Tullah, and after eight weeks in hospital he had recovered sufficiently to return to his camp at the mine. But his heart was now weak and dropsy set in. He was taken to hospital and sustained by pensions in the sunset of his life. He died in Hobart on the afternoon of 7 June 1912. That evening an old friend of his wrote to Sticht: 'I was with him when he died and he wished me to send to you for his funeral expenses'. The company sent a wreath, and paid the undertaker and the parson.

Steve Karlson, the kindly Finn, died in 1904 in his fiftieth year. After he had lost his share in the Iron Blow he sluiced for gold in the creeks of Lyell. In 1894 he discovered gold below the site of the Stitt River railway bridge at Rosebery, but made little money. In the copper boom he found copper near the site of the railway bridge across the Pieman, and called his mine 'Cutty Sark' after the famous China tea clipper. He crossed to Renison Bell where he was sluicing alluvial tin until a year before his death. He contracted cancer of the tongue and ended his life in pain and poverty.

Michael McDonough, alone of the discoverers, enjoyed the fruits of his toil. Bushman, prospector and miner, he roamed the coast for ten years before he returned to his old mine and worked for wages as an underground miner. Here Crotty met his old mate and more in kindness than wisdom made him acting manager of the South Lyell mine. When Crotty presented him with a packet of valuable North Lyell shares, Mick gave away some, handed the others across the bar for beer and resumed his wanderings. In 1906, cooking breakfast over a camp-fire at Balfour, he fainted and fell in the fire. He was carried forty miles on horseback to a doctor, who amputated his left arm and severed two fingers of his right hand; his prospecting days were over. The government of Tasmania granted him a good pension, and the Mt Lyell Co. bought him a small farm at Ulverstone, where he spent his remaining days. In April 1919, at the age of fifty-eight, he broke his leg and died soon after the accident. The local newspaper knew nothing of his name and began its brief reference to his death with the cold, impersonal words, 'the man McDonough'.

There was something grand about the way the discoverers did not plead for charity or bemoan their hard lot. On the other hand, William Dixon, who lived on his dividends in a lovely villa at Hawthorn, asked the Mt Lyell Co. to reward his services to the field by making a levy on every share in the company. When Bill McDonough died, Dixon announced to the Melbourne newspapers that he, not McDonough, discovered Mt Lyell and that the company should grant him a pension. Dixon was blessed with a wonderful physique and enjoyed his fortune to a ripe, old age. It was his fervent wish that when he died he might be laid to rest in a coffin of sweet-scented Huon pine, the most precious of the timbers of the west. He kept the coffin under his bed for years, and when he died in Melbourne in 1940, in his ninety-first year, his wish was honoured. It was surely a miracle of endurance that this mightiest of Linda packers should live longer than all the giants who trod that mountain trail.

Old F. O. Henry reached his three score and ten, but he passed through many lean times and went close to bankruptcy before his Mt Lyell shares carried him to wealth. A corpulent, long-bearded, frock-coated little man who loved his pinch of snuff, Henry spent his last years in a brick mansion with long verandahs and tower by the sea at Strahan. The sign 'Pioneer Storekeeper and Universal Provider', which was painted on his stores at Strahan, Queenstown, Gormanston and Kelly Basin, had become a legend in the west, but the heart of the jolly little man was not behind the counter. He once confided that he was born to be a statesman but doomed to be a grocer. He died in January 1916.

No contrast could be greater than the fate of the six pioneers of Mt Lyell. The three simple, naïve and generous discoverers died in public hospitals, in poverty or humble circumstances. The three shrewd, patient and intelligent men who inherited the mine, died in spacious villas or fashionable hotels. Karlson had neither money nor cunning, but he outstayed the McDonoughs who lacked even patience. Crotty, Henry and Dixon had money, shrewdness, patience and an inspired faith in the mine which enabled them to cling to their shares for thirteen years before they received their reward. But for their perseverance, Mt Lyell might have been a forgotten gold mine, overgrown by scrub and saplings.

When Michael McDonough died, the Mt Lyell Co. had paid £3,637,000 in dividends. This may seem small in terms of modern money values, but in the years before 1919, when the great age of Australian mining had passed, only six companies* had paid more than £3,000,000 in dividends; and possibly no industrial company had passed that sum. Mt Lyell had lost its place, however, as one of the world's great copper mines. Although the largest mines of 1919 were producing far more copper than the largest mines of 1899, Mt Lyell was producing less ore and less copper than in the first years of the new century. In the first decade of the century the Mt Lyell Co. averaged 8,350 tons of blister copper a year, but in the last years of World War I the company produced only 70 per cent of this amount.

From 1898 to 1906 the Mt Lyell Co. was the leading copper producer in Australia, but in 1907 Wallaroo-Moonta regained the lead for a year. Great Cobar, N.S.W., Mt Morgan, Hampden Cloncurry, and Mt Elliott, Q., also flourished in this richest era of Australian copper mining, and at least one of these mines produced more copper than Mt Lyell every year between 1911 and 1920. Then in 1921 Mt Lyell again became the leading copper producer in the Commonwealth and except for three war years, when Mt Isa smelted copper, it held that distinction until 1953. Thereafter Mt Isa boomed as a copper-field, becoming one of the world's great producers and dwarfing Mt Lyell.

*Broken Hill Proprietary, Mt Morgan, Great Boulder, Mt Lyell, Ivanhoe Gold Corporation, and Golden Horseshoe.

24

Rosebery: A Tale of Despair

In a normal year the mines at Rosebery, twenty miles north of Queenstown, support fifteen hundred people in one of the most prosperous mining towns in Australia. Rosebery's sparkling prosperity, however, is of recent vintage. For thirty years a baffling metallurgical problem depressed the field, and that problem was not grasped until World War I, when the Mt Lyell Co. formed three idle mines into Mt Read and Rosebery Mines Ltd.

Diggers found the first gold on this field in the Ring River in June 1891, during the Zeehan boom. When the first chamois full of gold was secretly deposited in the vaults of the Zeehan bank the news was whispered abroad, and that evening the first miners rolled their swags and stealthily slipped out of the roaring silver town and down the dark muddy track to Dundas, the starting point of the northerly trail to the new diggings. Within a month some four hundred diggers were washing gold in a deep valley below the long, snow-capped range of Mt Read.

Diggers who followed the creeks up Mt Read in search of the reef which shed the alluvial gold found free gold in the gossan outcrop which marked the Mt Read mine. While one party crushed the gossan in a two-head battery, other prospectors pegged the adjacent mountain side in ten-acre gold leases.

In 1893 Jimmy McDonald, who lived in a bag humpy near Ringville, packed prospecting tools and a bag of oatmeal on his back and battled five miles north to thick forest at the foot of Mt Black. There he found alluvial gold and boulders of zinc lead-sulphide. He floated the Rosebery Prospecting Association —Lord Rosebery was British Prime Minister of the day—and

240

after trenching for twelve months he found the zinc-lead ore body which has been the vault of Rosebery's wealth to this day. McDonald thought the zinc-lead was the source of the gold and he re-floated his association into the Rosebery Gold Mining Company.

Back at Mt Read, at Christmas 1894, wiry Joseph Will, old tin scratcher and Mt Lyell gold digger, found an inch-wide seam of gossan on Mt Hamilton, a spur of Mt Read. He blasted the gossan and to his delight the first sample assayed 60 per cent lead, with 22 ounces of gold and 365 ounces of silver a ton. Below the gossan lay rich sulphide ore, carrying zinc, silver, lead and gold in similar proportions to McDonald's Rosebery mine. The Hercules Gold and Silver Mining Company was floated in Launceston and pack-horses carried ore to the Dundas railway station. Mainland smelters recovered the gold and silver.

At the close of 1895 the Hercules and Rosebery mines faced a serious financial problem. There was not enough oxidized ore, rich in gold and silver, to finance the driving of tunnels and the building of tramway, mill, or smelters. Without cheap transport and smelters the poorer sulphide ores which seemed to comprise the body of the mines were valueless. The mines urgently required capital at a time when even the radiant prospects of Mt Lyell mines did not excite Melbourne or London investors. Moreover, the high percentage of zinc in the mixed sulphide ore posed a serious metallurgical problem. Customs smelters not only refused to pay for the zinc; they exacted penalty charges when the ore contained more than 10 per cent zinc. The average Rosebery ore contained 27 per cent zinc and it was so intimately blended with the galena and iron pyrites that it defied payable treament. With that cheerful optimism which characterized Australian mining, the Hercules and Rosebery companies continued to explore their mine in the hope that the lead would increase and the zinc diminish in the deep levels of the ore body.

In January 1897, when the initial success of Mt Lyell smelters interested English investors in Tasmanian copper mining, the Rosebery Gold Mining Company was refloated in England as the Tasmanian Copper Company. The South Rosebery Company which held the adjoining lease was refloated in Launceston with an issue of gaudy pink and carmine share certificates in the name of the Primrose Mining Company; Primrose was the family name of the Earls of Rosebery. In 1897 the No. 6 tunnel of the Tasmanian Copper Company broke into a copper lode, four hundred feet below the outcrop, and the Primrose Company in shallow trenches found that the adjacent ore body had entered its lease. The discovery of a good copper lode in the depths of the Tasmanian Copper Company's mine sucked this zinc-lead field into the whirlpool of the copper boom and Rosebery was an honoured guest at this feast of mad speculation. Hundreds of leases were pegged and more than fifty companies were floated in a ten-mile belt between the Cutty Sark mines at the Pieman bridge and the Curtain-Davis mines near Montezuma Falls.

Copper was the magic word for investors; and company promoters in their zeal for raising money magnified splashes of copper into 'ore bodies as promising as North Lyell'. They carefully concealed the huge quantities of zinc in many mines, and ignored the metallurgical problems which zinc imposed. In later years Mark Ireland, manager of the Primrose, recalled that shareholders in many companies 'had a better chance of being struck by lightning than receiving a dividend'. The boom was in share-buying rather than mining, and it centred more in Launceston than the mining camps of the west.

The Tasmanian Copper Company, sharing with the Primrose the one strong lode on Rosebery, decided to erect copper smelters. In 1897 it claimed that its ores averaged 2.34 per cent copper, 13 ounces of silver and 0.15 ounces of gold to the ton. The manager, B. P. Eckberg, was strangely silent about the deleterious zinc which permeated most of his ore body. The smelting of copper ores which contained more than 20 per cent zinc entailed expensive fluxes, large furnaces, and a heavy loss of gold and silver. It seemed incredible that smelters should be designed for such a mine.

As Mt Lyell had set the fashion in pyritic smelting, the Tasmanian Copper Company glibly decided to adopt this difficult process. Bushmen cleared and excavated a smelting site near the Stitt River and constructed long water races from the neighbouring creeks. Smelting machinery had already been ordered in England when Harold Wilson, the new general manager, made the timely discovery that the mine was too poor to make smelters pay. He estimated that 400,000 tons of ore were in sight, but this ore carried 21 per cent zinc and a mere 0.75 per cent copper. The scrub grew over the smelter site; the water races clogged with silt; and Wilson left London to examine new processes for treating zinciferous ores. He found no solution, and his company directed its energy to new mines—the old Blinman copper mine in the far north of South Australia and a copper mine near Williamsford.

The closing of the Tasmanian Copper Company's mine was the signal for the collapse of the Primrose and the smaller Rosebery mines; and when the phalanx of the Emu Bay Company's railway navvies moved across the Pieman and through the forest to Rosebery, less than forty miners were at work on a field which, two years earlier, was to have yielded a fortune to Emu Bay shareholders.

At Mt Read, the wind-swept mountain four miles to the south, the Mt Read and Hercules companies worked the zinc-lead ore body with spasmodic success. In 1899 the Hercules Company had completed its haulage tram from the mine to Deep Lead (Williamsford), the terminus of the two-foot gauge North East Dundas tram which zigzagged eighteen miles to Zeehan. The haulage line rose 1,642 feet in one mile and was said to be the largest and steepest self-acting tramway in the world. Down this haulage the Hercules and Mt Read companies exported a small tonnage of gossan, rich in gold and silver and free from zinc, to smelters at Zeehan and Dapto, N.S.W., at some profit. But the bulk of their ore, the zinc-lead sulphides, was as difficult to treat as the ore of the ill-fated Tasmanian Copper Company. While that company was excavating its smelters site at Rosebery, the Hercules Company was said to be planning zinc-silver smelters on the Emu Bay railway, twenty-two miles from Burnie, where deposits of limestone and ironstone flux lay close at hand. In the furnace, lead purchased from the Magnet mine, twelve miles from Waratah, might drown the high zinc content of the Hercules ore and separate the zinc from the lead. The Hercules directors apparently shelved this plan. In 1899 they decided to ship two hundred tons of sulphide ore to the

German works of Beer Sondheimer for trial smelting. That year the Mt Read Company exported 117 tons of sulphide ore to be treated by the Ellershausen process in England. Presumably the trial was promising, for next year an English syndicate was negotiating to erect large works in the Ring Valley and treat the zinc-lead ores from the Mt Read and Hercules mines in return for half the profit.

Meanwhile the Hercules Company caught the copper craze. In a third tunnel in the mountain miners found a small copper lode alongside the zinc-lead ore body, and in a lower tunnel they found a large deposit of copper pyrite. An expert visited the mine and his prediction that the copper would replace the zinc at depth was grand news for the shareholders and directors. The manager now wanted to build pyritic smelters and he chose first the banks of the Ring River and then the Pieman as suitable sites. Alas! the diamond drill revealed that the zinc was as strong as ever and that only 30,000 tons of 3 per cent copper ore lay in sight. In truth zinc permeated almost all the ore in the Mt Read and Hercules mines and these companies had to solve the zinc problem or abandon their mines.

The Mt Read Company sold its last ore in 1901, and paid no dividend to its British and Belgian shareholders. The Hercules Company was more fortunate, mining 15,000 tons of gossan, that averaged 10 pennyweights of gold, 22 ounces of silver, 9.47 per cent lead and no zinc. Most of this gossan yielded a profit of £3 a ton, but the sulphide ore, carrying 27 per cent zinc, was less profitable. It carried less than half as much gold and silver as the gossan and the company received nothing for the zinc and even paid a penalty of 12s 9d a ton to have it removed.

The German smelters at Zeehan saved the Hercules mine from closing down. In 1897 the Metallgesellschaft of Frankfurt-am-Main and one of the world's richest companies, the Deutsche Bank of Berlin, subscribed £80,000 and formed the Tasmanian Smelting Company to smelt those silver-lead ores previously shipped to Germany. In 1898 this company erected smelters at Zeehan. The chimney stack, slag dump, and rusting ruins of this once large enterprise lie beside the Strahan railway line a mile from Zeehan. Opposite the smelters is the overgrown pine garden that once surrounded the three-storied house where Max Heberlein, the brilliant German general manager from Montana, U.S.A., directed these works. Heberlein soon discovered that the Zeehan and Dundas mines could not keep his smelters working at full capacity and that the Hercules, Mt Read, and Tasmanian Copper Company's mines had more silver-lead ore than any mine on Zeehan. They could feed the Zeehan furnaces for years if someone devised a cheap method of separating the lead from the zinc. Heberlein's brother Ferdinand had tackled this problem and, with Thomas Huntington, invented the famous Huntington-Heberlein process, which rapidly spread to silver-lead smelters throughout the world. After 1901, when the Huntington-Heberlein furnaces at Zeehan began to treat the sulphide ore at greatly reduced cost, thousands of tons of Hercules ore arrived for treatment. The new process recovered the lead, silver and gold but lost the zinc. Heberlein's successor at Zeehan was pessimistic about the prospects of extracting the zinc: 'A satisfactory recovery of all four metals in a metallurgical way seems impossible'.

While the richer silver-lead ore from the Hercules mine was being smelted at Zeehan, 31,000 tons of ore assaying more than 40 per cent zinc were shipped to Germany, where the zinc was recovered and the lead lost. No matter where the Hercules Company sold ore, either all the zinc or all the lead was a dead loss. Nevertheless, the mine gave work to more than a hundred men and in 1903-4 paid a 1s dividend on every 2s 6d share. Some shareholders had waited eight years for that return.

At this time Robert Sticht, directing his company's west coast explorations, was impressed with the chance of amassing a fortune for his company by devising a cheap method of saving the zinc. He sent Luke Willams to inspect the Primrose, Mt Read, and Hercules mines, and Williams was impressed with the size of their ore bodies. At Queenstown in 1905 Sticht began to experiment with samples of zinc-blende and galena concentrate in the hope of improving Heberlein's process. In experiments he lost three-quarters of the zinc in the fumes and a quarter of the lead in the slag. He continued the test on a pocket of the ore from the Mt Lyell open cut, which carried 25 per cent zinc and 10 per cent lead. The results were so promising that he patented 'an improved process for the treatment of complex sulphide ores' and began to test a hundred tons of Mt Read ore secretly railed to Queenstown. As the North Lyell mine opened out and the search for new mines wilted, these experiments lapsed, and the Mt Lyell Co. thought no more of the Read-Rosebery mines.

In 1905 the two Rosebery mines were re-opened; and when ore contracts were signed with the Tasmanian Smelting Company, aged shareholders feverishly searched their tins and old chests for the long-discarded shares. The small township on the button-grass hills revived, and in the next eight years Emu Bay trains carried almost 100,000 tons of zinc ore to the Zeehan smelters. These sales kept the companies solvent but yielded not a penny to the groaning shareholders.

Meanwhile the Hercules Company, cut off from its German market by a world glut of zinc concentrates, attempted to reduce the miners' wages. For almost two years, the men camped at Mt Read, the wettest and coldest town in Tasmania, and refused to work the mine. When the company recruited new miners to break the strike, such an alarming proportion of bottle washers, rag dealers, artificial flower makers, and hotel boots made the free trip from Melbourne in the party of 'skilled miners' that the mine could not be manned. In 1907 the mine resumed work and sent lead ore to Zeehan and zinc ore to Germany. It was a rich little mine, for despite the huge wastage of un-recovered metals and the good ore that was given to the railways for ballast it yielded 2s 6d in dividends to the holders of every 2s 6d share. In August 1909, when the Zeehan smelters shut down for two years, the Hercules was the only zinc mine in the district rich enough to keep working.

The mines of Zeehan, not the smelters, had failed. Only four Zeehan mines had sunk deeper than 300 feet, and below that level the ore so decreased and mining expenses so increased that the companies mined at a loss. The smelters were too large for the field. They starved for want of ore and in their lifetime smelted only 445,000 tons of ore, as much as the Mt Lyell smelters treated in a busy year.

In July 1911, after the government had intervened, the Zeehan smelters re-opened and employed 250 men to smelt the ores of Rosebery and Zeehan. But the zinc mines still knew no answer to the baffling problem: 'How can we save both the zinc and the lead?' By 1913 the Hercules had given away 39,000 tons of zinc, worth £3,100,000 at the present price. This fortune lay in black dumps at Dapto and Zeehan and in Germany—a dead loss to the company which mined it and often to the company which smelted it. Like the old Mt Lyell Gold Mining Company which worked a copper mine for gold and silver, the Hercules Company worked a zinc mine mostly for silver and lead. The Hercules was a new Mt Lyell which offered immense wealth to the metallurgist who could extract all the metals.

Bowes Kelly, grey-haired and entering his sixtieth year, was as alert as ever for large mines which languished through weak management. The Hercules was such a mine. Between 1898 and 1913 its shareholders had paid 6d a share in calls and received 6s 6d a share (£36,323) in dividends—but a mere fraction of the profits which this mine would present to any company favoured by good fortune and a clever metallurgist. The Launceston directors and their managers had never worried about metallurgy except to draw comical plans for imitation Mt Lyell smelters. Quick profits was the drunken pilot of their enterprise. The mine was drained, worked, sampled, mullocked and explored with the same amazing inefficiency. Successive mine managers, in an endeavour to reduce the cost of mining, had not filled the hollow stopes with mullock; and through the years rock caved in, wrecked the stopes, and flooded or endangered most of the workings.

In 1912 the prospect of wresting a fortune from the three zinc mines of the Read-Rosebery field captured the imagination of Bowes Kelly and his friend, Lindsay Tulloch, a genial Launceston merchant who had been a director of the Mt Lyell Co. since 1897. For years they had held shares in these mines and they now began to buy bundles of cheap shares on the stock exchange. They decided to gain control of the field, engage the best metallurgist in Australia, and try the modern German zinc-saving processes on the ore of the three mines.

It was beyond their power to capture control of the Tasmanian Copper Company, a London company, but Tulloch was already chairman of the Primrose, and with Kelly he held sufficient shares and public confidence to attempt a bold coup on the Hercules, the largest mine on the field. In August 1912, at an extraordinary meeting of the Hercules Company in Launceston, Kelly caused a sensation by moving that the shareholders be empowered to replace any directors before their term of office expired. Despite heated criticism from Senator Clemons, the chairman, Kelly carried the day and in November he was duly elected chairman and Tulloch vice-chairman of the board of directors. The new board immediately consulted a New South Wales expert, G. H. Blakemore, who advised it to merge with the Primrose mine and the Zeehan smelters and smelt its ore at Zeehan. P. S. Morse, a Newcastle metallurgist, visited Germany and predicted that certain dezincing processes might prove economical at Zeehan. The Tasmanian Smelting Company was eager to merge with the Rosebery mines, for they were now the leading silver-lead mines in the island and alone could save the smelters from the wrecker. If the metallurgist at Zeehan could recover the 13,000 tons of zinc from the slag dump and the zinc which daily hissed from the furnaces in a stream of molten slag, his company would earn its first profit in fifteen years. The Tasmanian Smelting Company and the Primrose and Hercules companies drew plans for a united company which would raise £75,000 to modernize the smelters.

Meanwhile the town of Zeehan was sinking fast.* At an election in 1913 there were 1,200 absentee voters on the roll. The townsmen knew that unless the smelters merged with the Rosebery mines, the few remaining Zeehan mines would be forced to ship their ore to the mainland. On the evening of 24 July 1913, while shareholders of the Hercules Company met in Launceston to consider the merger, a large crowd gathered outside the office of the *Zeehan and Dundas Herald* to hear a verdict, vital to the life of Zeehan. When the Warden read out the cable and announced that the Hercules would merge with the smelters, the Zeehan Military Band struck up a lively air, and rockets and the whistles of mines and smelters swelled the tumult.

---

*Eileen Joyce, the celebrated concert pianist, was born in Zeehan in November 1912. Her father, a woodcutter for the smelters, joined the exodus from Zeehan, taking his family to Boulder, W.A.

Said the Warden to the cheering crowd: 'It is the greatest event in the history of Zeehan'.

But before Zeehan could become a flourishing zinc smelting town, it had to face the challenge from Rosebery, a scattered settlement of a few hundred people. In 1907 the Tasmanian Metals Extraction Company, subsidiary of a wealthy British chemical corporation, had contracted to buy the ores of the Tasmanian Copper Company and treat them with the new bisulphite process. Behind a tall barbed-wire fence and carefully guarded gates, it built extensive works along the Rosebery-Williamsford road; and late in 1912 it crushed, roasted and treated the first load of ore from the mine across the valley. It treated ore for three months and shut down for alterations. In October 1913, when the Zeehan smelters finally closed pending the raising of capital in London, the Metals Extraction Company re-opened its reduction works and seized its great chance to monopolize the ores of the entire zinc belt. It worked for three months and closed again for repairs. Critics saw through the fog of secrecy which concealed the works and knew that the process had failed.

Meanwhile Loftus Hills, assistant government geologist, was writing the first of four outspoken reports on the mines. He defined the geological formation, predicted that the zinc-lead ore bodies would descend to sea level and traced the zinc-lead sulphide belt for seven miles in a north-south line. His optimistic report on the mineral wealth of Rosebery plus the failure of the bisulphite process would have flung the field into Kelly's grasp but for a new curse, the curse of war, which suddenly smote the hapless mines. The gathering storm so hardened the money market in London that the proposed merger of the Hercules, Primrose and Tasmanian Smelting Company was not consummated. War cut off the Australian zinc mines from their markets in Germany and Belgium, and made the working of new zinc mines an act of folly. Kelly and Tulloch's slowly maturing plans were plucked from their hands. The Tasmanian government confiscated the idle Zeehan smelters, and Rosebery and Mt Read became ghost mining towns.

Ever since 1898, when the designing and selection of sites for copper smelters was a fashionable sport among the mining men of Rosebery, the ores of this field had defied every chemist and metallurgist. The mining companies had denied that the puzzle existed or they had approached it faint-heartedly. Although German scientists at Zeehan and Frankfurt, Australians at Dapto, Bendigo, and Mt Lyell, and British scientists at Rosebery, Swansea and London had studied this problem, no man could profitably extract both the zinc and the lead.

The extensive ruins of the Tasmanian Metals Extraction works, hidden by stunted timber on the hill above Rosebery station, symbolize this first phase in the history of the field. They resemble an ancient multi-terraced fort, once guardian of the valley, now razed and surrounded by bush. Twisted steel girders, piles of moss-covered bricks, concrete pits and tailings dumps litter the site; and some of the machinery—a lofty retort, the crushing rolls with large, spoked iron wheels, and long boilers on which are imprinted the names of famous manufacturers of London, Sheffield and Erith—stands on the very ground where once it throbbed or steamed. About £160,000, more than £750,000 in present-day money, had been lavished on this futile enterprise by 1914. That was but part of the price of mastering the complex ores of Rosebery.

Loaded with shares in idle mines, Kelly and Tulloch sought ways of recouping their investment. The Mt Lyell Co. might provide the answer. If it entered the field it could amass large profits for its own shareholders as well as the zinc companies. It could explore the mines and carry out metallurgical research at a cheaper cost than any other Tasmanian company. From Lake Margaret it could supply the mines with probably the cheapest power in Australia. These advantages convinced the other directors that the field was at least worth inspecting.

So Murray went to Mt Read and Rosebery to prepare a report on the mines. After hundreds of samples had been assayed at Queenstown, he estimated that the mines had ore reserves of 805,000 tons, of which less than one-third was 'actually in sight'. Sticht reported favourably, knowing that recent advances in the electrolytic treatment of zinc in the United States and the flotation of zinc ores at Broken Hill gave promise of solving the twenty-year-old enigma.

In September 1915 Kelly and Tulloch attended meetings of the Hercules and Primrose boards in Launceston and discussed the terms on which they would sell. The Tasmanian Copper Company, believing that the failure of the Metals Extraction works at Rosebery had dissolved their contract to sell all ore to that company, joined in the discussions. Finally the three companies agreed to give the Mt Lyell Co. the option of buying their mines within the next nine months on either of two conditions. Firstly, Mt Lyell could pay them 275,000 new Mt Lyell shares and liquidate debts amounting to nearly £40,000. Secondly, it could form the zinc mines into a separate company in which it would receive 29 per cent of the initial issue of shares, the remainder going to the three zinc companies. The Mt Lyell Co. would then finance the new company until capital was raised by the issue of debentures.

Kelly and Tulloch returned to Melbourne in the steamer and revealed these terms to their fellow directors, Hunt and Templeton, in the Mt Lyell board room. After a long discussion in which the high price of the mines was criticized, the board accepted a working option on the mines. Five hundred tons of Rosebery ore were promptly bagged and sent to Broken Hill for experimental treatment at the Zinc Corporation's plant.

Broken Hill led the world in the profitable treatment of zinc-lead sulphides. At the turn of the century, however, three out of every four tons of ore that came up the shafts defied treatment and were stacked in huge dumps along the line of lode: dumps that would mark the grave of Broken Hill unless the zinc, silver and lead could be separated cheaply. In 1902 G. D. Delprat, the general manager of Broken Hill Proprietary, invented a process that promised to extract the treasure in the £30,000,000 dump. He added oil, salt cake and other chemicals to a tank of pulped ore, and pumped in air through a blower at the bottom. He was delighted to observe that particles of mineral clung to the rising air bubbles and overflowed the tank while the barren particles sank to the bottom. His company erected the first efficient flotation plant in the world and recovered a fortune in zinc and lead from the long-despised dumps. Other Broken Hill companies devised other flotation processes with sensational results.

The Rosebery ore was more complex than the Broken Hill ore. The grain size of its constituent minerals was so small and the various minerals were so intimately blended that the zinc and the lead could not be recovered economically in a flotation plant. But improvements in crushing machinery and the development of a new technique of selective flotation were slowly paving the way for the treatment of complex ores. Kelly and Tulloch foresaw these advances when they began to buy Hercules and Rosebery shares before the war; and it was natural that when they had interested the Mt Lyell Co. in their mines, their first step would be to test the ore at Broken Hill.

A. T. Fry, a metallurgist at Zinc Corporation, tested the ore in an experimental flotation plant and recovered most of the precious metals. The answer to the dilemma was in sight. In June 1916 the directors of Mt Lyell decided to exercise the option. They formed a company called the Mt Read and Rosebery Mines and issued 345,000 fully-paid £1 shares, of which the Hercules Company received 120,000, the Tasmanian Copper Company 100,000, the Mt Lyell Co. 100,000, and the Primrose 25,000. Newspapers hailed the merger as one of the most important events in the history of Tasmanian mining. In foggy Rosebery and snow-clad Mt Read there was jubilation, whilst Zeehan was hopeful that her old smelters might become a huge zinc works. The small parties of tributors who had held the silver-field together hoped that the hydro-electric schemes which would operate the zinc works would supply cheap power to the mines. Optimism swept the west.

The new company shipped a hundred tons of Rosebery ore to the United States where the Anaconda Company had just erected electrolytic zinc works at Great Falls, Montana. In 1917 Sticht returned to his old haunts to watch the experiments. He reported that the experts agreed that the ore was amenable to treatment and that 22,000 horsepower would work the plant. Using the electrolytic process and harnessing power from the rushing rivers, the west coast would be the most economic region in Australia for mining and treating zinc ore. Only five years previously, high coke and coal freights had made western Tasmania one of the costliest regions in the world for producing marketable zinc.

Crotty seemed the best location for a large hydro-electric project. Huntley Clarke took his men down to the derelict one-pub town and examined the head of the deep gorge where the King River cuts between Mt Jukes and Mt Huxley. In the summer of 1917-18, under Clarke's direction, the company spent £10,000 in diverting the river, examining its bed and clearing the site for a dam. Clarke envisaged a concrete dam, 180 feet high, which would form a great storage lake stretching nearly ten miles up the valley. At Harris' Reward, an old gold mine three and a half miles below the dam, a power station would generate 45,000 horsepower for transmission to Zeehan, twenty-four miles away.

In December 1917 the government agreed to carry out this ambitious scheme and supply Mt Read and Rosebery Mines with 25,000 horsepower. The Mt Lyell Co., preparing for the day when the new dam would submerge a long stretch of its North Lyell railway, began to search for an alternative route to haul timber to its mines. The government suggested that a ferry would bridge the gap. The company was reluctant to sanction a scheme that would make the loss on the railway even more alarming and it toyed with the idea of constructing a new stretch of railway above high-water mark. A surveyor traced a route which crossed the gorge on the dam wall, and ran up the Tofft River to rejoin the old line, four miles from Linda. He said that in all his experience he had not seen such wild country for a railway. A short deviation line might cost £150,000, he added.

While the company was pondering over this problem, the government grew cold on the King River scheme. Committed to a heavy expenditure on public works, it wanted to give priority to those electric schemes which benefited the more populous parts of the island. This financial difficulty was aggravated by technical uncertainty. There was a danger that in the limestone country just south of the dam site, a large volume of water might seep through subterranean channels and escape down the Andrew River.

On 21 May 1919 the Premier of Tasmania, the Honourable W. H. Lee, and the Treasurer, Sir Elliott Lewis, met the Mt Lyell directors at Collins House, Melbourne, and discussed alternative sources of power. The directors were anxious to press on and sent their surveyors out to search for a small power scheme. At Lake Rolleston, eight miles north of Lake Margaret, Clarke found that 22,500 horsepower could be harnessed for £1,250,000. In December 1919 the government agreed to pay 40 per cent of the cost of construction.

And now the stage was set for the construction of a great zinc mining industry, an industry that might outgrow Mt Lyell in the fullness of time. Mt Read and Rosebery Mines had drilled 12,000 feet in exploration work and opened up their mines for large-scale working. They had extracted more than 80 per cent of the zinc and lead in flotation tests at Broken Hill and electrolytic tests at Great Falls, U.S.A. They had secured an option to buy the Zeehan smelters for £15,000. They employed an American named Crutcher to investigate the treatment of the zinc ore in a laboratory at Queenstown. They negotiated with R. B. Caples, a clever metallurgist at the huge Anaconda works, and as soon as he reached Tasmania he would erect a pilot plant and then the large plant at Zeehan. In 1924 the Zeehan works would be producing fifty tons of electrolytic zinc a day, and mines, mill, refinery and railway would be employing nearly a thousand men at Zeehan, Rosebery, Williamsford and Mt Read.

These plans were suddenly jeopardized. In February 1920 representatives of Mt Read and Rosebery Mines and the Electrolytic Zinc Company met in Melbourne to discuss a merger. The Electrolytic Zinc Company of Australasia had been formed by four Broken Hill zinc producers during the war, when they were unable to sell their concentrates to German and Belgian zinc works. With large stocks of unmarketable concentrate on hand, they decided to refine their own zinc. The Electrolytic Zinc Company proceeded to build zinc works along the waterfront at Hobart, bought cheap hydro-electricity from the government, and sold its output of zinc to the British government under an eight-year contract. In 1918, after the new works had sold their first pure zinc, the directors approached Mt Read and Rosebery Mines and offered to discuss a merger. Bowes Kelly, always an optimist, rejected the overture.

When the Electrolytic Zinc Company renewed its offer some time later, the Rosebery directors were not so confident. They

Drilling underground at Mt Lyell

Drilling in the open cut at West Lyell

sensed that if they carried out their plans, Rosebery might become another Crotty. In an official statement they said that the ore in sight would only last ten years and did not justify the investment of £1,250,000. This was certainly a valid argument, but it was just as valid in 1916 when the Mt Lyell Co. decided to enter the field. Sticht had realized that Rosebery was essentially a speculative venture, and in 1916 he had warned his directors that they were paying too much for an interest in the mines. But the directors thought otherwise and rejected his advice.

Robert Sticht and Herbert W. Gepp had long and frank discussions on the terms of the merger. They agreed that the prospective value of the mines to the Electrolytic Zinc Company should be the sole factor in determining their price. This was fair enough. After all, Broken Hill, mining a quarter of the world's zinc, could supply the Hobart works with cheap zinc concentrate for thirty or forty years; and if the cost of landing a Rosebery zinc concentrate at Hobart exceeded the cost of landing an equally rich Broken Hill concentrate there was no point in the Electrolytic Zinc Company buying the mines.

On this reckoning Mt Read and Rosebery Mines received 350,000 £1 shares in Electrolytic Zinc. The Mt Lyell Co. agreed to take 210,000 of these shares as payment for both the £180,000 which it spent in developing the mines and its holding of 100,000 shares in Mt Read and Rosebery Mines. It was also entitled to buy 90,000 £1 preference shares in Electrolytic Zinc, leaving 60,000 for the shareholders in the three smaller Rosebery companies. The Mt Lyell Co. thus became the second largest holder of ordinary shares in the Electrolytic Zinc Company and was granted two seats on that company's board.

There was bewilderment in Zeehan on 31 July when news of the impending liquidation of Mt Read and Rosebery Mines ricocheted through the forlorn town. For several years, many a crowded public meeting had urged the government to assist in establishing zinc works at Zeehan, and hundreds of people clung to the town waiting for construction to begin. They were somewhat consoled when they heard that zinc ore would still be railed from Rosebery and Williamsford to the site of the Zeehan smelters, where a grinding and flotation plant would prepare a

53 per cent zinc concentrate for shipment to Hobart. Moreover, the lead, silver and gold would be roasted and smelted at Zeehan, thus restoring a ready market for local ore.

But these plans did not mature. The dilapidated smelters played a minor role, roasting a small tonnage of concentrates and employing few men. Zeehan's long main streets began to creak with empty shops, halls and houses. Visited by the mysterious fires that crackle farewell to all old, well-insured mining towns, it became a melancholy ghost town, living on its memories. The *Zeehan and Dundas Herald* died in 1922, in its thirty-second year of publication, and the silent presses whispered that Zeehan would rise no more.

Nowadays, while the Rosebery mill rumbles day and night, its people wonder why the Mt Lyell Co. deserted the field. They forget the sixteen long years that passed between Mt Lyell's withdrawal and the completion of the flotation plant at Rosebery, years in which the Electrolytic Zinc Company undertook arduous research on separating the lead from the iron pyrites. They forget that if the Mt Lyell Co. had carried out its plans to build a power station at Lake Rolleston and zinc works at Zeehan its enterprise would have been wrecked by metallurgical difficulties or low zinc prices. In the 1920s the Mt Lyell Co. required all its financial strength to survive a prolonged crisis on the home front, let alone fight a losing battle in the mines across the mountains. It was lucky to escape with more than the money it spent on the field.

Rosebery is one of the great success stories in Australian mining. It is a triumph of persistence and courage in the face of great metallurgical difficulties. The Mt Lyell Co. made nothing out of the field but it played a conspicuous part in establishing it on a sound footing. 'They have introduced the very elements which were so sadly lacking before', wrote Loftus Hills, the geologist, in an impartial tribute in 1919. Mt Lyell replaced the policy of gouging out the rich ore with a long-term policy of systematic diamond drilling and metallurgical research. It had the vision to see that the field might have the seeds of greatness, and that with luck, might rise above the dismal era of burrowing for silver and lead.

25

The End of an Era

The new technique which revived Rosebery breathed new life into Mt Lyell. It gave promise of extracting the copper from millions of tons of schist rock that was too poor to be smelted profitably in a blast furnace. For years this ore had defied payable treatment. At the turn of the century two companies had installed rock-breakers, Cornish rolls, vanners, jigs, and agitators in an attempt to separate the copper from the barren rock by the system of water concentration. Their mills were so inefficient that one enterprising metallurgist later worked the tailings below the mill at Crotty for a handsome profit. The mills were scrapped and pyritic smelting remained the only economic method of recovering copper from the rock of the field.

Delprat had made flotation practicable in 1902 when the North Lyell Co. was panicking at Crotty. If this process had been applied to copper ore with instant success, North Lyell could have concentrated its ore at a huge profit and conquered its gasping rival. But the first copper was not successfully floated until 1912, when the United States led the way. The new flotation mill recovered far more copper than the old gravity concentration mills, and within five years, pilot plants were working on the chief Australian copper-fields.

L. V. Waterhouse, a clever Broken Hill metallurgist, erected the first flotation plant at Queenstown. In February 1916 he fed Comstock ore into the mill and eliminated more than 70 per cent of the barren rock. The same year he concentrated low-grade bornite from North Lyell and began to enlarge the plant. Within three years his oily bubbling flotation tanks were treating a ninth of the output of the mines and producing from poor

257

ore a concentrate carrying 10.5 per cent copper. As flotation was cheaper than direct smelting, Waterhouse was eager that all ore should be concentrated before it was smelted. Sticht, however, refused to change his famous technique of direct smelting. In 1919 Waterhouse resigned, and crossed to the mainland where he won a fortune in gold from tailings dumps in Victoria and the river flats of New Guinea. A financial crisis led to the metallurgical change for which Waterhouse had fought. Towards the end of the war the nations ceased to stockpile strategic metals, and the price of copper collapsed like a concertina. The year 1918, when the company earned a net profit of £247,000, marked the end of the boom in copper prices. By 1920 the company was earning no profit from the mines, and at the close of the year it was producing copper at about £100 a ton and selling it for little more than £80. Mt Lyell faced extinction. On 24 March 1921 the directors announced that unless the price of copper improved or working costs were reduced substantially, the company would close its mines. They invited the men to consider two unpopular proposals. Firstly, as only half the contract miners had bothered to work on Saturday morning since the introduction of a 44-hour week in the mines, the directors suggested that the miners work 40 hours one week and 48 hours the next, thus reducing absenteeism on Saturdays and increasing output. Secondly, they proposed to reduce wages and salaries by 10 or 15 per cent. Even if the men made this sacrifice, the shareholders would receive no dividends and the company would mine at a loss.

The union delegates refused. They told the company that wages were inadequate and that the company should tender its proposals to the Arbitration Court. The directors, realizing that the court would reject the company's application, invited the unions to confer with them in Melbourne. Nineteen union delegates and four directors met at Collins House to search for a compromise.

Old Bowes Kelly addressed the gathering. He said that Mr Justice Powers, in rejecting a similar application from the North Nuggety Ajax gold mine, had emphasized that it was necessary 'to keep this living wage as a thing sacrosanct, beyond the reach of bargaining'. The judge, moreover, had refused to allow underground miners to work more than 44 hours a week. It was hopeless, argued Kelly, for the company to approach the Arbitration Court. The union delegates gave Kelly a sympathetic hearing and relented in their stand. They offered to work 40 hours and 48 hours on alternate weeks, to assist the company in securing two hundred more underground men, to reduce absenteeism and increase efficiency. The directors then agreed that if the London price of electrolytic copper did not drop below £70 a ton for fourteen consecutive days, the company would work for six months in the hope that living costs and working costs might fall. On 8 May 1921 the members of every union except the Amalgamated Society of Engineers endorsed this plan.

Next day the Combined Unions Executive over-ruled this vote and rejected the directors' offer. This mainland body demanded that the Arbitration Court, the constitutional authority which the company had always upheld, should sanction any change in conditions of employment. Moreover, they recalled that during the war the company had enjoyed 'an era of unparalleled prosperity' in which the men did not share. This latter charge was false. For fifteen months the company paid a generous bonus to all employees, thus adding almost £30,000 to the wages bill. Moreover, the company had spent a huge sum in improving living and working conditions at Mt Lyell. Mainland union officials, it seemed, were greedy for their pound of flesh even if three townships were ruined, the fortress of Tasmanian unionism razed, and five thousand people deprived of their sole means of livelihood. The directors had no alternative but to close the mines. On 20 May they reluctantly announced that all mining and smelting would cease in a month.

In June, at the request of Mr Justice Powers, the company agreed to postpone the closing, while a Sydney accountant estimated how much the mine was losing. The accountant found that if wages and the price of copper remained static the company would lose £18 16s 1d on every ton of copper it produced. In a year the company would lose £95,972, the equivalent of about 1s 5d a share. Mr Justice Powers then conferred with the directors and unionists, but the days passed by without any solution in sight. On 29 June, deadline day, no word had come from Melbourne, and Sticht was forced to take the drastic step. All day anxious groups of miners crowded around the notice board to read the fateful notice:

> All ore-breaking operations will terminate with the afternoon shift today.
>
> *R. C. Sticht*
> GENERAL MANAGER

In Melbourne, that afternoon, Mr Justice Powers knew that if the dispute was not settled immediately there would be a rapid exodus from the field. He forced the two parties to agree. He permitted the alternate 40-hours and 48-hours week in the mines, and decreed that current wages be paid until December. For six months Mt Lyell was reprieved. Its inhabitants did not know how close they had been to destitution. 'At times', wrote the secretary, 'it looked as if there was no hope of anything but a complete cessation of all operations.'

In the last half of the year the company rode the storm. The new hours increased output of ore, and by November 94 per cent of the miners worked on Saturdays. In December the underground men voted unanimously that the system of working on alternate Saturdays be retained, and it operated for years. The cost of living in the district fell and made possible a reduction of wages in the following year. It was lucky for Tasmania that Mt Lyell survived. Between the autumn and spring of 1921 unemployment trebled so that sixteen out of every hundred unionists in the island were out of work. As the largest industry in Tasmania, Mt Lyell was a wind-break against the economic gales, and had it collapsed, the island would have experienced greater hardships than in the depression of the early nineties. It is certain that before Christmas one in four Tasmanian wage-earners would have been out of work.

It required more than the economies which Mr Justice Powers had sanctioned to keep Mt Lyell alive. In 1922 the company had to revise its method of smelting and foresake the technique which had made it world-famous. Coke was so dear and copper so cheap that even 10 per cent North Lyell ore could not be smelted at a profit. Pyritic smelting and the Iron Blow were doomed. The triumph of the flotation process was complete. R. M. Murray, the acting general manager, and R. P. Roberts, his American metallurgist, decided to concentrate all but the richest ore in the mill and smelt the concentrate in the furnaces without the aid of pyrites. Henceforth the flotation tanks eliminated 70 per cent of that silica which hitherto had fused with the iron in the heat of the furnace and poured down the drain as molten slag. The crushing mill and flotation plant turned 6 per cent ore into a concentrate of 15 to 18 per cent copper; the furnace removed more waste rock, until the matte contained nearly half copper; and the converter vessel poured out blister copper, 99 per cent pure. In 1900 eleven large furnaces stood in stately array in the long smelting buildings and devoured lumps of ore straight from the mine. Now one small furnace stood alone, smelting copper concentrate that had been roasted into black cinders in the adjoining sintering plant.

Near the smelters stands the monument to the vanished era of direct smelting—a great black slag dump, more than sixty feet high, half a mile long and covering forty-acres of the valley. The bare, coloured hills, stripped of all trees, shrubs and peat until only the skeleton of bedrock remained, also stand witness to the era when clouds of sulphur drifted over the smelters. Although the new method of treatment checked the sulphur scourge, allowed gardens to flower, and tallow-wood, cheesewood, dogwood and small green shrubs to fight their way back on to the more sheltered ranges, it painted a new scar on the landscape. Tailings from the twenty-six million tons of pulped ore that passed through the mill have turned two rivers into grey industrial gutters, silted up the beautiful lower reaches of the river where the barges glided up to Teepookana, and formed a long spit in Macquarie Harbour.

The Mt Lyell open cut had become a deep oval crater on the side of the hill with eleven narrow ledges where men cleaned up the remaining few thousand tons of accessible ore. Underground the water level was rising slowly through 450 feet of workings to the floor of the quarry. In all, four and a half million tons of overburden and four million tons of ore had been mined from the open cut, while underground the company mined one and a half million tons, of which one-third came from the adjacent South Lyell ore body. The ore contained nearly 71,000 tons of copper, 12 million ounces of silver and almost 358,000 ounces of gold; only two mines on the famous Bendigo and Ballarat fields yielded more gold. The mine was not the fabulously rich copper deposit which its pioneers visualised, and it produced only a very small part of the copper that has so far been won from the field; but it was the metallurgical key to the field until Broken Hill forged a new and better key.

Robert Carl Sticht did not live to see the last days of pyritic smelting. He was lying in a Launceston hospital dying of cancer when his famous system was superseded, but he gleaned the poignant news from Murray and nodded his approval. He died a few weeks later, on 30 April 1922; he was sixty-five.

Sticht had left the United States intending to spend two years in the backwoods mining camp, but he remained for the rest of his life. He became the potentate of the third largest town in Tasmania, ruling his realm from a two-storied brick mansion which stood on a steep hill high above the valley of tarred roofs. Here he entertained all the notable visitors who came to the field, and here, in his inner sanctum, he lived the scholar's life. He gathered one of the finest private libraries in the Commonwealth and a celebrated collection of Dürer woodcuts, Rembrandt etchings, medieval parchments, Reformation tracts and priceless specimens of early printing, now the property of the State Library and National Gallery of Victoria.

Those who first met him in his later years were surprised to find that he was more like a lovable old German professor than a shrewd, dynamic mining magnate. He was short and stocky in build, kind and contented of face, with plump cheeks, bushy moustache, and a thick patch of sleek snowy hair on each side of his bald head. He spoke in a quiet, polished way with no tang of the Yankee in his voice, but he was obviously proud of his American nationality, for on days of celebration he flew the star spangled banner from his flagpole on the hill. His great quality was his energy, his zeal for work. Supervising the firing of the new converters, he worked until he fell asleep on the earthen floor through utter exhaustion, to be awakened later by a shower of sparks that singed his clothes. And in the early years of smelting he often walked down the track from the smelters at three or four o'clock in the morning.

Sticht was sympathetic and kind. He was accessible to the grimiest labourer from the smelters, or the bearded prospectors who hailed his Daimler rail car as it sped between Queenstown and Burnie and handed him ore to examine. His popularity was such that in 1914, when he made his first trip back to the United States, his railway journey to Burnie was like a triumphal procession with groups of people at sidings along the line and moving farewells from townsmen at the larger stations. But Sticht eschewed the limelight and gave away thousands of pounds in acts of charity that rarely met the public eye. On the other hand, if he thought anyone was imposing on him, his pen was barbed. An incident of 1902 revealed this trait. The boys who trucked the ore at the Blocks mine went on strike, so the manager approached the Mt Lyell Co. and bought a draught horse to haul the trucks down the tunnel. When the truckers returned to work, the manager, having no further use for the horse, tried to sell it back on the spurious grounds that Sticht had sold the horse to stop the strike from spreading to his mine. Sticht took up his pen, wrote three polite sentences in which he refused to buy the horse, and finished his note thus: 'The unintelligent effrontery which prompts you to assign the reason for the transactions which you do in your letter, affords me an explanation of why you have not been getting on better in this locality'.

Some years later William Dixon, the lion-hearted prospector, returned to Mt Lyell after a long absence and was ushered into Sticht's office. 'Ah! Mister Sticht', said Dixon boastfully, 'you should have seen the Mt Lyell mine at its best! When I left, there was icicles of silver, mahn, stickin' out av' the roof.' Sticht replied with a smile: 'I should have been as delighted to see those icicles of silver, Mr Dixon, as I am to meet you'. Dixon, blind to the twinkle in Sticht's eye, was full of praise for him. 'Glory be to God, phwat a grand mahn he is!'

In 1903 Sticht received a salary of £5,000 a year — earning as much in a week as a smelter hand in a year. Taxation and inflation have so undermined higher incomes that a modern professional man would need to earn one million dollars in 1990 to enjoy the equal of this income. Sticht, however, died in straitened circumstances. He bought the Copper Reward mine at Balfour in the belief that the shallow surface lodes resembled the giant lodes of Butte, Montana, U.S.A., and reputedly lost £70,000 before he realized his error.

His great fame was waning when he died. In 1903 he was the best known man in Australian mining, and the one Australian metallurgist whose renown was world wide. But fifteen years later he was more an historic figure than a man of the hour. Mt Lyell was no longer a giant of Australian industry; mining had lost its glamour; and pyritic smelting was only practised in six widely scattered parts of the world. Even so, the American *Engineering and Mining Journal* paid tribute to his reputation by beginning its obituary with the words: 'The name of the late Robert Sticht was familiar throughout the world as that of a distinguished mining and metallurgical scientist'.

The death of Sticht, the end of pyritic smelting, and the closing of the Mt Lyell mine—these events of the autumn of 1922 marked the end of an era.

Tightening the Belt

Russell Mervyn Murray, who succeeded Sticht as general manager, was a native of Colac, a western Victorian town which his grandfather had pioneered during the pastoral exodus from Tasmania in the 1830s. In 1900, after graduating from the University of Melbourne as a civil engineer, Murray made several requests for employment with the Mt Lyell Co. At first Sticht refused them on the grounds that a large company risked its efficiency in training inexperienced students; then he relented and offered Murray a position as draughtsman and assistant surveyor in the mine office at Gormanston. Murray hurried across to Strahan, readily exchanging the luxury of 'Borongarook', a spacious homestead overlooking the hills and lakes of Colac, for an iron hut in one of the most desolate and wind-swept towns in Australia. He stayed at Mt Lyell, not for the customary brief term of the young engineer, but for the remainder of his life, becoming a unique figure among the captains of Australian mining, a general manager whose whole working life had been spent on the one field.

Murray was twenty-nine years old in 1906 when the sudden death of Batchelor gave him a chance to prove his worth. He was acting manager for a year, supervising the work of nine-hundred men before he was officially appointed manager with the title 'Engineer-in-Charge of the Mt Lyell Company's mines'. Five years later, his calmness and courage in directing rescue operations in the North Lyell mine won him the Royal Humane Society's silver medal and the respect of many a miner who viewed each manager as his enemy. The miners showed this respect by electing him Warden (Mayor) of Gormanston municipality in 1920, and although he soon moved into Sticht's old residence at Queenstown, they elected him Warden each year until his death.

When he sat in his office, eyes alert, fingers twitching the corners of his moustache as he carefully framed his sentences, he at once gave the impression of solidity and caution; and in fact his chief mental qualities were of that type. He had an unusual grasp of detail that enabled him to detect inefficiency or error at a glance; an analytical mind which won him recognition as a leading exponent of industrial legislation in the Arbitration Court; and a logical and realistic outlook that was far removed from the radiant optimism of the mine managers who congregated at the Federation Hotel when he first came to Gormanston.

The new general manager needed all these good qualities, for the North Lyell mine was the only west coast mine that worked continuously throughout 1921, and the only large Australian copper mine that worked continuously in 1922. Australian mining had reached its lowest ebb since the gold discoveries of 1851, and in this slump no section of the industry fared worse than copper mining. The Wallaroo and Moonta field collapsed, giving South Australia its lowest copper production for seventy-eight years; Mt Morgan was idle for many months; the expensive machinery of the smelters at Great Cobar was sold as scrap iron; the copper smelters at Chillagoe were operated by the Queensland government at a heavy loss; and the Cloncurry field in North Queensland, formerly the largest producer in Australia, yielded only 325 tons of copper—3 per cent of its output in 1918. The value of Australian copper production, which was higher than any other mineral except gold in 1916, fell by 80 per cent in five years.

The collapse of copper prices on the world market wrought this damage. In six years the price of copper was halved, the sharpest fall occurring between 1920 and 1921 when the average price fell from £110 to £75. The closing of many mines, however, was hastened by the greed and short-sightedness of their owners, who tore out the rich ore while the price was high and neglected the search for new ore bodies and the systematic working of the mine. Such mines were already disembowelled before they were drawn and quartered by world prices.

In this gloomy setting Murray was appointed general manager. He stamped out the inefficiency which had characterized Sticht's last years. He abandoned more than a third of the company's mining lease and cut the pay-roll so drastically that in 1922 the company employed an average of only 942 men, a thousand less than in pre-war years. Likewise, the directors reduced the cost of administration and strengthened their reserve funds so that the company could survive any new slump in the price of copper. In 1924 they sold the last of the company's shares in Electrolytic Zinc. In 1926 they dismantled the Port Kembla coke works, which produced barely enough coke to feed one blast furnace, and sold 75,000 shares in Wallaroo-Mount Lyell Fertilisers.

The company tore up the North Lyell railway. It had been a white elephant since the closing of the Crotty smelters, carrying firewood and mining timber for the company's mines, and occasional loads of coal, timber, and copper concentrate for the Consols and Blocks mines. After 1918, when the logging industry near Darwin began to decline, the annual railway deficit grew heavier. Except on picnic days so few passengers used the line that a weekly rail motor easily satisfied the simple needs of Kelly Basin's eight residents and Finnigan's 'Shamrock' Hotel. In 1924 the company received permission from Parliament to dismantle thirteen miles of railway between Darwin and Kelly Basin; and on 13 January 1925 the last train steamed out of the Kelly Basin station, whistled farewell to the deserted waterfront and swayed along the grass-grown railway track that twisted up the timbered gullies. Three years later a fettler and his family left the landscape of razed brick and masonry that once was Crotty, and the last train moved slowly towards Linda, loading rails and sleepers on its way. For some years motor trucks crawled along the railway formation to Kelly Basin, but fire destroyed the wooden bridges, trees fell, scrub encroached and cuttings slipped. The magnificent steel bridge designed by John Monash to span the King River near Crotty still stood, but nobody came to admire it.

Despite these economies, the company made an average annual profit of barely 2 per cent on its operations at Mt Lyell over a six-year period. At annual meetings it became common for shareholders to murmur that the company seemed to be in business merely to keep men in employment. They inferred that the company should sell out and pay a handsome liquidation dividend on each share. The directors faced this truth, though not in the same spirit, for they felt affection towards the towns which they had pioneered. They knew too that the alternative plan of closing the mine until the price of copper rose was risky; the Wallaroo and Moonta Company, by temporarily closing down, had lost more money in keeping the mine and machinery in order than it would have lost by working at full pressure. And so Mt Lyell battled on, depleting its limited reserve of rich ore, and hoping against hope for an early rise in the price of copper.

In these crucial years profits from the company's fertilizer works, the second largest makers of superphosphate in Australia, fell sharply. The struggling wheat farmers, vexed by the high price of fertilizer, began to form large co-operatives and make their own superphosphate at cheaper prices. In 1927, in Western Australia, the company wisely united with a farmers' co-operative and formed a company called Mt Lyell Farmers' Fertilisers Ltd. Half of the farmers in the state acquired a direct interest in the new company. In Victoria, however, the Mt Lyell Co. failed to come to terms with the farmers' movement, and in self-defence had to amalgamate with other chemical works in a new company called Commonwealth Fertilisers and Chemicals Ltd.

Despite the fall in fertilizer profits the Mt Lyell Co. made more money from manufacturing than mining in most years of the 1920s. A wartime company, Metal Manufactures Ltd, which was formed in 1916 to make Australia self-sufficient in copper wire, copper sheets, brass tubes and copper alloys was the rising source of profit. After the Mt Lyell Co. had refused overtures from W. L. Baillieu to invest in the new company, it changed its mind, subscribing a quarter of the £80,000 capital, and acquiring a larger interest in the new factory at Port Kembla than the original shareholders—British Insulated Cable Co., Electrolytic Refining and Smelting Co., and the two Queensland copper companies, Mt Morgan and Hampden Cloncurry. Like all the powerful metal fabricating industries that sprang up during World War I, Metal Manufactures rapidly enlarged its plant and paid large dividends as the Australian market expanded. More important, the tariff duty on imported copper which protected the new company enabled Mt Morgan and Mt Lyell to sell it copper at a higher price than the world price.

It was more than coincidence that the rapid rise of copper manufacturing in Australia was accompanied by a decline of copper mining. The wave that lifted manufacturing was the same wave which submerged marginal mines. That wave was the tariff, which had risen from a mere billow in the first year of the Commonwealth to something like a tidal wave in the late twenties. The Mt Lyell Co. was shielded from the full impact of the rising tariff, because it eventually sold almost half of its copper to the Port Kembla factory at the higher tariff-propped price and reaped a share of the actual manufacturing profits. This advantage, however, fell short of the burden which the tariff heaped on the cost of producing the company's copper, especially that large portion sold overseas. Five leading economists, studying the effect of the policy of tariff protection on export industries in 1929, estimated that it added 10 per cent to the general cost of production. Industries such as Mt Lyell paid in effect a tax of roughly 10 per cent on the portion of their product which they sold on the world market.

Hardening of the arteries contributed to the plight of the Mt Lyell Co. The early directors were young, creative, ambitious men who seized every chance and took any risk in their zeal to increase the wealth of the company. In the early 1920s, however, the board consisted of elderly, cautious men who not only lacked the drive, but the large share interest in the company which characterized the early directorate. The growing importance of the company's manufacturing interests and the company's comparative poverty tended to cultivate conservatism and the desire for security at a time when bold plans were essential. Although Murray had pruned the dead branches, the company was not healthy.

In 1927, however, the retreat halted; the company marched forward again. It carried out two expensive projects which sliced the cost of producing copper. It built an electrolytic refinery at Queenstown, and drove a long haulage tunnel from the mill to the North Lyell mine. Looking to the future, the company resumed the long delayed search for new ore bodies.

Since 1911 the Electrolytic Refining and Smelting Co. had refined the blister copper from Mt Lyell and separated the copper, gold and silver in its works at Port Kembla. When copper mining collapsed Mt Lyell kept the works alive, paying a seventh of the cost of producing copper in refining charges. In 1926 this expense induced Murray to visit refineries in North America to see whether it would pay to build a refinery at Queenstown. He learned that Lake Margaret's cheap power would enable the company to copy the efficient refinery at the Trail works in British Columbia, which cut out the intermediate step of smelting blister copper in an anode furnace. H. Y. Eagle, sent out from New York to supervise the construction of a £75,000 refinery, drew the first cathode of copper from the precipitation tank on 12 May 1928. Henceforth, the sheets of cathode copper were shipped to Port Kembla, melted into wire bars at the refinery, and railed to the adjacent factory of Metal Manufactures. The black slime that contained gold and silver was packed in steel drums and shipped to Port Kembla for final treatment.

The North Lyell tunnel, the second project in the company's new campaign, holed through a fortnight after the first copper left the refinery. Like the refinery, the idea of a long haulage tunnel through the steep ridge that separated the Mt Lyell mine and the smelters had been suggested by Dr Peters in 1893; and like the refinery, doubts about the future postponed the plan until it was eventually forgotten. Another American optimist, Lamartine Trent, proposed a deep North Lyell tunnel. His surveyors, preparing for the day when he would seize the Queenstown smelters, designed a long tunnel that would link the smelters with the North Lyell mine. The late Pierre Chaperon, who used to travel on the footplate of a special locomotive to Kelly Basin and spend the week-end with Trent's family, owned a blueprint of the tunnel, which closely followed the route finally selected in 1926.

When Trent left the field, his plan was forgotten. For a quarter of a century, every lump of North Lyell ore was handled eight times between the underground workings and the ore bins of the smelters. A miner drilled and blasted the ore on to

Twenty-ton truck and mechanical shovel, West Lyell open cut, 1958

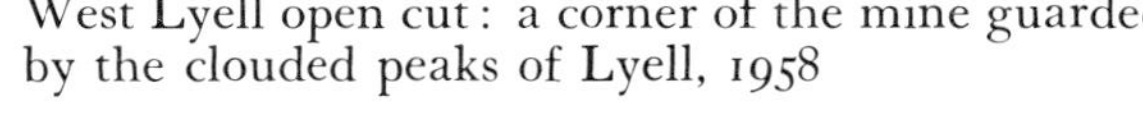

West Lyell open cut: a corner of the mine guarded
by the clouded peaks of Lyell, 1958

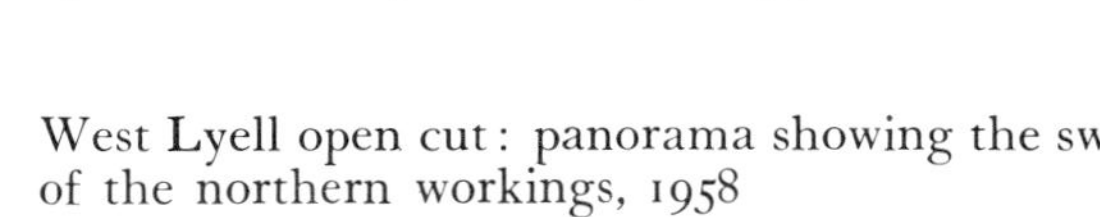

West Lyell open cut: panorama showing the sweep
of the northern workings, 1958

the ground of the stope; a labourer shovelled it down the ore pass to the drive; a 'trucker' filled his iron truck and pushed it along the rails to the cage; the engine driver hauled the cages to the surface; a horse hauled the rake of trucks along the tunnel to fresh air; a steam locomotive hauled the little trucks along the ridge to the ore bins at the top of the haulage tramway; larger trucks were filled with ore and lowered down the haulage by cable; and another steam locomotive carried it around the gully to the ore bins at the reduction works. A deep tunnel that could drain the mine and carry all the ore straight from the deep workings to the crushing plant would save a huge sum in manpower, steampower and electricity.

There was no valid reason why the tunnel should not have been constructed about 1906; but somehow the idea was not seriously considered until 1926 when it was necessary to equip the idle Blocks shaft with pumps and ore bins to facilitate the working of the deep levels of the North Lyell mine. One day G. F. Jakins, the mine superintendent, and his assistant engineer, E. Barkley, were discussing the problem when the idea of a tunnel arose. The idea was strengthened by a letter from Murray enthusing about the long transport tunnels which he was seeing in his tour of United State mines. In the meantime Jakins estimated that the scheme would pay for itself within three years, and Barkley surveyed a tunnel between the mill and the 1100' level of the mine. When Murray returned from America, he was shown plans of a tunnel that would be nine feet high, nine feet wide and, including the branches, one and a half miles long.

In 1927 'Johno' Pearton, the underground foreman, and James Hornsey, the surveyor, began to direct the driving of the tunnel. Day and night for fourteen months, men working at both ends of the tunnel slowly converged until the barrier of rock was only a few feet wide. At 2.10 a.m. on 26 May 1928 the fuses were lit for the last firing, and when the carbide lamps of the opposite miners gleamed across the pile of shattered rock there was high excitement. By mid-morning the tunnel makers were playing spectacular football, mine-end versus smelters-end, with Rafferty as referee, barrels of beer up-ended beside the goal-posts, and all the signs and trappings of a monster temperance rally. On 4 September the first electric ore train rumbled down the brightly lit tunnel, and the Queenstown miners were carried through the tunnel to their places in the mine.

When the tunnel went through the North Lyell mine was the only payable mine on the field. For years pessimists bemoaned that the days of the mine were numbered, but again and again a new drive or drill hole would find enough rich ore to quieten their fears. Now an area little larger than a city block was dissected by more than twenty-six miles of drives, levels and cross-cuts—enough to run an Olympic marathon—and probed by more than four hundred diamond drill holes, most of which penetrated the rock for hundreds of feet. The chance of finding another large ore body on the lease grew smaller every year.

If the North Lyell mine would soon be exhausted, where else could the company find ore? Professor J. W. Gregory, a geologist of renown, had said in 1903 that the chance of finding other mines as rich as North Lyell was remote. This advice and the stream of copper which continued to gush out of the deep reservoir in the North Lyell mine deterred the company from exploring for new ore bodies. In the following twenty-five years the company did virtually no prospecting outside the seven mines where large ore bodies were known to exist, spending far less money in prospecting at Mt Lyell than in searching for new mines in other parts of Tasmania.

In 1927 Dr Loftus Hills, the leading Tasmanian geologist of the day, completed the first geological survey of the field since Gregory's report. He suggested that certain areas were favourable for the deposition of ore, but the company, preferring to play safe, continued to explore those poor ore bodies, discovered in the boom. It drilled the three Tharsis mines and the Prince Lyell and found that the mines were still unpayable. There remained the idle Comstock mine which had been worked by the company for nine years and closed in the scare of 1922. It carried at least half a million tons of $3\frac{1}{4}$ per cent ore, which could be profitably treated if the price of copper was high. In 1929 a favourable price induced the company to open the mine and extend the railway which zig-zagged up a gorge of the Queen River. The small town of forty or fifty dwellings, dilapidated through years of idleness, was renovated and re-peopled.

K. A. Cameron, later the managing director of Mt Morgan, was manager of the Comstock, and old Herbert Muir, the former manager of the North Lyell mine, was his storeman. Muir's rise and fall was typical of his generation of mine managers who flocked to mining when it offered the greatest industrial career in the land, and were stranded when the industry declined. After Muir left the North Lyell mine, he fossicked around several copper mines on Mt Jukes, bagging samples of the richest ore from the dumps of the Proprietary mine and sending it by pack-horse and train to the Queenstown smelters. The cheques from the smelters were too small, and Muir crossed to the mainland, destitute but cheerful. He re-graded railway yards in Victoria, managed a gold mine in Western Australia and a copper mine in Queensland and scratched for tin in the furnace heat of the Northern Territory. In 1923, after months of unemployment, he wandered back to the old field to work as a timber-man in the mine he once managed, finally settling in the valley of the Comstock.

Muir saw the Comstock mine produce more ore in eighteen months than the North Lyell mine had produced in all the years of his management. Although the Comstock ore had to be hauled five miles to the crushing mill and was much poorer than the North Lyell ore, it yielded a substantial profit. Encouraged by this success and the low cost of using the North Lyell tunnel, the company decided to work the large deposits of $1\frac{1}{2}$ per cent ore in the Crown Lyell and Royal Tharsis mines. The mill, flotation plant and refinery were enlarged to handle the increased output, and a second power station was erected a mile below the main station at Lake Margaret. As the company treated more ore, the cost of treating each ton grew smaller; and ore which even the most ruthless promoter would have sneered at in 1900 became profitable when worked on a large scale.

The new period of expansion, beginning in 1927, lifted Mt Lyell from the rut and placed it in the forefront of Australian mining. In the years 1926-30 the company made £1 million profit and paid an average yearly dividend of 13 per cent. It treated more ore and produced more copper than ever before. As the first Australian company to use mill tailings instead of barren rock to fill the depleted workings underground, and the first company to rise a shaft, the 866 feet Royal Tharsis shaft, it led Australia in modern mining technique. The progress of the mill under the brilliant South Australian, Max E. Playford, was acclaimed by metallurgists. Thus in the world-wide depression, when the price of the red metal sank to the lowest level in history, Mt Lyell was braced for the shock, and worked at full speed, though mining at a loss.

The depression years were a heyday for underground mining at Mt lyell. In 1935, the vintage year, more than half a million tons of ore were mined underground and eleven hundred men worked in the mining department alone. Mt Lyell was the largest underground ore producer in Australia, and though dwarfed by some of the mechanized open cuts of the United States it ranked twenty-second among the world's copper producers and seventh amongst the copper companies outside America.

27

The Long Trail

When the depression hit Australia, Bowes Kelly was still coming into Collins House each Thursday morning to take his seat at the massive table in the board room. For half of his life he had been a director of the Mt Lyell Co. and now in mellow old age he was as devoted and enthusiastic as ever. In his late seventies he was an impressive old gentleman, with square shoulders which the years could not bow, snowy head, small steely eyes and closely trimmed white beard and moustache. Those who glanced at his black morning coat and his seemingly clerical collar could be excused for mistaking him for a dignified old prelate of the church; on closer acquaintance, however, his powerful handshake, his slow expressive manner of speech, his occasional mispronunciations, and his strong physique marked him more as an outback squatter.

In 1924 Kelly resigned as chairman of the board, and George Swinburne's signature replaced the lofty, rotund hand that had appeared for thirty years on the minutes of directors' meetings. Kelly continued to visit Mt Lyell whenever his health would allow, making the journey rich in the memories and landmarks of his life. He made his last journey in 1928 along the Emu Bay railway, built by the luckless company he had helped to float in the zenith of the Lyell boom; past the overgrown Chester siding that led to the deserted open cut; past the working mines of Rosebery which he had taken over before World War I; past the rusting Dundas railway and the small black slag dump which marked the site of his first large investments in the west; and so into shabby Zeehan, the derelict silver city which his speculation had originally boomed. Thirty-eight years ago in that

275

muddy main street, crowded with miners, sharebrokers, and tethered pack horses, Kelly's gaze had first fixed on the bare peaks of Mt Owen and his imagination had been fired by the story of the immense gold mine on the foothills of that mountain. And so he continued his journey past the old German smelters, now roasting the zinc ores of Hercules and Rosebery, past the deserted town of Argenton where Dr Peters had anxiously watched the smelting of the first Lyell copper in 1893, and on to the familiar railway which inspired his quarrel with Crotty.

At Mt Lyell, Kelly was eager to see the old and the new. When the power station was being built at Lake Margaret, he had insisted on scrambling up a rocky gorge to see the lake. And on his last visit to Queenstown he insisted on seeing the electrolytic refinery, though he was so infirm that he had to sit on a chair to view the new plant.

In his lifetime Kelly had two great chances to win a fortune. Broken Hill, the first chance, was a gift, but its long life and entry into steel making were not the fruits of chance. The pastoralists who controlled the mine in the 1880s, realizing that there were no silver-lead experts in Australia, made one of the most important decisions in Australian history; they went abroad for their managers, returning with Schlapp, Patton, Stewart and Delprat. The directors who shaped this policy at Broken Hill applied it with even more success at Mt Lyell. Kelly, Jamieson and Knox seized the opportunity which the Launceston company had lost, engaged more experts from the United States at salaries which amazed the parsimonious directors of other mines, and followed their advice to the letter. For two decades Mt Lyell was acclaimed as one of the most efficient mining companies in the world; and in April 1910, when the astute correspondent of the London *Times* wrote two glowing articles on the company, he confessed that he was unable to find anything important that could be criticized. 'The company', he added, 'is often said to be the best managed concern in Australia; the reports and balance sheets certainly justify this claim.'

Although Kelly and his friends owed much to excellent management, they owed more to their passion for gambling. They gambled for profit and they gambled for pleasure, playing two-up with gold sovereigns and much laughter at the close of the weekly board meeting. With wealthy mines in their control such inveterate gamblers could have easily rigged share prices and sold out in the boom, but they resisted the temptation. Kelly, to his credit, was far more interested in developing new mines than in playing the share market. In Tasmania alone he invested heavily in risky mines at Zeehan, Dundas, Rosebery, Mt Read, Derby, Balfour, King Island, Mt Lyell, and the cement works at Maria Island, all enterprises in which the chance of failure was strong. A man who chanced poverty in promoting industries that gave employment, directly and indirectly, to tens of thousands of people, in an age when governments were not great employers of labour, deserved great riches; and the old saying 'fortune favours the brave' was true for most of Kelly's life. In his last years, however, he must have lost heavily. At his death in October 1930 he owned a mere fraction of his former wealth, his chief possession being 'Moorakyne', a dilapidated but ornate Italian-style mansion next to the old Government House in Glenferrie Road, Melbourne.

Bowes Kelly served longest on the board of the company, but seven other men were directors for twenty years or more. William Jamieson, a Scottish migrant who was a jackeroo on a sheep station and a government surveyor until the Broken Hill Proprietary mine handed him a succession of four-figure dividends and the position of first general manager, joined the board of the Mt Lyell Co. in 1893 and served until his death in 1926. Lindsay Tulloch, the company's last Tasmanian director, and one-time director of the Mt Lyell Gold Mining Company, died in 1918 after twenty-one years' service. Colin Templeton, Melbourne accountant and an original member of the famous Adelaide Prospecting Syndicate which pegged out a huge area of Kalgoorlie, including the three richest mines, was elected to the board in 1912 and served for twenty-eight years. The same length of service was given by P. C. Holmes Hunt, who, like his predecessor, George S. Swinburne, was an Englishman who had come to Melbourne as a gasworks engineer; Hunt was chairman when he died in 1941. K. M. Niall, pastoralist, one-time mining engineer and son of a former chairman of Mt Morgan, succeeded Hunt as chairman, and at his death in 1953 was in his twenty-fifth year as director. D. York Syme, a shipowner who joined the board a year before Bowes Kelly died, served for thirty-three years; and Sir Robert Knox, whose father sat on the board with Bowes Kelly, has been a director for twenty-six years. Thus Kelly's record still stands.

One of Kelly's cherished schemes which was not completed in his lifetime was a road linking Hobart and the west coast. After 1897, when he began to spend much of the summer at 'Norton Mandeville', his newly-acquired pastoral property in the Gretna district, a hundred miles across the moutains from Mt Lyell, he found that to reach the mines, he either had to make an unpleasant steamer trip from Hobart to Strahan or make the tiring journey from Hobart to Queenstown on four different railway systems, a 380-mile journey that took thirty-five and a half hours. He became a strong advocate for a road or railway from Hobart to the west, and although private railway syndicates died his enthusiasm did not languish.

Long after motor vehicles were competing with railways throughout Australia, railways remained the only means of inland communication on the west coast. At the end of 1921 Australia had seventy-five motor vehicles for each 5,000 people, but the 5,000 people on the Lyell field had only one solitary van, which had to be loaded on a railway truck to leave the district. The old overland trails that fanned out from Mt Lyell were narrow, winding corduroy tracks, bad for pack-horses or small drays and utterly useless for motor vehicles. The railway to Strahan remained the only link with distant civilization, and the arrival of the evening train with mails and papers and passengers was always greeted ceremoniously by railway officials in braided uniforms and a large crowd of curious sightseers.

In 1918 Hobart businessmen agitated for a road to Queenstown, and their arguments were echoed at large meetings on the west coast. At Queenstown indignant speakers declared that their town, economically and socially, was a suburb of Melbourne, and that it was cheaper and quicker to travel from Queenstown to Melbourne than to Hobart. They insisted that the west coast would remain the lost province of Tasmania until a road was built across the mountains. But Jimmy Campbell, a notorious demagogue who used to lean a ladder against his tumble-down shop in Orr Street and clamber on to the roof to address passersby on the events of the day, scorned the idea of a road. 'We want no dog track', he shouted. 'If the government refuses to build a railway, the citizens of Queenstown should secede from Tasmania and become part of the Federal Territory.' Although few people supported this threat, the storm of protests forced the government to authorize preliminary surveys of the road.

Colin Pitt, the government surveyor, finally chose with a few small deviations the route which the late T. B. Moore had selected for a road from Lake St Clair to the mines of Heemskirk in 1883. But years elapsed between the first survey and the commencement of work, and Jimmy Campbell nearly tumbled off his roof as he excitedly voiced the anger of the west coast. In 1928 work on the road began in leisurely fashion and by February 1930, 240 men were camped along the route between Derwent Bridge and Lyell. A year later the Hobart *Mercury* was delivered in Queenstown on the day of publication for the first time in history, after a party of motorists had walked twenty-two miles through mud and snow to bridge the gap between the roads. On 19 November 1932 the fifty-one mile gravel road was officially opened at the King River bridge, three miles from Linda, and the sense of utter isolation that had dominated the people of Lyell for a generation almost vanished. The new road enabled passenger buses to travel the 159 miles from Queenstown to Hobart in seven hours, and it enabled road freighters to snatch a part of the Melbourne-Strahan trade which was once carried on by ship; but it possibly destroyed some of the friendly spirit and community liveliness that acute isolation bred.

In February 1937, after heated regional rivalry, reminiscent of the railway war, had been voiced in Parliament, the government completed a twenty-mile road which skirted the Great Lake to the west coast road and gave Launceston direct communication with Queenstown. In October 1937 a twenty-six mile road from Queenstown to Strahan was opened, and four years later Queenstown and Zeehan were linked by road.

By World War II old inhabitants of the west coast were lamenting that the character of the region was deteriorating. They continued to express their wonderment that someone could leave Queenstown one morning, return the next evening, and announce that he had just been to Hobart. 'You certainly get round', was the kind of congratulatory comment they made; and they would follow it up with eager questions about the journey which made the traveller feel that he had just crossed the world rather than the island. On the other hand newcomers to the west coast did not share in the wonderment; to them the region was still isolated. If they drove a car into the west coast, they had to drive back the way they had come— along a narrow, gravel road winding through the forest. If they set out from Melbourne—and the financial and commercial ties with Melbourne were still strong—they found that the easiest and quickest way to visit Mt Lyell was virtually the old way: the overnight steamship from Melbourne to Burnie, the Emu Bay railway from Burnie to Zeehan, and the direct road, opened in 1941, across the ranges from Zeehan to Queenstown. If they wished to visit Rosebery or Williamsford or Tullah, they had to go on the old railways; no road led into these mining towns.

The real advantage of motor vehicles over locomotives was their potential mobility. Whereas the locomotive needed expensive permanent way and rails, the motor vehicle normally needed an inexpensive road. On the west coast, however, dense forest and mountainous terrain and fast streams and rivers made the making of roads a costly task. Moreover, the sparseness of population, indeed the slow decline of population, gave the Tasmanian government no sharp incentive to spend a lot of money on building roads through lonely forest. The effect of motor vehicles on the west coast was therefore relatively slow, with one strong exception. In large open cuts the motor vehicles had an overpowering advantage over the old railway or horse tram that had once been essential. Railway tracks in an open cut would easily be damaged by the daily blasting, but the rough road which motor vehicles used in an open cut could withstand the pummelling or be easily repaired. Motor lorries in an open cut had a flexibility which the rail-bound locomotives could never attain, and lorries could also climb steep hills or make sharp turns that would have vanquished a locomotive. Thus, when Mt Lyell turned again to open-cut mining in the 1930s, motor vehicles were capable of tilting the scales from loss to profit.

28

Mining in the Mist

The old town of North Lyell straggled along Philosopher's Ridge and looked out, in fine weather, on the thin sheet of ocean in the west and the white lighthouse on Cape Sorell. In pride of place stood Long and Sidler's eighteen-roomed hotel, a rambling, wooden building with a tarred roof held firm against the wind by rocks blasted from neighbouring mines. The lights of the bar shone long into the night and welcomed the miners in their wet blueys as they came off shift, swinging their lamps down the track from the northern mines. Around the hotel were stores, butchers, bakery, barber, surgery, school, post office, stables, boarding houses and several hundred galvanized iron huts, tents and bag humpies. The town was surrounded by mines, of which the nearest was the small South Tharsis quarry; and when the bell tolled for the daily blasting people hurried for shelter before the flying stones began to drum on nearby roofs.

Forty years later the huge terraces of the largest metalliferous mine in Australia would slice into the ridge for half a mile to the south and skim the top off the old Lyell Tharsis mine to the north; and the administrative and assay offices, machine shop, blacksmiths' forges and change house of the new mine would stand in the heart of the deserted town, on ground still littered with broken bottles from 'Paddy' Long's hotel.

This transformation of the landscape was the long delayed result of tunnels driven by a London company, Copper Mines of Mount Lyell West, whose seventy-acre lease stretched from the southern outskirts of the town to the overburden dumps at the Mt Lyell mine. The first manager of West Lyell was Bowes

Kelly's younger brother, Aloysius, who directed in intensive search for an extension of the Mt Lyell ore body; a few yards north of the haulage line are the rail-covered shaft and rotten boiler which mark the site of this unsuccessful quest. Moving to the head of Zeplin's Gully, a quarter of a mile to the north, the company drove the Russell tunnel westward into Philosopher's Ridge. At 729 feet the miners discovered a body of grey copper ore, which averaged 2.35 per cent copper in the following 150 feet.

In December 1900 Charles McCulloch presided over the annual meeting of Copper Mines of Mount Lyell West in London, and in a speech that was a welcome contrast to the optimism or trickery of the average company report of that era frankly admitted that the Russell ore body was 'absolutely unworkable by itself', although it might be smelted profitably with other ores. Even this humble claim was doubted at Mt Lyell, where the extravagance of the company and the boasts of Ogilvie, a jolly champagne-loving giant of seventeen stone who had succeeded Kelly as manager, made the West Lyell workings more an object of amusement than serious discussion. Thus when Ogilvie attended a meeting of the directors of the Mt Lyell Co. in Melbourne and offered to sell his company's mine for £60,000, he was greeted with expressions of amazement. As Alfred Mellor said, relating the interview to Sticht: 'The value placed upon the property was a decided staggerer to the Board'. When Ogilvie justified his price by claiming that there were 300,000 tons of 3 per cent ore in the West Lyell leases, the directors, believing that the leases held only scattered patches of poor ore, again exchanged smiles of incredulity.

So Ogilvie vanished and West Lyell sold no ore, abandoning its leases in 1913. These leases served as useful ground for dumping mullock from the Blow, and in time of drought the Kelly shaft watered the boilers in the adjacent compressor house. Meanwhile the shabby settlement at North Lyell, having survived the fire which destroyed its two-storied hotel in 1905, and having out-lived the companies which had tried to evict it from their leases, fell prey during World War I to a violent gale which spread-eagled half of the buildings far down the Linda Valley.

In 1927, when the efficiency of the flotation mill made poorer ores payable, the Mt Lyell Co. explored the low-grade deposits of copper known to exist on the leases of the old Comstock, Prince Lyell and three Tharsis companies, but did not touch the Russell tunnel. As the West Lyell Company sold no ore and allowed no journalists or strangers to inspect its workings, old employees of the Mt Lyell Co. thought that the company had found no ore. Even when L. K. Hudspeth, secretary of the mine office, handed Murray a small red book describing a large body of low-grade ore in the West Lyell lease, the general manager, treasuring memories of Ogilvie's optimism in the bars of Gormanston, naturally dismissed the book as boom-time journalism.

In November 1933, however, five years after the low-grade mines had been explored and were sending ore to the mill, the forgotten workings were rediscovered. The possibility of quarrying a large deposit of 1 per cent ore in the Prince Lyell lease on the western fall of the ridge prompted the engineers to investigate whether the Prince Lyell ore extended as far east as the Russell tunnel. Like all long abandoned workings in wet country, the tunnel mouth was partly blocked by mud and slurry which dammed the water to a depth of several feet. The dank-smelling tunnel was drained, and for several weeks lamps shone across the water, and the splash of gum boots and the hollow sound of hammers chipping samples from the wall echoed down the long drive. To the amazement of the mine staff, a long stretch of tunnel averaged $2\frac{1}{2}$ per cent copper, suggesting an ore body similar in size and richer in copper than the adjacent Royal Tharsis mine. Ogilvie's name was redeemed at last.

To explore this new ore body the company drove south from No. 1 level of the Royal Tharsis mine and broke into the workings of the old Russell tunnel. A stope was opened up in the heart of the West Lyell ore body, and by the winter of 1934 ore was being trucked back along the drive to the Royal Tharsis ore pass for delivery to the mill. Meanwhile a long, inclined diamond drill hole, bored up from the Russell tunnel, indicated that the ore persisted to the surface.

The mine officials now realized that much of the ore body

could be mined cheaply in a large open cut, and in order to design the mine they divided the known copper-bearing area into squares of fifty feet, boring shallow test holes at the corner of each square. On this bare, rocky, undulating ridge, littered with patches of black peat and charred stumps, the only level ground above the Russell tunnel was the old North Lyell cricket pitch, and here the first holes were bored. The mosaic of drill holes revealed that a large area of copper-bearing ground, larger than the Mt Lyell mine in surface dimensions, lay just below the thin layer of peat and gravel. In September 1934 the company knew that a million tons of $2\frac{1}{4}$ per cent copper lay above the Russell tunnel—enough to begin a shallow open cut. Miners began to break the ore, and men shovelled it into small motor trucks which ran along an old railway formation to the Royal Tharsis shaft. To September 1935, West Lyell produced 60,000 tons of 1.86 per cent copper, of which 16,000 tons had been mined in the short-lived underground workings.

Great riches were not expected of the new mine. It might prolong the company's life for three or four years and they would be very profitable years if the company did not spend too much on mechanical open-cut equipment. To save heavy capital expenditure the company hired a fleet of three-ton Ford trucks from Perpetual Trustees in Hobart and transferred a one-yard electric shovel from the Crown Lyell mullock quarry. This primitive equipment dwarfed the wheelbarrows and horse-drawn trams which hauled ore in the old Mt Lyell open cut and in 1936 it handled 345,766 tons of ore, nineteen thousand more than the Blow yielded in its busiest year. Within two years the output had leapt to 825,236 tons, which, added to the underground output, made Mt Lyell the first metalliferous mining company in Australia to mine a million tons of ore in a year.

Between 1935 and 1938 the average grade of West Lyell ore fell from 1.73 per cent to 1.15 per cent copper. This sharp decline was partly due to the tendency of the ore body to be poorer below the zone of surface-enriched ore, but more to the policy of enlarging the open cut to include poorer deposits of ore. A rise in the price of copper made the 1 per cent copper ore in the Prince Lyell lease payable, and to mine this ore as part of the existing open cut a large intervening deposit of poorer ore had to be removed. And so the mine grew deeper and wider. New terraces or benches were blasted out of the hillside, and old plans were abandoned as the mine assumed dimensions which no one had predicted in 1934.

The company rapidly mechanized the mine to handle the huge output. Three-ton trucks gave way to five-ton trucks, and these were replaced by ten-ton trucks, which in turn were scrapped for nineteen-ton semi-trailers. Caterpillar-tracked shovels which lifted one cubic yard of rock were replaced by shovels capable of lifting two and a half cubic yards. In 1943, when 1,372,000 tons of ore were mined, eight mechanical shovels, nineteen trucks and two bulldozers worked day and night, while a fleet of seven buses carried workmen to the mine.

As a copper producer West Lyell reached a pinnacle in the three years, 1941-2-3, when its annual production exceeded ten thousand tons of pure copper—far more than any other mine on the field had produced in a year. In these war years, when Australia for a time was desperately short of copper, the company concentrated all its machinery on the richest parts of the ore body and curtailed its campaign of removing the waste rock. Once the available rich ore was exhausted, the open cut began to wilt. At the end of the war the ore body above the Russell tunnel had been robbed of its richest ore, the average grade of the ore had fallen to 0.59 per cent, and the company had made a loss on its mining operations for the year 1945. The life of the field was endangered.

The company carefully reviewed the situation and concluded that the mine had a reserve of thirty-four million tons of low-grade ore, averaging about 0.7 per cent copper and sufficient to last for twenty years. To secure this ore the company must remove eight million tons of overburden or waste rock that surrounded the ore body—a long task that would increase the cost of mining at the very time when a substantial reduction in costs was essential for survival. Obviously the mine had to be streamlined to handle the greater tonnage of rock and handle it efficiently. The directors, not deterred by a bank overdraft of £600,000, ordered expensive heavy equipment—a fleet of trucks and bulldozers and a huge jaw crusher that could instantly crush four-ton boulders into rocks measuring less than a foot in diameter. Miners began to push the abandoned upper benches further into barren rock to make room for new benches at depth.

In 1949 the company began a second and greater mechanization drive that infused even more efficiency into the mine at a time when rising costs could have crippled the enterprise. G. F. Hudspeth, the mine superintendent, inspected open cuts in the United States, and on his advice the company began to spend heavily on mechanized equipment that could mine even more cheaply. The barren rock that had to be moved to enable the company to get to the copper ore was moved in increasing quantities. In 1945 one ton of waste rock had been mined for every five tons of ore; in 1953 nearly five tons of waste rock were mined for every five tons of ore, and £478,000 was spent on mining waste rock alone. Within eight years the annual output of mined rock had grown from 1.7 million to 2.8 million tons and huge dumps of mullock had buried many of the gullies that ran down from the mine.

The new machinery which enabled the company to remove a huge tonnage of overburden had transformed the open cut by the early 1950s. The small shovels had gone, and five-yard shovels towered in their place like long necked dinosaurs, and scooped jagged boulders weighing five tons into their buckets. The long low semi-trailers had gone; and twenty-two American Euclids, shod with tyres as high as a man, made a deafening roar as they bounced and swayed along the roads to the crusher or the dumps. The miner, hanging on his rope and working the rock face with bar or jack-hammer, had vanished; and his younger brother stood in the cab of a clanking, tall-masted churn drill or travelled around the mine in a compressor wagon, drilling outsize boulders dislodged by the firing of the churndrill holes. The small army of mechanics, welders and blacksmiths now worked in a grey building as large as a city hall, an engineer's lotus land, with a long line of grease pits and lathes and forges so modern that the old garage on the hill seemed like a grimy barn by contrast. And old Bill Lyden, whose famous fight precipitated the strike of 1911, no longer plodded with his gang through the mist. He retired in 1953, and his modern

The ore pass at the open cut

The reduction works, with Mt Owen on the skyline and Sticht's black slag dump on the right

counterpart drove around the mine in a truck and talked to his foreman by wireless.

The open cut by then was shaped like a huge semi-circular amphitheatre 3,700 feet long and 2,000 feet wide at its greatest dimensions and consisting of seven wide benches rising in steps of forty or fifty feet. The mine was an ever-changing landscape. In winter, it was a quagmire of pools and small lakes; in summer, a pattern of white, dusty roads; in creeping mist, a gloomy prison surrounded by wall upon wall of grey rock; in sunlight, as bright as a painting by Picasso with splashes of grey, yellow, fawn, brown, orange and mauve in many shades; at night, a dark hollow that was partly lit by the scattered lights of churn drills, shovels and trucks, and far dimmer than the orange lights of Queenstown shining in the valley.

It was little short of a revolution that tough, schistose ore carrying only 0.6 per cent copper could be worked at a small profit; for similar ore that carried three times as much copper was hopelessly unpayable forty years before. Mechanical equipment had slashed the comparative cost of mining; the development of grinding machinery and the flotation process reduced dramatically the cost of extracting the copper; and the exhaustion of the world's small, rich mines and the growing demand for copper in an electrical age made it profitable to mine huge deposits of low-grade ore. Even with these factors making poor ore payable, this large body of 0.6 per cent would have repelled any company if Mt Lyell had been an uninhabited wilderness. A new company might have spent £20,000,000 on reduction works, mining equipment, machine shops, houses, railway, hydro-electric station and technical skill before it was ready to produce a ton of copper, and then the mine might never have repaid the investors. The Mt Lyell Co., however, had all these advantages and was therefore in a strong position to work the lowest-grade copper mine in the world.

While the drills were probing beneath the mountain ridge and rediscovering the West Lyell ore body, a new phase was dawning in the metallurgical history of the field. Since 1916 a grimy Dwight Lloyd sintering plant had stood alongside the smelter flue, roasting much of the sulphur from the copper concentrate. In all copper reduction works, sintering was the intermediate step between flotation and smelting. It turned powdery concentrate that looked like sloppy cement into small black lumps, and in this form the concentrate melted quickly in the furnace instead of being blown as dust up the chimney stack by the intense heat and air pressure.

In 1934 the problem of replacing the dilapidated sintering plant prompted R. M. Murray, after consultation with the smelter superintendent, to experiment by mixing lumps of sinter with the concentrate and tipping the lot into the furnace. They gradually increased the proportion of concentrate until it exceeded the sinter. A quarter of the copper concentrate was blown out of the furnace and along the brick flue leading two hundred yards uphill to the foot of the chimney stack. Eventually, a dust-collecting apparatus devised by the company's small research team became so efficient that only two and a half of the fifty-two tons of valuable fluedust escaped up the chimney each twenty-four hours. The sintering plant closed down in 1934, and was shipped to the Wiluna goldfield in Western Australia.

In a less sensational manner the abolition of sintering repeated Sticht's bold experiment of 1896, both in the exact technical nature of the change and in the way in which it defied the accepted axioms of metallurgy. It not only saved the high cost of replacing the sintering plant and the daily cost of sintering, it also reduced the coke bill by using as fuel in the furnace the sulphur previously discharged in the sintering plant. The return to semi-pyritic smelting and the successful smelting of a wet concentrate into a matte of 40 to 45 per cent copper made the furnace one of the most efficient in the world. Nevertheless, it is a freak process and when D. H. Wilsdon, the present metallurgist, went around the world to investigate smelting techniques he found widespread disbelief that a blast furnace could smelt such a puggy concentrate without serious trouble.

While the sintering plant was being scrapped the company's metallurgist successfully extracted pyrite from the waste sludge that flowed from the flotation plant into the river. This grey moist powder, averaging 48 per cent sulphur, became an important product and by 1938 the company was producing 50,000 tons annually for export to the fertilizer works in Melbourne. When war was declared, and raw sulphur from Italy became unprocurable and imports from the United States declined, Mt Lyell's pyritic concentrate proved a valuable substitute and would have proved even more valuable but for the problem of transport; during and after the war, while farmers were desperate for superphosphate, a stockpile of sulphur lay in huge rain-washed dumps at Queenstown and Strahan, awaiting transport to the mainland. Later, improvements to the Mt Lyell railway and the wharves at Strahan, and an improved shipping service opened the bottleneck.

Curiously, the vital changes launched in 1934—the production of pyrite for the making of fertilizer, the return to semi-pyritic smelting, and the opening of the big open cut—were all revivals in new garb of the company's practices of the early 1900s. They were soon followed by another vital change—the decline of the underground mines which had been the chief vaults of the copper since the first years of the century. The scarcity of miners accelerated their decline. The North Lyell mine, the prize of the field, declined rapidly from 1938; Crown Lyell was closed in 1942; and two years later the Comstock mine was closed by the shortage of skilled miners and the expense of hauling the ore on a narrow-gauge railway down a long, winding gorge.

The resignation of 'Johno' Pearton in 1944 heralded the end of the underground era at Lyell. He was almost a legend in Australian mining. He was blue-eyed, bald, semi-literate, tough, aggressive, rum-loving, and fond of a brawl in a pub even in his sixties. A miner of the old school, he had a wonderful knowledge of practical mining, an uncanny eye for dangerous ground, arms of steel that had won him many hammer-and-drill contests in the Linda Valley forty years earlier, and an overpowering personality that won for him the self-styled position of underground manager. In the stopes, in a temper, he would throw his hat on the ground and stamp on it; in danger he was quiet and self-possessed, a born leader whose courage made him a hero of the North Lyell disaster and the right-hand man of R. M. Murray thereafter.

Russell Mervyn Murray retired in the same year as Pearton,

and his career was even more a mirror of the way mining had changed on the field. He had come to Mt Lyell in 1900 when the company was predominantly engaged in quarrying ore; as mine manager from 1906 to 1922 he had personally been responsible for developing the biggest group of underground mines in Australia; and then as general manager from 1922 to 1944 he had completed the cycle by directing the swing from underground back to open-cut mining. He retired just when the annual underground output, which had exceeded 500,000 tons less than a decade previously, had slipped to 100,000 tons.

He had guided the company through times that were more difficult though less spectacular than Sticht's. While Sticht deservedly had an international reputation as an innovator, it was Murray who made more drastic changes in the operations at Mt Lyell. Indeed, in the early 1920s his efforts had probably saved the field from closing, and once closed it is doubtful if it would have been reopened for many years if at all. Most employees of the company, especially the old ones, sensed this and displayed unusual gratitude and affection when they met him around the plant.

Murray had acute arthritis in his last years and could only walk with the aid of sticks; he died in January 1945, only four months after his retirement, at 'Penghana', the general manager's house at Queenstown. He was aged sixty-six, the same age as his successor, Arthur Howard Prichard Moline. Both Moline and Murray had been born in western Victoria, had studied civil engineering at the University of Melbourne, and as young engineers in the early 1900s had both lived at Gormanston. But unlike Murray, who had spent his mining career with the one company, Moline had the wandering career typical of the mining engineers of his generation. He had managed many small ventures including the Y-Water tin mine at Emmaville in New England, the well known Cocks Pioneer gold and tin workings at Eldorado in north-eastern Victoria, and the Taranaki oilfield in New Zealand, before returning in 1931 as Murray's assistant after an absence of some twenty years from the field. Moline was general manager for four years, retiring when he was over seventy. He was to be prominent in the uranium boom of the early 1950s, and it was fitting that a man who had been king in so many mining towns should in old age have a mining town named after him—Moline in the Northern Territory.

The new general manager was Hugh M. Murray, eldest son of R. M. Murray. Born at North Lyell when his father was the young mine manager, Hugh Murray passed through the University of Melbourne and on to the research laboratory at the company's flotation plant in 1929. He became mill superintendent in 1935, general superintendent in 1944 and general manager in 1948. He won recognition as one of the nation's leading mining men in 1952 when he was selected as sole representative of the mining industry on the Atomic Energy Commission.

When Hugh Murray took office the West Lyell open cut was dominating the field, and the underground mines were the haven for a small band of ageing men who much preferred a miner's light to sunlight and a roof overhead to the sky overhead. In 1949 even the magnificent North Lyell, the greatest of the underground mines, ceased to produce. Since its discovery by the roadmakers just over half a century previously, it had yielded more than 4,900,000 tons of ore averaging 5.5 per cent copper and carrying in all 252,000 tons of copper. James Crotty had no idea that it was to prove such a rich mine; even the original North Lyell Co. in its last months of independence had no idea of the value of the mine whose wealth it was squandering, and in fact nineteen of every twenty tons of ore that came from the mine had not even been discovered when the Mt Lyell Co. took over the mine in 1903.

The Royal Tharsis was now the only underground mine and employed about one hundred men at the time of its closing. In 1954, for the first time in more than sixty years, no underground mine was working on the field. All that could be heard in the vast warren of old workings was the dripping of water and the occasional creaking of timber, and those eerie sounds were magnified by the surrounding silence.

29

Decay and Boom

Mining is full of the unexpected, of sudden wealth and rapid decay. All mining fields must eventually die and most old men of the west knew this from bitter experience. In seventy years they had seen populous towns rise with all the airs and signs of permanence and then collapse so completely that only the tombstones remained. Kelly Basin, Crotty, Argenton, Balfour, Mt Read, Ringville, Darwin, North Lyell, Trial Harbour, Magnet, Heemskirk, Teepookana and Dundas were wiped from the map; Corinna and Lynchford had only a few families; Zeehan, Linda, Strahan, Gormanston, Williamsford and Waratah were mere shadows of their former selves; and numerous small towns had vanished and left no trace of their shanties, store or pub. Of the western towns, only Queenstown and Rosebery withstood the passage of time.

Indeed, without an element of luck, the Lyell field might have perished in one of the many crises. Sticht thought in 1897 that the field would probably outlive his own life. In 1904, however, the Mt Lyell mine was so impoverished that he thought that two or three years would see the end of the field. In 1908 vistas of long life were opened in the deep levels of the North Lyell mine, and this optimism lasted until, shortly before his death, the crash in copper prices heralded the most dangerous crisis of all. In the 1930s the world-wide depression and the accompanying dip in copper prices again endangered the mines. A few years later the declining reserve of rich ore in the underground mines would have threatened the life of the field but for the discovery of the shallow low-grade copper of West Lyell. And at the end of World War II the poverty of the West Lyell copper and the areas of barren rock that surrounded and over-laid it threatened the field again. A local business man or house-owner did not have to be neurotic to envisage, during this suc-cession of crises, that Queenstown might easily become a sleep-ing village either haunted by pensioners or quite deserted before the close of the twentieth century. It was easy to imagine the time when visitors would walk up the overgrown railway track and, standing on the broken arches of the Empire Hotel, see the shadows move across the black dump of slag and the stumps of the chimney stacks, and see the evening sunlight gleaming on the mountain of mullock that surrounded the deserted mines.

The streets showed the scars of the ups and downs. In the 1890s Queenstown had emerged swiftly from a valley of snake-infested swamp and forest into a town of 5,500 people, with hotels and banks and halls that would not have seemed out of place in a provincial city. In the following decade the smelters and quarries dispensed with hundreds of men, and the town's population had fallen to 3,700 by 1911. The decline accelerated after World War I; and men who knew the town in 1900 and returned twenty-five years later found that the population had nearly halved, that many shops and hotels had closed and hun-dreds of houses and huts had disappeared leaving a scattered town with many vacant lots and walls that were shabby with peeling paint. The vigour of the underground mines during the depression of the 1930s revived the town, increasing the popula-tion by 1,200 in seven years and enabling it to displace Burnie for a few years as Tasmania's fourth largest town. Then came the war and the population slipped back to 3,500, recovering to 4,400 in 1952.

Queenstown at least had a stability that the mining towns on the other side of the ridge could not match. By 1950 they held less than one-quarter of the population which they held in 1910. The town of North Lyell was no more; Linda was little more than a name; and wind and fire left Gormanston with a few shops, one hotel, the old miners' hall, post office, school, fire station and less than five hundred people—a mere mountain outpost of Queenstown. The Queenstown miners once walked for more than an hour through all weathers to reach their mines; later the North Lyell tunnel, the Comstock tram and then the motor buses enabled them to reach the mines as quickly as the men from Gormanston. And so the mining valley, having gloomier surroundings, a worse climate, and an inferior social life, could not halt the exodus when its one advantage of proximity to the mines was overcome. In 1950 what remained of Gormanston was freshly painted, though it took more than paint to offset the bare rocky valley and the predominance of galvanized iron that sent a shudder down the spine of the passing tourist.

The stranger who passes through the Linda Valley now sees nothing but mullock tips to suggest that the bare hills once enfolded a famous mining field. But up the gullies and out of sight of the road are scores of old tunnels and waterlogged shafts; eroding tram formations and narrow pack tracks, silted water races and broken concrete walls, and hundreds of small excavations which mark the site of the miner's huts. Embedded in dirt and clay are rotting lease pegs, rusty mining steel, beer bottles, patent medicine bottles, and purple cordial bottles with glass marbles as stoppers. The wreckage lies thickest in the creek between the North Lyell mine and the site of the Blocks, where the chaos of smashed bricks, rusting iron, and wrecked trolleys seems like the ruins of war.

The old Mt Lyell open cut is the most impressive scar in the valley with its sheer jagged wall of multi-coloured rock. The mouth of the tunnel which produced the silver bonanza is still visible, and the adjacent cutting where the little mill stamped for gold is a graveyard of overturned ore trucks. The lowest tunnel where the men walked to the shaft is blocked with silt and rubble, and the concrete change house where hundreds of men gathered each afternoon at the changing of the shift is a crumbling roofless ruin.

On the west coast today a bushwalker venturing far from the roads would be entitled to think he was penetrating virgin forest until, suddenly, he came across the remains of an abandoned railway. At many hidden points are earthen railway platforms with thick scrub growing where once people waited for trains, deep railway cuttings that nourish trees nearly as tall as the cuttings, and the charred stumps of bridges that once carried trains over deep gorges. As late as 1906 the western network of eleven railways, eight of which were privately owned, formed one of the most comprehensive transport systems of any region in Australia. By the late 1950s only four of those railways were still working. Today only one railway remains and even part of that has been abandoned.

The railway from Mt Lyell to the bay at Strahan had probably been busier in the 1950s, on the eve of its death, than ever before. The traffic in pyrite from the smelters to the coast was so heavy that it taxed the railway's capacity. One cause of inefficiency was the old Abt locomotives, which could haul 110 tons along most of the railway to Strahan but only 60 tons up the cogged Abt section. Accordingly from 1953 the company used English diesel locomotives to haul loads of 150 tons on the half of the line nearest the port. Though the passenger traffic on the line was now trifling, with barely a dozen paying passengers in some weeks, the pyritic concentrate filled about twenty trains a week. In addition much of the company's copper was railed to Strahan, and the returning trains carried coke, explosives, and general supplies.

Diesel locomotives revolutionized the mountain railway. They could not hope, however, to defeat motor trucks if ever the winding road from Queenstown to Strahan were widened, straightened, and sealed. In 1963 the Tasmanian government began to remake that road and the railway was doomed. On Saturday, 29 June 1963, the company's first Abt locomotive, which had been running on the railway since 1896, drew the last passenger train from Queenstown to the music of its own whistle and the Queenstown Pipe Band. The last goods train ran on 2 August. Most of the rails were pulled up, the railway yard at Queenstown was converted into a carpark for the company's new self-service store, some of the rolling stock was given to historical societies and museums, and all the railway employees were transferred to other jobs. The Mt Lyell Mining and Railway Company did not change its seventy-year-old name; it became one of the few railway companies that owned no railway.

Some of the railwaymen were taught how to drive a truck and placed at the wheel of the small fleet which the company placed on the Strahan road. Sly critics thought it was suicidal

to allow on to a public highway men who had spent their working life on a railway that averaged only fifteen miles an hour
in its fastest years. Moreover they were let loose on a road that
was still being remade, was muddy in winter and dusty in
summer, and required four hundred changes of gear on each
return trip. The danger of meeting a railwayman driving a
truckload of explosives on a skidding road aroused a lot of
conjecture in Queenstown, but by April 1966 the trucks on that
road had travelled one million miles without an accident.

Queenstown, like Albury or Kalgoorlie, had been a break-of-
gauge railway junction. Alongside the 3′ 6″ track was a network
of 2′ gauge which carried ores, fluxes, coke, and firewood to the
smelters. These narrow railways at Queenstown once gave work
to 450 wagons and nine small locomotives, mostly Krauss
locomotives from Munich and distinguished by a spark catcher
resembling a Turkish mosque. The surviving sections of narrow
track were also dismantled in 1963, leaving only the narrow
tramway on which a rail motor ran to the isolated Lake Margaret power station; even that was replaced by a road in 1964.
In 1964 the company estimated that it was saving about
£140,000 a year by changing from railways to roads.

Meanwhile the small port of Strahan had lost its other railway, the dilapidated government line which had run to Zeehan
for more than sixty years; the railway had been lately menaced
by drifting sand near the surf of the Southern Ocean but had
been menaced even longer by an absence of passengers and freight.
Zeehan, soon after losing its line to Strahan, lost its private line
to Burnie when the old Emu Bay Railway Company moved its
northern terminus from Zeehan to Rosebery in the early 1960s.
Then with the closing of the Farrell silver-lead mine at Tullah
and the dismantling of the little Farrell railway, the Emu Bay
lost the last of the many railways which had fed it with traffic.
Could the Emu Bay survive? It had never seemed likely to be
the one railway that would survive. What strength it possessed
seemed to come from its freedom from road competition and
that freedom was increasingly challenged. In 1953 a road from
Zeehan reached Rosebery and the Emu Bay railway lost its
monopoly of communications with the only busy mining town
which it now served. In 1964 the new Murchison highway

linked the west coast and Burnie on the north coast, and captured much of the passenger and goods traffic from the Emu Bay. A year later, however, the railway dramatically dismissed the predictions that the new road would kill it by paying its first dividend to ordinary shareholders. That dividend had been so long delayed that all but a few of the original shareholders were dead, and many people who inherited shares in the company had understandably lost their share certificates and not bothered to replace them, believing that they were almost valueless. There was much advertising in Australian newspapers for lost certificates when news of the Emu Bay Railway Company's maiden dividend was announced in 1965. The heavy mineral traffic from the Rosebery zinc-lead-silver mines was still the mainstay of the railway, but diesel locomotives had achieved what the steam locomotives had never achieved—a good profit.

Curiously the decline of the railways coincided with a revival of mining on the west coast. The decade 1956-66, which saw the decay of so many of the landmarks in the region, saw also the busiest and most successful phase of mineral development since the metal boom of 1906-8. Whereas that boom affected scores of small mines and hundreds of prospecting ventures, the new boom revolved around a few big mines.

Mt Lyell continued to be the most populous and productive mining field on the west coast, and in the mid 1960s was producing more copper than ever before. In each year from June 1963 to June 1965 Mt Lyell mined more than 13,000 tons of copper, whereas in most of the post-war years output of copper had hovered around 7,000 or 8,000 tons. That expansion was aided by favourable copper prices, improved metallurgical methods, the mining of ore that carried 0.7 per cent copper compared to the 0.6 per cent ore of the 1950s, and above all by heavy investment in enlarging the open cut and the reduction works; in the year 1957-8 and thereafter the company was able to mine and treat more than two million tons of ore, a record for an Australian base-metal or gold mine though a record that was soon to be snatched by Mt Isa Mines.

The additional copper came from more machines rather than more men. Nevertheless in the 1960s Queenstown held as many people as at any time in the past and covered a larger area than ever before. New streets of houses sprang up both north and south, and they now stretched, in tight array, two miles down the narrow valley and up so many hills and gullies that only a high-altitude aerial photo could take in all the settlement. The town was so freshly painted that, from the surrounding hills, it resembled a mosaic of red roofs with odd dabs of green, blue and grey. Despite its isolation, it had all the facilities for a strong community life: eighteen halls, ranging from the old Salvation Army hall and the bookmakers' hall to the modern theatre and a lavish war memorial hall; six hotels, all large two-storied buildings more than half-a-century old, and two new motels; two radio stations and two television masts that relayed pictures from the other side of the island; a golf course on the river flats, and the churches, lodges, bands, sporting clubs, common to every Australian town.

The heart of the town had not quite lost the atmosphere of the 1890s, though new public buildings had been built in recent years. When Orr Street, the main street, was quiet or deserted, it resembled the old mining towns of the wild west of the United States, with wooden verandah posts stretching in unbroken line on each side of the road, old-fashioned shops of wood and iron, and a background of razorback hills and stark mountains walling in the town. This antique air persisted on Saturday evenings in summertime when the silver band played from a hotel balcony or the highland band paraded the streets while people lined road and pavement. But when darkness fell the neon signs began to glow, and modern cars and taxis crowded the kerbs; and the frontier town vanished in the bustle of the twentieth century.

For working men and their families Mt Lyell had long offered a high level of social security. The company had maintained full employment, cheap housing, a good standard of living, and an unrivalled health scheme; for some forty years it is doubtful if the employees in any other large Australian mining field had received such a high proportion of the wealth won from the mines. In the same period no Australian mining field had been so free from social and economic upheaval as Mt Lyell, and in that achievement the attitude of union leaders and men had been as important as the attitude of the company and its staff. Even so, the sense of security on the field could not be complete unless it was reinforced by the prospect of a long life for the mines. Local confidence in the longevity of the field came partly from the simple fact that it had lasted so long and survived so many crises; that brand of confidence was real but not entirely logical. Well-founded confidence could only come from knowledge that the field held a vast tonnage of copper ore, as yet unmined. To discover that ore was now an expensive and risky task; the ore deposits that poked their head above the ground or lay at shallow depth had presumably all been found.

Hitherto, geologists had found little payable copper at Mt Lyell, a circumstance which can be attributed as much to the failure of the company to test their theories as to the failure of the theories themselves. Only the expensive drilling programme set in 1940 by the brilliant Irish-born geologist H. J. C. Conolly was tackled with any energy; and it was not completed. Geophysical surveys had been nearly as disappointing; between 1934 and 1938 a large area was tested with a method capable of detecting sulphide ore bodies and mineralized areas lying fifty or sixty feet below the surface. The presence of too much iron pyrites in the ground impaired that survey and a later survey near the Comstock mine. Even so, it yielded a low-grade ore body which takes its name from the discoverer E. L. Blazey and is mined in the West Lyell open cut.

In this century Mt Lyell lived basically on the discoveries of the previous century. It worked out the rich ore bodies, then turned to the poorer ore discarded by the small companies after the boom. With the exception of the New Development Ore Body in the North Lyell mine—a discovery which was assured once the main North Lyell ore body was being worked—no important ore body was found in the half-century after 1901. And yet, before that year, fourteen companies discovered good deposits, mostly in the vintage years 1897 and 1898, without the aid of geologists. The success of the wasteful and extravagant mining boom is not hard to explain. Some forty companies subdivided the few square miles of ground that surrounded the one known ore body and criss-crossed the country with a hundred tunnels and shafts and furlongs of trenches after the manner of a feverish treasure hunt. They probably found most of the large deposits of copper that came within three hundred feet of the surface. As these companies liquidated, and as the drills and shafts had to go down deeper to explore new ground, it was inevitable that the extent of prospecting and the rate of discovery should be far less than in the palmy days of the field. As only one company survived to prospect an area that once received the attention of forty, and as this company had to spend as much as £15,000 on one of scores of diamond drill holes, prospecting was restricted by lack of money.

Early in the 1950's the Mt Lyell Co. set up its own geological department and employed a permanent team of diamond drillers. Money spent on the search for new copper deposits soared. From 1956 to 1962 the company joined with the Electrolytic Zinc Company in exploring the long-neglected country to the south, using a helicopter to carry men, food, and prospecting gear to trackless country and then building roads to carry in drilling equipment; the quarter million pounds spent by the two companies yielded nothing of value. At Mt Lyell itself in the decade 1956-66 the company put more effort into the search for new lodes than during the previous fifty years. The finding of a new ore body in the Crown Lyell area led to the revival of underground mining. Systematic drilling found so much ore in the vicinity of the West Lyell open cut that the company soon had larger ore reserves than at any other time. Furthermore the company learned so much about the geology of the field that the chances of predicting accurately where copper may exist were enhanced. The new emphasis on searching for copper may well be looked back on as the most important event in the post-war history of the field.

It was not Mt Lyell but a ramshackle township to the north-west that was served up as champagne on Australian stock exchanges in the early 1960s. Until recently the euphonious name of Renison Bell was virtually unknown outside the west coast, though everyone who visited Queenstown had to pass it in the long era when the railway was the only approach. Gold and tin had been discovered near Renison Bell during the silver boom of 1890, and later prospectors cut tracks through undergrowth and forest or set the bush alight in summer in order to find the patches of tin hidden by scrub. Many bags of alluvial tin were carried by pack-horses from Renison Bell to Zeehan, and some prospectors vowed that the new field needed only a railway to become a new Mt Lyell. The railway came in 1900. In fact the navvies making the railway for the Emu Bay company dug a cutting in the centre of the Renison Bell lease and exposed the main lode of tin so clearly that prospectors and promoters could see it clearly from the comfort of the slow-moving train. But no boom followed in the guard's van of the first trains.

Each day the train dropped off a bundle of newspapers at Renison Bell for the several hundred miners who were hidden in the forest. Water races were built around steep hills, and miners played the nozzle of powerful hoses on to alluvial tin or crumbling gossan outcrops and collected the heavy mineral in sluice boxes. Alluvial tin was easy to mine but the richest patches were soon rooted out. The difficult and vital step was to extract the tin from the hard rock, and a few companies erected batteries to crush the tinstone. The biggest mill—twenty stamps driven by electricity generated by a water-wheel—was erected on the edge of the railway line in 1909 by a company proudly calling itself the Renison Bell Prospecting and Mining Company No Liability. The mill was much noisier than the passing trains and for a few years more profitable. In 1913 the small Hobart company that owned the mill paid five dividends in the space of six months; and then came trouble. The mills of other small companies such as the Boulder and Central and Montana swelled the output though hardly the profits of the field. By 1914 the brief flurry of activity was almost over.

Travellers who passed Renison Bell soon after World War I saw few signs that the tin-field would recover. A torpor bathed the scattered tin camps like a Scotch mist. From the train one might see an axeman standing still beside a fallen log or a prospector ruminating on a bag of tin at a railway siding. The torpor was of course exaggerated because Renison Bell was so isolated and its life so humdrum that everyone in sight of the railway track stopped work when a train passed by. Even so, lethargy and hopelessness characterized the settlement; a few prospectors and mine managers insisted that the lodes were valuable and that the post-war slump in the price of tin would cease, but their optimism seemed like a mental windcheater worn to keep out the weather.

Renison Bell was repeating the history of Mt Lyell. Both fields had begun with alluvial miners scratching out a living by harnessing waterpower to mine the soft oxidized rock near the surface. Both fields had moved to the stage where small companies erected batteries to crush the harder oxidized rock. The batteries in both fields were too large and ambitious for the amount of ore they had to treat. The directors of the companies were too anxious to pay dividends instead of conserving profits for the expensive tasks ahead. Thus when both fields had treated most of the oxidized ore that formed the cream on the ore bowl (the oxidized ore being richer in minerals and cheaper to mine) they faced crisis. They next had to treat the pyritic or sulphide ores. Those ores were deeper and harder, and therefore more expensive to mine. They were also poorer in metals, and what metal they held was more difficult to extract because the pyrite wrecked the efficiency of the standard treatment processes. Mt Lyell had reached the sulphide problem by 1890, the Renison Bell field by 1914, and on both fields the existing companies had no money with which to face the problem.

Mt Lyell, as we have seen, defeated the crisis in the space of a few years. Renison Bell, however, took about half a century to grapple with, let alone defeat, the crisis. While Renison Bell had one enormous advantage in the railway that passed by, it had several disadvantages. It lacked Mt Lyell's ideal metallurgical solution—pyritic smelting. Its lodes did not lend themselves so easily to the cheap and deep open-cut mining which was one of the saviours of the old Mt Lyell mine. Its lodes lacked the large zone of rich sulphide ore which so aided the Mt Lyell Co. in the late 1890s. Above all the times when the two fields needed huge sums of capital for exploration and erection of plant were very different. While Mt Lyell had called for capital at a time when mining speculation was glamorous, Renison Bell began to need capital just when Australia's mining market was beginning a long slump; the period 1914-54 was a relatively dismal period for investment in new base-metal mines and prospects in Australia. Not only were investors reluctant

Diamond drilling in search of new copper deposits at Mt Lyell

The West Lyell open cut in 1966 resembled a vast amphitheatre

to finance the risky exploration of new mineralized areas but most mining companies which had money were also reluctant to explore.

Renison Bell fell asleep. One by one the companies went into liquidation, and fossickers and small parties alone produced a little tin. The decay was useful in one way, for it paved the way for the formation of a company which owned nearly all the useful tin deposits and therefore could, if necessary, work the field on the large scale so essential for success. The new company, Renison Associated Tin Mines, was formed in January 1934 with offices at Devonport. Its paid-up capital of £21,000 was trifling but at least it owned a huge area of potentially valuable ground.

The most prominent and enthusiastic men in the new company were the O'Deas: P. O'Dea, an old Renison mine manager with intense faith in the field, and his son Gavin, an insurance salesman. Both father and son had a turn as legal manager and also general manager of the new company and were prominent on the board. In the late 1930s, O. T. Lempriere, for long a leading ore-buyer and tin trader in Australia, became chairman of the Renison company and helped to finance its activities. By the start of World War II a small treatment plant—battery and flotation cells—was working noisily at Renison Bell. Though more than half of the tin escaped with the sludge from the mill, the company soothed the handful of shareholders with an occasional dividend.

To mine the tin deposits of Renison Bell on such a humble scale was as unsatisfactory as making a modern motor car in a plant no bigger than a suburban cinema. The larger the scale on which ore could be mined and treated at Renison Bell, the lower the cost of mining and milling each ton of ore and therefore the higher the profit. The directors of Renison Associated Tin, holding their long board meetings at night in Devonport, realized this fact. They also knew that a long line of geologists ranging from Hartwell Conder to Loftus Hills had argued that a huge tonnage of low-grade ore existed at Renison Bell. The problem was firstly to raise money to drill systematically in order to learn if such deposits really were there. The second problem would then be to raise a huge sum of money to mine and treat such deposits.

In the late 1950s mining exploration was reviving all over Australia. The entry of overseas companies into the search, and the favourable price of most base-metals, created the climate of which Renison Bell had long been dreaming. Various companies inspected the Renison deposits, and were variously impressed. Accordingly in 1959 Renison Associated Tin suggested that the Mt Lyell Co. should acquire a half interest in the company and finance systematic drilling of the deposits. The deal was arranged in a few days. It was to have curious effects on the subsequent history of the Mt Lyell Co., as the following chapter will show. Meanwhile Mt Lyell spent heavily in diamond-drilling the tin deposits. The results were impressive. By 1963 it was clear that Renison Bell was at least another Mt Bischoff.

Beneath forest and scrub lay a huge tonnage of tinstone averaging 0.7 per cent tin—the same assay as West Lyell, with this vital difference that the tin was worth more than two and a half times as much as copper at ruling prices, The Mt Lyell Co. began to plan a mill treating 350,000 tons of ore a year at Renison Bell and a new suburb of houses at Zeehan. The project was completed in 1967; and Renison was soon to rival Mt Lyell in profits though its scale of operations were smaller than Lyell's. Here was one of the biggest tin mines in the world.

Renison Bell and Mt Lyell were not the only fields which expanded in the 1960s. The Electrolytic Zinc Company's mines at Rosebery were vigorous and profitable. Further north the massive deposits of iron ore long known to exist on the Savage River, between Mt Bischoff and the Pieman, were being developed by Japanese and American money into a major export industry with a long pipeline to carry crushed ore to a pelletizing plant near Stanley on the north coast. And not far from Mt Bischoff the large tin ore bodies at Mt Cleveland were being vigorously explored by a company controlled by the Aberfoyle company which had grown rich by mining tin and wolfram in north-eastern Tasmania. The history of the west coast had turned a full cycle, and the tin which had led to the first booms and so much of the courageous prospecting and pioneering was again the most glamorous metal.

The new boom made the west coast a more productive mining region than at any time in its history. But it did not make the west coast a more populous region than at the turn of the century. The era when mining booms were synonymous with huge rushes of men has virtually passed. Whereas in 1900 the picks, shovels, hammers and hand-drills were the main tools of construction, today one man and a machine often do the work which twenty men did in the past. Moreover in 1900 the costs of transport were so high that the region supplied most of its own fuel, and thousands of men were employed in firewood camps. Today, in contrast, the main fuels—hydro-electricity, petroleum, coal and coke—are imported to the west coast and give work to few men in that region. Finally, smelters existed in 1900 near most big western mines and gave work to several thousand men, but by the 1960s Mt Lyell had the only smelters and refinery, and even its refinery was closed in 1965. Much of the work which the western mines created therefore was performed elsewhere. Those scattered families who owned blocks of land in the overgrown main streets of old western mining towns, and who had long hoped that those ghost towns would some day be resurrected into cities, did not become rich landlords in the new mining boom.

30

The Bidders

There was a time when every British investor who knew any-thing about mining shares knew the name of Mt Lyell. There was also a time when most journalists in Australia probably knew enough about Mt Lyell to edit any snippet of news that came through the telegraph. After World War I, however, the field less and less attracted the news-seekers. No scandal arose in the affairs of the company to interest the public. The annual dividend except in rare years was no longer one of the largest declared by an Australian public company. No dramatic discovery of mineral attracted the imagination of men in far-off streets, no long strike or industrial dispute occurred, and even news of mining accidents became less frequent with the waning of the underground mines. The items from Mt Lyell that reached the national news were usually oddities; it was said annually on Good Friday to be the one Australian industry that worked at full pressure that day; in other seasons snow was blocking the highway, or too little rain was falling—or too much.

The ownership and control of the Mt Lyell Co. attracted no public attention. Over the years tens of thousands of people had held shares in the company, but only a handful took a positive and vocal part in the affairs of the company. In 1892 a few Broken Hill investors had held 55 per cent of the shares and naturally they appointed the directors; they chose themselves. Within a year they had lost their majority, and within ten years they did not own 5 per cent of the company's shares. Nevertheless the increasing band of other shareholders, scattered throughout Australasia and Britain, were content that

306

the original directors should continue to direct the company. When a vacancy on the board occurred through death or resignation, the other directors chose the new one; if the new nominee was not already a shareholder he simply bought a small parcel of shares to qualify himself for a seat on the board. Like the boards of most public companies, the Mt Lyell board was thus self-perpetuating, like a club. Every year, of course, several of the directors automatically had to stand for re-election at the annual meeting of shareholders, but they were unopposed. Only once since the formation of the company had there been a contested election; that was in 1896 when Crotty's candidate was easily defeated. In all other years the shareholders, with occasional isolated complaints, accepted the policies the board had made and the dividend it had declared. For long periods Mt Lyell had exactly the same board. There was one span of thirteen years (1897-1910) when the board was unaltered.

Stability was one characteristic of the Mt Lyell board. The kind of man who sat on the board, however, did slowly change with time. The early directors were mostly self-made men who had won a fortune through mining speculations. On the other hand the later directors had made their names more as successful managers of businesses than as creators of individual fortunes, and they were usually professional men; thus three of the five directors were engineers by profession in the year 1962, when the ownership of the company was on the eve of a dramatic series of changes. The five directors at that time had between them an aggregate of nearly ninety years on the board; all were Melbourne men; all sat on various other boards; and all held only token shareholdings in the Mt Lyell Co. Sir Walter Bassett, the chairman, was a consulting engineer; Sir Robert Knox was an industrialist and merchant and son of a former director, William Knox; D. York Syme belonged to an old coastal shipping firm; N. K. S. Brodribb, C.B.E., was a former Director-General of munitions for the Commonwealth government; and F. Peter Johns was chairman of the century-old engineering firm of Johns and Waygood. They met regularly in Melbourne and made the company's policy.

The company's head office had always been in Melbourne; first in Queen Street, then from 1915 to 1961 in Collins House (for long the financial castle of Australian mining), and lastly in William Street. The company also possessed an office in London, where an advisory board met regularly. After the merger of 1903 that board consisted of the four former North Lyell directors and when vacancies occurred the Melbourne board chose the new London director. Shortly before World War I, when most of Mt Lyell's copper was sold in Europe and five of every six Mt Lyell shares were held in the British Isles, the company maintained a busy office in Palmerston House, Old Broad Street, London. By the late 1920s the majority of Lyell shares had passed from British to Australian and New Zealand investors, and by 1951 only 11 per cent of the company's shares were held on the London register; that year the London board met for the last time. There seemed no prospect at that time that the company would ever again be regularly advised, let alone controlled, from London.

In management, as in the board room, the company had unusual stability. Since 1893 there had only been four secretaries: the kindly and skilful Alfred Mellor who died after a fall on the deck of an Adelaide-bound mail steamer in 1911, D. G. Lumsden who gained his first experience of the field when Crotty appointed him secretary of the North Lyell Co. in London in 1897, R. V. Parsons who took office in 1937 after Lumsden died on a visit to his native Scotland, and L. G. Naismith, secretary since 1955. Likewise the company had had only four general managers at Queenstown: Robert Sticht, R. M. Murray, A. H. P. Moline, and Hugh M. Murray. Continuity in managerial policies came also from the fact that each secretary and each general manager— except the first—had long experience with the company before his ultimate promotion. Furthermore, Hugh Murray, and the man who was to succeed him, Geoffrey Hudspeth, were sons of former employees of the company and were born at Mt Lyell.

The ranks and roles of the company's shareholders were less stable. Instead of hundreds of shareholders there were now thousands; they were scattered across the globe; they knew less about mining and Mt Lyell than the earlier shareholders; and they could not easily organize themselves into a lobby to

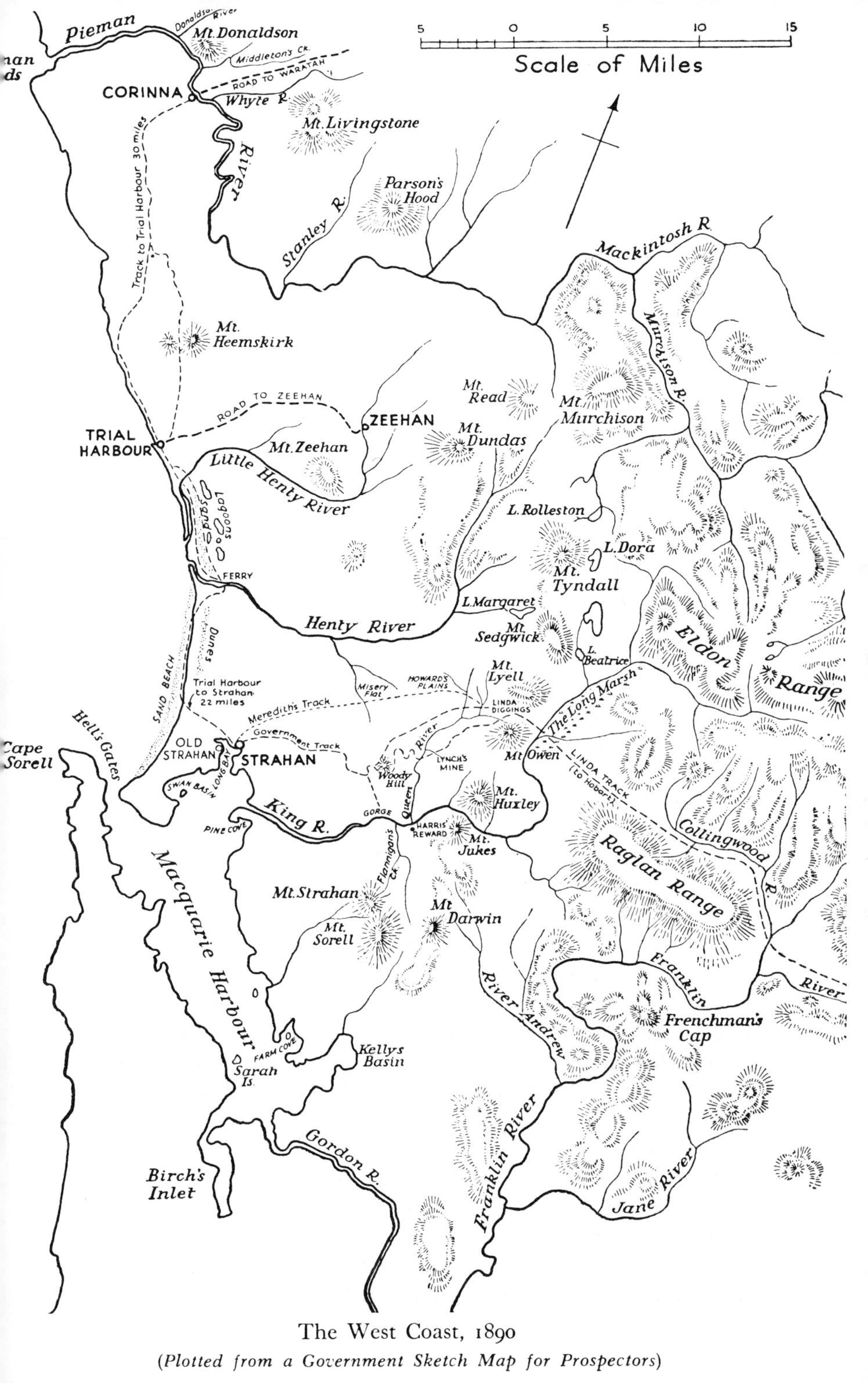

The West Coast, 1890

(Plotted from a Government Sketch Map for Prospectors)

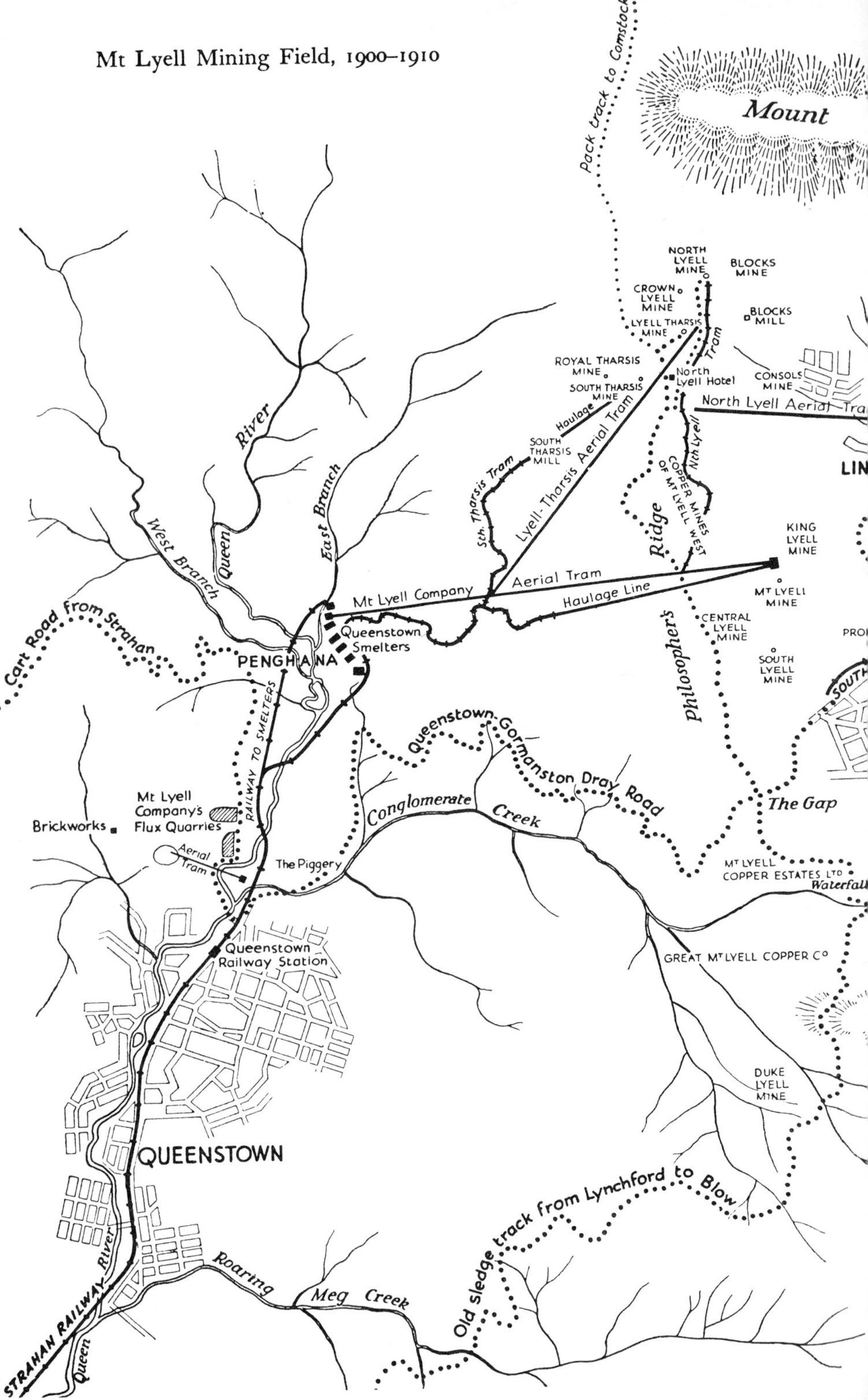

Mt Lyell Mining Field, 1900–1910
Pack track to Comstock
Mount
NORTH LYELL MINE
BLOCKS MINE
CROWN LYELL MINE
BLOCKS MILL
LYELL THARSIS MINE
ROYAL THARSIS MINE
North Lyell Hotel
CONSOLS MINE
SOUTH THARSIS MINE
North Lyell Aerial Tram
LIN
Haulage
Lyell-Tharsis Aerial Tram
SOUTH THARSIS MILL
Sth Tharsis Tram
Nth Lyell Tram
COPPER MINES OF MT LYELL WEST
Ridge
KING LYELL MINE
River
East Branch
Queen
West Branch
Aerial Tram
Mt Lyell Company
Haulage Line
MT LYELL MINE
Philosopher's
CENTRAL LYELL MINE
PRO
Cart Road from Strahan
Queenstown Smelters
PENGHANA
SOUTH LYELL MINE
SOUTH
RAILWAY TO SMELTERS
Queenstown-Gormanston Dray Road
The Gap
Conglomerate
Creek
Brickworks
Mt Lyell Company's Flux Quarries
Aerial Tram
The Piggery
Mt Lyell COPPER ESTATES LTD
Waterfall
Queenstown Railway Station
GREAT MT LYELL COPPER Cº
QUEENSTOWN
DUKE LYELL MINE
Roaring
Meg Creek
Old sledge track from Lynchford to Blow
STRAHAN RAILWAY
Queen River

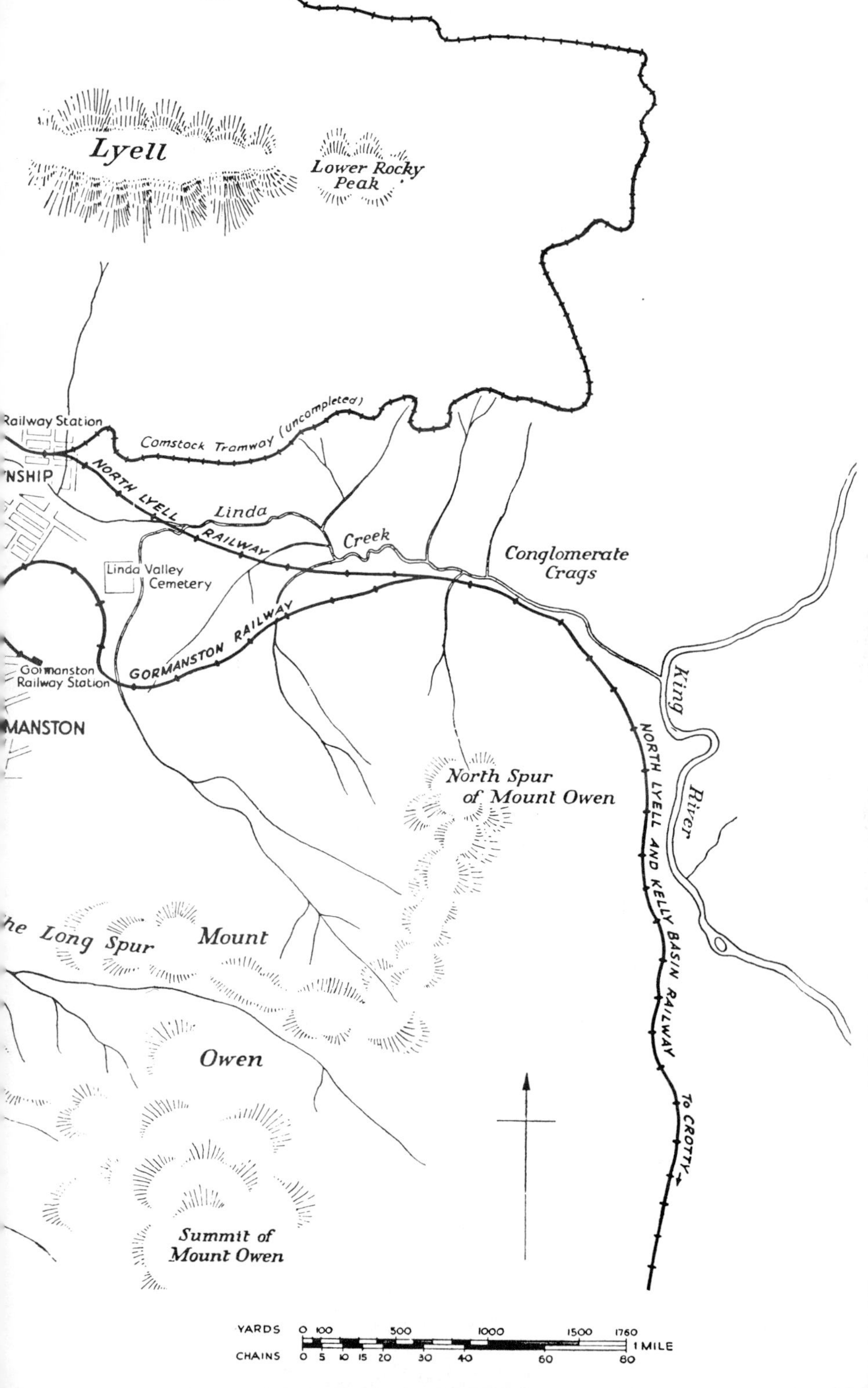

Lyell
Lower Rocky Peak
Railway Station
Comstock Tramway (uncompleted)
NORTH LYELL RAILWAY
Linda
Creek
Conglomerate Crags
TOWNSHIP
Linda Valley Cemetery
GORMANSTON RAILWAY
Gormanston Railway Station
GORMANSTON
North Spur of Mount Owen
King River
NORTH LYELL AND KELLY BASIN RAILWAY
The Long Spur
Mount
Owen
Summit of Mount Owen
To CROTTY
YARDS   0 100   500   1000   1500   1760
                                                          1 MILE
CHAINS   0 5 10 15 20   30   40   60   80

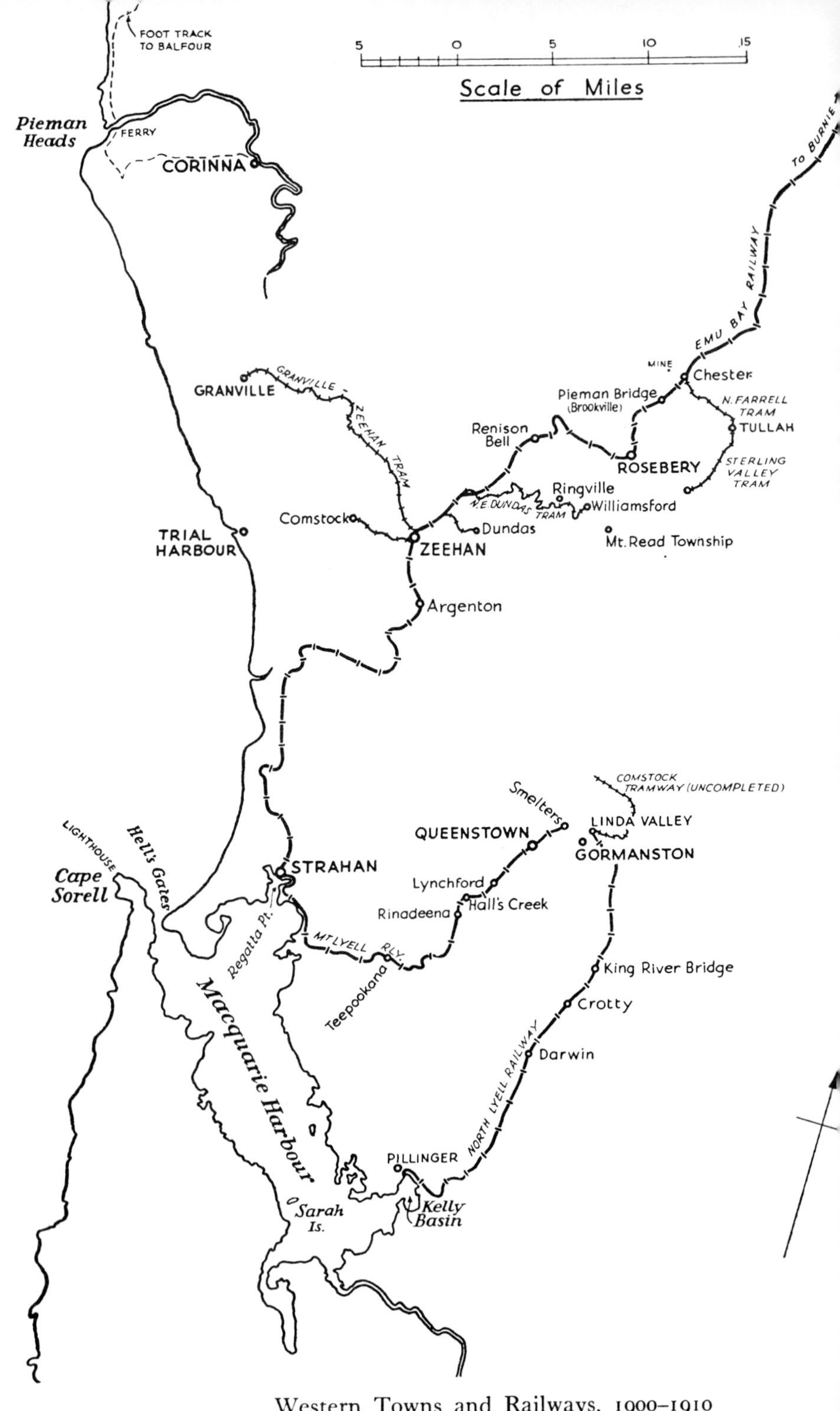

Western Towns and Railways, 1900–1910

impose their policy on the board. The abdication of the shareholder from active control of the company was taking place in thousands of other public companies in the English-speaking world, but the dispersal of the shares into small lots and many hands went further in the Mt Lyell Co. than in almost any other Australian industrial company. In 1962 the five biggest individual shareholders in Mt Lyell held between them less than 5 per cent of the company's shares, and if a dissatisfied shareholder had decided to organize a ticket of rival candidates for seats on the board he would have had to enlist the support of hundreds of scattered shareholders even to form a block of 25 per cent of the votes.

The interest of many shareholders in the copper-field was short-term. They hoped their Mt Lyell shares would yield them quick profits on the stock exchanges; they were birds of passage alighting briefly on the share register and then migrating elsewhere. On the other hand the directors' policy under the leadership of Sir Walter Bassett in the 1950s was to take a long view of the mine and its prospects. They believed—and for a time they were correct—that by investing heavily in new equipment the field could be more prosperous and have a more assured future. In pursuing this policy they were aided by a nest of eggs gathered over the years. The nest held a valuable list of shares in profitable industrial companies: in Metal Manufactures, a powerful company based on Port Kembla, which turned most of Mt Lyell's copper into sheets, tubes, wires and cables; in Imperial Chemical Industries of Australia and New Zealand; and in four fertilizer companies: Commonwealth Fertilisers and Chemicals (Vic.), Cuming Smith and Mt Lyell Farmers' Fertilisers (W.A.), Wallaroo-Mount Lyell Fertilisers (S.A.) and Australian Fertilizers (N.S.W.); the Mt Lyell Co., through these holdings, was powerful in the Australian fertilizer industry and had been so for nearly sixty years. Mt Lyell's shares in these companies had a face value in 1962 of nearly £4 million—the real value was much higher—and the dividends from these shares that year were £300,000. In many years the company received more profit from these shares than from its mining activities; sometimes when the mines worked at a loss the nest egg enabled the company to pay a dividend. Again, if the company needed capital to expand the mines at a time when capital was not easily found, it could dip into the nest or borrow from banks on security of those assets in the nest.

Amongst the handful of shareholders who attended the company's annual meetings in Melbourne were a few who from time to time suggested that the company should cease to use these profitable investments to reinforce and subsidize the mine. They argued that all Mt Lyell's shares in fertilizer and other manufacturing companies should be presented to the shareholders, leaving the mine to stand on its own. If the company were to adopt this advice the future of the mine would be less certain. On the other hand some shareholders, who as individuals were naturally more concerned about their own pocket than the homes and jobs of the thousands at Mt Lyell, believed that such a policy would give them a much higher dividend and a higher market price for their shares. That argument seemed valid in many years of the 1950s; indeed the shareholders would have gained in the short term—but lost considerably in the long term—if the company had gone into liquidation, closing the mine, selling everything that was saleable at Mt Lyell, and selling too the prized portfolio of outside shares; the total proceeds of such a sale would have given the shareholders a liquidation dividend far exceeding the ruling price of their shares on the stock exchanges. Fortunately for Mt Lyell, and fortunately for the shareholders, their suggestions were not followed by the board. Ultimately the company's mining assets, both at Mt Lyell and nearby Renison Bell, improved enormously in market value and potential; and much of that improvement had come from the company's traditional policy of using the portfolio to strengthen and develop the mines.

Those shareholders who wished to break open the nest egg won allies in the late 1950s. Takeovers became a common part of commercial life, and scores of empire-building companies found that the quickest and cheapest, if not always the safest, way to expand quickly was to buy out existing companies. The companies ripest for a takeover were those which had substantial negotiable assets but, because of their conservative financial or dividend policies, had a deceptively low value on the stock exchanges. Mt Lyell was such a company. An ambitious bidder only needed to offer the thousands of Mt Lyell shareholders a good premium for their shares, and most of the shareholders probably would have quickly accepted the offer. The mining field and the company's assets elsewhere would then be in the control of a new owner, who might be more interested in Mt Lyell's nest egg than its mines, thus endangering the life of the mines. The board of the Mt Lyell Co. was increasingly aware of the risk of a takeover.

In July 1961 Imperial Chemical Industries of Australia and New Zealand successfully offered to buy all shares in Commonwealth Fertilisers and Chemicals, one of the largest private companies in Australia. As the Mt Lyell Co. was a big shareholder in the fertilizer company, it received £311,000 in cash and 964,000 £1 shares in I.C.I.A.N.Z. This takeover drew public attention even more to the nest egg; it therefore probably made the Mt Lyell Co. even more vulnerable to an outside bidder. In November 1961 the directors announced that they would divorce most of the investment portfolio from the mining company. Accordingly a second company known as Mount Lyell Investments was prompty formed with the same paid-up capital as the old. The twin companies had the same chairman, Sir Walter Bassett, and at first the same shareholders because each shareholder in the Mt Lyell Mining and Railway Company was given without payment an equal number of shares in Mt Lyell Investments. The shares were distributed in March 1962, the new company was quoted separately on the stock exchange, and the dividends which the new company promised to pay were guaranteed in effect by the valuable portfolio of fertilizer and metal-manufacturing shares which it held—a portfolio which on some estimates was worth at least £10 million. The old Mt Lyell Co. continued to function; its main assets were the Mt Lyell copper-field, the shares in the Renison tin-field, and the bulk of the I.C.I.A.N.Z. shares which formed a useful insurance policy. While the new policy weakened the Mt Lyell Co., it seemed to ensure that the company would not be taken over by an ambitious company which was more interested in gaining industrial investments than in carrying on the mines.

To prevent such a takeover had presumably been the main purpose of forming Mt Lyell Investments, though the directors gave no reason for their decision.

Mt Lyell Investments had a short life. It caught the eye of the master of the art of the takeover, a young company known in 1963 as Bitumen and Oil Refineries (Australia) Limited and known now as Boral. Only a decade previously Boral had been a much smaller company than Mt Lyell. Its main income had flowed from an oil refinery at Matraville near Sydney, but by swallowing a diverse range of other companies it had grown like a sunflower. It had taken over the old shipping firm of Huddart Parker and an assorted bag of coal mines, engineering and chemical plants, road-making and bitumen-making firms. Now, in April 1963, Boral turned to Mt Lyell Investments, offering 7s 2d in cash (or an alternative offer of Boral shares and cash) in return for each 2s 6d share. Whether Boral was interested simply in expansion and a good financial bargain or whether it was more interested in acquiring the fertilizer shares held by Mt Lyell Investments is not clear; the takeover bid was successful, and later Boral sold at a handsome profit nearly all the shares it had bought. Mt Lyell thus ceased to own any part of the fertilizer industry. Today the name of Mt Lyell has even vanished from the titles of the fertilizer companies in South and Western Australia, though as relics of the era when Mt Lyell was the best-known name in Australia's superphosphate industry one can still see on old railway sidings or general stores across the wheat belts a few faded metal signs proclaiming the virtues of a product that has vanished.

The capture of Mt Lyell Investments in 1963 did not weaken the old Mt Lyell Co. It seemed rather to confirm the wisdom of divorcing the investment wing from the mining wing of the company's operations. But while Mt Lyell was no longer a prize because of its industrial shares, it curiously now became a prize because of the tin-mining shares it held. The exploration of the tin lodes at Renison Bell in the early 1960s had given such dramatic results that in the eyes of some investors the tin leases were more valuable than the busy copper mines. And the simplest way in which an outsider could control the tin was to acquire a majority of shares in the Mt Lyell Co.

The Patino family had owned rich tin mines in the Andes mountains in Bolivia. During World War II, when the rich tin zone of South-east Asia was captured by the Japanese, Bolivia was probably the biggest miner of tin in the world. Tin dominated the Bolivian economic life, and the Patino Mines and Enterprises Incorporated dominated Bolivian tin until the company was expropriated by the government in 1952. Long before that setback the Patino family had become international mining magnates with headquarters in Avenue Foch in Paris and the strength to survive serious setbacks. They held useful interests in Malayan mines through the British Tin Investment Corporation, and strong interests in tin smelters at Penang in Malaya and Liverpool and Redruth in England through Consolidated Tin Smelters, of which His Excellency Don Simon Iture Patino of Paris was president. These inter-married companies had such power in the world tin markets that any potentially big tin deposit interested them and a potential producer of the size of Renison interested them very much. They decided in 1963 to approach the shareholders of the Mt Lyell Co. with an offer to take control of Mt Lyell and its remaining interests.

The Patino companies gave formal notice to Sir Walter Bassett at his office in Melbourne at 5 p.m. on Friday, 25 October 1963 just after the stock exchanges had closed for the week-end; until that day Sir Walter had heard virtually nothing to suggest that Patino was interested in Renison. He made the unprecedented step of convening a meeting of the board for the following day, a Saturday afternoon, to consider the offer.

At a time when increasing foreign ownership of Australian companies was stirring political controversy, the idea of a foreign group of companies taking over one of the oldest Australian mines excited wide comment. The fact that the bidding companies had had Bolivian associations seemed to add a layer of mystery and intrigue to the affair in the minds of newspaper-readers. In the streets of Queenstown there was uneasiness and a flood of rumours. In Melbourne and Sydney the issue was discussed scores of times in editorials, financial columns and news stories. The final answer lay with the scattered shareholders and they gave no inkling of what they would do.

The Patino offer to the Mt Lyell shareholders was not particularly generous. It was followed, however, by a bolder bid. On 3 December 1963 Boral, the company which had captured Mt Lyell Investments, offered to buy shares in the Mt Lyell Co. The Mt Lyell board firmly advised shareholders to accept the Boral offer, partly because it was a higher offer but more because it seemed likely to ensure that ownership of the Mt Lyell Co. would remain in Australia. Patino did not match the new bid, and withdrew its offer. By the end of the first week of 1964 the owners of half the shares in the Mt Lyell Co. had accepted the new offer, and ultimately more than 60 per cent of the shares passed to Boral. After more than seventy years of independence the Mt Lyell Co., once one of the largest three non-banking companies in Australia, became a subsidiary of another company. Three directors of Boral joined the Mt Lyell board and sat with three of the Lyell directors; the secretarial and managerial staff of the company was unchanged; and the head office remained in Melbourne though Boral was a Sydney company.

Australian control of Mt Lyell was soon to be challenged again. Within six months Boral sold half of its Lyell shares and soon after sold the remainder, making a handsome profit from its second short excursion to Mt Lyell. The buyer of these shares, at a price of more than £4 million, was the Sydney subsidiary of Consolidated Gold Fields Limited of London. It thus acquired more than 60 per cent of the shares in Lyell, the remainder being held by several thousand individual investors and companies in Australasia and Britain. Once again the board of the Mt Lyell Co. was changed, the Boral directors giving way to directors nominated by Consolidated Gold Fields: J. B. Massy-Greene, G. J. Mortimer, B. W. Andrew, and S. L. Segal. The new directors sat with three members of the old Mt Lyell board—Sir Robert Knox, F. Peter Johns, and Sir Walter Bassett who continued to be chairman.

The company which had swallowed Mt Lyell was a mining giant. Consolidated Gold Fields controlled beach-sand deposits and coal mines on the Pacific coast of Australia. It controlled or worked gold and platinum and uranium and diamond and tin and coal mines in South Africa. In the United

States it controlled zinc mines and treatment plants and an engineering plant. Its products ranged from aluminium beer barrels to diamonds, and the 136 companies in its organization employed nearly 100,000 people—so reported the company's chairman, Sir George Harvie-Watt, Bart, in brochures issued to his employees in 1966 'in the hope that they will contribute towards maintaining our family ties'. It was not easy to persuade third-generation miners and smelter men on the west coast of Tasmania that they had 'family ties' with mine managers and miners in Johannesburg and Tennessee.

Consolidated Gold Fields had been formed in London in 1887, primarily to mine gold at Johannesburg; and the dynamic man on its first board was Cecil Rhodes, the mining magnate and empire-builder. So the company whose founder had for long been the epitome of the empire on which the sun never set had taken over the field where legend affirmed that the rain never stopped. There was a stronger, less meteorological, link. Consolidated Gold Fields could not have become wealthy at the close of the last century without J. S. MacArthur's cyanide process, which was indispensable for extracting gold at Johannesburg. Nor perhaps would the Mt Lyell Co. have survived early in this century but for the mistakes which the same MacArthur had made for the rival North Lyell Co. at its Crotty smelters. If MacArthur had won in Tasmania the same degree of metallurgical success which his ingenuity had won in South Africa, then the North Lyell would have conquered the Mt Lyell Co., and control of the field would thereby have passed to London. In fact the transfer of control to London was postponed for sixty years. Curiously the ambitions of the prospector and promoter, James Crotty, that the copperfield should be controlled from London and that the Mt Lyell railway should be abandoned, came to pass at the same time, though hardly in the manner he intended.

31

Prince Lyell and the Long Crisis

It was often said that the west coast offered at least two remarkable sights. One was the small coastal steamers, arriving to load Mt Lyell's copper and butting their bow against the mill tide racing through the narrow throat of Hell's Gates. The other sight was molten orange slag pouring from the furnaces on a cold night at Queenstown. Whereas one scene illustrated vividly the isolation of the west coast, the other showed the influence of fire metallurgy on the history of the copperfield. Both scenes, familiar since the closing years of the last century, were about to vanish.

Macquarie Harbour, always risky for coastal ships, was now doomed. The cost of sending each ton of copper away in small ships was high. The fee for insuring the ships against wreck was also high. Though the harbour was no longer used for bringing general supplies to Mt Lyell it still brought the coke for the smelters and the steel balls which were used in large numbers to crush the ore. Even in the 1960s two ships called about every fortnight and carried away from Strahan the blister copper to the refinery at Port Kembla and pyritic concentrate—a by-product—to Melbourne where it was converted into sulphuric acid at the fertiliser works near the mouth of the River Yarra.

At times the the two steamships met trouble in the shallow water covering the sand bar outside Hell's Gates. Again and again they bumped on the sand. On Sunday 26 May 1968 the *Kumalla*, ploughing across Bass Strait towards the west coast of Tasmania, received a radio message that the water on the sand bar was too shallow for her to enter the harbour. She

320

changed course, returning to port. The sand bar was dredged, and the two ships were able to resume their regular voyages. When the port was finally closed to cargo vessels in January 1970, and jurisdiction over the port of Strahan was handed from the local Marine Board to the distant port of Hobart, it was widely believed that sand had choked the port. In fact Burnie was the conqueror. A larger port with a safe approach from the ocean, it could accommodate the big cargo vessels which Mt Lyell now required.

Mt Lyell was mining more and more copper. In the last year of the 1960s it produced a record 18,000 tons of blister copper, or more than double the output of Sticht's best year. The furnaces, however, were outdated. Furthermore, they could no longer cope with the volume. There was no alternative but to dismantle them. On Christmas eve, 1969, the fire in the smelters went out for the last time. Plans to rebuild a larger smelter did not eventuate. Henceforth the final product of Mt Lyell was a copper concentrate emerging as a wet slurry from the flotation plant and containing about 25 per cent copper. A damp greyish sand, it was carried in large trucks to the new terminus of the Emu Bay railway at Melba Flat, near Zeehan, and then sent in trains some eighty miles to the waterfront at Burnie where it was shipped to smelters at Port Kembla and increasingly to the Mitsubishi smelters in Japan.

The new sequence of production needed more transport than in the past. A small revolution in transport was taking place. As the final product of the company was now a sand in which only one part in four was copper, an output of say 18,000 tons of copper required the carrying away of four times the tonnage previously shifted. In addition, a big tonnage of pyritic concentrate was taking the same route, being carried by truck along the bitumen road to Melba Flat and then by railway to Burnie. There Mt Lyell and its neighbour Electrolytic Zinc shared the large expense of a new factory built in 1970 to convert the pyritic concentrate into sulphuric acid. The name of the new factory was North West Acid, and within a few years it left an acid taste in the owners' mouths. Its sulphuric acid, the raw material of fertilisers, could not compete with raw sulphur imported from overseas.

The abandoning of the old port and the old smelters were signs of optimism. Mount Lyell, which had many times been on the verge of extinction, was enjoying a new Spring. The price of copper ran to a series of peaks in the late 1960s. In the year ending June 1970, the company's net profit of $5.7 million equalled a return more than 100 per cent. Some shareholders must have been pop-eyed when they received a letter announcing that for the twelve months the dividend was 60 per cent. Employees also shared in the high prosperity, and on a pay day just before Christmas of 1970 they received their bonus.

High copper prices were especially needed because the field was in the expensive process of turning again to underground mining. The days of the big open cut were numbered. It was so steep and deep that it was almost unworkable. In its early years the people living down in the valley could see, on the top benches of the West Lyell open cut, the lights of the heavy trucks and engine-driven shovels doing their work; but the moving lights became fewer as the open cut went deeper. By 1970 it was the biggest hole in Tasmania, with ledge after ledge descending nearly 800 feet below the point where the open cut had been commenced. The ten tallest skyscrapers in Australia could have been dropped into the hole without the top of any of them being visible from the valley.

The copper ore was known to persist far below the bottom of this gaping quarry. By 1966 ore was found to extend at least 2,000 feet below the original top of the open cut. Diamond drills revealed that the orebody, at depth, did not shrink. Nor did it become poorer in copper. Would this copper support a bigger scale of mining than hitherto carried out on the field? A costly effort was begun in 1966 to drill two deep holes that would investigate whether the big copper orebody persisted for say 3,000 feet or some three fifths of a mile from the original top of the open cut. These bore holes, if successful, would go well below the level of the sea.

At the company's offices the progress reports of the drilling were read eagerly, week after week, for they were unravelling the long-term future of the field. Unfortunately one drill hole, slowly approaching the target area, entered faulted ground and came to a halt. The other hole was more than compensation. It discovered copper at considerable depth, passing through more than 100 feet of ore averaging a pleasing 2.76 per cent of copper. These expensive holes revealed enough for the time being. Since then no other hole has been drilled to such a depth.

This massive orebody dipping far below the open cut was an extension of the West Lyell orebody but could only be worked as a new mine. It was given a new name, being called Prince Lyell after a failed and forgotten company which was floated in the boom of the 1890s. In effect much of the West Lyell orebody had veered, at considerable depth, into Prince Lyell's old ground.

Prince Lyell was now the hope of the field. By 1968 it was known to hold at least 27 million tons of payable ore carrying almost 2 per cent copper and a far larger amount of poorer ground which, if the price of copper remained high, would also be mined. The company had received a heart transplant—or so it seemed.

There was at least one obstacle. The company would have to change once again from the open cut to the underground. Nearly all its mining equipment was about to become value-less. After all, how could rumbling 50-ton Euclid trucks with tyres as high as the roof of a normal car, do their work in the cramped spaces of an underground mine? Likewise much of the workforce would have to be retrained because the under-ground was a different world requiring new skills. A big sum of capital would also be needed to prepare deep Prince Lyell for the mining of a daily output of ore dwarfing the tonnages produced by the company's underground mines worked decades ago. The new mine would be profitable only if it was highly mechanised and worked on a big scale.

In Sydney, plans for the new Mt Lyell were officially announced in July 1968. It was a proud month for Sir Walter Bassett. Approaching the end of his time as chairman—he was second only to Bowes Kelly in his tenure of that post—he saw no reason why a determined man in his mid seventies could not prepare the company for the twenty first century. With a strong will, an engineer's faith in what the latest technology could do, and a touching belief in Mt Lyell and its people, he consented to speak to the press ('those bounders').

With his everpresent walking stick—he had been badly wounded when his aircraft crashed near the French battlefront in the First World War—he tapped the floor for emphasis as he enthused about Mt Lyell. When he spoke of its future he pointed his stick firmly to the sky and when he explained that the company would go underground he jabbed his stick downwards. He was not the person to encourage critical questions. In his quiet, emphatic way, he announced that Mt Lyell would raise some 30 million dollars by the sale of new shares and by loans from banks. Within five years the company would reach the big annual output of 25,000 tons of copper, and nearly all of it would come from underground. In old age Mt Lyell was about to break all its records.

Prince Lyell spread confidence. More than 200 houses were built to attract skilled employees. An air service was operated from Queenstown to Tasmanian cities. The population rose towards 5,000, making the town the seventh biggest in the island.

Meanwhile an all-out effort was made to prepare the underground orebodies. The old North Lyell tunnel, running from the mill and smelters in the Queen Valley right into the mountain, was a point of access not only to the planned workings of the new Prince Lyell but also to another orebody, the Cape Horn, recently discovered after a geophysical survey. Cape Horn was the prominent crag on the western face of the Mt. Lyell mountain, a wet and blowy headland long familiar to miners walking to work at the distant Comstock in days gone by. The hidden orebody, far below the crag, was first mined in 1969.

The North Lyell tunnel was extended more than one mile in order to serve as the gateway to the new Cape Horn mine. Another route to the new mines was constructed. Known as the Main Decline, it was a steep vehicle road for hauling ore from deeper areas. The access to the very deep workings was to be a new shaft, the widest and deepest so far planned for the field. Its big steel headframe was erected and the sinking of the shaft was commenced in 1971.

To open these remote underground workings was the equivalent of building a network of narrow roads underneath a mountain. It was expensive and slow. By 1972, however, four of every ten tons of ore was coming from the new underground. Next year, the most productive in the field's history, eight out of every ten tons came from the underground mine.

The life of the West Lyell open cut was almost over. Those who had spent most of their working life in that rainy and windswept quarry knew that they had won a victory over a harsh environment. Year after year the big trucks had worked all through the night, often driving close to the rocky edges and their precipitous drops. Don Martin, recalling his Euclid truck, thought that only once had he been forced to stop work by the thick fog which occasionally settled. In very wet years, 130 or more inches of rain could fall on the open cut, and the trucks would roar through deep pools of water, but work was not halted just for rain.

In daylight the open cut was increasingly in the shadow. As it went deeper, the shadows grew. In the end, in those deep workplaces where the mechanical shovels tipped the broken rock into the trays of the waiting trucks, the winter sun rarely penetrated. By 1972 the open cut was almost worked out.

Geoff Hudspeth. the general manager, who was born on the ridge now mutilated by nearly forty years of quarrying, thought a closing ceremony was called for. On 31 August, about noon, he prepared to light what he said would be the last blasting of rock in that vast hole from which 100 million tons of copper ore and waste rock had been removed. A small crowd, invited to see the ceremony, gathered at the top of the open cut and peered down. There was Hudspeth, at the bottom, wearing the steel hat which all miners were legally compelled to wear. His career was almost over, he had little use for his white hat. Waving it to the crowd gathered high above him he placed it near a rocky ledge and lit the fuse and retreated, leaving his hat to be blown up.

A photo is preserved of spectators standing at the top. Some carry furled umbrellas—the coat of arms of the West Coaster. A few men are even wearing suits, ties and felt hats for such an important farewell. Who is that old man, standing so straight? His face can just be recognised. It is old Bill Lyden, now more than ninety years old. He had worked in the original Mt Lyell mine, was the target in the big strike of 1911, and much later was the boss of a gang in this very hole—a smaller crater then. Now he was watching yet another mine reach its end.

With the new Prince Lyell and other underground mines blasting out the ore, the field was flourishing. Pay was high. The field was believed to have a longer life mapped out than ever before. To add to the comfort, copper prices leaped during the Middle East crisis late in 1973. It was almost as if copper was beginning to chase the surging price of oil. For nine months the price of copper was spectacularly high. Even though it slumped before the financial year ended in June 1974, the Mt Lyell Co. concluded the year by recording a record profit of $7.2 million. Such a bumper year—allowing for the changing value of money—did not appear again.

While the price of copper fell further, wages and the prices of explosives and all other materials were soaring. The world was in a new period of inflation, coupled—to the surprise of economists—with slower economic growth. Copper, a favoured metal during building booms because it was so much used in heavy engineering and in electrical wires and cables, suffered in these quieter years. Moreover part of its market was eaten away by aluminium. Mt Lyell was bruised by these changes.

The underground expansion announced by Sir Walter Bassett in 1968 had been based on the hope, reasonable at the time, that the price of copper would remain high. It turned out to be one of those freak times when copper was as dear as tin. Such a fluke could not last. Likewise the underground workings were being equipped with a network of railways just when a few other Australian mines were beginning to bring large rubber-tyre vehicles into deep workings: a new era in underground transport. Mt Lyell was soon forced, at heavy expense, to abandon its imported locomotives. In hindsight the faith in high copper prices and in underground railways was understandable but costly.

Brian Massy-Greene, an experienced businessmen who succeeded Bassett as chairman, quickly learned to be skilled at announcing bad news. For the year ending June 1975 he revealed that the mine was working at a heavy loss. There was one compensation. He and his colleagues, predicting that copper would fall, had shrewdly sold Mt Lyell's copper at a favourable price even before the copper left the mine. Through this gamble the company made a massive profit of $8.5 million on the London Metal Exchange, thus financing a dividend when the mine in theory was working at a loss.

The losses increased. The field was in jeopardy. Loans had to be paid off, money had to be found for wages. To raise cash the company decided in February 1976 to sell its controlling interest in the attractive Renison tin mine lying just across the ranges. Set aside for a rainy day, this valuable asset, when sold, did not yield enough to cope with the cloudburst. The proceeds from the sale of Renison shares could not prop up the Mt Lyell mine for even twelve months. Soon after the sale, the price of tin and therefore the Renison shares jumped. The Mt Lyell Co. wished it had held onto them. But even if it had chanced to receive a larger sum from its Renison shares it would not have climbed out of danger. The danger was long-term.

To save money the workforce was cut. Few of the people who resigned or retired were replaced. In two years the number of employees fell from about 1,400 to 1,050. The construction program launched back in 1968 was not yet finished but could no longer be financed. Even the sinking of the big Prince Lyell shaft to the required depth—the very lynchpin of the expansion—was halted.

The people on the mining field were not prepared for this change of mood. Believing that Lyell's future was bright, they had bought, extended or refurnished houses, often borrowing the money. Now, when they thought of moving elsewhere, they could hardly find a buyer.

Many shopkeepers and employees still hoped that copper, with its unfathomable ways, would save Mt Lyell by rising in price. It began to rise in the winter of 1976 and then quickly fell. The world had far too much copper. All those economists and conservationists who had said that an over-populated world would soon run short of copper and other metals were wrong.

There was another way of explaining Mt Lyell's plight. The world was entering a new, puzzling wave of inflation. In the years 1972 to 1976, Mt Lyell was harmed more by the galloping wages than by the price of copper. In four years the price of copper actually rose by 16 per cent but the cost of labour at Mt Lyell rose by 103 per cent. The nation's high rate of inflation was choking Mt Lyell which, selling on a world market, could not reply by raising its price.

Charles Copeman, who was to succeed Sir Brian Massy-Greene as chairman of Mt Lyell, recalls that at the head office in Sydney a decision was actually reached to close the mine. At the last moment a brave compromise was patched up. To save the copperfield the company called for savings of a severity not seen since the crisis of 1922 when Sticht-style pyritic smelting was ended. The directors resolved to mine only the rich ore. They regretfully abandoned as unpayable all those ore-reserves which earlier were the source of hope. They decided to lower the monthly production. The mill too would save money by closing down during the weekend when penalty rates of pay were high.

Other cuts were needed. The future of the Lyell engineering shops was questioned. For decades they had solved crises by making or repairing a variety of broken machines at short notice. To wait while new parts of essential machines came from Melbourne or Sydney would have forced the closure of the mine or mill for weeks on end, and so the company ran its big fitting shops, heavy engineering shops, foundry, carpenters' shop and other tradesmen's shops, with one of the biggest intakes of apprentices in the island. In this emergency, the company no longer could afford to be self reliant in engineering. The big West Lyell workshop was closed and only vital services were retained.

Such changes could be made only if 344 employees lost their jobs almost immediately. The names were selected, a painful task. The list included more than 100 skilled trades-men, 85 semi-skilled assistants, and numerous assayers, surveyors, clerks and other white-collar employees. The actual miners were safe; their output was urgently needed. On 4 November 1976 the news of the retrenchment was made public. There was shock. Many of those who were handed a written notice that they would soon be out of work were flabbergasted. In the main streets some of the owners of small businesses did not fully realise how desperate was the situation. They were dumfounded when they realised that many of their best customers—some owing money—would have to leave the town.

Unless these jobs were abolished, the company estimated that it would lose the massive sum of $21 million for the financial year now under way. The alternative was to close the mine. Maybe it could be placed in the hands of the caretakers and re-opened later—if the price of copper recovered. The news of the sackings—the word 'retrenchment' came later—did more than any event in the last half century to sour industrial relations. The young president of the West Coast Trades and Labor Council, Russell Maher, had no inkling of the drastic cutbacks. He felt outraged. Coming on top of the cuts in the workforce made quietly through the effluxion of time, and therefore largely voluntary, these dismissals were harder to accept because they were compulsory and sudden.

The reduction in the company's workforce from 1,400 to a proposed 730 in the space of two years shattered all confidence in the future of a town in which seven of every ten homes were owned or being purchased by employees of the Mt Lyell Co. In Australia, sackings on such a scale were less common in the 1970's than later. That they should happen at Mt Lyell with its long tradition of benevolence was shattering. Decade after decade, boys of fourteen or sixteen had started work in the mine or machine shop, knowing that if they wanted to stay they probably would have a job for life. There had even been a period when the company employed men over eighty in simple jobs on full pay. A well-known employee had been so crippled with arthritis that he was lifted into the bus that took him to work, but for years he was allowed to continue a daily job that he could no longer carry out. The privilege of still earning a living even when too frail had virtually ceased by the 1970s, but was part of the tradition of goodwill. Now the goodwill was draining away as men aged thirty were suddenly told that their job would be gone by Christmas.

The bewilderment was increased because the decision to retrench came from people seen as outsiders. The senior managers were no longer local men who had been born on the field or had given it most of their working life. Geoff Hudspeth, a Lyell man right down to the toe of his gumboot, had retired as general manager some three years ago, thus ending an unbroken line of general managers who were seen as belonging to the field. He was replaced by Terry Lanz and then by David Sawyer. For the first time in perhaps half a century an unusual gap was perceived between managers and men. In fact the gap was probably much narrower than in the typical big enterprise in Australia because the general manager of Mt Lyell lived in the town; and so even if he was new he was soon known by sight to most people and by name to hundreds. Mt Lyell's unique tradition of 'local' managers had come to an inevitable end—just before the field faced its biggest crisis. No matter how hard a new general manager worked to bridge the gap, he could not bridge it quickly.

The company, if the mine was to be continued, had no alternative but to make these savings. To explain them, however, was not easy. David Sawyer was willing to talk at length with deputations of unionists and townspeople on the fate of Mt Lyell, but his task was simply to say 'no'. There was no money with which to say 'yes'. Privately he was called 'the butcher' though later it was realised that he faced an impossible task and that he carried it out courageously and honestly. If by chance, Hugh Murray or Geoff Hudspeth had still been in charge of Mt Lyell their word, their explanations, would have been accepted more readily. But they would have found it almost impossible to retrench so many people whom they had known since childhood.

In the last weeks of 1976 the atmosphere was a strange mixture of resignation and indignation. Many of the employees who, for reasons of family or finance or their own career, thought it sensible to remain at Mt Lyell wanted to fight.

Those who thought of leaving often faced financial difficulties in leaving. Married men who found jobs at Whyalla and the Pilbara now faced the question of what to do with their house. The property market—there was no estate agent in the district—was almost dead. Eventually some relief came when the Tasmanian government set aside money to buy at low price the houses of some 22 breadwinners who wished to leave the district in search of work.

In Canberra, within a week of news of the sackings, the Senate had set up a Select Committee, virtually a rescue committee, consisting solely of Tasmanians and chaired by Senator R. C. Wright. It gave hope to the town. Several weeks later, firm help came unexpectedly. The Federal Government devalued the Australian dollar by a stark 17.5 per cent. That immediately gave Mt Lyell an added income from copper sold overseas.

Meanwhile so many men had left of their own accord that the company had vacancies to fill. It was able to reverse some of its retrenchments and continue employing half of the men who had been given notice. This reduced the anxiety: it did not completely remove it. Within the trade unions was a feeling that the company would give in to pressure. Early in the new year a ban imposed on overtime by the biggest union, the AWU, disrupted the mine for six weeks. By reducing the mine's output and revenue, it possibly increased the likelihood of the mine closing altogether. A stop-work meeting became almost a fortnightly event. By June 1977 the company had lost a total of 8,245 man-hours through stop-work meetings, a form of protest which had not been common at Mt Lyell.

The drastic changes had saved a big sum of money but the Prince Lyell still worked at a loss. Charles Copeman, the mining engineer who took over as chairman on the first day of 1977, could see no way of avoiding large losses unless the price of copper rose or governments gave aid. Most industries in Australia received some form of aid. Many factories received a tariff protection of at least 100 per cent. Mt Lyell received no aid. Indeed, even in this slump in copper prices, it would have been earning a profit but for the various government policies which, in aiding some industries, indirectly harmed mines.

An inquiry by the Industries Assistance Commission made a preliminary recommendation that the Federal Government should help Mt Lyell. It suggested a temporary loan. A small part of the loan came from the Tasmanian Government. The final report of the Commission appeared in 1978. It did not envisage Mt Lyell becoming reasonably profitable in the long term. Nor could it see a strong case for subsidy. Australia had plenty of profitable copper mines: Mt Lyell was essential for Tasmania but not for Australia.

The crisis was now in its third year. The mine was surviving only through a succession of short-term arrangements. Queenstown existed partly on hope. The hope was that in the end the Fraser government would relent and pay a long-term subsidy whenever copper prices were low. On Wednesday 23 August 1978 the acting prime minister, Doug Anthony, disclosed the verdict: a joint Commonwealth-Tasmanian scheme to provide a maximum of $7.6 million in the hope of keeping the mine alive for almost two years.

The news spread around the town and into the remote recesses of the mine. It was heard with elation. Jack Sheehy of the Commercial Hotel, one of the first to hear, put on free beer at 4.30 pm. Almost everybody in the town, though it was winter, prepared to celebrate in the main street after darkness. At 7.30 the company's siren sounded, and the church bells were rung for three minutes. At 8 p.m. more than 3,000 people were said to be standing in Orr Street or nearby. There was a religious ceremony of thanksgiving in the open air, many speeches from the balcony of the Queenstown Hotel, and music from the Scottish band and the silver band. Bags holding balloons and sweets and whistles were given to what one reporter called 'the awestruck and gaping children'. The event was reported throughout Australia, for the woes of this isolated district and its sentences of death and last-minute reprieves were meat for the news-gatherers.

Good news arrived unexpectedly three months later. The world price of copper, after years of slumbering, stirred and jumped. The mine was breaking even. Gold was also rising dramatically, converting the small quantities of gold in the ore into a valuable asset. The mine made a profit month after month. The benefits of a smaller, more efficient workforce were visible. In 1980 the Mt Lyell Mining and Railway Company not only paid back the loans received from Canberra but paid shareholders their first dividend for five years.

While Lyell had been gasping for breath, Renison Bell was running with the wind. The mine which the Mt Lyell company had developed and then been forced to sell was now a bonanza. It was the largest underground tin mine in the world. It employed more than 500 compared to Mt Lyell's 700. In the five years ending June 1981 Mt Lyell had made a combined loss of some $10 million—the three years of light profits did not atone for the two years of heavy losses. In contrast Renison had made a profit of $169 million before tax and nearly $100 million after tax. A sign of the changed status of Mt Lyell was that in 1981 it was submerged in a new company carrying the name of Renison. In one sense the pup swallowed its parent.

On 27 July 1981 the Mt Lyell shares ceased to be traded in their old name. The company ceased to have its own board representing its shareholders, for now it was wholly owned by a new company called Renison Goldfields Consolidated. The new company was a merger of four separate mining companies previously listed on stock exchanges in their own name: Consolidated Gold Fields, Mt Lyell, Renison and AMC, which was the world's largest producer of mineral sands. Previous shareholders in Mt Lyell received, in return for their Lyell shares, a corresponding number of shares in the new company. The Mt Lyell Mining and Railway Company still existed but was wholly owned by the Sydney company, Renison Goldfields Consolidated. That in turn was half-owned by the London company, Consolidated Gold Fields Limited until 1990 when it was bought out by another English firm, Hanson plc.

The people of Mt Lyell gained some security from the merger of 1981. The profits of the prosperous Renison tin mine, it was hoped, could be called upon to prop up struggling Mt Lyell in the event of another crisis. Renison's tin, however, did not earn the high profits of the previous decade. In several years of the late 1980s it was even inferior to Lyell in profits.

There was always the hope that a richer orebody would be found at Mt Lyell. Knowledge of the rocks in which the copper was deposited—maybe 600 million years ago—had increased in quick bursts. Ever since Mervyn Wade had become the first resident-geologist in the early 1950s, the hope grew that a richer discovery was possible. Where exactly the new copper could be found was the tantalising question. At least two competing theories tried to explain how the copper of Mt Lyell had arisen and how it might therefore best be sought at depth. There was not enough evidence for one theory to conquer the other.

It was beyond dispute that the field held far more copper than almost anybody had predicted. It continued to surprise mining engineers by its capacity to disclose new and big orebodies when existing mines were approaching exhaustion. The copper known to exist at Mt Lyell in 1900 was multiplied many times over. The copper known to exist in 1940 was multiplied many times over. The early mines, the North Lyell and the Mount Lyell, were still remembered as mighty producers but they were utterly dwarfed by recent mines. A ladder of the top six producers of copper in the field's history is dominated by the modern mines. Thus of all the copper mines that had worked up to June 1991, West Lyell was the top with a total output of 420,000 tonnes of pure copper, Prince Lyell was second with 331,000 tonnes of copper. Then came North Lyell with 249,000 tonnes in its long working life. After a long gap came the old Mt Lyell mine with 72,000 tonnes, closely followed by mines whose heyday was in the 1970s—Crown Lyell & 12 West with 64,000 tonnes, and the Cape Horn with 58,000 tonnes.

As so much additional ore had been found in old and new orebodies in recent years, it was reasonable to believe that much more could be found in a field that was not adequately explored. There lingered in the minds of some geologists the reasoned hope that while the company was struggling to survive, a much richer orebody was perhaps waiting to be found — if only the large sums could be set aside to search for it.

The potential copper-bearing ground was large, and as late as 1970 the senior geologist Kerry Reid reported that an accurate geological map of the surface of whole area did not yet exist. Knowledge of the deeper ground was inevitably sparse, for such ground was expensive to explore. In the 1980s two deep holes drilled from the gorge of Conglomerate Creek—far below the corkscrew bends of the Gormanston road—tried to find a southerly extension of the copper field. Finding useful clues rather than copper, they cost a total of $1.4 million.

If a richer mine could not be found the poorer existing mines had to be made payable. Now it seemed that every strip of fat had been sweated from the Mt Lyell organisation, rendering it lean and efficient. The only trouble was that copper prices in real terms were even lower than before. Not since the depression of the 1930s had they been so low. In August 1982 the mine and mill were closed for six weeks. Not even in the crisis of the previous decade was such a drastic step taken. Later that year, to save the heavy working losses, another three weeks of shut-down were called for. The mining field was close to permanent closure when the Tasmanian government offered a small loan if the company kept going for the first six months of 1983.

The gesture was made superfluous. The price of copper rose quickly and the Australian dollar was devalued—twin items of good news that had rarely arrived at the same time. Such news was too good to last. Copper fell again. Australia's high rate of inflation in the early years of the Hawke government added to the company's costs—costs which could not be recouped from the sale of the copper shipped to Japan for final smelting and refining.

The axe was still poised above the town. By the winter of 1984 it seemed certain to fall. In the space of three years Mt Lyell had lost close to 15 million dollars. Max Roberts, the chairman of Renison Goldfields Consolidated, said in Sydney that the time had come to cut the loss. In the twenty years since his parent company had bought a controlling interest, the total profit on the investment in the Mt Lyell field had been worse than nothing. The question was how to close the mine in a way that was least damaging to all those families who for so long had depended on it. In 1984 the closing of the mine was definitely fixed for the end of the following year.

One visitor to the Prince Lyell mine at this time was Paul Johnson, the distinguished English author. He noted in his diary his impressions of the underground workings: 'Atmosphere quite different to South African mines. No frills. No deference to superiors. Very dark. Deep mud, very difficult to walk in, like Western Front in Great War'. Though it must have been a day when water in the deepest workings was not draining freely, his notes summarised the mine's accumulation of problems.

The mine had reached the stage where drastic works were needed if it was to remain alive. The North Lyell tunnel which since 1928 had been the main drain of the under-ground workings—conveying mine waters from the depths of the range to the low-lying Queen River—could no longer serve that purpose. If the Prince Lyell mine was to go deep-er, well below the level of the North Lyell tunnel, a new pumping station was called for. New underground highways were needed to enable heavy items of drilling and mining equipment and the ore trucks to go deeper. Maybe a total of $5 million dollars had to be spent even to keep up the supply of ore. What was the point of spending such a sum simply to reach a deeper part of the orebody that would probably involve the company in heavier losses?. It made no sense.

To close Lyell and create so much unemployment, however, made no sense to the Tasmanian government. Robin Gray, the Premier, offered help. In the summer of 1984-85 another res-cue operation, bolder than all the others, was devised. To raise the capital to open up a deeper part of Prince Lyell, the so-called 40 Series, the company sold its own hydro-electric station at Lake Margaret to the government for $5 million. Gray also offered a loan of $5 million. So the money was found to go deeper.

This was only the start of the cost-cutting. The expenses of working the mine had to be sliced again. In Japan the Mitsubishi company agreed to lower the smelting charges. At Mt Lyell the workforce considered a plan called self-help, and a mass meeting in the Queenstown Memorial Hall accepted a package that would save more money. The electricity in the home—always a subsidy from the company's own hydro station—was no longer so cheap. The rent on the company-owned houses was raised. The salaried staff agreed to return to a 40-hour working week and to take no break for morning tea. The wages' employees agreed to drop their claim for a 38-hour week. Peter Reid of the Trades and Labor Council saw this as a defeat for the union movement and its traditions but he could see no alternative. The result was to extend the life of the mine for four more years. The new closing date was December 1989.

Mt Lyell employees who went to 'the mainland' noticed the contrast between the fast tempo of work at Mt Lyell and the slower pace in the capital cities. They noticed the massive creation of jobs, many of them ephemeral, by the new Hawke government. Some felt slightly peeved that artificial jobs could receive a heavy subsidy from Canberra but nothing was set aside for real jobs earning export revenue for a nation urgently in need of exports. More important, there was a feeling that the Labor Party, once a religion of the west coast miners, now belonged to a new breed of city people. To the indignation of most people on the west coast, the Labor Party also prevented the expansion of those local hydro-electric schemes which provided jobs for those who could find no work in the mines. The new green movement had few disciples in Queenstown and Gormanston. That Labor allied itself with the opponents of economic development was a slight not understood or forgiven on the west coast.

Mt Lyell had long been a national stronghold of the Labor Party. Most residents were proud of their townsman Eric Reece who moved to Queenstown from Storeys Creek as a schoolboy in 1917, went away and then came back to work in the smelters from 1933 to 1935. Widely respected as a union organiser for the AWU, he won a seat for Labor in the Tasmanian Lower House in 1946. He must have been the minister for mines for a longer period than any politician in Australian history. Premier of Tasmania in all but three years of the seventeen years from 1958 to 1975, he continued to keep in touch with Queenstown and knew the nick-

names and first names of most of the older residents. He
personified the political loyalties of the west coast. In the
light of this long Labor tradition, a transfer of political loyalties was almost impossible to imagine. The impossible
happened. In the state election of 1986 the voters of Mt
Lyell gave a high personal and political vote to the Premier,
Robin Gray, a Liberal and not even a west coaster.

The mine was now approaching the end, according to the
death certificate written for it in advance. Almost as if by
miracle the mine became highly profitable again. The devalu-
ation of the Australian dollar meant that Mt Lyell received
more in Australian currency for the copper it sold to Japan.
The painful reducing of the cost of mining and milling copper
also paid its reward. In the first six months of 1986 the profit
was $11.5 million, though the profit soon turned to loss.

Michael Ayre, the general manager who thought he would
see the final closing of the mine, now made the detailed
plans for a further extension of the mine's life. The copper
ore remaining in the Prince Lyell was massive, a national
asset. Why should it be abandoned? Plans were made for
another burst of capital expenditure to enable the Series 50
and 60 levels to be worked: in short the mine was going
much deeper. As the ore could not cheaply be hauled by
motor trucks from such a depth the Prince Lyell shaft was
employed as the main hauler of ore and a conveyor belt carried the crushed ore across the hills to the treatment plant at
Queenstown. For these works Renison found $18 million, and
the Tasmanian government offered a loan at the ruling rate of
interest and promised to defer the collecting of payroll tax
and royalties. In effect the mine was a complicated partnership between the company and the Tasmanian government.

The new deal was approved by Parliament in 1987. Thus
the mine won an extension of life until June 1994—so long
as the world price of copper did not fall too low and so long
as the workforce became even more efficient. The workforce
gained an efficiency which would have astonished miners of
thirty years earlier. Each tonne of deep ore, however, did not
yield quite the amount of copper predicted. More savings had
to be made. Another 100 jobs were abolished. By now the

workforce was a mere 450, or 1,000 less than the workforce existing when the chain of crises began some 15 years earlier.

In July 1991 the general manager, Keith Faulkner, gained the union's consent to a change which the old underground men would have fought to the end. He introduced the 12-hour working shift for most of the underground miners. Curiously this drastic change was preferred by most men who broke the ore and trucked it. In a typical week they now worked three days out of seven. As they earned about $60,000 a year they could count themselves amongst the highly-paid manual workers in Australia. How many years their jobs would last they did not know. Many hoped in 1992—the time of writing this chapter—that the mine would somehow stay alive by steadily going deeper. The present plan is that the mine will close sometime during the year 1995-96.

In those numerous years during which Mt Lyell seemed close to death, its towns suffered. Queenstown in the early 1970s was spread over a wider area than ever before. Every valley had its houses, with iron roof usually painted a vivid red or green, and in the south end of the valley the houses extended more than half a mile beyond the previous fringes of the township. On a warm day in summer the noise of motor mowers could be heard the length of the valley. On a cold night in winter the smoke could be sniffed from a thousand house-chimneys where woodfires were burning.

The copper crisis almost hammered flat this flourishing town. Storekeepers wondered whether to sell at a loss and leave the town. Most of the old firms stood firm for they had faced many such crises. Mt Lyell would 'come good again' they said: 'it always does', they added. Those who had issued easy credit to customers felt the pinch. In some shops, many goods set aside and partly paid for on the lay-by system were never collected. The purchasers had left the town. Every church, club, lodge and sporting body at Mt Lyell suffered from the exodus of people.

In the shrinking towns the four senior football clubs could not survive. To the dismay of loyalists the Smelters merged with Queenstown City while Lyell and Gormanston merged later. Gormanston in its heyday owned a cramped football ground without one clump of grass and and took pride that its footballers were far better than the gravel surface on which they played. Syd Coventry played there just after the First World War, before going across Bass Strait to Collingwood where he won a Brownlow Medal and captained a chain of premiership teams. Ian Stewart, winner of three Brownlow Medals between 1965 and 1971, had spent his childhood in Gormanston.

Gormanston the town was a walking miracle. It had survived disasters and uncounted crises. By the 1970s it needed more than a miracle to survive. The closure of the big West Lyell mine, which lay just inside Gormanston's municipal boundaries, deprived the town of its main source of revenue. Another blow was the glut of houses in Queenstown, and it persuaded some folk to move down from Gormanston, virtually abandoning their old house. One by one the Gormanston amenities closed—the general store, the post office, school, the last church. The Mt Lyell Hotel was simply abandoned. The council chamber was burned down, and the six members of council, four of whom were women, met in the deserted post office with the secretarial help of a part-time officer who helped the remaining residents by bringing fresh milk and bread from Queenstown.

Whether the former inhabitants lived in Queenstown or in another part of Tasmania they still saw themselves as 'Gormie people'. In 1992 in Queenstown the parish priest observed that so many of the faithful in his flock were what he called 'Gormie people'.

The town was almost dead but the spirit lived. The Gormanston municipality—and it covered a lot of bushland and valley as well as its own rocky streets—was left with only a hundred or so people when in 1986 it gave away its independence and amalgamated with Queenstown in a new municipality called Lyell. A plaque standing at one of the hairpin bends on the road between Gormanston and Queenstown commemorates the merger. The names of the reigning wardens of Gormanston and Queenstown—Jack Rowe and Bruce Dilger—appear on the monument.

It is rare in Australia for a municipal merger to be commemorated. Some activities, however, would not be merged. For nearly ninety years each of the two towns had celebrated its own picnic on the public holiday so allocated. For the twin towns it was the equivalent of Cup Day for Melbourne. Though Gormanston faded away it refused to join in the Queenstown picnic. Instead it held its own picnic by the bridge crossing the King River, on the road towards Hobart. When that old bridge and picnic ground were permanently flooded by the big King River hydro-electric scheme during 1991, the plausible idea of sharing in the Queenstown picnic—always held by the beach at West Strahan—was again rejected as disloyalty. On 31 January 1992 the Gormanston picnic was moved to a new ground on the shores of Lake Burbury, and in the cold mist the organiser Ritchie Burns made a speech proclaiming that he and his fellow-organisers would not give in. This was the afternoon before one of the most-discussed state elections in Tasmanian history. It was a tribute to Gormanston that the Premier of Tasmania, Michael Field, was there to open the new picnic ground and that Robin Gray, the previous Premier, was there to open the picnic itself.

Gormanston still has a few houses, even Linda has a few, and they sit in that bleak valley along which a glacier had once moved, slowly melting away in ancient Aboriginal times. The final death of the ghost towns appears to be not far away, but a few of the 'Gormie people' swear that their town will revive and that the rocky slopes will be lined with new holiday houses a few years after water has completely filled the new hydro-electric lake at the foot of the valley. Many of the deserted home-sites are definitely not for sale. 'Gormie', their owners say, 'will rise again.'

32

The Changing Face of the Moon

In the early towns of Western Tasmania people knew that mining was sometimes a destroyer of beauty as well as the provider of daily work. Marie Pitt, who lived in a windswept village on Mount Read, wrote poems revelling in the scent of the white blossom of the leatherwood and the song of the mottled mountain thrush; but she had no hesitation in praising the axemen who 'slew the pine and sassafras'. There was no outcry—only congratulations—when a new mine scarred a beautiful hillside or a forest was chopped down for firewood. In heavy undergrowth the main weapon of the prospector was a tin of wax matches, and in summer he cheerfully set the countryside alight to see if mineral deposits lay beneath the scrub and fallen logs. This was seen as the price of progress. Everyone wanted progress because it meant food instead of hunger.

Most people came to the west coast for the work, not the scenery. As Charles Whitham of Queenstown wrote wistfully in 1923: 'most of our western folk would rather see a racecourse, a crowded danceroom, or a billiard-saloon, than the prospect from a hill overlooking Macquarie Harbour, with its winding bays and the changing light on its waters'. When on a fine public holiday he set out to walk in the hills he was looked at almost pityingly.

Mt Lyell's denuded landscape was quickly accepted. A few people complained but most understood that this was the price to be paid for a good standard of living. The landscape was damaged the most during the early period of full pyritic smelting. Then the ore from the Mt Lyell mine, so rich in

342

sulphur, was tipped straight into the blast furnace. Every ton of copper ore carried about 48 per cent of sulphur. More than half of the sulphur, as Sticht noted, 'distills out of the furnace as sulphur vapour'. Each year some 200,000 tons of sulphur dioxide poured out the big chimneys on the hillside and floated with the wind of the day. For a mining field of that size the pall of sulphur in the air was incredible. A modern smelterman would marvel at such a sight. In Canada the big Inco nickel smelter, treating a massive tonnage of ore and said to be the world's biggest emitter of sulphur dioxide, produces only about 700,000 tonnes of sulphur dioxide a year.

When the flotation process and semi-pyritic smelting took over in 1922, much of the sulphur was eliminated in the mill rather than in the blast furnace. The clouds of sulphur dioxide diminished. They were still substantial, and some householders who grew vegetables in the path of the smelter fumes would lose cabbages when freak weather allowed the sulphur to settle on the garden. In general the sulphur was less of a menace after the metallurgical process was modified in 1922. An occasional small shrub, a lonely clump of rushes, and a thin layer of moss found their way onto the bare hills.

The copper smelters were finally closed in 1969. It was not yet known whether the absence of fumes would hasten the return of vegetation. The effect was slow but favourable. More plants crept onto the bare hills and valleys. Their tenacity was amazing. Some grew alone, with no other living plant to be seen within a radius of a hundred metres. Ten years after the smelter closed, the effects of the cleaner air were especially noticeable to people who had lived for many years on the mining field. To outsiders, however, the slopes seemed unbelievably bare.

Twenty years after the smelter closed, the effect was remarkable. Plants were invading the bareness, an advancing army of plants, though the bareness was still predominant. Visitors still thought it was like the face of the moon—and wondered why it was so stark until they were told that Robert Carl Sticht had 'painted' it. Oldtimers thought the landscape was becoming too vegetated. When they saw the sunset glowing on the hills they deplored the scatter of plants amidst the brilliant areas of coloured rock and clay.

The growth of plants on the denuded hillsides was still impeded by scarcity of soil. Every movable piece of clay had been washed downhill long ago. When the seed of a rush or tiny shrub took root and began to grow, there was still a high risk that heavy rain would undermine its perilous toehold. Another impediment to growth was the presence in the surface rock of tiny quantities of lead and zinc and copper which had probably been carried away in the smelter smoke and deposited on the rock. Decades of sulphur dioxide had increased the acidity of the surface rock, and the acidity gave young plants an access to the aluminium already present in the rock. The effect was toxic. Nearly three quarters of a century of copper-smelting had thus set up a variety of obstacles which opposed the return of the native plants.

One of the first plants to return was the cord rush with its handsome cluster of sharp vertical leaves. Here and there the cord rush took root, all alone amidst the barren rock. Normally found near streams and lakes it appeared more and more on these wet barren hills and liked them. Blackwood and acacias reappeared, including the shiny-leaf wattle. The mountain snow-berry found its spot. Green patches of soft moss, at first the size of a finger nail and later the size of a large hand, made their home near trickles of spring water. So the tiny colonies of plants extended their territory, leapfrogging across the bare hills. The Mt Lyell Co. began to plant thirteen kinds of native plants in chosen areas.

Curiously a few mementoes of the old rainforest still dot the hills, and it is surprising to come cross the thick knee-high stumps still in place, though decaying. These stumps have been weathered into a dull grey by countless storms. They are the only remains of the myrtle, blackwood and King Billy pine trees that must have been chopped down for building-timber or firewood no later than 1896.

While the closing of the smelters had eased the pressure on the surrounding landscape, the mills of the treatment plant increased their pressure. The rock-crushers, ball mills and flotation plant continued to handle millions of tonnes of ore. After the tiny percentage of copper was removed a mighty amount of crushed rock had to be disposed of. The waste sludge and tailings were released into the Queen River as a thick grey liquid. Flowing through Queenstown the grey sludge with its sharp aroma of chemicals eventually reached Macquarie Harbour. There, at the mouth of the King River, it formed a sandy delta which by 1990 covered some 250 hectares. More than 90 million tonnes of sands lay in that delta, and some of the sand was visible from the tourist launches crossing the harbour on their way from Strahan to the Gordon River. The sand contains 0.16 per cent of copper. Someday much of that copper will probably be recovered.

By the 1970s the barren landscape and the grey river of Queenstown were becoming two of the most photographed symbols of pollution in Australia. The Green movement had arrived, with its almost religious worship of nature. In Tasmania, it selected Mt Lyell as its object lesson of what not to do. Any idea of building a new copper smelter had to be abandoned. Another demand from the conservationists was that the pouring of sands or tailings into the Queen River should be halted. The alternative way of disposing of the tailings would be costly. In a nearby mountain valley the company would have to build a large reservoir into which the tailings could be pumped. The demand for such a tailings dam became vocal, though the demand was primarily from people who did not live on the west coast. Local people accepted for better or worse the environment created by their own work.

A call to purify the Queen River and build a tailings dam became louder in the late 1970s, just when the whole mining field was in danger of being closed by the low price of copper. Plans for a dam were drawn up and costed. The additional expense of the tailings reservoir would have tilted the scales and closed the mine. Even a smallish dam, frugally built on the Princess Creek downstream from Queenstown and capable of holding only the tailings produced in the space of five years, was estimated in 1990 to cost $6 million. There was increasing pressure on the Tasmanian government which in turn put pressure on the mining company, but the ultimatum to build the tailings reservoir was not delivered. When in 1985 Tasmania's parliament passed a bill with the hope of prolonging the life of the mine for another five years, it did not enforce strict environmental rules. To implement them at Mt Lyell would have required a large subsidy from the taxpayers.

In 1989 five Green candidates won seats in the lower house of parliament. They were to hold the balance of power until 1992. In that political climate the future of the mine was even cloudier, and when the leading green members, Dr Bob Brown and Christine Milne, made a formal visit to the mine, a confrontation with underground miners was expected. It did not occur: the strongest pressure on Mt Lyell came from outside organisations. Some wilderness groups wished to ban all mining on the west coast. The finding of a major gold deposit on the Henty River, near Queenstown, in 1989 was seen by some observers as a last chance to open a mining field on the west coast.

The finding of mines was already curbed by the setting up of national parks and world heritage zones on the west coast. Now one fifth of the island was out of bounds to prospectors and miners, and the proportion was expected to increase. As for the practice of allowing a grey river of tailings to pass through a charming rainforest, that was persistently denounced in the greener political climate. If Mt Lyell in 1990 had needed urgent support in order to survive, that support probably would not have come because in Tasmania the Labor government depended on the votes of the Green group in whose eyes Mt Lyell was better dead than alive.

In 1992 the election of a Liberal government led by Ray Groom gave Mt Lyell what appeared to be a another short reprieve. According to the plan announced on 26 March 1992, Mt Lyell will finally close sometime during the year ending in June 1996—or exactly 100 years after the beginning of pyritic smelting. 'The new agreement', said Mr Groom, 'obliges the company to spend about $5 million on its environmental management program.' The plan included the 'revegetation of the mine site'. The mining leases would eventually be handed back to the Tasmanian government. The prospect of another mining company taking over the field or exploring for more copper was to be encouraged, not precluded.

Meanwhile the clumps of vegetation on the steep bare hills will slowly expand. When the mine is finally closed the river will cease to be grey, and slowly the marine life will return and on the river's edges the vegetation will appear, at first thin and sparse. The creeks and rivers will continue to serve as a drain for the acidic water flowing, in this region of high rains, from the massive dumps of broken rock standing near the abandoned open cuts at Mt Lyell. Part of this water with its copper, lead, zinc and iron will flow east into Lake Burbury—the dam of the hydro-electric scheme completed in the gorge of the King River in 1992. How the mineralised water will affect the trout being released in the lake is not yet known. To reduce the metals trickling down the Comstock and Linda Creeks to the new lake, the flow is being partly diverted westerly to the Queen River. In a steep terrain often drenched with rain, the flow of acidic and mineralised waters will be a risk long after the mine is closed.

If Mt Lyell's climate and terrain had been different—if it had been a hot, dry and flattish terrain like Kalgoorlie—the acidic waters would have been coped with. And yet terrain and climate were initially amongst Mt Lyell's assets. For long they had saved a fortune in the costs of energy— both firewood and hydro-electricity—and in the cost of draining the underground workings and the disposal of tailings. Mt Lyell might have closed long ago but for the economies it made by virtue of cheap hydro-electricity—the product of high rainfall and steep terrain—and by the cheaper mining costs arising from the ease with which the company could open-cut copper inside the steep slopes. In geography, nearly every asset is also a liability. Towards the end of its life Mt Lyell was becoming conscious of the liabilities of its region.

At one time few tourists in Tasmania visited the west coast but now they come in a procession of buses, cars, motor-bikes and campervans. Most are astonished to find such a strange landscape. Many are shocked, but some are pleasantly surprised, especially if they see the sun shining on the bare hills and on the rocky mountain tops. One of the country's leading artists, Jan Senbergs, trapped some of the magic and weirdness of Mt Lyell in a series of paintings completed in 1983. Mr Sticht's old house, standing on a crag like a little Rhineland castle, and looking out towards the smelters and the bulging hills, will be seen in the major art galleries long after the field is closed.

The hills of Mt Lyell represent both a disaster and a triumph, for it was here that probably for the first time in the history of the world the ancient hope of mankind—to smelt hard rock with the aid of virtually no fuel—was achieved. Without Sticht's smelting process the field would not have been worked on as large scale from the 1890s. The bare hills were the penalty for all the jobs he created and the wealth he tapped. One patch of bare hillside should, if at all possible, be preserved. It would then continue to puzzle, anger, delight or astonish visitors, attracting them in their hundreds of thousands and so keeping the town alive.

Appendix

MT LYELL OFFICIALS 1892-1992

DIRECTORS

D. E. McBryde	1892
Joseph Clarke	1892-1894
Aloysius Kelly	1892
Bowes Kelly	1892-1930 (*Chairman*, 1892-1911, 1914-1924)
Hon. William Knox	1892-1910
William Orr	1892-1894
William Jamieson	1893-1926 (*Chairman*, 1911-1914)
W. D. Reid	1895-1896
J. C. Syme	1895-1912
Joseph Dowling	1896
Lindsay Tulloch	1897-1918
E. Neale Wigg	1911-1913
Colin Templeton	1912-1940 (*Chairman*, 1928-1937)
P. C. Holmes Hunt	1913-1941 (*Chairman*, 1937-1941)
Hon. G. S. Swinburne	1913 and 1918-1928 (*Chairman*, 1924-1928)
K. M. Niall	1928-1953 (*Chairman*, 1941-1951)
D. York Syme	1929-1962
Sir Harry Lawson	1937-1952
Sir Robert Knox	1940-1971
Sir Walter Bassett	1948-1974 (*Chairman*, 1951-1969)
N. K. S. Brodribb	1952-1963
F. Peter Johns	1953-1980
O. G. Meyer	1962-1964
E. R. Griffin	1964
T. A. Webb	1964
Sir Brian Massy-Greene	1964-1976 (*Chairman*, 1969-1976)
S. L. Segal	1964-1975
B. W. Andrew	1964-1972
G. J. Mortimer	1964-1975

J. M. Mackay	1972-1973
D. E. Ainge	1973-1976
G. M. Niall	1974-1980
B. C. Ryan	1975-1977
L. W. Skelton	1975-1980
K. Wood	1975-1980
T. F. Lanz	1976-1977
A. C. Copeman	1977-1980 (*Chairman*, 1977-1980)
A. D. Hemingway	1977-1980
G. G. Northcote	1977-1980
G. R. J. Guise	1980

GENERAL MANAGERS

R. C. Sticht	1897-1922	D. P. C. Sawyer	1975-1978
R. M. Murray	1922-1944	R. M. Patterson	1978-1982
A. H. P. Moline	1944-1948	M. W. D. Ayre	1982-1988
H. M. Murray	1949-1966	R. J. Brainbridge	1988-1989
G. F. Hudspeth	1967-1973	K. E. Faulkner	1989-
T. F. Lanz	1973-1975		

MINE MANAGERS

O. G. Schlapp	1892-1894	B. M. Phillips	1974-1975
R. W. Powell	1894-1895	D. Taylor	1975-1976
L. C. Clark	1896-1900	R. M. Patterson	1976-1978
W. T. Batchelor	1901-1906	M. W. D. Ayre	1978-1982
R. M. Murray	1906-1921	R. P. Callaghan	1982-1987
G. F. Jakins	1921-1948	B. Atkinson	1987-1987
G. F. Hudspeth	1949-1965	R. J. Wright	1987-1988
J. K. A. McLeod	1965-1967	K. R. Faulkner	1988-1989
B. V. McDougall	1967-1970	L. O. Rossetti	1989-1991
V. Jumppanen	1970-1973	P. A. Myers	1991-
R. P. Callaghan	1973-1974		

METALLURGISTS

R. C. Sticht	1895-1897	W. A. Gosman	1929-1931
G. F. Beardsley	1897-1903	W. Hart	1934-1935
A. L. Dean	1904-1913	D. H. Wilsdon	1944-1967
R. P. Roberts	1913-1928	Jack Sutherland	1968-1969

SECRETARIES

St John Biggs	1892	B. H. Lord	1970-1971
Alfred Mellor	1892-1911	W. F. Mizon	1971-1975
D. G. Lumsden	1912-1937	J. King	1975-1976
R. V. Parsons	1937-1955	S. J. Welch	1976-1980
L. G. Naismith	1955-1970		

Bibliography

Most of the evidence on which this story is founded comes from the private records of the Mount Lyell Mining and Railway Company. As these records are not open to public perusal, and as this history is written for popular rather than academic tastes, I have not inserted footnotes on each page. To compensate for their absence I have made the bibliography of public sources as detailed as possible, dividing it into three chronological sections. In referring to newspapers or year-books I mention the years for which I used them rather than the longer period during which they were published. In recording books and parliamentary papers I mention only those from which I gleaned evidence that was useful in writing the history. I do not enumerate, for example, parliamentary papers on Lyell which were not sufficiently important to be woven into the narrative.

Chapters 1 to 9 — 1854–1896

COMPANY RECORDS

These records begin with the Mount Lyell Mining Company, 1892. Thereafter, the gaps are few and of little importance.

Regular Reports

Reports to shareholders, published half-yearly from 1892 to 1916, and annually thereafter. The half-yearly reports run into forty or more pages, containing the detailed reports of chairman of directors, railway engineer, metallurgist and mine manager.

Mine manager's letter-books, and weekly reports to directors, 1892–6.

Metallurgist's weekly reports, cables and letters to directors, 1895-6.

Progress reports of railway engineer, 1894–6.

Minutes of directors' meetings, 1892–6.

Share registers of the company.

Special Reports and Papers: among the most important are

Reports on the mine by H. H. Schlapp and John Howell; and reports on the ore by G. Board of the Port Pirie refinery.

Reports on the Mt Lyell mine by E. D. Peters, T. A. Allan and A. Montgomery, 1893.

E. D. Peters' papers and reports, including his weekly reports to the directors, his report of the smelting test at Argenton in May 1893, and his 115-page report on the proposed smelters, 11 July 1893.

William Knox's report on his trip to the United States and Europe in 1893; and a large sheaf of his papers, cables, weekly reports and correspondence on this trip.

Reports on the railway route by F. A. Cutten, Napier Bell, and James Johnstone, 1893–4.

Brief notes on the early activities of the company, written in 1944 by H. J. Clarke of Strahan, who worked on the railway survey.

Summary of board minutes and other historical events, 1892 to 1908, compiled by A. J. Syme, who worked at head office from 1897 to 1948.

Reports on the construction works at smelters site by H. H. Schlapp, consulting engineer, 1894–5.

Circulars and correspondence in the Crotty-Kelly dispute 1895–6.

PARLIAMENTARY PAPERS OF TASMANIA

There are copies of these papers in the State Archives, Hobart, and the State Library of Victoria. With one exception, No. 75 of 1881, they are bound in the *Journals* of the Tasmanian House of Assembly.

1860: No. 4, Report on the Exploration of the Western Country, by C. Gould

1862: No. 26, Report on Macquarie Harbour, by C. Gould.

1863: No. 9, Report on the Exploration of the Western Country, by C. Gould.

1876: No. 42, Report on the Country around Mount Bischoff, by C. Sprent.

1878: No. 51, Report on the Mineral Resources of the West Coast, by C. Sprent.

—— No. 85, Correspondence on Great Western and Corinna Tin Mining Companies.

1881: No. 75, Leg. Council, Boat Expeditions round Tasmania, 1815–16 and 1824.

—— No. 82, Progress Report on the Mines of the West Coast, by G. Thureau.

—— No. 91, Select Committee on the Resources of the West Coast.

1882: No. 89, Report on Tin Mines, Mount Heemskirk, West Coast, by G. Thureau.

—— No. 99, Select Committee on the Tramway from Macquarie Harbour.

1883: No. 56, Report on the Country between Lake St Clair and Macquarie Harbour, by T. B. Moore.

1885: No. 129, King River and Mount Lyell Goldfield, by Commissioner Glover.

1886: No. 146, Report on Linda Goldfield, by G. Thureau.

1887: No. 58, Deputy Surveyor General's Report (on Tracks).

1890: No. 129, Reports on Mines, by A. Montgomery.

1892: No. 119, Select Committee on the Mt Lyell Tramway Bill.

1893: No. 68, Select Committee on the Mt Lyell Company's Leases Bill.

—— No. 96, Select Committee on the Mt Lyell and Strahan Railway Bill.

The *Annual Reports* of the engineer of roads and the secretary of mines are also valuable documents, bound in the volumes of parliamentary papers.

NEWSPAPERS AND JOURNALS

Newspapers are the most important source of information from 1862 until the Mt Lyell Co.'s records begin, thirty years later. Their value lies less in the writings of their journalists than in the reports of explorers, mine managers, companies, and legal judgments, which they publish in full.

Daily Telegraph, Launceston, 1888, the year in which the Mt Lyell Gold Mining Company erected its battery.

Hobart Gazette contains lists of shareholders of new mining companies registered in Tasmania.

Hobart Mercury

1859–62, for Gould's journeys and the New Zealand diggings. The issue for 14 May 1862 contains the most valuable of all Gould's reports, describing his daily movements on the journey in which he discovered Mt Lyell.

April–June 1878, for the discovery of gold at the Pieman River.

May 1896, for daily evidence in the lawsuit, *Dixon* v. *Henry*. The judgments, amounting to some 30,000 words, are recorded in the *Mercury* on 23 July 1896.

July-August 1906; controversial reminiscences of P. E. Karlson and M. McDonough.

Mount Lyell Standard: In 1896–7 it published the reminiscences of T. B. Moore, J. Crotty, J. S. Karlson, M. McDonough and Jimmy Elliott, all prospectors in the Lyell district in the early 1880s. The articles of the first four men are marked by many contradictions and much bickering.

Tasmanian: The northern Tasmanian newspapers were better informed on mining than the southern papers, and this Launceston weekly was the main source for the years 1881–91. It often reprinted from the *Launceston Examiner* copious and generally reliable reports on western mining, both by itinerant correspondents and occasional travellers. There was little news on Mt Lyell until the rich strike of June 1886, when news of the Linda diggings became more common, though it was often vague. The *Tasmanian* reported the 'jumping case' at Waratah on 12 February 1887, and usually published the fortnightly reports of the manager at Mt Lyell from 1887 to 1891.

Tasmanian News, 1889–91, for detailed half-yearly reports of the Mt Lyell Gold Mining Company.

Weekly Examiner, forerunner of the *Tasmanian,* for Bischoff news, 1875.

Zeehan and Dundas Herald: from the first issue in October 1891 it provides a valuable record and carries several historical articles. In 1892, 1896, and 1897 it published long reminiscences on the early days of Heemskirk and the Pieman. Con Curtain, a former prospector and author of most of these articles, also contributed an article on his old friend, Tom Currie, on 28 June 1909. It is the most detailed source on Con Lynch's expeditions.

The *Age* and the *Argus,* Melbourne, published official reports of Melbourne mining companies operating in Tasmania, together with details of numerous lawsuits over Lyell shares.

Australian Mining Standard, Melbourne: a reliable source on the Zeehan boom, 1891.

British Australasian, London, reports the activities of Australian promoters in Britain, 1892–3.

The Economist, London, for Australian financial conditions, 1890–3.

Location of Newspapers: Files of the above Tasmanian newspapers, and many more, are available in the State Archives, Hobart. Files of the *Argus, Age, Economist, British Australasian* and *Australian Mining Standard* are in the State Library of Victoria, which also has certain Tasmanian newspapers. Zeehan Mines Pty Ltd has files of the *Zeehan and Dundas Herald* in the old Grand Hotel at Zeehan. At Queenstown the Mt Lyell Co. has a file of the *Mount Lyell Standard* from 1896 to 1898, and the Robert Sticht Memorial Library, Queenstown, has a battered file for the year 1900.

E. Morris Miller, 'A Historical Summary of Tasmanian Newspapers', Tasmanian Historical Research Association, *Papers and Proceedings*, vol. 2, no. 2, March 1953.

MANUSCRIPTS

IN STATE ARCHIVES, HOBART

Minutes of the Executive Council, 1862.
Colonial Secretary's Files: Fox-Young period, vol. 87, file 546, correspondence on appointment of government geologist, 1856–9; Gore-Brown period, vol. 6, file 39, correspondence on Gould's second western expedition; Gore-Brown period, vol. 34, files 375, 384, correspondence on Gould's third western expedition, and the subsequent search for gold.

IN MITCHELL LIBRARY, SYDNEY

Notes on 'Philosopher' Smith, written by his son, R. E. Smith, in 1947.
The Meudell Papers, containing the only known copies of four early reports on the mine, by J. R. M. Robertson, F. G. Duff, R. Bennett, C. W. Marsh, 1887–91.

IN PRIVATE POSSESSION, QUEENSTOWN

Notes and reminiscences on the Lyell field in the 1890s by the late W. L. Rhodes, who carried the mails from Strahan to Lyell before the railway went through.
Answers to historical questions, compiled by J. Boyd and D. L. Best for a radio session on 7QT, Queenstown.

BOOKS AND BULLETINS

Bedford, Randolph: *Naught to Thirty Three* (Sydney, 1944). The autobiography of a journalist who visited the west coast in the 1890s.
Ireland, Mark: *Pioneering on North-East and West Coast of Tasmania, 1876 to 1913* (Launceston, undated).
Lawson, G. A.: *The Past and Present Position of the Mineral Industry on the West Coast of Tasmania* (Melbourne, 1896). A flimsy handbook on the prospects of the Lyell mines.
McLintock, A. H.: *The History of Otago* (Otago, 1949).
Meudell, G. D.: *The Pleasant Career of a Spendthrift* (London, 1929). The recollections of a Melbourne sharebroker.
O'Sullivan, Very Rev. D. J.: *Memories of the Lands of the Southern Cross* (n.d., copy in Mitchell Library). The author was a priest at Zeehan in the early 1890s.
Penn-Smith, Frank: *The Unexpected* (London, 1933). The author spent some years prospecting on the west coast.

Peters, Eleanor B.: *Edward Dyer Peters* (New York, 1918), quotes the letters which Dr Peters wrote to his wife from the Blow.

Prior, S. H.: *Handbook of Australian Mines* (Sydney, 1890).

Reynolds, John: *Discovery of Tasmania, 1642* (Hobart, 1942).

Rickard, T. A.: *Stamp Milling of Gold Ores* (New York, 1897), includes chapters on Australian gold batteries.

Russell, M.: *Mount Lyell Mines* (London, 1896), written to sell the copper-field to London investors, includes a description of his first visit to Lyell in 1891.

Sholl, Martin: *A Handy Book to Tasmanian Mining and General Investment* (Launceston, 1882), has a list of Heemskirk mines.

Taylour, W. H.: Brief notes on the early history of Lyell, based on articles which he edited for the *Mount Lyell Standard* in 1896–7, are appended to J. W. Gregory's *The Mount Lyell Mining Field* (1905).

Tilley, Wilberton: *The Wild West of Tasmania* (Zeehan, 1891), written to inform and encourage shareholders of the new silver-field.

Waterhouse, L.: *South Heemskirk Tinfield*, vol. 21 of the Tasmanian Geological Survey, 1916.

Whitham, Charles: *Western Tasmania* (Hobart, 1924). An austerity edition was published by the Robert Sticht Memorial Library, Queenstown, in 1949. The historical chapters carry the scars of hasty compilation (the small section on Lyell consists of quotations from various pens, loosely thrown together), but some of his chapters on the scenery are as good as any Tasmanian writings of his generation. I agree with E. T. Emmett, a former director of the Tasmanian Tourist Department, that there is probably no better guide-book in Australia. It has accurate notes on early explorers and the minor mining fields.

Chapters 10 to 18 — 1896–1903

COMPANY RECORDS

Regular Reports

Half-yearly reports to shareholders.

Weekly reports to the general manager from the mine manager and metallurgist.

Confidential letters and reports from the mine manager to the general manager.

Minutes of board meetings.

Letters and cables from the general manager in Queenstown to the secretary in Melbourne, and vice versa. The most important of the company's records, this two-way correspondence often ran to more than 4,000 typed quarto pages annually.

Special Reports: among the most important are

Reports on all working Lyell mines by L. C. Clark and W. Cundy, 1900–1.

Papers on negotiations with North Lyell Company: records of Launceston conference, February 1903; correspondence of London secretary; W. Knox's cables and letters on his negotiations with the North Lyell board in London.

Letter-book of the manager of the South Tharsis mine.

Letter-books of the *Mount Lyell Standard,* containing copies of letters written by the editor and published between 1896 and 1899.

Records of the North Mount Lyell Copper Company

Minute-books of the Melbourne board, 1898–1900.

Letter-books of the mine manager, 1897–1901.

Correspondence of L. C. Trent, general manager, 1901–2: a large bundle of letters to shareholders, newspapers, the mine manager, and London and Melbourne directors. Some letters cover thirty closely typed pages.

Correspondence of F. D. Mitchell, 1901–3, containing more than a thousand typed pages, mostly written when the author was managing director at Crotty.

Miscellaneous correspondence: important letters to D. J. Mackay, J. S. MacArthur, Hector McDonald, and J. P. Madden, 1900–3.

Official reports: verbatim accounts of meetings of shareholders and debenture holders, 1902–3. The report of the final meeting in July 1903 covers over seventy typed foolscap pages.

Miscellaneous documents: ore and matte shipments from Kelly Basin; railway reports; insurance policies; ore contracts; smelting returns; lists of shareholders, etc.

PARLIAMENTARY PAPERS OF TASMANIA

1896: No. 58, Select Committee on the Mt Lyell and Strahan Railway Bill.

—— No. 80, Select Committee on the Great Western Railway and Electric Ore Reduction Company's Bill.

1897: No. 60 and 71, Memoranda on the West Coast Railways, by F. Back.

—— No. 68, Select Committee on the North Mount Lyell and Macquarie Harbour Railway Bill.

—— No. 74, Select Committee on the Tasmanian Central and West Coast Railway Bill.

—— No. 75, Select Committee on the Great Midland and West Coast Railway Bill.

1898: No. 2, Entrance to Macquarie Harbour, by Napier Bell (see also paper 61, 1890).

—— No. 55, Branch Line from Rosebery to Lyell: Opinion on its legality.

1903: No. 29, Census of Tasmania, 1901.

The *Annual Reports* of the secretary of mines (including reports of inspectors of mines) and the *Statistics of Tasmania* are also useful papers.

NEWSPAPERS AND JOURNALS

Mount Lyell Standard: An enterprising and fairly reliable newspaper with reports on all mines, lists of share prices, reports of shareholders' meetings, interviews with mining leaders, and a comprehensive account of the growth of the field; it died in 1902 after losing a libel action.

Zeehan and Dundas Herald: A lively daily, competing with the *Standard*, it reported the important developments on Lyell and serves as a useful corrective to the *Standard*.

British Australasian, London.

Mining Journal, Commercial & Railway Gazette, London.

The Economist has some first-class articles on Lyell, especially August-September 1900.

Melbourne *Evening Herald*, Sydney *Bulletin, Australian Mining Standard, Champion, Clipper, Argus, Age*, and the *Review of Reviews* sometimes have original comments or reports on the field, though they frequently seem to have borrowed from the papers of the west coast.

Special pictorial editions on Lyell: *Australian Mining Standard*, 1 July 1898 (92 pp.); *Critic* (Adelaide), 1 January 1900; *Clarion* (Melbourne), 7 January 1899, edited by R. Bedford.

MANUSCRIPTS

IN STATE ARCHIVES, HOBART

Correspondence between the Premier and the Great Western Railway Company on the right of the Emu Bay Company to build a railway to Lyell. September-October 1897. Premier's Office Records, vol. 87, file 84.

Prospectuses of Great Mt Lyell Copper Company, Mt Lyell Copper Estates, Mt Lyell Comstock Copper Company, Emu Bay Railway Company Debentures Issue, 1899. Premier's Office Records, vol. 108, file 25.

IN PRIVATE POSSESSION, MELBOURNE

Letters of the late L. K. Hudspeth, answering queries on the years 1898–1914.

Historical notes of T. W. Haynes, a former manager of the Mt Lyell chemical works.

BOOKS

Bridges, Roy: *From Silver to Steel* (Melbourne, 1920). The official history of The Broken Hill Proprietary Co. Pty Ltd.

Clark, Donald C.: *Australian Mining and Metallurgy* (Melbourne, 1904). A comprehensive technical description of Australian mines and smelters.

Felstead, S. T.: *Horatio Bottomley* (London, 1936).

Gordon and Gotch, *Australian Handbook* (London—annually). Useful from 1890 to 1904.

Gregory, J. W.: *The Mount Lyell Mining Field* (Melbourne, 1905). A geological study.

Greville, E.: *Year Book of Australia*. A privately owned almanac which recorded the annual reports of Australian stock exchanges in the late 1890s.

Nash, R. L.: *Australasian Joint Stock Companies' Year Book* (Melbourne, 1898, 1899, 1900, 1902, 1904, 1907, 1909, 1914). A financial record of all companies to which both British and Australasian capital was subscribed.

Peters, E. D.: *The Principles of Copper Smelting* (New York, 1907), and *The Practice of Copper Smelting* (New York, 1911).

Ware, John: *Tasmania's Eldorado, Strahan, Macquarie Harbour* (Hobart, 1908). A small tourist tract with historical notes.

Cyclopedia of Tasmania (2 vols, Hobart, 1899, 1901). Contains biographical notes on hundreds of Tasmanians.

Chapters 19 to 30 — 1903–1966

COMPANY RECORDS

Regular Reports

The same routine correspondence, as for Chapters 10–18—1896–1903, together with letters from the Melbourne secretary to the London board, and weekly reports of the manager of the Rosebery Mines (Geo. Barker) and the Hercules Mine (C. Moxon), 1916–19.

Special Reports and Papers

Papers on fertilizer works.

Notes on manuscript draft of J. W. Gregory's 'Mount Lyell Mining Fields', by R. C. Sticht and W. T. Batchelor, 1903.

Boxes of correspondence, cables and reports on the company's exploration campaign, 1903–12: Blue Tier, Mt Read and Rosebery, Waratah-Pieman, Queensland Copper Mines, West Coast mines, Jukes-Darwin, Norfolk Range-Balfour, Macquarie Harbour-Port Davey.

Correspondence between the company and the Amalgamated Miners' Association.

Reports on the North Lyell disaster, 1912: B. Sawyer (local superintendent) to Sticht; R. M. Murray to Sticht (a graphic account of day-to-day rescue operations); typescript of evidence given to Royal Commission.

Notes on the history of ore treatment by R. M. Murray and D. H. Wilsdon; notes on geology by J. M. Alexander.

Production statistics compiled by W. Proctor, former metallurgical accountant at Mt Lyell.

Crates of papers on Mt Read and Rosebery mines, 1913–20, including all important reports on the mines, ore treatment, hydroelectric surveys, and negotiations with the Tasmanian government and the Electrolytic Zinc Company.

Books of newspaper clippings from Tasmanian, Victorian, and English newspapers. Although the clippings are often arbitrarily selected, they include useful articles.

PARLIAMENTARY PAPERS

Tasmania

1900: Report on Mineral Field near Mt Black, Ringville, Mt Read, and Lake Dora, by the government geologist (in secretary of mines report).

1913: No. 2, Report of the Royal Commission on the North Mount Lyell Mining Disaster.

—— No. 8, Report on the Mount Lyell and North Mount Lyell Mines, by A. Montgomery.

1920–1: No. 51, Select Committee on the Mount Read and Rosebery Mines' Leases Bill, 1920.

1924–5: No. 22, Select Committee on the North Mount Lyell and Macquarie Harbour Railway Bill.

Commonwealth of Australia

1927: No. 193, *Report* of the Tariff Board on a Copper Bounty.

NEWSPAPERS AND JOURNALS

Zeehan and Dundas Herald: The daily paper for Lyell, 1902–22, but its coverage of Lyell news is poor compared with that in the late 1890s.

American Engineering and Mining Journal, has good notes on Australian mining in the 1920s.

Transactions of the American Institute of Mining and Metallurgical Engineers, vol. 106 (1933): article on the electrolytic refinery at Queenstown, by R. M. Murray.

BOOKS AND BULLETINS

Amalgamated Miners' Association of Victoria and Tasmania: *Reports* of Annual Conferences, 1899–1912 (Mitchell Library).

The Australian Mineral Industry: annual reviews 1948–65, Bureau of Mineral Resources.

Conder, Hartwell: a review of Tasmanian mining, with statistics, in the *Tasmanian Handbook*, Hobart, 1914.

Hills, Loftus: Reports on Mt Read-Rosebery Field, *Tasmanian Geological Survey Bulletin*, 1915–19, Nos. 19, 23, 31; good notes and statistics on the history of the field.

Mount Lyell Practice, 1915; articles by R. C. Sticht, G. W. Wright, R. M. Murray, G. F. Jakins and L. J. Coulter, reprinted from *Proceedings* of the Australasian Institute of Mining Engineers, 1916.

Progress Quarterly Report of Mineral Industry of Tasmania (Mines Department, Hobart); useful record of Lyell mines, especially for the years 1900 to 1914.

Russell, H. A. H.: *Mount Lyell Mining Manual* (London, 1907); a tract containing financial details of surviving Lyell companies.

Stevens, Horace: *The Copper Handbook* (New York, 1900 onwards); contains a list of the world's leading mines in volumes 1 to 11.

Walch's *Tasmanian Almanac* (Hobart, 1863–1953).

Weed, W. H.: *The Copper Mines of the World* (New York, 1908).

Zeehan School of Mines, *Annual Report for 1905*, is a 170-page handbook on western mining.

Chapters 30 to 32 — 1967–1992

I especially gained from information in the Report of the Senate Select Committee on Mount Lyell Mining Operations, 3 December 1976; from the company's submission to that committee; a recent paper by Ian B. Wood, Renison's environmental manager, on 'The Mount Lyell Mining and Railway Company Limited, An Environmental Case Study'; geological reports and production statistics compiled by Murray Flitcroft; the Mt Lyell Company's books of newspaper clippings, 1967-92; and the published proceedings of the Royal Society of Tasmania's symposium, *Landscape and Man: The Interaction between Man and Environment in Western Tasmania*, Hobart, 1977. I also learned much from a tour of the mine with Peter North; from discussions with many employees including officials of the West Coast Trades and Labor Council led by Peter Reid; and discussions with municipal leaders including Bruce Dilger. I thank the general manager, Keith Faulkner, and his staff for their unfailing co-operation.

Index